SHAKESPEARE

BOOKS BY IVOR BROWN

✱

Novels

YEARS OF PLENTY
LIGHTING-UP-TIME
MARINE PARADE

Satires

MASTER SANGUINE
THE GREAT AND THE GOODS

Politics

THE MEANING OF DEMOCRACY
ENGLISH POLITICAL THEORY
LIFE WITHIN REASON

Criticism

FIRST PLAYER
PARTIES OF THE PLAY
MASQUES AND PHASES
NOW ON VIEW
I COMMIT TO THE FLAMES

Word-Books

A WORD IN YOUR EAR
JUST ANOTHER WORD
SAY THE WORD
I GIVE YOU MY WORD
NO IDLE WORDS
HAVING THE LAST WORD

IVOR BROWN

SHAKESPEARE

THE REPRINT SOCIETY
LONDON

FIRST PUBLISHED 1949
THIS EDITION PUBLISHED BY THE REPRINT SOCIETY LTD.
BY ARRANGEMENT WITH WM. COLLINS SONS & CO. LTD.
1951

PRINTED IN GREAT BRITAIN BY
CHARLES BIRCHALL AND SONS, LTD.,
LONDON AND LIVERPOOL

ACKNOWLEDGMENTS

The author is most grateful to the following authors, executors and publishers for permission to quote from the under-mentioned works:

- J. DOVER WILSON: The Essential Shakespeare (*University Press, Cambridge*)
- E. FRIPP: Shakespeare, Man and Artist (*Oxford University Press*)
- MRS. GRANVILLE-BARKER: H. Granville-Barker's "Prefaces to Shakespeare (Coriolanus)" (*Sidgwick and Jackson*)
- J. HARBAGE: Shakespeare's Audience (*Columbia University Press and Oxford University Press*)
- W. SOMERSET MAUGHAM: The Summing Up (*William Heinemann*)
- MISS D. E. COLLINS: G. K. Chesterton's Life of Dickens (*Methuen & Co., Ltd.*)
- EDWIN MUIR: Robert Burns, editor W. Montgomerie (*Maclellan Ltd., Glasgow*)
- G. B. SHAW: Preface to the Dark Lady of the Sonnets (*Constable & Co.*)
- C. SPURGEON: Shakespeare's Imagery (*Clarendon Press*)

CONTENTS

CONTENTS

'*With the plays and sonnets in our hands we know much more about Shakespeare than we know about Dickens or Thackeray.*'

G. BERNARD SHAW

'*Reverence is often no more than the conventional homage we pay to things in which we are not willing to take an active interest. The best homage we can pay to the great figures of the past, Dante, Titian, Shakespeare, Spinoza, is to treat them not with reverence, but with the familiarity we should exercise if they were our contemporaries. Thus we pay them the highest compliment we can; our familiarity acknowledges that they are alive for us.*'

W. SOMERSET MAUGHAM

'*A play that has never found a theatre, actors, audiences, is not really a play at all. A dramatist is a writer who works in and for the Theatre. (It is a significant fact that all considerable dramatists play an active part in the first productions of their plays, and never accept the legendary role of the wistful little author whom every one in the playhouse ignores). . . . A dramatist must have actors and audiences in order to realise himself: thus he must come to terms with the Theatre of his time.*'

J. B. PRIESTLEY

CHAPTER I

The Shakespeare Wonder

THE use of the word Wonder for a thing most strange, for something almost miraculous, is well planted in our language. Wild country, for example a landscape abounding in crags and crevices and revealing Nature in a Gothic mood, provided our ancestors with a store of Wonders. Such views they often deemed ' horrid,' by which they meant fiercely bristling; but, horrid or handsome, these glimpses could thrill our fathers to the Wonders of such a scene. Thus Derbyshire had its Wonders of the Peak, as the Eighteenth Century travellers described that county's summits, crevices, and caverns. In the same way, the Age of Reason, so ready to be rapt as well as rational if the Man of Feeling was given proper guidance and encouragement, discovered William Shakespeare of Stratford-upon-Avon, the Warwickshire Wonder.

To his own age he had been the ' dulcet singer,' the good companion in ' a cry of players,' the ' patterne of all wit.' John Webster, author of *The Duchess of Malfi*, and dismissed by Bernard Shaw as the Tussaud Laureate, mentioned Shakespeare as one of several leaders—not as *the* leader—in his profession. He singled out for praise, rather casually, and in the manner of a headmaster writing a good report for a pupil, Shakespeare's ' right happy and copious industry.' No acknowledgment there of any supremacy of genius! The tributary verses of the First Folio had, naturally, to say more than that, and in 1630 John Milton actually introduced the word ' Wonder ' to the lexicon of what was later called Bardolatry, the worship of the Avonian Bard.

> Thou in our wonder and astonishment
> Hast built thyself a live-long Monument.

But, for nearly a century after his death, Shakespeare remained more a theme for criticism by the few than a subject of adulation by the many. Dryden acclaimed him, but also criticised and rewrote him. The man of Stratford, with his neglect of classic canons, was something barbaric to the civil wits of the Restoration. His plays were garbled on the stage and performed far more for the roles they provided to the actor than for their truth in character or for the beauty and the music of their verse. And then, with mounting speed and power, acknowledgment of the Shakespeare Wonder swept across England and the world. In 1769 Garrick, by summoning London to the first Stratford Festival, confirmed what Rowe, Pope, Johnson, and the other editors and commentators had begun to tell the reader. Bardolatry, the worship of the Wonder, was on the move, never to halt again.

The Wonder, as we see it now, is simply this: that no writer of any land or age has ever had popularity and renown on such a colossal and astounding scale. There is no civilised, or even faintly civilised, nation which does not read, study, perform, salute (and actually enjoy) the works of William Shakespeare. Even the warmest admirers of ' Sweet Mr. Shakespeare ' in his own day could have had no conception whatever of the renown and even worship which their gentle hero was to win.

The growth of that renown was slow, then steady, then staggering. In his own time Shakespeare was liked and esteemed, but there was no suggestion that he abode nobody's question, out-topp'd knowledge, was myriad-minded, had a ' boundless, cloudless human view,' and was the superman that subsequent adoration has made him seem. Early praise of him, indeed, now seems rather sticky in its stressing of his dulcet quality. Francis Meres (1598) called him mellifluous and ' hony-tongued ' and made allusion to his ' sugred sonnets.' In the same year Richard Barnfield praised his ' hony-flowing vaine ' and in 1599 John Weever proclaimed

Honie-tong'd Shakespeare when I saw thine issue
I swore Apollo got them and none other.

Spenser, too, in his verses on Willy,

> From whose pen
> Large streams of honnie and sweete Nectar flowe,

may have been alluding to Shakespeare. However that may be, William was soon a favourite of the student-class. In the Cambridge plays of the turn of the century, performed at St. John's College, 1598-1602, *The Pilgrimage to Parnassus* and *The Returne from Parnassus*, there are several references to the sweet charms of Shakespearean poetry. One character of the earlier piece, ' Sicke-thoughted Gullio ' (melancholy was then, as often, one of the affectations of the intelligentsia), wooed with ' shreds of poetrie gathered at the theators.' ' We shall have nothinge but pure Shakespeare,' protests Ingenioso, his ' bounden vassall to commande,' and asks in what ' vayne ' he should compose amatory verses for his friend. Gullio, both doting and punning, replies,

> Not in a vaine veine (prettie, i'faith!): make mee them in two or three divers vayns, in Chaucer's, Gower's and Spencer's and Mr. Shakspeare's. Marry, I thinke I shall entertaine those verses which run like these;
>
> > Even as the sunn with purple coloured face
> > Had tane his laste leave on the weeping morne, etc.
>
> O sweet Mr. Shakspeare! I'le have his picture in my study at the courte.

The lines quoted are the opening of Shakespeare's *Venus and Adonis*. Gullio adds later, ' Let this duncified worlde esteeme of Spencer and Chaucer, I'le worshipp sweet Mr. Shakspeare, and to honoure him will lay his Venus and Adonis under my pillowe.' From this we gather three things, that pictures of ' sweet Mr. Shakspeare ' were then readily available, that he was, by 1598, in our modern slang, ' Pin-Up Boy ' of the students and Inns of Court wits—or at least of some of them— and that there was a point in continually ' Mistering ' him. Was

the long and at last successful struggle to get back the Shakespeare Coat of Arms becoming a public joke ? Had Shakespeare's service of the Earl of Southampton become a jest
among the sneering tattlers ?

In the last play of this series, *The Returne from Parnassus*,
Part II, Shakespeare is rebuked by the character Judicio for
being too light, too much obsessed with sex.

> Who loue's not Adons loue, or Lucrece rape ?
> His sweeter verse contaynes hart-trobbing line,
> Could but a graver subiect him content,
> Without loue's foolish lazy languishment.

Later actors of Shakespeare's fellowship, Kempe and Burbage,
are introduced to pay a larger tribute. Dismissing the scholars'
plays as over-learned, allusive, reeking of midnight oil, Kempe
says :

> Few of the vniuersity men pen plaies well, they smell too much
> of that writer Ouid, and that writer Metamorphosis, and talke
> too much of Proserpina and Iuppiter. Why heres our fellow
> Shakespeare puts them all downe, I and Ben Ionson too. O
> that Ben Ionson is a pestilent fellow, he brought up Horace
> giving the Poets a pill, but our fellow Shakespeare hath given
> him a purge that made him beray his credit.

The last sentence refers to a scene in Jonson's *The Poetaster* and
the complicated Battle of the Poets, it need not be followed
up now. The salient fact about Shakespeare's reputation in
1601—the date given to this passage by Sir Edmund Chambers
—is that the actors esteemed his practical stagecraft and his
theatrical appeal to the general public, while the students made
a cult of his amatory verses and habitually called him ' sweet.'
It is odd that he should be rebuked for lack of ' graver subject '
when *Hamlet* may already have been acted, for Chambers gives
1600 as the year of production for *Hamlet*. The bleak and
severe Shakespeare of the great tragedies, the essential
Shakespeare to many, was mainly to come, but it is a queer
judgment that could see nothing but ' loue's foolish lazy

languishment' in the author of the historical plays. Were Richard II, the Bastard in *King John*, Hotspur, and Falstaff nothing?

Between 1600 and the author's death in 1616 allusions to his fame are fewer. Perhaps the author of *King Lear* and *Timon of Athens* had disappointed the devotees of his honeyed vein. With the tributes in the First Folio edition, tributes by his fellow-actors Heminges and Condell, by Ben Jonson, Hugh Holland, L. Digges, and John Mabbes, there is the strong promise of immortality:

> Be sure, our Shakespeare, thou canst never die
> But, crown'd with lurel, live eternally.

The insistence on 'sweetness' is now less. Hunt called the plays 'dainty,' but dainty was a stronger word then than it is in our times, when Ye Olde Tea-Shoppe offers its 'dainty teas,' which generally means teas with nothing solid to eat. Furthermore, Jonson sounded the note of victory abroad and palms across the sea.

> Triumph, my Britain! Thou has one to show
> To whom all scenes of Europe homage owe.

This immediately preceded the ever-quoted

> He was not of an age, but for all time.

The glory was proclaimed. Milton's Sonnet came seven years later. The Shakespeare Wonder was born.

But Folio verses were bound to be flattering. They were there, after all, to sell the book as well as to celebrate the man —and the man had so far never stood on any pinnacle, save the honey-pot of the students' esteem, in his own life and time. Kempe's reference to Shakespeare 'putting them all down' was aimed at the classical scholars of the Universities. Ben Jonson ranked higher. There was never any suggestion of burying Shakespeare beside his rivals in Westminster Abbey. Beaumont, now deemed scarcely considerable at the highest level, might lie there. Stratford-upon-Avon could keep William's bones.

There was for many years no Shakespeare Wonder in Stratford itself. His family stayed on quietly. Sightseers and pilgrims were not yet on the move, but in September, 1634, one Lieutenant Hammond records a visit to the tomb:

In that dayes travell we came by Stratford vpon Avon, where in the Church in that Towne there are some Monuments which Church was built by Archbishop Stratford; Those worth observing and of which wee tooke notice of were these . . . A neat Monument of that famous English Poet, Mr. William Shakespeare; who was borne heere.

And one of an old Gentleman a Batchelor, Mr. Combe, upon whose name, the sayd Poet, did merrily fann up some witty, and facetious verses, which time would nott giue vs leave to sacke up.

Hammond and his friends did not stay long. Nor were they much followed. Stratford was then far from achieving its present status of a Mecca. The glory spread slowly; how slowly is shown in the notebooks of the Rev. John Ward, who was Vicar of Stratford from 1662-81. After some gossip about Shakespeare (' he was a natural wit without any art at all ') Ward mentions his London successes and his wealth—' Hee spent att ye Rate of £1000 a year, as I have heard.' Then he says:

Remember to peruse Shakespears plays and bee vers'd in them that I bee not ignorant in that matter.

Can one visualise the present incumbent of the parish church of Stratford-upon-Avon making a note that he must really remember to have a look at Shakespeare? Ward's jotting on this point shows plainly how little Stratford at that time cared about its hero. Here was the vicar of the very church which, having Shakespeare's tomb, is now a magnet to all the myriads of the faithful, confessing that the plays by the tenant of that sepulchre meant little or nothing to him.

The start, locally, was sluggish. But the Shakespeare family themselves had dwindled away and only through a married sister of William's, Mrs. Hart and her children, did the line continue. So there was no rallying point for Bardolatry there. It was not until the eighteenth century that Stratford woke up slowly, rubbed its bewildered eyes, and found itself famous. ' Local lad makes good ' is regarded by the county newspapers as an eternally saleable ' story.' And did ever local lad ' make better ' than William Shakespeare ? When Garrick held his Shakespeare Festival in 1769 and rallied London to Avonside, there to drink, feast, race, let off fireworks, and do everything for Shakespeare (short of acting his plays), Warwickshire had at last discovered the Shakespeare Wonder and a Shakespeare Cult was founded.

The visitors to-day, as far as I can judge from frequent observation, enjoy the trip and derive a genuine pleasure, even a rapture, from treading where Shakespeare, as they fancy, trod, and sitting where he may, quite probably, have sat. I have noticed, during my wanderings in Stratford-upon-Avon, a kind of spinal ecstasy thrilling in the frames of the most faithful and rising to illumine their faces as they make contact with some bench or pew in cottage, school, or church which may possibly have been the recipient of their William. They enjoy listening to the Avon waters ripple against the Clopton Bridge, that genuine antique. This noble sweep of stone was the young man's gate to glory when he left the town and met his eye on his periodical returns with money in his purse and investments, as well as lyrics, in his mind. I recommend the Avonside walkers to pause awhile below the bridge on the left bank, especially when the river is running strongly, and watch the queer back-eddy which Dr. Caroline Spurgeon so acutely noted and referred back to a passage in the early poem *Lucrece*:

> As through an arch the violent roaring tide
> Outruns the eye that doth behold his haste,
> Yet in the eddy boundeth in his pride

> Back to the strait that sent him on so fast
>   In rage sent out, recall'd in rage, being past,
> Even so his sighs, his sorrows, make a saw,
>   To push grief on and back the same grief draw.

' Back to the strait that sent him on so fast.' This queer reversal of the water's flow certainly happens, just under the arch nearest the London side. But perhaps it happens under many bridges. The anti-Stratfordians will certainly claim that it does.

So the world travels to the Avon, a river which Shakespeare never mentioned by name. Avon water has been solemnly bottled and sent over to America to anoint the foundations of a new theatre. There is no other such literary or theatrical pilgrimage in the world, no comparable Mecca of the Muse. The Shakespeare Wonder is unique in its drawing power. No other writer has better served the tourist agency, the hotel manager, inn-keeper, caterer and salesman of mementoes as well as the publisher and printer, actor and manager. No other writer has evoked a tithe of the editions, commentaries, emendations, speculations, and down-right lunacies that have been begotten by the Shakespeare Wonder. Shakespeare stands alone in his spawning of cranks and bores as well as of erudite scholars and devotees of genius. Prizes and scholarships abound in his name: what copious prize-winner at school ever left without a leather-bound Shakespeare ? That itself was often won by giving the right answers to problems of the play, by interpreting this word or phrase, or by ' estimating the value ' of that incident or character. All this has its irony, since Shakespeare wrote of school with a weary heart, as a place reluctantly attended. There is a real echo of personal animosity in the lines spoken by Berowne, who is generally accepted as one of the self-projections of the poet:

> Study is like the heaven's glorious Sun
>   That will not be deep-searched with saucy looks;
> Small have continual plodders ever won
>   Save base authority from others' books.

This may have been a drive at Ben Jonson, so weightily erudite. More probably it is a cry from the heart of one who never enjoyed a weighty dullness in others, least of all in a dominie. The pedagogues have had their revenge in full, since too many of them have achieved the master-miracle of making the thymy-scented pastures of ' Eng. Lit.' arid and tedious as an asphalt yard and of turning the Shakespeare Wonder into the Shakespeare Bore. I am happy to think that the teaching of Shakespeare is now much more lively and better related to the warm life of the playhouse than when his plays were just a section of ' Eng. Lit.,' a dry chunk of the curriculum, and the raw material of examination papers.

Another aspect of the Wonder has been the annexation of Shakespeare as their particular prophet by almost every sect of worshippers, philosophers, and politicians. Saint and devil have vied in quoting Shakespeare to their purpose. He can be toasted at Birthday junketings and on ' Immortal Memory ' occasions with equally sincere fervour by Catholics, Protestants, and Agnostics, by Optimists and Pessimists, by Aristocrats and Levellers, by the most chaste of pietists and by those who inwardly agree with Ally Sloper's Dook Snook that ' a dirty mind is a continual feast.' By the method of your citation you can make him Fascist or Jacobin with ease, since he railed as bitterly on the fawning courtier and at fur-robed oppression as ever he did upon the slippery leaders of the stinking mob. He spoke, with some feeling, against schools and their peda-gogues; but he spoke for all schools of opinion and that with the apt, the brief, the memorable phrase. Thus Shakespeare has given to every type of person the perfect line wherewith to summarise and to extol the drift of his opinion and the practice of his life.

In any fair-sized library ' Shakespeareana ' make up an entire department, no mere shelf or case. The literary editor of a newspaper, listing his arrivals ' for review,' usually finds that more books about Shakespeare are turned out during each year than are written in the same period on all the other figures and pillars of English Literature put together. Then why, you may say, write another ? To that I would make the old plea of safety in numbers. Were there only nine good books about Shakespeare, one would have to be chary of attempting a tenth. But where all types of nuisance, as well as of excellence, have broken in and trespassed, another pair of feet may be more easily pardoned. At any rate one can modestly suggest that since so much fantastical vapouring, so much turgid rubbish, has been emptied over Shakespeare, in addition to the critical deposits of the truly great and shrewdly fond, another book is the less culpable.

The flood of books is partly due to the existence of a Shakespeare Mystery as well as of the Shakespeare Wonder. During the last hundred years a persistent and increasing number have denied that the works of Shakespeare were, or could have been, written by the man from Stratford. They claim that his name was used as a mask or shelter by some aristocrat or Very Important Person, since direct contribution to the stage and to its suspect world of motley was, for such great ones, deemed harmful to dignity and dangerous to a career. The notables selected for this honour have been Francis Bacon, Lord Verulam—first at the starting post and still carrying the most money—Edward de Vere, Seventeenth Earl of Oxford, Roger Manners, Fifth Earl of Rutland, William Stanley, Sixth Earl of Derby, Sir Walter Raleigh, Sir Edward Dyer (better known, perhaps, as lyricist of ' Down among the dead men '), Mary Countess of Pembroke, and less notable and certainly a strange choice—a Miss Anne Whateley, of whom I shall have more to say with another reference, concerning the lady's heart rather than her hand.

The pleading of the causes and the deposition of ' the man Shagsper '—it is customary to use this, seemingly contemptuous, spelling when kicking the actor off the poet's plinth—have exercised some able people as well as some very odd ones. But always their fervent disloyalty to Stratford is based on an equally fervent loyalty to the author of the plays: the anti-Stratfordians are not denigrators of the poet; they see themselves as rescue-parties allotting the glory where they believe it to be due. This must be saluted as an honourable exercise, whether you agree or disagree with the theories and attributions that are advanced. Their hobby or passion has set people conjecturing, deciphering, tampering with graves, and even communing with the spirit world. It has evoked endless ingenuity. Indeed Shakespeare has been a fascinating riddle to the doubters, giving them as much recreation as the creators of cross-word puzzles could ever have provided. They have hunted down indications of authorship in the lineation of the First Folio, hints which could only have got there if the true author had stood over the printers continually and decided the placing and spacing of every syllable in the book; that is a task, I think, for which the supposed Notable would scarcely have had time or patience, a task also which would have at once betrayed to all in the printing-house the secret which he was supposed to be hiding from the present and yet intimating to posterity.

I shall explain later on my attitude to the Shakespeare Mystery; namely, that Shakespeare of Stratford came into close touch with play-writing aristocrats and may have taken over some plots of theirs or amended some of their scripts, but that his own handiwork is unique and unmistakable. We need not take a rudely dismissive view of the anti-Strat-fordians. Nor, indeed, does Stratford itself do so. In the debates at Mason Croft, headquarters there of the British Council, the heretics have been welcome combatants. Their case, when properly stated, has to be considered and not kicked downstairs with the curt contumely once deemed sufficient by the orthodox. For the moment I only mention the Shakespeare Mystery as a contributory element of the Shakespeare Wonder and as a prolific source of the recent additions to the already massive deposit of Shakespeareana on our shelves.

All this could never have happened without one precedent condition; namely, the absence of a clearly and consistently stated point of view in Shakespeare's work. In literary fame there are always two kinds of favourite; one is the author who delights a certain type of reader holding certain strong opinions and predilections; the other has a wide and even universal appeal. The former's work must have a definite and little-changing quality of mood and doctrine. The second, the beloved of all, must have a knack of changing ground, of responding sunnily to sun and moodily to rain, of seeing the best in all conditions of men and of society. He can, if you drive the matter that far, be muddle-headed—and Shaw did not hesitate to dismiss Shakespeare's brain as a feeble instrument matched with his own. But what the universal favourite must have is the knack not only of saying to perfection ' what oft was thought but ne'er so well expressed ' but also of finding the verbal formula and the verbal music which make the echoing, resonant, unforgettable summary of all varieties of simple human emotion.

There are words, and patterns of words, which run with the ear and catch the sympathy of mankind: those words and patterns may be seized by care or by instinct or by a happy blend of both. If a writer has no single, strong doctrinal urge, but responds quickly to the beauty or the bitterness of things seen and felt, and has the supreme verbal felicity, the mastery of rhythm, and the flash of phrase so completely possessed by Shakespeare, his immortality is assured. ' A plague of opinion. A man may wear it on both sides like a leather jerkin.' So, on both sides, Shakespeare wore it, but not with any leathern austerity. He gave to every shade of thought the tint and the music that were its due. He saw Nature whole, from cowslip to cataract, and wren to hurricane, and sang it so.

The writers of striking opinion or notable particularity have their henchmen. The Browning Societies may have faded away, leaving, one hopes, many less socially cohesive but none the less devoted Browning readers. The Ibsenites may dwindle, but the Shavians are a multitude. It is true that, when an author is old enough, even his enemies relent: especially does that occur among the gently-inclined British, in whose country failure can actually be the door to popularity as nowhere else in the world. Such posthumous or belated victory has its ironical, even its humiliating, side, when an author comes to be widely applauded by those who have neither understanding of, nor sympathy with, the message that he has been trying to deliver.

If Shakespeare had been a messenger or a reformer, he would never have been the general darling. When fame did at last overtake him, he would have seen, if he had still been there, the infuriating spectacle of muddle-headed partisans applauding him for the wrong reasons and completely reversing the course of his opinion in the whirl of their friendly folly. When Cauchon and the Archbishop, Inquisitor and Soldier, Warwick and Stogumber, Dunois, Charles, and Executioner all laud the canonised Saint Joan with chants of adoration, in the epilogue of Shaw's play, the Maid has the sense to know the depth of her defeat. ' Woe unto me when all men praise me! ' she exclaims. And the great play ends with the radiance of her figure and with the cry upon her lips, ' O God that madest thy beautiful earth, when will it be ready to receive thy saints ? How long, oh Lord, how long ? ' The Inquisitor had said that the simpleton had never understood a word of her trial. Now she knows that none of the clever ones, still mumbling their formulae in 1920, has understood a word of what she told them in the early fifteenth century.

Despite his frequent obscurity of phrase and bawdiness of jest, the world has virtually canonised, in a secular and literary way, the name and nature of William Shakespeare. Of course there must be much among the faithful that would madden him, did he have to return and meet the adoration. But, on the whole, he would not be distressed by complete misunderstanding of a message, for the good reason that he never was a messenger. He had always had the capacity to turn on himself and laugh at his own moods and notions. He could look upon a lecherous world, ulcered with sin, snarl with a wolfish pessimism, and then wheel round to behold a daffodil in the wind, become ' sweet Mr. Shakspeare ' once more and write romantic masquerades. He could work on *Twelfth Night* and *Hamlet* side by side, perhaps in the same year. He could practise a careful economy in his own life and yet pour out his admiration on the wastrel Antony.

As a Scotsman, fascinated by the elusive figure of William Shakespeare ever since Arnold Bennett counselled a boy-reader to try Frank Harris's *The Man Shakespeare* as an alternative to the respectable dummy of Droeshout's portrait and Lee's life, I have naturally had the Burns parallel often in my mind. Burns, of course, has never had the universal veneration paid to Shakespeare; he was the hero of a small nation. But the members of that nation have been great wanderers and colonists and so the 25th night of January is celebrated, with whisky, if possible, and with sentiment always, in scores of places many thousands of miles from Ayrshire. The stiffest English, too, have somehow acquired the habit—I cannot discover how or why or when it began—of crossing arms and clutching hands when not quite sober (or, if sober, wholly embarrassed) and in this posture chanting ' For Auld Lang Syne ' on solemn occasions and especially on New Year's Eve: this they do although they could not translate ' auld lang syne ' into English if you asked them. There has been, in short, a Burns Wonder, though not on the scale of the Shakespeare Wonder, and the reason for it is simply that both men give satisfaction all round by superb articulation of the common stuff of the human heart.

To use Shaw's phrase, they have made the ordinary senti-ments ' sound magnificent by mere brute faculty for their art.' As Edwin Muir has very well put it, he (Burns)

is a myth evolved by the popular imagination, a communal poetic creation. He is a Protean figure; we can all shape him to our own likeness, for a myth is endlessly adaptable; so that to the respectable this secondary Burns is a decent man; to the Rabelaisian, bawdy; to the sentimentalist, sentimental; to the Socialist, a revolutionary; to the Nationalist, a patriot; to the religious, pious; to the self-made man, self-made; to the drinker, a drinker. He has the semi-miraculous power of making any Scotsman, whether generous or canny, senti-mental or prosaic, religious or profane, more whole-heartedly himself than he could have been without assistance; and in that way perhaps more human. He is comforting, a necessary figure; as comforting as the tatties and herring and as necessary as the whisky whose odours rise in a sort of incense to his memory every 25th of January. He greases our wheels; we could not roll on our way so comfortably but for him; and it is impossible to judge impartially a convenient appliance to which we have grown accustomed.

It astonishes me that Muir added,

We cannot imagine Wordsworth or Shelley or Tennyson or Shakespeare turning into a popular myth.

The first three I grant him. But is there no popular myth of Shakespeare? Is there no Protean William, all things to all men, fulfilling Rabbie's task of making them whole-heartedly themselves? The Shakespeare Wonder could not have happened without such a myth. (Muir and myself are not using myth in the sense of falsehood but of storied truth.) The Shakespeare Myth began to be built in the eighteenth century when the legends and anecdotes were collected or invented; these tales were well adapted to put William on the stool of repentance, a sinner like Rabbie and the rest of us, poacher, tippler, lover out of wedlock, piece of common clay. Heroes must be lowly and fallible if they are to win a universal suffrage, first humble and then successful. Human nature has a way of doting on men like Dick Whittington, whose success-story so fascinates the British that they have given him the supreme honour of heroic rank in fairy-tale and pantomime. He was poor, he plodded on, he was kind to animals (except rats) and he 'made good' to the extent of a wealthy marriage and mayoral status.

For the general public Shakespeare and Burns are in this admired class. They start in a lowly way and they reveal the frailties of the flesh. The first has a rustic marriage in haste and proceeds to his Dark Lady of the Sonnets; the second has his barnyard lasses before he moves on to conquer capital and Clarinda too. 'Brisky juvenals' both, they grow up to renown and to win—so the legend has it—by strength of genius and by size of heart. Yet the legend always requires some remaining proof of the old Adam. In Burns's case that was easy enough to find. But in Shakespeare's instance there was less to work upon. The Rev. John Ward had to attribute the death to a fever following excessive drinking at a merry meeting with Ben Jonson and Michael Drayton. This yarn crops up half a century after the event and there is no supporting evidence. Ward was a notoriously inaccurate gossip who dabbled in such ' news ' as that Milton was crypto-Papist and frequented Catholic clubs. What is interesting is the welcome given to this kind of gossip by those who would never attend such merry meetings themselves.

The righteous seem to enjoy signs of continuing devilry in their heroes; or else they carefully adjust their spectacles to miss the offence. Shakespeare's obscenities and obscurities alike are pardoned. Many of the obscenities are easily overlooked because they are also obscurities; the punning in gross matters is often (luckily for teachers) extremely involved and jests remain unrecognised. Both men could be difficult. (Some of the language of Burns can be as unfamiliar to many modern Scots as to the English.) But difficulties are forgiven by a reader otherwise entranced. In the theatre the listener, waiting for Perdita and Autolycus, will put up with the strange tangle of words and anarchy of syntax which mark some early passages of *The Winter's Tale*. Taken at ordinary playhouse speed these lines are incomprehensible. But the play moves and lives. So who cares ?

The sentimentalists, even the most strict in ethical code, surrendered to the man who could sing

> The heart's aye the pairt aye
> That maks us richt or wrang.

An errant minstrel may always atone for his lapses by a drive at the simple and innocent emotions. Let him throw in a bonnie lassie with a love as red as roses and as dulcet as a melody that's sweetly played in tune and then the reverend clergy of England and even the thrawn presbyters of Scotland will surrender, as the priests of Egypt fell before Cleopatra of old; they will, in Shakespeare's own phrase, bless him when he is riggish.

So there, in outline, is the Shakespeare Wonder, enhanced,

as an intellectual curiosity, by our lack of certainty about Shakespeare the Man. This book of mine will solve nobody's problem, if certainties are sought. But few will be foolish enough to insist on a certain solution. All excursions in discovery of Shakespeare are essays in conjecture and any one may compete. One might say that Shakespeare has been buried under the mountain of his greatness: the temptation to try, once more, to dig him out is urgent; the justification must be the devotion as well as the curiosity of the digger. Only true affection can qualify for further delving at the scanty facts for further work upon the many fancies.

If one has been, during nearly all of one's reading and play-going life, Shakespeare-haunted, one may surely be excused an effort to make flesh of that tremendous ghost, despite the myriad experiments already made. Devotion, as I said, must be there and some freshness of approach. The cult of freshness may lead merely to a spirit of fantastical surmise, which vice I shall endeavour to avoid. But I can, I think, fairly claim to have used the most obvious approach of all, the theatre-door. It is surprising how many Shakespearean scholars have neglected this, or at least underrated its invitation. With their eyes fixed upon the editions and the texts, they have too much abstracted the playhouse-poet from the boards and tiring-rooms, the rehearsals and arguments and squabbles, the storming, jealous actors and the fits of temperament amid which so much of his energy must have been spent.

I remember that I once wrote and spoke on the secret history of modern plays, i.e. all the previous comings and goings, the tussles over casting, the arguments, rewritings, inventions of new act-endings and the like, and expressed surprise that any clear and excellent result could ever emerge from such a Bedlam. A well-known Shakespearean scholar commented that the theatre could not possibly be such a mad-house as I had painted it. Little he knew! No doubt things were less complicated then, both in organisation and psychology. There were no film contracts and no lures of the Radio to disturb the company; there was no assiduous cultivation of ' publicity '; all of his fellowship may have been simply players and less self-consciously ' artists.' Had they names to assert and maintain, wrangling, even to the eighth of an inch, over the lettering of a bill ? But strain and stress there must have been, post-mortems after failures, box-office calculations, rows over costing and casting, recriminations and rivalries of many a kind.

The scholars will argue over a syllable in Quarto or Folio, solemnly debating to the last letter whether Shakespeare wrote it. How can we know ? What a dramatist writes, they should understand, is constantly discussed, adapted, modified or strengthened, cut or expanded, during rehearsal. We are handicapped from the start since we have none of Shakespeare's manuscripts to look at; in that case how can we possibly tell what additions and deletions took place ? The actors of his team may frequently have suggested a line or a passage. His own editors guaranteed the plays in the First Folio to be ' absolute in their numbers,' but the scripts had been in usage for many years and at the players' mercy. It is idle to suppose that the text we have is pure Shakespeare, the Will, the whole Will, and nothing but the Will. The scholars suggest the hands of other poets and playwrights here and there. Why not the hand of Burbage, the star-actor of the fellowship ? People with back-stage knowledge will see things in Shakespeare which the professors miss, while they will be less inclined to pore over the inessential verbal point. It needs both sorts to make a commentary. It is the actor, for example, who will most appreciate the wondrous bounty of an author who could toss some of the most glorious lines and speeches to Second Murderers and Minor Barons.

What a fine confusion must Shakespeare's life have been! By the Thames he was wresting beauty from a bear-garden, competing with a raree-show of bull-baiting and blood-boltered carnival amid a welter of lusty living, loving, and carousing. By the Avon he was carefully investing what he won in London. To look for the essential Shakespeare is immediately to be confronted with the major and ever-engrossing Elizabethan mystery. The question is, concisely, this. How could an epoch so brutish and so cruel in its pursuit

of power and pleasure have been so delicate in its pursuit of
the tender passion, the verbal beauty, and the musical
harmonies which were always so ravishing to Shakespeare's
sensibility ?

How close can we come to that London of 1600 which was
at once scaffold, whipping-post, bawdy-house, baiting-ring,
music-box for ' heavenly harmony,' and platform of the sons
of Apollo ?   Often there have been these associations, these
queer cousins among human doings and desires, but scarcely
ever were they packed so close together as in Elizabeth's tiny
London and especially on the Southwark shore of the busy,
music-ringing Thames.

It is an undrained, unwatered, fetid London, with plague
ever waiting to pounce, its scavengers the rats and kites and
carrion-crows.   Yet the wits who are being rowed over from
the Inns of Court are dressed in the exquisite foppery of the
world.   Their talk is carved into conceits.   They have lutes and
voices and they sing lyrics as fine-spun in beauty as any ever
wrought by this most lyrical of nations.   Done with their
voyage and their madrigals, they join the stench and squalor of
the Paris Garden mob and enter the Globe to hear the mightiest
of lines, the tenderest of songs, the dying fall of an iambic on
some boy-player's lips, word-music which went whispering
out of Southwark into the air-stream of the ages and is now
for ever on the lips of men.   Two lines of a Shakespeare Sonnet
sum up the paradox of the City and the time in which the man
was working,

> How 'gainst this rage shall beauty hold a plea
> Whose action is no stronger than a flower ?

Life raged, coarse as a hurricane, about the roots of English
poetry then: but the flower held.

That is one reason why this Shakespeare Wonder appeals
especially to me.   To seek to probe this paradox of beastliness
and beauty is adventure enough.   Curiosity, steeled by a
combative loyalty, is the spur.   Combative, because every man
fights for his own Shakespeare: loyal, because without

devotion nobody would take the trouble to retread so much hard-trodden ground. What William Shakespeare wrote (in all sincerity, I think) to Henry Wriothesley, Earl of Southampton, in the preface to *Lucrece*, I make bold to apply to him, who is my subject, ' What I have done is yours; what I have to do is yours: being part in all I have, devoted yours.' In short, this is a lover's book.

CHAPTER II

' Unwillingly to School '

ONE fact alone is known for certain about the boyhood and youth of William Shakespeare. By ' known for certain ' I mean supported by contemporary documentary evidence. The existence of such evidence does not, of course, guarantee its accuracy and, when we come to examine Shakespeare's marriage, we shall see how ready are some scholars to disparage or explain away a contemporary documentary statement when it does not suit their book. But there seems little reason for disputing the announcement in the register of Stratford Parish Church attached to the date April 26, 1564, that William, son of John Shakespeare,* was then baptised. Except for hearsay and conjecture nothing more is known of this infant until we reach the tangled affair of his wedding in November, 1582. His actual birthday is unknown. April 23 has been assumed, perhaps for reasons of symmetry and aptitude. It was the day of Shakespeare's death and is celebrated also as the day of St. George of England.

Something is known, and much more has been argued, about the parents of this child, who was so hugely to enrich the world of poetry and, in a more material way, the township of his birth. John Shakespeare the father was the son of Richard Shakespeare, yeoman of Snitterfield, a village lying three and a half miles to the north-east of Stratford. John had married, probably in 1557, Mary Arden, youngest daughter of Robert Arden of Wilmcote in the parish of Aston Cantlow. Extensive researches have been made by specialists into the previous history of the Shakespeares and the Ardens. For those who are mainly interested in John and Mary's third

*There were several variant spellings of Shakespeare. I have kept to the most familiar one for convenience sake.

child, William, it is unnecessary to recapitulate all that has
been dug up about the yeomen of Snitterfield and about the
comparative grandeur of the Ardens. The significant fact is
that the Shakespeares were solid tillers of the land and mer-
chants of its products: so too were some of the Ardens, since
younger sons of the landed gentry were then compelled to
fend for themselves.

> The lot of younger sons was proverbially a hard one. Both
> law and practice combined to keep the estate unbroken, from
> one generation to another, in the hands of the eldest son and
> heir, for the maintenance and perpetuation of the family
> name. Younger sons had to accept what provision could
> be made for them, to engage in agriculture or to sink into the
> class of mere adventurers.

Thus John Semple Smart in his valuable book, *Shakespeare—
Truth and Tradition*. He goes on to quote illustrations from
Shakespeare's own plays of the plight of younger sons. Orlando,
in *As You Like It*, complains that his father, Sir Rowland de
Boys, left him but ' four thousand crowns ' and that his elder
brother kept him rustically and stalled him like an ox. Smart
also cites Poins in *Henry IV*, who was a second son of a noble
house but lacked ' visible means of subsistence,' except in so far
as his Prince bestowed them.

The Ardens of the senior succession were lordly people
indeed, pre-Conquest notables, accepted by William the
Conqueror, retaining their Warwickshire lands, rising with
Simon de Montfort, battling with the House of York, and
recovering lost territory under Edward IV. Their big house
was Park Hall near Birmingham. Though Mary Arden's
branch of the family were junior and so had to be self-
maintenant, there is ample proof that all of her branch were
on easy terms with the nobility and gentry of the Midlands.

It is essential to remember this when we are trying to visualise
Shakespeare's boyhood. Human nature being in these
matters fairly constant, Mrs. John Shakespeare's conversation
must have included a good many references to the Arden
past, the Arden tradition, and the Arden lands. (In *As*

You Like It, William Shakespeare's Forest of Arden play, the youngest son is the hero and there is restitution of rights to the unfortunates at the close: also the woodland society is, on the higher levels, ducal.) The urgency with which Shakespeare, as soon as he was professionally successful, fought to win (or to recover) from the Heralds' College a Shakespeare coat of arms is significant and partly explained by the Arden blood in him.

John Shakespeare had, to keep his end up, laid claim to some past family splendour, referring to an antecessor honoured by Henry VII. But not much detail was offered. The plea was favoured by Sir William Dethick, Garter King-of-Arms, in October, 1596, and confirmed in 1599. The motto was ' Non Sans Droict ' (Not without Right). The crest contained a silver spear and falcon. In 1599 it was officially added concerning the Shakespeare arms, ' We have lykewise uppon an other escutcheone impaled the same with the Auncyent Arms of the said Arden of Wellingcote ' (i.e. Wilmcote).

So honour therein was satisfied, and both sides of the family could feel that young William had done them well by the pressure of his personality, connection and finances in London, and that Wilmcote Ardens and Snitterfield Shakespeares were equally admitted to the status of armigerent gentility. It was a solution all the happier since the financial troubles that had befallen the family in Stratford during the two previous decades were now less pressing. The son had made himself ' Sweet Mr. Shakespeare ' among the wits and grandees of the capital, and Master Shakespeare, Non Sans Droict, of New Place, the principal house of his home-town. Whether or not the boy had disgraced himself in his teens, he was certainly, Mary Shakespeare could reflect, a good scion of the Ardens now. A harlotry player ? A motley to the view ? Perhaps, but decently far away. Here in Warwickshire he was a man of property, an investor, one of the crest-and-motto Shakespeares whose antecessor had done so well for Henry VII. If one of the nobler Ardens, passing through Stratford, on the verge of the Arden lands, called in for a glass of wine with John Shakespeare, there could no longer be much condescension. The glover in a poor way of business, as John might have been called in the 1580's, was up again. In the enjoyment of this sunset John lived till 1601 and Mary till 1608.

Theirs was not, on the whole, a healthy family, although they themselves lived to a good age, judged by Elizabethan standards of longevity. William was the third child. Two sisters, Joan, born in September, 1558, and Margaret, born in November, 1562, had died in infancy. So William's early months must have been watched with a careful anxiety. A son had come at last! Was he to go so quickly too? Plague visited Stratford three months after the boy's birth. There were 237 deaths between July and December. There must have been great alarm and much hurried retreat to country farms. William survived and was followed by Gilbert (1566) and Joan (1569). Then came Anne (1571), who died at the age of eight. Then Richard, 1574, and Edmund, 1580; these two died at twenty-nine and twenty-seven respectively. The toughest life was that of the second Joan, who, as Mrs. Hart, died at the age of seventy-seven. William, who lived to be fifty-two, was the second in tenacity. His only son, Hamnet, died at the age of eleven in 1596. His three grandsons, by his daughter Judith Quiney, all died young, and by 1670 he had no direct descendants at all. The Shakespeare blood only flowed on through Joan Hart and her descendants. (See Appendix I.)

Mary Shakespeare must have lived laborious days and been hardened to the preparation of the funeral meats and trappings as well as of the layette. Three daughters, one son, and a grandson died during her life-time. Looking at the records of the Shakespeare group, one notices the lethal power of the early months of the year. There was much dying in April, when William himself was smitten in his middle age. That, of course, is always, to some extent, the case. The cold strengthens with the lengthening day and many a time have Birthday celebrants at Stratford felt a wind with fangs and claws come prowling across the Clopton Bridge with a sharp, pneumoniac menace. The body has been cheated of sun for seven or eight months and in the sixteenth century the winter diet was a murderous ally of the winter weather.

The absence of root-crops meant a great slaughtering of

stock at Michaelmas, when the grass began to lose its quality. The breeding-stock was spared; the rest had to be slain, salted, preserved, owing to the absence of winter-feed. There were no potatoes in Shakespeare's boyhood and British people have recently learned with suffering to how great an extent a modern diet is based upon this crop. Salt meat, salt fish, and wholemeal bread were the staples of Tudor England. For vegetables there was the cabbage-patch and, of more relish, leeks and onions. If mention in the plays is any fair test of what is working in the writer's consciousness, vegetables meant little to William Shakespeare. He mentions no carrots (save once in a pun on the Latin word ' caret '), no cauliflowers, no spinach, no sprouts: turnips and cabbage appear once each. When Shallow entertains Falstaff, the menu is some pigeons, a couple of short-legged hens, a joint of mutton, and kickshaws. If we take the last to be sweets or savouries, there are no vegetables mentioned. Pigeons were a great resource of the Tudor larder in winter, and I have been told that, if you eat pigeon every day for a month, you die. Not much caring for pigeon, I have never put this grave (or graveyard) matter to the test. But presumably the legend has some basis in the less than salutary effects of continuous application to pigeon. Dr. Martin Mitchell in his book on *The Shakespeare Circle* actually links pigeon-meat with the Ardens:

> Incidentally, the difficulty of fresh meat in Winter and Spring helps to explain the large numbers and huge size of the pigeon houses then so much in use. They often held up to 600 or 800 couples (Mary Arden's pigeon house at Wilmcote, still well preserved, could accommodate 650 pairs). The privileged clergy sometimes had pigeon lofts actually above the chancel but under the roof of the Church, as may be seen to-day at Elkington and Overbury, near Tewkesbury.

Salt meat, salt fish, few vegetables. The winter table was monotonous. There was, accordingly, a common deficiency of Vitamin C, and in consequence of that scurvy was a general affliction. Shakespeare's son-in-law, Dr. John Hall, who married his elder daughter Susanna, was not only the principal

medical man of his area, but an author.   He has left, under
the admirable title of *Select Observations On Human Bodies*, his
case-book.   He wrote in Latin and in detail.   There is a
lamentable gap in that he fails to say anything of his father-
in-law's condition before death and of what overtook him.
But there is much about his patients in general.   Scurvy was
usual: the doctor's own wife had it.

Hall's methods were severe.   He purged his patients
vigorously and set them vomiting.   Dr. Mitchell records the
doctor's orders.   Sometimes this attack on the trouble seems
to have been well earned.   There was Squire Beaufoi, who ate
' great quantities of creame ' at the end of his ample supper
and was given ten vomits and three stools, ' which answered
desire.'   Then there was the Countess of Northampton, who
in March, 1620,

> fell into that dropsy called anasarca with swelling of the face
> and feet and was cured as followeth: " . . . a decoction
> (containing 28 herbs and drugs).   First day 8 stooles.   The
> second day 18 and the third 15 without any losse of strength."
> Then for 5 mornings an electuary.   Then another decoction
> in white wine, 6 ounces in morning and 4 ounces at night
> causing her " well to sweat."   " And every third day she was
> purged with another mixture . . .   after which she was
> perfectly cured and brought to a good colour in 20 days
> space."   The Countess was the daughter and heiress of Sir
> John Spencer, Lord Mayor of London, " the Rich Spencer "
> as he was called.

It was no light matter to take orders from Dr. Hall.   His
' practice ' was evidently of a high social tone and must have
brought a decent income to the comfortable and well-gardened
and spacious house in Old Town still known as Hall's Croft.
Hall gratified the nobility and gentry by his cunning removal
of their itches.   Lady Underhill who ' felt as if it were biting
of ants in many parts of her body and these from scurvy ' was
relieved of this pest and ' highly praised the apozeme as
if it wrought by enchantment.'   (An apozeme was an in-
fusion of herbs, an electuary a powder mixed in honey or
syrup.)   Hall's use of plant juices to cure scurvy was sound

enough, but the general methods of the time seem frightening and even filthy now. Those who called in the doctor might be ordering some very odd medicaments when they did so.

Pigeons were not only much in the larder: they were used as conductors of poison in case of plague. In cases of Bubonic, live pigeons were laid with the fundament naked to the sore, those dying being replaced. The cure-all known as a Mithridaticum—since Mithridates was supposed to have made himself poison-proof—contained viper's flesh among its fifty ingredients, and the unguents and plasters used by Hall bring us right up against the magical (and nauseating) pharmacopeia of the Witches in *Macbeth*, and the mumbo-jumbo of Jonson's *The Alchemist*. Mitchell records that

> One of Hall's applications included the webs of spiders and a little powder of nut shells. A poultice was made of ' swallows nests, dirt, dung and all, boiled in oil of chamomel and lillies, beaten and passed through a sieve, to which was added white dog's turd one ounce, the meal of linseed and foenugreek, each one ounce, ointment of Diathea and hen's grease each half-an-ounce—and so make a poultice—it is applied hot.'

> We find such preparations as water of frog's spawn for gouty fomentations, also a powder of earthworms and the white of hen's dung in white wine.

> Shavings of ivory were often used. ' A fume of horse hoofs burnt, restored a patient as soon as it was brought to her nostrils.' One powder for fainting was so good, says Hall, that he always carried it about with him.

On the whole it must have been easy for a delicate child to dwindle on the diet of the time and to remain unmended by the curative practice of the day. William Shakespeare, following two cases of infant mortality in his family, exposed to risk of plague, and surviving to be the second eldest of a large and somewhat brief-lived family, must have been anxiously watched and fairly healthy too in an age of poor nutrition and of primitive medicine.

Hall was a Cambridge man and had studied in France. He

rose to high repute. His methods were probably far in advance of some used by the rougher country doctors when Shakespeare was a boy. One shudders at considering what happened to mothers in a long, hard labour, or if struck with fever afterwards. Mary Arden (Mrs. John Shakespeare), who lived for exactly fifty years after the coming of her first child, and had seven live births, must have been a hardy woman: for that was longevity in those days.

No incontestable fact, as I said, is known about William Shakespeare's life between the day of his baptism in Stratford and the announcement in Worcester of his intended marriage. He flourished where his two elder sisters had faded. He obviously went to school. As there are no pupil lists of Stratford Grammar School at the time of his boyhood, we have no evidence that he went there and no evidence that he did not. The chances are, naturally, that he did. Where else would he go ? His father, though a prominent citizen and reasonably prosperous, at least during William Shakespeare's boyhood, would not disdain the free education there offered. And what was the alternative ?

There is no reason to think that Shakespeare enjoyed his schooldays. Few children of that period can have done so. The lessons were dull, the discipline severe. Looking backward from the autumnal years that gave us the last, romantic plays, Shakespeare could idealise the innocence of boyhood at play, regardless, like Thomas Gray's Etonians, of future doom,

> Two boys that thought there was no more behind
> But such a day to-morrow as to-day
> And to be boy eternal.

The simple bliss is further pictured (by Polixenes in *The Winter's Tale*).

> We were as twinn'd lambs that did frisk i' the sun
> And bleat the one at the other: what we chang'd
> Was innocence for innocence: we knew not
> The doctrine of ill-doing: no, nor dream'd
> That any did.

But those are tales out of school. The journey towards the desk is several times described as slow and sad. 'Creeping like snail unwillingly to school' and 'Toward school with heavy looks' are familiar to all. Bianca, in the Pedant Episode of *The Taming of the Shrew*, exclaims,

> I am no breeching scholar in the schools,
> I'll not be tied to hours nor 'pointed times.

And the leaving of school is seen as a happy business in the same play. Elsewhere there is emphasis on the bliss of escape when, the school broken up, ' each hurries to his house and sporting place.' Convention always envisages the school-child as attending lessons with sluggish resentment, but Shakespeare certainly stresses the reluctance and nowhere suggests that his pedagogues gave him light or leading.

The chief masters at Stratford Grammar School in his time were Walter Roche, who left in 1571 to become a lawyer and remained in legal practice in the town. Next came Simon Hunt (1571-1575), who had Papist leanings at a time when these were dangerous. He appears to have been badly ' ragged,' left for Douai and Rome, and became a Jesuit. He died in Rome in 1585. He was followed by Thomas Jenkins, who, being Welsh, may have originated the character of Sir Hugh Evans, the parson-dominie of *The Merry Wives of Windsor*. It was of Evans that Falstaff complained that he called cheese and butter Seese and Putter and so ' made fritters of English.'

It is significant that there is a scene in which Sir Hugh examines young William Page in elementary Latin. Because William is a simple lad and Mistress Quickly drags in the phrase ' Hang-hog is Latin, for bacon, I warrant you,' referring to hunc, hanc, hoc, the Baconians have seized on this certainly rather pointless scene in order to maintain that we are being given a hint as to the true ' Hang-hog ' author. Sir Hugh is in the play a droll, but his form of education is dull enough and one cannot imagine his original kindling a spark in his pupils.

Another schoolmaster in the plays is Holofernes in *Love's*

Labour's Lost. The curate Nathaniel praises him, it is true, as a good instructor of youth, but he turns out to be a monstrous word-spinner, a devotee of pedantic Latinity and a mouther of polysyllabic jargon. Had he a model in Stratford? Shakespeare may have elsewhere knocked against this type of classical prig who rejoices to hear the afternoon called ' the posterior of the day,' a phrase that seems to him ' well-culled, sweet, and apt.' Holofernes has lived long on the alms-basket of words, says the clown Costard, and goes about, nose aloft, sniffing out false Latin. The character is rarely so amusing on the stage as one expects: at least that is my own experience as a playgoer. But that holds of much in this comedy which reads better than it plays, so that producers are driven to all sorts of inventions and fantastications in order to keep the fun alive. But what exquisite reading it contains! And the final songs, of Spring and Winter, are the perfect voice of English country, as full of blossom and glimmer as of stolchy mud, with April's bird-pipings and girls' chatter set against December's sniffs and coughs and soughing of the icy wind.

John Brinsley's *Ludus Literarius* or The Grammar Schoole (1612) gives a grim picture of the discipline imposed through ' jerks ' of the rod and by detention. There was no idea in Brinsley's mind that the boy eternal knew not the doctrine of ill-doing: there was no Original Virtue, as Shakespeare saw it, in his philosophy. He spied Original Sin and believed the birch to be its divinely appointed remedy. The Devil was in the boys and had to be flayed out of them. The Puritan attitude to childhood was dourly expressed in Lewes Bayly's *Practice of Pietie*,

> What is youth, but an untamed beast? All whose actions are rash, and rude, not capable of good counsel when it is given; and ape-like, delighting in nothing but in toys and baubles? Therefore thou no sooner begannest to have a little strength and discretion, but forthwith thou wast kept under the rod and fear of parents and masters: as if thou hadst been born to live under the discipline of others, rather than at the disposition of thine own will. No tired horse was ever more willing to be rid of his burden, than thou

wast to get out of the servile state of this bondage—a state
not worth the description.

There were sensitive schoolmasters, as Dover Wilson reminds
us in *Life in Shakespeare's England*: one Willis, an exact contemporary of Shakespeare's, paid a very fine tribute to Master
Gregory Downhale of Pembroke Hall in Cambridge, who at
Christ's School in the City of Gloucester stirred reverence and
love in his pupil and, adds Willis, ' made me also love my
book, love being the most prevalent affection in nature to
further our studies and endeavours in any profession.' There
is no evidence that Shakespeare ever met one of Downhale's
kind or encountered such a liberal attitude to the young idea
and such a victory over young affection. The nearest that he
comes to praising a pedagogue is in Nathaniel's compliment
to Holofernes, but Nathaniel is described later as ' a foolish,
mild man,' a kindly neighbour and good at bowls, but unlikely to be a judge of men: Holofernes is shown as a pompous
and loquacious booby.

Willis's striking salute to a schoolmaster stands out as a
rarity. The boys in Marlowe's mind are subject

> To Pedants that with cruel lashes flay them

and that is the common note. Brinsley's sour regimen was laid
out in detail. The masters and ushers were inquisitors.

So always at such playing times before the exeats, the master
and ushers to view every form through; and then to cause
them all to sit still whom they remember to have been
negligent or faulty in any special sort worthy of punishment,
and to do some exercise in writing besides; either those which
they have omitted before or such as wherein they cannot be
idle. But herein there must be a special care when they are
thus restrained from play, that either master or usher, if it can
be conveniently, have an eye to them that they cannot loiter;
or some one specially appointed, to see that they do their
tasks. Also that they be called to an account the next

morning whether they have done the tasks enjoined, under pain of six jerks to be surely paid.

Further on he lays down an elaborate technique of corporal punishments and includes such odious discourse as this:

> Finally, as God hath sanctified the rod and correction, to cure the evils of their conditions, to drive out that folly which is bound up in their hearts, to save their souls from hell, to give them wisdom; so it is to be used as God's instrument to these purposes. To spare them in these cases is to hate them. To love them is to correct them betime. Do it under God, and for Him to these ends and with these cautions, and you shall never hurt them: you have the Lord for your warrant.

We need not assume that Stratford's Jenkins was a man of Brinsley's detestable kind, but the common discipline was severe and there is no trace in Shakespeare's writing that ' the boy eternal ' was happy in the classroom.

Brilliant men have been dull in school, but it is difficult to believe that Shakespeare found learning onerous. The essence of his life was speed. He rose rapidly to be Johannes Factotum in the theatre: he rapidly soaked himself in the Renaissance classicism which came gushing out triumphantly in *Venus and Adonis* and *Lucrece*. His life was a continuous hustle of acting, managing and composing plays and poems as well as of looking after property in London and Stratford and yet he left not a blot in his papers. The adult mind was exceptionally clear and quick. Why suppose that the boy could not cope precociously with Hunt and Jenkins and their ' Hang-hog ' Latin lessons ?

The best authority on Stratford life is Fripp, who applied himself with relentless industry to all Stratfordian records and documents. In *Shakespeare, Man and Artist*, he left us two volumes of immense research warmed by devotion. Like most of the Shakespeareans he fashions William according to his own predilections and those predilections are not always mine. But I regard Fripp's work as insufficiently acknowledged. He helps one better than most to picture a small boy's hard life in the sixteenth century. A lad had to be up and clean and at school by seven in winter and six in summer, when ' an act of corporate worship' opened the day. There was a pause at nine for breakfast, then lessons till eleven. There was a two hours' break for dinner, taken at home, and then lessons from one till five, with two half-holidays a week in term, and forty days in the year of total vacation. It was a long day for a small boy, especially as the children were expected to lay the table at home and wait on their parents before they had their own meal. Small wonder then that he went ' toward school with heavy looks.'

On the other hand there is no indication in Shakespeare's writing that he bore sad memories of home. His sympathies are with the elders ' stooping with their children's oppression' and he alludes to

> unbridled children, grown
> Too headstrong for their mother.

There is a well-known passage in *Measure for Measure* about the kindly parents,

> Having bound up the threatening twigs of birch
> Only to stick it in their children's sight
> For terror, not to use, in time the rod
> Becomes more mock'd than feared.

Was that his memory of John Shakespeare's domestic practice or a description of his own ? I get no suggestion of an oppressed childhood. He may even have been a little spoiled, being the first son after two casualties.

Dr. Plume, Vicar of Greenwich, recorded in 1657 some talk of Admiral Sir John Mennes and his early memories.

> He (Shakespeare) was a glover's son. Sir John Mennes saw once his old father in his shop, a merry-cheekt old man that said, ' Will was a good honest fellow, but he dared have crackt a jesst with him att any time.'

The roseate hues and blithe good temper of Shakespeare senior may well be authentic. The boys who appear in the plays, though often in tragic surroundings, are generally alert, self-confident, precocious children. The theatre-boys had, no doubt, to be given effective lines in parts which would show up well. The pert back-answer was a special gift to them. Master Macduff's observations on the fate and frequency of those who swear and lie are an example. When allowance has been made for the kind of smart talk in which the ' little eyases ' would score with the audience I retain my feeling that Shakespeare wrote from recollections of a free childhood in a liberal home, compared with which school was dull and gloomy.

Nor was it, I am convinced, an illiterate home. Waves of controversy have rolled over John Shakespeare's mental attainments. The anti-Stratfordians, who want to reduce their pet villain, Shagsper the Actor, the Clown from Stratford, to the lowest level of illiteracy, so that he must be disqualified from any claims to authorship, have had great larks with a dung-heap outside the house in Henley Street. For leaving this, twelve years before William's birth, John and two neighbours, Reynolds and Quiney, had been fined. Sanitation was never a strong feature of Elizabethan life and it has little enough connection with the ability to read and write. One may surmise that if Stratford had had fewer of what Milton called ' sewers that annoy the air,' and more closed-up drains and conduits, there would have been fewer flies and fewer deaths of infants. But what of that ? The dung-heap argument smells chiefly of a desire to discredit Stratford at all costs.

It is further and more reasonably claimed that John left no signature: we have his mark in the borough records. But so have we the mark of others who were well able to write and left their signatures. Smart, in his *Shakespeare—Truth and Tradition*, cleared up this point for all time.

The belief that there was nothing derogatory in signing with the cross, or with such symbols, lasted through the Middle Ages and into the time of Elizabeth. Evidence from Stratford itself is not wanting. John Shakespeare had a next-door neighbour, Adrian Quiney, father of Richard Quiney, the poet's friend. Adrian Quiney could write very well and dispatched several letters to his son in London. He asks that the key of his study may be sent home, in order that he may seek there for certain documents, and talks garrulously of lambs, colts, and knit hose at Evesham Market. But in the records of Stratford Council, and on the very page where John Shakespeare makes a mark, Adrian Quiney also makes a mark. This obviously literate Adrian Quiney had also shared the dung-hill and the fine in 1552! So plainly that offence against public health, by modern standards, was no proof of inability to hold a pen and cover paper with intelligible markings.

Furthermore John Shakespeare held several public offices, including that of Borough Chamberlain or Treasurer. He had his own business as a glover and leather merchant to run, and the idea that all this private and public business could be conducted by an ignorant bumpkin working with tallies is very difficult to believe. Would an Arden have been likely to marry the unlettered oaf whom the anti-Stratfordians love to depict? The idea of ' a bookless neighbourhood,' as Tudor Stratford has been described, can be dissipated easily. The parson who baptised William Shakespeare, John Bretchgirdle, had a large library and bequeathed books in English and Latin to the sons of William Smith, a draper and Councillor of Stratford, whose house must have been on the same social and cultural level as that of John Shakespeare, glover and Councillor too.

Nor do Shakespeare's plays suggest illiteracy as normal. Jack Cade in *Henry VI* is anti-literate, and wages a proletarian war on such bourgeois institutions as Grammar Schools and paper-mills. But the servitors in the plays can read and write: Maria in *Twelfth Night* is a first-rate scrivener. Mistress Quickly can write out a reckoning, and Mopsa the Shepherdess in *The Winter's Tale* buys printed ballads because she loves to study them. The rude mechanicals and amateur actors of Athens, obviously English country types, can read their own parts. To follow Smart on this topic is to be well convinced that the conception of Stratford as a gross hamlet buried in dung and ignorance is ridiculous. Nor, as a matter of fact, is it necessary to the anti-Stratfordian case. If some notable person were trying to father his plays on a suitable second, he would naturally select a ' stooge ' of some admitted education; otherwise the trick would have taken in nobody. To reduce Shakespeare and his origins to the level of illiterate barbarism is not only against the evidence: it does not help at all the case for Bacon, Oxford, or whoever may be the chosen figure behind the supposed mask of William.

Ample has been written about Shakespeare's riverside boyhood, the fishing and bathing in the Avon, the following of sports, the watching of the flight as some lordly falconers released their ' tassel-gentles ' to ' stoop ' upon the partridge or the mallard, the winter day behind the hounds at work, the observing with compassion of poor Wat, the hunted hare. Of the writers of his period Shakespeare was the most concerned for the victim of the sport. His quickness to appreciate all excellence of skill made him aware of the huntsman's craft and of the hounds' true quality: he knew, too, that the hounds do not come unscathed from the chase. Here is a passage from *Venus and Adonis*, not often quoted, that rings of a day in the thorny coverts:

> Here kennell'd in a brake she finds a hound,
> And asks the weary caitiff for his master;
> And there another licking of his wound,
> 'Gainst venom'd sores the only sovereign plaster;
>   And here she meets another sadly scowling,
>   To whom she speaks, and he replies with howling.
>
> When he hath ceas'd his ill-resounding noise,
> Another flap-mouth'd mourner, black and grim,
> Against the welkin volleys out his voice;
> Another and another answer him,
>   Clapping their proud tailes to the ground below,
>   Shaking their scratch'd ears, bleeding as they go.

Still, they are better off than poor Wat, the description of whose plight is more familiar,

By this, poor Wat, far off upon a hill,
Stands on his hinder legs with list'ning ear.
To hearken if his foes pursue him still:
Anon their loud alarums he doth hear;
    And now his grief may be compared well
    To one sore sick that hears the passing-bell.

Then shalt thou see the dew-bedabbled wretch
Turn, and return, indenting with the way;
Each envious brier his weary legs doth scratch,
Each shadow makes him stop, each murmur stay;
    For misery is trodden on by many,
    And being low never reliev'd by any.

Yet we need not associate all Shakespeare's country lore, as many do, with Avon and its water-meadows. He travelled much as an actor and knew his England. The London to which he went was only a small town by our standards: he could leave it easily on foot and would be rapidly out of it on horse. He had only to take an afternoon stroll from his first place of work north of the river to the knolls and meres of Islington, then famous for its duck and later for its water supply, to see the archers at practice and the fowlers at their sport. He could brush up his botany by going no further than what was Piccadilla or Peckadilla then, and is Piccadilly now. (The name is probably derived from the country house owned by a prosperous haberdasher and ruff-maker: a peckadill or pickadil was a ruff and the rich man's mansion came to be known as Pickadilla Hall.) Gerard the Herbalist found many simples ' on the banks of Piccadilla.' It is needless to suppose that, whenever Shakespeare mentioned beast, bird, and flower, he was thinking of Warwickshire. His London was a little urban island amid marsh and forest, whose citizens could go a-birding as easily as they could go to the play.

At the same time in his life, presumably early, he became a student of land and its enemies. A picture of weedy desolation is most vividly described by the Duke of Burgundy in *Henry V* (v, ii). Of France he says,

Her vine, the merry cheerer of the heart,
Unpruned dies; her hedges even-pleach'd,
Like prisoners wildly overgrown with hair,
Put forth disorder'd twigs; her fallow leas
The darnel, hemlock, and rank fumitory,
Do root upon, while that the coulter rusts,
That should deracinate such savagery;
The even mead, that erst brought sweetly forth
The freckled cowslip, burnet, and green clover,
Wanting the scythe, all uncorrected, rank,
Conceives by idleness, and nothing teems
But hateful docks, rough thistles, kecksies, burs,
Losing both beauty and utility.

The man who put such detail into that passage knew something of a farm run down and of land ' in bad heart.'   William Bliss in *The Real Shakespeare* stresses Shakespeare's close acquaintance with gardening and weeding.   The boy was obviously fascinated by the snail and shocked by the depredations of the caterpillar.   The latter is frequently associated with weeds, especially as a symbol of corruption and decay in the commonwealth.

Why should we, in the compass of a pale,
Keep law and form and due proportion,
Showing, as in a model, our firm estate,
When our sea-walled garden, the whole land,
Is full of weeds; her fairest flowers chok'd up,
Her fruit trees all unprun'd, her hedges ruin'd,
Her knots disorder'd, and her wholesale herbs
Swarming with caterpillars ?

On the other hand, his delicate observation was sympathetically awakened by the snail, who, when hit,

Shrinks backward in his shelly cave with pain,
And there, all smother'd up, in shade doth sit,
Long after fearing to creep forth again.

No man can be a great poet without intense sensitivity. Shakespeare's attention was continually held by the tiniest things in nature, especially by the wren, ' the most diminutive,' the wren ' with little quill,' smallest of British birds. He was fascinated, too, by the drops in the cowslip's bell and by ' the tender horns of cockled snails,' than which only Love is ' more soft and sensible.'

So the picture I fancy—and, of course, we can claim no more than fancy for our Shakespeare glimpses—is of a small boy kept busy yet happy in the home, going unwillingly to school, despite ability to master his lessons, healthy enough amid unhealth, carefully watched by parents proud of their eldest child, having a good, well-tended time in a socially ambitious household. He was happiest, perhaps, when left alone to watch things. That he was sensitive and easily put to shame is one of Dr. Spurgeon's derivations for the numerous allusions to change of facial colour. She writes (*Shakespeare's Imagery*, p. 58):

Shakespeare's intense interest in the human face has never, I think, been adequately noticed: its frowns and wrinkles, smiles and tears, the tint and shape of the nose, the tension of the nostrils, the eye, its colour and character, 'in flood with laughter,' sparkling, sun-bright, quick, merry, fiery, mistful, dim, lack-lustre, heavy, hollow, modest, sober, sunken or scornful; the peculiar beauty of the eyelid, the betrayal of the gnawing of a nether lip, the dimples on a child's chin, and, above all, the way in which he continually makes us *see* the emotions of his characters by the chasing changes of colour in their cheeks.

There again it is the minute details, the downy curtains and fringes over the azure-veining of the eye, that are so precisely noted and so perfectly described.

The further conjecture is made by Dr. Spurgeon:

Shakespeare is so conscious of the betraying change of colour in the face, as the signal flag of various emotions, fear, anger, astonishment, pleasure, and he so vividly and constantly describes it either directly or by means of an image, that I cannot help surmising that he himself, like Richard II, was fair and flushed easily, and that possibly in youth he suffered from the ease with which, under stress of feeling, he betrayed his emotions through blushing or pallor.

A recent snub from the schoolmaster, more stinging than ' a jerk,' would add to the reluctance of the morning's journey; those who flush quickly suffer both the pain that caused the colouring and the laughter of those who see and mock the blush.

What the boy learned at school is clearly traceable in his plays. The subject has been often treated and a clear, succinct statement is to be found in Fripp's first volume. There are a number of Shakespearean allusions to Lily's *Short Introduction to Grammar*: the significant scene between Sir Hugh Evans and William Page draws directly on Lily and the other Shakespearean schoolmaster, Holofernes, also quotes him. Holofernes has this learning at his fingertips, *ad unguem*, which leads to the clown's (not very brilliant) punning on *ad unguem* and dunghill, a possible echo of some old schoolroom joke: for the jape is on the schoolboy level and dunghills were familiar in Stratford. Had not John Shakespeare been fined for carelessness in this regard ?

It is noticeable that Latin quotations are frequent in the early plays, when Lily's Grammar would be most in mind. *Titus Andronicus* and *The Taming of the Shrew* each have one direct allusion to Lily's lesson-book and Caesar's Commentaries are quoted in *Henry VI*, Part 2. Virgil, Horace, and Seneca also left their mark. But Ovid was the boy's particular favourite and remained so: William so drenched his mind in Ovid that Francis Meres made his famous declaration (in 1598) that ' the sweet, witty soul of Ovid lives on in honey-tongued Shakespeare: witness his Venus and Adonis, his Lucrece, his sugred Sonnets among his private friends.'

Ovid—and the Bible! Contrasts indeed, but the double addiction to the sensuous romances of the Roman, exiled so long and so bitterly for the licence of his writing, and to the legends of Jehovah and his chosen people, stories in which the moral is continually stressed, reveal once more the width of

Shakespeare's relish. The Chronicles of the Jews were implanted in his mind: his parallels, similes, and images prove that time without number. Yet he was not, apparently, a consistently or deeply religious man. His pessimism, when in spate, was of a pagan kind and death, for example, allured him more as a sleep and a forgetting than as the gateway to another and more vivid life. The truth surely is that he was gripped both by a good story and a flashing or a thundering phrase. Ovid, whether taken in the Latin or in Golding's translation, gave him warm, pulsing narrative. The Genevan Bible of his young tuition proclaimed its lessons, as it put forth its legends, with the added magic of an English prose that was rapidly moving to full stature.

It is not impossible that Shakespeare went to the University. The fact that his name occurs in no Students' roll does not settle the issue. These rolls were then very loosely kept and instances have been brought forward of several men who left no trace in the books of Colleges which they are known to have attended. But, if the boy had gone to Oxford, as was natural to a Stratfordian, living only forty miles away, the legends would surely have picked the fact up and some triumph of wit or deed of young audacity would have been added by the eighteenth-century gossips to the Shakespeare Myth.

I surmise that the young Shakespeare, however gifted, was never a headmaster's pet and might not have appeared to Jenkins as meriting scholastic promotion. Unless Jenkins had been unusually acute he could easily have passed over a preoccupied, rather difficult boy, resentful of pedagogic routine, with a dream-life of his own which he satisfied in private reading, in countryside diversions, and in unofficial ' nature study.' That kind of boy does not stride up the educational ladder with the easy motion achieved by others possessing a more patient character and more readily accepting the curriculum. Nor does that kind of boy appeal to the makers of legend. While Jenkins might have liked a more docile, concentrating type of ladder-climbing pupil, the builders of anecdote certainly preferred the poacher and the tippler to make a basis for their tourist-fetching yarn of the Avonian Will, the Lad of the Village, the devil for adventure. I visualise a boy intolerant of dull teaching and becoming increasingly restless as he realised how much his mind and fancy outraced the slow plodding of the dominie: but not a whining, self-pitying, or dismal type. There was escape in reading and in roaming beside the river, where ' boy eternal ' could look forward with ' sparking and delight ' to ' such a day to-morrow as to-day.'

CHAPTER III

'I Came to Wive'

WE can come back from supposition to fact, to the second documented fact in William Shakespeare's life, namely his marriage. For nothing that intervened between baptism and banns have we any certain authority. But when the young man had reached the age of eighteen and a half he was again in the records of ecclesiastical information. And once more we plunge straight into a puzzle.

On November 27, 1582, an entry was made in the episcopal register at Worcester. This set down the issue of a marriage licence to William Shaxpere and Anne Whateley of Temple Grafton. On the next day two yeomen of Stratford, Fulk Sandells and John Richardson, agreed to pay forty pounds should any legal consideration arise to prevent the marriage of William Shagspere and ' Anne Hathway of Stratford in the Dioces of Worcester maiden.' What was sought was a marriage between these two after a single reading of the banns instead of after the usual three. It was the object of Sandells and Richardson to indemnify the Bishop and his officials for any action or suit arising from the grant of this special licence. They were, in fact, guaranteeing the absence of let or hindrance such as consanguinity or previous marriage would provide.

Of Anne Whateley nothing is known, except that Whateley is a familiar Warwickshire name. The Shakespearean pilgrim, driving by road to Stratford through Banbury, can rest and refresh himself at the Whateley Arms in the main street of the latter town. Anne Hathway or Hathaway is also not a well-documented figure, but, if her grave-stone in Stratford Parish Church bears a correct inscription—and why should it be either wrong or falsified ?—we know at least that she was eight years older than her husband. She outlived him by seven years, died on August 6, and was buried on August 8, 1623, exactly three months before his immortality was assured by the publication of the First Folio of his plays. The statement of her age, 67, is definite.

She was probably the daughter of Richard Hathaway, a farmer of Shottery, a village now very nearly embodied in the town of Stratford from whose centre it is about a mile away. Richard Hathaway had died a year before the Shakespeare wedding, and Anne, his eldest child, was then left with a stepmother, Joan Hathaway, and three half-brothers who were still children. The assumption is that they lived at Hewlands Farm, Shottery, the house now shown to the public as Anne Hathaway's Cottage. With a well-kept garden in front and with a typical Warwickshire orchard behind, it makes the pleasant target of a stroll, especially on a fine day in blossom-time. Some of modern Shottery's architecture suggests that chaos has come again, but the cottage, which naturally needed repairs and alterations in the course of the centuries, may very well have been the scene of Shakespeare's approach to matrimony.

Anne had good enough reasons for wanting to be married. She was twenty-six and still ' maiden,' as the Worcester Register states: that was a mature age in those times and, if she were going to have a husband at all, there was a case for speed. (Shakespeare's daughter, Susanna, was married at the age of twenty-three and her daughter, Elizabeth, became Mrs. Nash at eighteen.) Life with a stepmother and a family of youngsters may have involved strained relations as well as hard domestic work in the not extensive premises at Shottery. To have a man of her own and a place of her own was not only a natural ambition for Miss Hathaway; it was an urgent need. So, if a highly attractive lad came her way, was she to reflect that eight years' difference makes an insuperable barrier ? No, not even if the word ' baby-snatcher,' or its Elizabethan equivalent, was frequent among the Shottery housewives and ' the spinsters and the knitters in the sun.'

Matters at any rate had gone too far for parting. Anne

Hathaway was three months with child when Sandells and Richardson descended on Worcester and offered security in order to procure an immediate wedding. So, when Shakespeare's eldest child, Susanna, was born in the following May and baptised on the 26th of that month, there could be no scandal. According to the run of Academic books on Shakespeare, whose authors, as a rule, are eagerly concerned to make him, as near as may be, a model citizen, there was nothing for reproach in what had occurred at Shottery or thereabouts in August, 1582. It was customary, they urge, for betrothal to justify cohabitation: the ecclesiastical rites of marriage came later and were a ceremony of double purpose: the blessing of the Church was thus assured on the spiritual plane and the material rights of dower were also confirmed for earthly comfort. The haste, we are told, was occasioned by the need to have the ecclesiastical ceremony performed before Advent, which was an off-season for marriages.

But what, then, of Anne Whateley, a licence to marry whom had been taken out by a William Shaxpere the day before the Shottery yeomen arrived with forty pounds—in those years a large sum, at least the equivalent of four or five hundred now—to see that nothing hindered wedlock with the pregnant Miss Hathaway. Orthodoxy, determined as ever to have no scandal, can and does bring forward two pleas; one is that this was another Mr. Shakespeare altogether, which is conceivable—since the Shakespeares like the Whateleys were a well-spread Midland tribe—but surely the arrival, altarbound, of two William Shakespeares on following days is a most unlikely coincidence. The other explanation is that ' Anne Whateley ' was a miswriting of Anne Hathaway or Hathway.

It is, of course, possible that the Clerk in charge of the records made a mistake. J. W. Gray in his ample study of the whole subject, *Shakespeare's Marriage and Departure from Stratford*, cites such errors in the register. Hiccox becomes Hitchcocke; Baker and Barbar are confused; Elcock has a variant Edgcock. Again, ' The bridegroom's name in a bond dated November 25, 1583, is Robert Bradeley: in the Bishop's

Register (folio 536) the name is Robert Darby.' Those con-
fusions seem to me easy and natural. But in the case of
' Shaxpere ' and his two Annes, the possibility of a secretarial
error is much less. We know that the spelling of names in
those times was sketchy. A Marlowe could also be a Morley
or a Marley at will—or rather at the haphazard choice of the
writer. In the case of Miss Whateley, however, there is the
perfectly definite statement that she came from Temple
Grafton, a tiny village five miles from Stratford. In the other
case of the bond, backed by Sandells and Richardson, the
woman's name is plainly stated as Anne Hathaway of Stratford.
Now however sleepy a clerk may have become during the
course of his day's penmanship and its refreshment intervals,
it is extremely unlikely that he would transliterate Temple
Grafton into Stratford. He might, let us admit, muddle
Hathway into Whateley: the letters are nearly the same in
each word. He might have been thus careless, though it is
a larger and less likely error than altering Elcock into Edgcock
or confusing a couple called Baker and Barbar. What is much
less credible is that a clerk could confuse two such wholly
different names as those of Stratford and Temple Grafton.
If there were any known connection between the Hathaway
family and Temple Grafton, the affair would be more explicable
on the lines of clerical error. But there is not.

I am inclined to believe that there was an Anne Whateley
of Temple Grafton and that she was beaten on the post by
Anne Hathway of Stratford (which included Shottery). The
latter lady had the stronger claim and powerful friends. The
suspicion that the young man, after an ' affair ' at Shottery,
had lost his heart elsewhere, would give further cause for the
haste with which the Hathaway champions descended, money
in hand, upon Worcester. It may sound like melodrama to
suggest that when Anne Hathaway heard of a rival in Temple
Grafton and of William's riding to Worcester, the registral
centre of the area, she sent her friends in rapid pursuit, so that
the entry for licence on one day was followed by the bond of
the next. But melodrama plots are occasionally realised in life
and one has to do a good deal of unsatisfactory explaining in

order to reduce poor Miss Whateley of Temple Grafton to the dim, sad status of a shadow born of a misprint.

Consider the situation. If any one thing can be certainly derived from the writings of William Shakespeare it is an extreme sensitivity to beauty and especially to beauty in persons. His work offers to the anthologist the supreme expression of every kind of sexual emotion, from the spring-clear devotion of a Juliet to the autumn fires of a Cleopatra, from purest passion to grossest lust, from the holy palmer's kiss of hand in hand to the ' paddling with reechy kisses ' in the bed of a ' bloat king.' The man with such an eye and such a heart must, in the flush of youth, have been a good deal more than susceptible, to use the trite word of later times. Shakespeare continually sang the ecstasy of love and continually sounded the warning against the violent excess to which it may lead.

> Oh love, be moderate: allay thy ecstasy,
> In measure rain thy joy: scant this excess.
> I feel too much thy blessing: make it less,
> For fear I surfeit.

(These lines are spoken by Portia, though most would, at a guess, attribute them to Juliet.)

The idea of surfeit and the damage it may wreck was ever in his mind. Polonius is uttering the opinion of many of Shakespeare's characters when he says,

> This is the very ecstasy of love;
> Whose violent property fordoes itself,
> And leads the will to desperate undertakings,
> As oft as any passion under heaven
> That does afflict our natures.

Furthermore, there is continual assertion in Shakespeare's writing of the devouring power of love. Sometimes, of course, as in the poems *Venus and Adonis* and *Lucrece*, this can be dismissed as part of a convention; Renaissance Classicism was rich in reference to the kindling flames of Eros' torch and to the shower of piercing darts with which Cupid will lacerate his victim. But there is more to it than poetic custom. No English poet, certainly, has ever so poignantly phrased the agony, as well as the ecstasy of passion, the dominion of its sweetness, and the torturing fears of those thus held in thrall. Listen to Troilus in his pathetic devotion to false Cressida,

> I am giddy; expectation whirls me round.
> Th' imaginary relish is so sweet
> That it enchants my sense: what will it be,
> When that the watery palate tastes indeed
> Love's thrice-repured nectar? death, I fear me;
> Swooning destruction; or some joy too fine,
> Too subtle-potent, tuned too sharp in sweetness,
> For the capacity of my ruder powers:
> I fear it much: and I do fear besides,
> That I shall lose distinction in my joys;
> As doth a battle, when they charge on heaps
> The enemy flying.

Swooning destruction and panic lest the surfeit of it all remove ' distinction ' and turn the lover to a lecher.

Those lines, one may surely believe, were written out of personal apprehension and personal rapture. Such music is not discoursed by a good, efficient dramatist with a useful turn of phrase: it springs from the sensuous delight and no less bitter disenchantment of a man who knew the full bliss and bondage of being passion's slave. There is no need to inform true Shakespeareans that their poet had known for himself the peak and the abyss. The truth leaps out from every vibrant syllable.

At eighteen, a young man of that quality may, indeed probably will, love rapidly, dispersedly, intensely. We do not dishonour Shakespeare if we imagine that he could be wooing in two villages at once—or at least within three months. It has been done often enough by ' brisky juvenals ' past and present. Or he may have been the party wooed. Anne Hathaway, as we have seen, had ample reason to be seeking a husband. Once her pregnancy was certain she would naturally press the harder for a legal and religious confirmation of her match, and young men so pressed may easily turn to other compassionate arms. When the blood burns, the soul, as we are warned, is prodigal of vows. Suppose Anne Whateley of Temple Grafton to have been the prettier of the two and closer to the young Shakespeare's age. It is no extravagant supposition.

Well, Anne Hathaway won. It is not known where they were married. There is no record of it where we should expect to find it, in Stratford Church. A local tradition, but not one reaching very far back, has mentioned Luddington Church three miles down the Avon from Stratford, but no reason can be found for this belief. J. W. Gray, considering the claims of St. Martin's, Worcester, wrote,

> On examining the register I found that the two missing leaves which contained the entries for several years, including the date of Shakespeare's marriage licence, had been cut out, the freshness of the edges of a small portion of the parchment still attached to the binding thread indicating removal at a comparatively recent date. The church officials have no information about the theft, the object of which is difficult to explain, but it has been suggested that it was the act of some person who had a mania for the possession of such memorials as the record of the poet's marriage.
>
> (*Shakespeare's Marriage and Departure from Stratford*)

The place, after all, does not greatly matter. It is certain that the Hathaway marriage did take place and that a daughter was born six months later; certain, too, that the marriage, whether happy or not, endured.

' Shakespeare's Other Anne,' if, as I believe, there was such a Miss, disappears from the story. I once wrote a little one-act play with that title about a surreptitious diversion of William's during one of his returns from London to Warwickshire: he calls at a farm near Temple Grafton to renew old acquaintance and finds that Anne Whateley's marriage is being prepared: her match now is with a smug schoolmaster. She is not very happy about it, and is certainly made restless by the renewed glimpse of the likely lad whom she had lost some years ago at Worcester. At Temple Grafton, according to my fiction, around the Whateley farm, Shakespeare had seen and sung his ' daisies pied and violets blue and lady-smocks all silver white and cuckoo-buds of yellow hue ' in meadows painted with delight. In the kitchen at another season he had met greasy Joan who keel'd the pot and Marian of red nose and raw Dick the shepherd and Tom the woodman. Outside were the staring owl and wanton cuckoo. Might he not, with old memories in mind, put them all into a play, or at least into a song in a play, which had the significant name *Love's Labour's Lost* ? The solemn scholars will, of course, have none of it and even dismiss me as insane. But, altogether apart from this further invention of my fancy, I shall not abandon my glimpse of Anne Whateley and shall even take leave to imagine that cuckoo ' word of fear, unpleasing to a married ear ' was a sound especially embarrassing and alarming to Miss Whateley's subsequent husband whenever Master Will was known to be back from London and at large in Warwickshire. The orthodox will sniff and even snort at such a surmise: but I make it.

We turn back to Stratford. Two more certain facts are known about William and Anne Shakespeare before the former turns up in London and is mentioned in connection with playhouse wrangles and the jealousies of the poets in 1592. Of the ten hidden years we know this, that a daughter of the couple, Susanna, was baptised on May 26, 1583, and that twins followed. ' Hamnet and Judeth, sonne and daughter to William Shakespere,' were entered as baptised in Stratford on February 2, 1585. The rest, as far as William is concerned, is a baffling and infuriating silence.

But we do know a fair amount about his parents' affairs during his boyhood and adolescence. There was financial trouble at the house in Henley Street and perhaps some social trouble too. John Shakespeare was a leather-dresser and a glover: he may have dealt also in wool and carried on some business as a butcher. But there is no proof of this and the glover's craft was his principal occupation: he used a drawing of a pair of glover's ' dividers ' as his sign and symbol when he made his mark. Eight years before William's birth he had bought a house and garden and croft in Greenhill Street, Stratford, and a house in Henley Street, now, after many vicissitudes and restorations, shown as the Birthplace. Here are signs of prosperity indeed. He was serving as Borough Ale-Taster in 1557, Constable in 1558, Affeeror (i.e. assessor of penalties not appointed by Statute) in 1559, and Chamberlain in 1562. To be Chamberlain was a large and responsible matter: after William's birth and during the plague in 1564 John Shakespeare was engaged in administering relief to the victims. Four and five years later the Borough Chamberlain was paying out nine shillings for the Queen's Players and twelve pence for the Earl of Worcester's Players on their visits to Stratford. (The Worcester Company seems to have been a cheap ' No. 3 ' crowd compared with the costly stars of the royal troupe, unless the Queen's men made a far longer stay!) He was still buying property (two houses with gardens and orchards) in October, 1575. And then the tide turned.

In January, 1578, John Shakespeare was one of six aldermen who failed to contribute to the furniture of three pikemen, four billmen, and one archer whom the borough, in need of better police than Dogberry, sought to enrol. Later in the year he was listed among the creditors of Roger Sadler and exempted from the weekly alderman's tax of fourpence for the relief of the poor. He failed to appear at Council meetings: he also failed to contribute when there was a town levy for purchase of arms. In 1579 the Shakespeares had to mortgage, for £40, the small estate of Asbies, part of the Arden property at Wilmcote. Mary was now contributing to meet the crisis. At the same time came domestic tragedy, as well as financial stress. ' Anne, Daughter to Mr. John Shakespeare,' died and was buried on April 9 at the age of eight, another victim of those English springs. The Chamberlain's Accounts carried this quiet entry, ' Item for the bell and pall for Mr. Shaxper's dawghter, VIII d.'

> And now his grief may be compared well
> To one sore sick that hears the passing-bell.

Thus William of poor Wat, the hare: he knew that bell.

Next the interest of John and Mary Shakespeare in two messuages at Snitterfield was conveyed to Robert Webbe. Still, life went on and its losses were made up. Edmund, eighth and last child of John and Mary, was baptised on May 3, 1580. William, just sixteen, saw his family go—and come. During the early 1580's John Shakespeare was a regular absentee from Council meetings. Early in 1586, and then later on in 1586, he was visited with writs, and on September 6 the Council records:

> At thys halle Willm Smythe and Richard Cowrte are chosen to be Aldermen in the places of John Wheler and John Shaxspere for that Mr. Wheler dothe desyre to be put owt of the Companye and Mr. Shaxspere dothe not come to the Halles when they be warned nor hathe not done of longe tyme.

Things were going badly indeed. In 1592 John Shakespeare's name appeared in a list of recusants who had also been previously presented ' for not comminge monethlie to the Churche.' It is all bad news, including the death of his grandson, Hamnet, son of William, in August, 1596. The passing-bell again!

Then suddenly the cloud seems to lift. In October, 1596, came a draft grant of Arms to John Shakespeare, and in the following May, William, already successful and wealthy, had purchased from John Underhill, for £60, New Place, the chief house in the town. Arms and the Mansion! Next year John and Mary were filing a bill in Chancery for the recovery of Asbies. In 1599 the grant of Arms was confirmed. In 1601 John was once more assisting the Council. In September of that year he died. Mary lived seven years longer. But both had seen the return of happy days. Both Ardens and Shakespeares were themselves again.

What is behind these facts ? A man may fail in his business

and perhaps John Shakespeare did have bad luck or lose grip: he seems also to have been litigious. Furthermore, there appears to have been a general dwindling of trade in Stratford during the last decades of the sixteenth century. To say so much stirs little argument. But the question of John Shakespeare's faith and the nature of his recusancy have bedevilled the disputation: inject religion and you always add venom to a debate.

Two completely contrasted opinions are put forward. First it is argued that the old faith lingered strongly in Warwickshire and that the Shakespeares were Catholics or crypto-Catholics: some of the Ardens certainly were. That family was deeply implicated in the Arden-Somerville Conspiracy of 1583, in which a relative of Mrs. Shakespeare lost his head to the executioner. According to the loathsome practice of the age the severed heads of Edward Arden and John Somerville were exposed on London Bridge that winter. This would cause nervousness, naturally, in Stratford, since the Ardens were a Warwickshire family. But those who strongly dispute the Catholicism of the Shakespeares can argue, as Fripp does, that an event of this kind would only terminate all relationship between John and the Catholic extremists of his wife's family.

One could be a recusant, or absentee from Church, and so risk a fine for two reasons, Catholicism or Puritanism. The punitive bishop of Worcester, Whitgift, who was promoted to Canterbury in 1583, had been a scourge of both extremes. John Shakespeare can hardly have been a ' stubborn Catholic,' since he publicly conformed during his first years of municipal office, swore the usual oaths of fealty to Church and State, and stayed in the Council while measures were being carried out in the Churches to implement the Reformation. He was Chamberlain when money was paid out for defacing images and for taking down the rood-loft in the Chapel of the Guild. Copes and vestments were sold during his tenure of office. It was when Whitgift turned on to the Puritans the heat which he had so powerfully projected against the Catholics that John Shakespeare's troubles began. The

Catholics' argument that he was, traditionally, a ' merry-cheek'd old man ' and that Puritans are sour of face is shallow enough. A man can be a Protestant and laugh. And his son can go to London and be an actor without necessarily being of the Roman faith. The statement made about William by the Rev. Richard Davies, nearly a hundred years after the poet's death, that he ' dyed a Papist ' is of little value, lacking all support. If it were true, the remark would seem to imply that William was not born a Papist and so came of a Protestant home.

William Shakespeare's will and burial suggest conformity: the tenor of his writings indicates a volatile temperament which moved between hilarious welcome of life and profound distaste for it At one moment he expresses, with a most livid conviction, a pessimism so profound that one can hardly believe him to have been happy in any Christian Church: in another he is so rapt by the beauty and the humours of life that he might congratulate even a tortured cripple on being the inmate of such a heaven upon earth. If the son cannot be placed in any catalogue of the creeds, so too does the father evade the easy label. The matter is further complicated by the known existence in Stratford of another John Shakespeare, a shoemaker who married a Margery Roberts on November 25, 1584: he was Ale-Taster in 1585 and Constable in 1586. There is undoubtedly a puzzle in the difficulties that beset the home in Henley Street. It seems to me likely that for some time John Shakespeare was a middle-of-the-way man in religion: in his earlier years, as Chamberlain, he both led in entertaining the visiting teams of actors, scarcely a task for a Puritan, and helped to strip holy buildings of Romish relics and sold copes and vestments, scarcely a task for a Catholic. Later he appears to have decided strongly one way or the other. In 1580 he was bound over, along with 140 other Midland men, to present himself at the Queen's Bench in Westminster with sureties for maintenance of the peace. Like many of the others he did not go and was fined £40 in all, a very heavy penalty, two-thirds of the price of New Place when that was purchased fifteen years later. Here was trouble indeed. Fripp is confident that the 140 were Puritan recusants. The Catholic writers, notably the Comtesse de Chambrun, take the opposite view.

We can only say for certainty that William Shakespeare's later boyhood was not spent in altogether serene domestic surroundings. He must have been oppressed, at the age of sixteen, with a sense of a threatened household and of his growing responsibility: as the eldest son he had rescuing work to do and within a decade of leaving Stratford he had triumphantly done it. But in the meantime he had married a woman considerably older than himself, begotten three children, left whatever profession he first adopted for the vicissitudes and possible disgrace of the motley, and taken his chance in a calling which had neither dignity nor profit to commend it: for the greater renown and rewards of the players were yet to come. Indeed, it was partly due to William's 'excellence in the quality he professed,' as Henry Chettle phrased it in 1592, that the status and substance of the actor were improved and increased.

At some time in the middle or end of the fifteen-eighties a very brave decision was made, and I can well imagine that a shattering family row was its companion. Here was the eldest son and potential prop of the family of John Shakespeare, here a husband and a father of three, abandoning his home, his work, his livelihood and making away to London in the trail of some 'harlotry players' who had fired his fancy and had possibly been fired in return by some written lines or by a feat of declamation on the part of this Warwickshire youngster. It is difficult to imagine Mistress Anne taking this resolve calmly. There would be little or no help from her now embarrassed father-in-law. And how much could her William guarantee to send home for the housekeeping ? If Anne had a tongue—and Frank Harris attributed to her the 'venom clamours' which Shakespeare was later to attribute to the scolding Adriana in *The Comedy of Errors*—she had cause to use it now, when she saw him risking everything for a caprice or an ambition that seemed to her idle and absurd. Could she not cry, with Adriana, as he went his way,

> His company must do his minions grace
> While I at home starve for a merry look.
> Hath homely age the alluring beauty took
> From my poor cheek ?

She saw security decline as the years advanced.   Homely to the Elizabethans meant plain to look upon, as it still does on the other side of the Atlantic, where the early meanings of so many English words have been better preserved than in their own country.   Some of the wife's bitterness against the new minions who had lured him away to London may be heard, perhaps, in Adriana's cry, bringing in the wood-notes of Shakespeare's constant arboreal observation:

> Thou art an elm, my husband,—I a vine,
> Whose weakness, married to thy stronger state,
> Makes me with thy strength to communicate:
> If aught possess thee from me, it is dross,
> Usurping ivy, brier, or idle moss;
> Who, all for want of pruning, with intrusion
> Infect thy sap, and live on thy confusion.

The usurping ivy of stage life was to become the crown of laurel, the idle moss was to be the purse of gold.   But how could Anne Shakespeare know it then ?

Was it a happy marriage ?   The orthodox are mainly agreed that it was.   If their William is to be England's model, gentle and serene, the exemplary citizen, then plainly the man must be a good husband who wins his meed of happiness in the home. Those who see their William as a wilder type, a wayward addict of beauty in all its forms, do not like the idea of a solid, bourgeois marriage in the background.   Surely the Lovely Boy of the early Sonnets and the Dark Lady of the later ones must have been far more to the poet than the farmer's girl he had left in paltry Stratford!   That is the kind of argument one meets, often with special and wholly irrelevant emphasis on Stratford's lack of sanitation, a point in which London was certainly not an exemplary borough and probably, owing to density of population, a worse offender than most country towns. The portrait of Shakespeare as Perfect Husband matched with Seemly Wife is seen in its glossiest colours in the work of Fripp. The other vision is of a wayward, melancholy, sensuous, impulsive genius, pushed into an unhappy marriage with a shrew by Sandells and Richardson, escaping to London, denying his wife further intimacy on his returns—an assumption based on absence of further children after 1585—refusing to pay her debts, and finally leaving the poor woman nothing but his second-best bed. This will be found worked out with some gusto by Frank Harris (*The Man Shakespeare and His Tragic Life Story*).

If you believe in an Anne Whateley who was left, as the modern music-hall song has it, 'waiting at the church,' it is natural to believe also that the hasty marriage with Anne Hathaway, so forcibly insisted on by her friends and relatives, began dismally. But there is no proof that everything went wrong thereafter and certainly the marriage lasted till death: if it was 'a marriage of true minds,' Anne Hathaway must have been an uncommonly able and well-informed woman, and of her intellectual gifts we know nothing. The Latin tribute on her grave, probably written by Dr. John Hall for his wife, Anne's daughter, the witty Susanna, alludes to the inadequacy of a tombstone as a return for the life-giving milk of a maternal breast and prays, formally, for a glorious resurrection and ascent to the stars. A marriage of true minds with her great husband is not suggested.

But marriages can work out well enough without equality of mental power: children unite parents and also, as the proverb reminds us, a certain quantity of personal separation may lead to fondness of the heart. Absenteeism in husbands can work to save a partnership as well as to destroy it. Shakespeare was an absentee from Stratford on the grand scale, fortunately for his own career and for the world's delight. There is no evidence that Anne ever followed him to London or brought the children with her: in view of the frequent ravages of plague, most common in the Capital, she would have been wrong to do so. Since we know that Shakespeare was at times a lodger with London families, e.g. about 1602 with Christopher

Mountjoy, a Huguenot tire-maker at the corner of Silver Street in Cripplegate, it is unlikely that he kept a regular home in London as well as in Stratford.   How often he took a Warwickshire holiday or carried some home-work back to the Avon we do not know.   John Aubrey, the seventeenth-century gossip, who got his talk of Shakespeare from the son of one of the actors in Shakespeare's team, stated definitely ' He was wont to goe to his native Country once a yeare.'   That seems likely enough.   The annual visit to Avonside may have sustained the marriage: but obviously Shakespeare had other affections on the banks of the larger river.   The Dark Lady, haunting plays as well as sonnets, is inescapable, and the continual reference to the bliss of love's ecstasy and the pains of its surfeit were not academic exercises or written merely to make good acting parts.   If ever a man poured his own heartbreak on to paper, it was William Shakespeare.   That, of course, has been disputed by the orthodox projectors of a model citizen and worthy husband.   I shall have more to say of this view when we go in search of the Dark Lady later on.

At this point in the argument much bandying of texts begins.   This raises the enormous question of the validity of such methods in the case of a dramatist.   No writer is more difficult to pin down in matters of doctrine than a dramatist. Even so explicit a playwright as Shaw might be completely misinterpreted by picking of quotations were it not for his prefaces which expound the matter in hand and usually pronounce judgment as well.   Shakespeare, with his ' boundless, cloudless human view,' his rapid changes of mood, and his ' swift and penetrating insight ' into the hearts of all and sundry, is an especially difficult case for the analysts of opinion.   Yet it is surely inevitable that every writer must in some sort declare himself.   His views and prejudices may well up through the choice of metaphor and simile.   From this evidence of imagery we derive that Shakespeare was gripped by the fascination of sports, especially hawking, and had the terminology of the law substantially embedded in his mind.   Further, if we can find a special run of affection or condemnation frequently visible in the texture of his work, we can reasonably assume

that these represent personal likings and loathings. It is hardly
to be disputed that Shakespeare hated fawning flatterers even
to the extent of disliking spaniels who were for him their
prototypes in the animal world. Fawning dogs, sycophancy,
and over-sweet foods are frequently linked in his imagery and
to argue some personal taste or distaste from these repeated
passages is sufficiently justified.

But can we derive from his plays, i.e. from speeches attributed
to fictional characters and suited to their particular 'humours'
and actions in the play, his feelings with regard to a most
intimate and private matter, the success of his own marriage?
Only, if passages stand out which seem to be well outside the
range of expression natural to the events and to the characters
which evoke and deliver them, only, too, if these passages have
a special urgency of emotion and proclaim, as far as any such
proclamation can be made, that they have tumbled straight
from the thoughts and passions of the author. Fripp announces
that 'Shakespeare delights in loves passionate and pure and
in happy young wives and husbands' and can wheel out
quite a cavalcade of stage characters to justify the statement.
But, since the dramatist was dealing so largely in the plot-
stuff of old romances, there is nothing remarkable in this.
Because, in a scene of pastoral revel (*The Winter's Tale*, IV. iii),
Camillo calls Perdita 'The queen of curds and cream'—
and this is a play written when Anne was well over fifty—
it is going rather far to announce, as Fripp does, as though
he were showering the blessings and commendation of the
Church on a young couple at the altar, 'We cannot doubt
Shakespeare's romantic passion for his " Queen of curds and
cream." '

The writers of the opposite school have frequently harped on
Orsino's advice in *Twelfth Night*:

Duke What kind of woman is't?
Viola Of your complexion.
Duke She is not worth thee, then. What years, i'faith?
Viola About your years, my lord.
Duke Too old, by heaven: let still the woman take

An elder than herself; so wears she to him,
So sways she level in her husband's heart:
For, boy, however we do praise ourselves,
Our fancies are more giddy and unfirm,
More longing, wavering, sooner lost and worn,
Than woman's are.

This may be a confession of truancy on the poet's part: it has some ring of personal experience and conviction and has no particular point upon Orsino's lips. More impressive, perhaps, are Prospero's views of marriage, since Prospero is usually accepted as a self-projection of Shakespeare in maturity, the poet on the brink of retirement. If the abdication from art's magic and the last, beautiful appeal for mercy and forgiveness are taken as essential Shakespeare, why should not Prospero's views on marriage also be regarded as authentic Shakespeare ? Nothing could be more explicit than his warning to Ferdinand:

Then, as my gift, and thine own acquisition
Worthily purchas'd, take my daughter: but
If thou dost break her virgin-knot before
All sanctimonious ceremonies may
With full and holy rite be minister'd,
No sweet aspersion shall the heavens let fall
To make this contract grow: but barren hate,
Sour-eyed disdain, and discord, shall bestrew
The union of your bed with weeds so loathly
That you shall hate it both: therefore take heed,
As Hymen's lamps shall light you.

That is strong speaking. To it Ferdinand, duly impressed, replies, not very lucidly, but with apparent force and sincerity:

As I hope
For quiet days, fair issue, and long life,
With such love as 'tis now,—the murkiest den,
The most opportune place, the strong'st suggestion
Our worser Genius can, shall never melt
Mine honour into lust; to take away
The edge of that day's celebration

When I shall think, or Phoebus' steeds are founder'd,
Or Night kept chain'd below.

The significant points are these. Prospero is generally
welcomed and honoured as the voice of the author. The
author had himself, as we know for certain, anticipated with
Anne the ' sanctimonious ceremonies ' that are minister'd
' with full and holy rite.' The defenders of Shakespeare as a
moral example and perfect Christian gentleman have carefully
explained that the plighting of troth, without journey to the
altar, was sufficient to justify sexual intercourse and that no
blame can be attached to the couple for the birth of a daughter
six months after the ecclesiastical marriage. Yet here is
Prospero-Shakespeare proclaiming, in the clearest possible way,
that such intimacy, without the full, holy, and sanctimonious
ritual, will be cursed of heaven and lead to a marriage that
is almost hell on earth. Why was this passage written with
such astonishing vehemence ? It really is not at all extravagant
to suppose that it was composed after some violent domestic
quarrel and that Shakespeare did have moods of bitter resentment against the woman who took a younger than herself,
did not sway level in her husband's heart, and was well below
his brain. At the back of his mind, as he wrote his last
romances, may have lurked a London memory of that other,
the ' whitely wanton with a velvet brow ' whose pitch-black
eyes and ebon hair were the model for two at least of his
great roles.

A line often cited as Shakespearean opinion is that of Parolles
in *All's Well that Ends Well*, ' A young man married is a
young man marred.' This follows closely on another line,
spoken by Bertram, which was once pointed out to me, by a
man of great reading, suffering and sensitivity, as the most
frightening in all Shakespeare's plays. It is simply this:

War is no strife
To the dark house and the detested wife.

It means that a man had better go and risk death than face
a bad marriage. It may, like the former line, have nothing

C*

at all to do with what happened at Shottery and later at
Worcester, but it has a terrible ring of resentment driven deep.

To the dark house and the detested wife.

Could soured gloom be packed more tightly and more terribly
into ten simple syllables ?

Defenders of the ' unhappy ever after ' point of view have
further emphasised some considerations of property and real
estate. They observe that when Shakespeare invested in house
property in Blackfriars in 1613 he made rather curious arrange-
ments. The Blackfriars Gate-House, which he bought as an
investment, not for personal use, was conveyed in joint ownership to William Shakespeare, of Stratford-upon-Avon, gentleman, and to three gentlemen of London, William Johnson,
John Jackson, and John Hemmyng (the last presumably was
Shakespeare's colleague who later was co-editor of the First
Folio). Sir Edmund Chambers (*William Shakespeare*, Vol. 2,
p. 164) deduces from the surviving documents that the three
Londoners were only trustees for Shakespeare, who paid the
purchase money and to whose use any further assurance was
to be made. He adds, ' Elton suggested that the object of the
procedure of 1613 was to bar Shakespeare's widow from a
right to dower on the property and this would certainly have
been the effect, as Chancery did not recognise a right of dower
out of an equitable estate.' Dower was the part of the husband's property which the law allowed to the widow for life. It
is assumed that Shakespeare arranged shared ownership (in
name) of Blackfriars Gate-House in order that any claims of
Anne's upon it should be made null and void.

Is much to be concluded from that ? Shakespeare may
surely have thought, without ill-will, that Anne would get
enough from her dower on the Stratford property and was not
at all the person to be burdened with the responsibility of
looking after a building and collecting rental as far away as
London. That seems a reasonable reply to the seekers after
evidence of hostility.

This party has naturally made the most of the curt allusion

to Anne in Shakespeare's last will and testament, in which his
elder daughter, Susanna Hall, was chief legatee, receiving New
Place, the Shakespeare family home in Henley Street, all ' his
barns, stables, orchards, gardens, lands, tenements and here-
ditaments whatsoever ' in Warwickshire and also the house
in Blackfriars. Towards the end of the will occurs this brief
sentence, ' Item, I give unto my wife my second-best bed,
with the furniture.' Simply that and nothing more. All the
rest of his ' goods, chattels, leases, plate, jewels, and household
stuff whatsoever ' went to ' John Hall, gent., and my daughter
Susanna, his wife.'

Those determined to discover a broken marriage can, of
course, make something ugly out of this. To us to-day, if we
look no further, that second-best bed may seem to indicate a
sardonic joke. But, unless Shakespeare's mind and temperament had been wholly warped by the distress of his last illness,
the very cruelty of the jest seems to place it beyond probability.
After all allowance has been made for the changes of taste
in jesting and behaviour that may have occurred between
Shakespeare's time and our own, it is very difficult, if not
impossible, to believe that the man to whose gently-mannered
good humour such tribute was paid by his coevals would
have died with this contemptible sneer upon his pen. Admit
that the comic spirit of the period could be harsh and unkind
in its puncturing of fools, bullies, and pretenders—the Malvolios
do not get off lightly—and even so we can hardly see the sweet
and gentle Shakespeare ending his life with so savage a quip and
with so unworthy a use of the retort discourteous.

The champions of an exemplary William Shakespeare have
their answers ready. Anne may have become an invalid by
this time, infirm of mind, incapable of administering an estate
of any kind. Of that there is no evidence, but it is possible.
What is certain, however, is that Anne was not disinherited
or left only with an inferior bed and some sheets. She had her
right of dower and this meant that she was entitled to a life-
interest in one-third of the testator's heritable estates on which
dower had not been barred or evaded (as it was, we have seen,
in the case of the Blackfriars Gate-House) and she would live,

if she chose, in the testator's chief house. Dower-houses, or secondary houses, were a convenient escape for cautious widows who did not wish to jostle their daughters-in-law: our ancestors knew as well as we do the discomforts and distresses of a shared home. Anne was at least certain of a room at New Place and of the medical and daughterly care of John and Susanna Hall, which may have been her chief need.

As for the second-best bed, there is often distinction in wills of the period made between first and second beds and the seconds were allotted without slur. It is known that there was a guest-chamber at New Place and the best bed may have been there. Or Shakespeare may have lain dying in the best bed while Anne moved to a room and bed of her own which she would rather have retained than the marriage-bed of her memories. It may be that the best bed went to John Hall and Susanna as new heads of the family. Or perhaps this second-best bed was a favourite bed of Anne's. There are plenty of reasonable explanations, any one of which may be the correct one. Those who choose to believe that Shakespeare died with the sarcastic ' crack ' of a particularly mean and spiteful kind have really nothing to give them cause save their own itch for a little scandal.

This is not to say that the marriage must have been idyllic. Shakespeare was away for long periods in London, where he was rapidly successful and admitted to the high, gay company of Lord Southampton's circle. His writings betray so frequently, so intimately, and so intensely both the delight in and the fear of sexual passion that it is unlikely in the extreme that he remained faithful throughout to his wife in Stratford. She was older by seven years. She must have resented so much absence, although she profited materially by the results, and she must have been suspicious.

If a copy of the Sonnets ever came back to New Place she could hardly help wondering what William had been up to and inquiring who exactly were his ' loves of comfort and despair ' and why he had to proclaim that ' love is too young to know what conscience is.' The Dark Lady bestrode the final Sonnets with her ebon-gleaming tyranny. Perhaps

William took particular care to forget this volume when saddling up for Stratford in his later years, but Anne, if she could read books—and there is plenty of evidence for wide-spread literacy in Stratford—must have heard of and at least dipped into *Venus and Adonis* and *Lucrece* which were the chief causes of her husband's early advancement to wealth and to renown. If she had so dipped, she must have wondered a little about the way in which his mind was working.

The vernacular of the English people contains the phrase ' a steady ' for a wife who abides by the home and puts up with the competition of more volatile creatures. ' A steady ' will have a tongue and use it: but she speaks out instead of walking out. I surmise that Anne was William's ' steady.' He could have had memories indeed of Anne Whateley, if my fancy about her be correct, of London ladies in general and of the ' whitely wanton ' in particular, the gipsy-coloured beauty who, as he said of dark Rosaline, would defy the hundred eyes of Argus to be out and do the deed. But William Shakespeare never ceased to be Avonian Will, as Garrick sang of him, the Warwickshire lad, the countryman, the house-holder, the man of property, the investor in malt and tithes and messuages here and there.

Anne fitted into that part of his full, varied, and even con-tradictory life. A wayward man and his ' steady ' can be happy despite an occasional hurricane of rows. Perhaps the shrewish wives of the early comedies did owe something to Anne's tongue. Prospero's strangely intemperate outburst on the disastrous results of exactly that conduct which had occurred in the summer of 1582 between Anne and William may very well have poured off Shakespeare's quill after a bad morning in the home. I can imagine him working at Stratford and interrupted by some irrelevant bickering when he knew he was at the very top of his form, when he was just coming on to the cloud-capp'd towers and gorgeous palaces of the ' Our revels now are ended ' passage and to the famous farewell to the great Globe itself. Did he compose that day amid storms ? The immediate precursor to the immortal ' revels ' speech is this:

Ferdinand   This is strange: your father's in some passion
             That works him strongly.
Miranda   Never till this day
             Saw I him touch'd with anger so distempered.

At the end of the famous passage, Prospero alludes to his vexation, his troubled brain, his beating mind, his need for solitude. The excuse for this in the play is the existence of a conspiracy which, as a master-magician and well-nigh omnipotent, he knows he can overcome with a mere hey-presto and a flourish of the conjurer's wand. This is surely inadequate cause for so powerful a piece of declamation about the miseries of wedlock entered without innocence. That passage has the smack of personal suffering. May it not have found its way into the text after a rumpus ? It might very well have been removed after the poet had written some unforgettable lines for Prospero-Shakespeare to deliver.

> Though with their high wrongs I am struck to the quick,
> Yet, with my nobler reason, 'gainst my fury
> Do I take part: the rarer action is
> In virtue than in vengeance: they being penitent,
> The sole drift of my purpose doth extend
> Not a frown further.

He followed this with that haunting jingle of the epilogue placing its sweet emphasis on mercy and indulgence. But the passage was not so removed and there, pricking our curiosity, it remains.

' And, when, alas, I came to wive.' Shakespeare may have felt the ' alas ' soon after the enforced wedding and at recurring intervals when tastes and tempers clashed. It would be a dull marriage that never knew ' a difference ' and unbroken harmony is almost inconceivable in the case of so keen a temperament as William Shakespeare must have owned. Homeward, it seems, he annually came from his winning of money and renown; and there was Anne, his ' steady,' worthy of her dower and of any bed she happened to prefer.

CHAPTER IV

The Hidden Years

NOW comes the great gap in our knowledge of Shakespeare's life, the gap which has given freedom of play to every kind of guesswork and even fantasy. We have not a single documented fact about William Shakespeare between the baptism of his twins Hamnet and Judith at Stratford on February 2, 1585, and the publication of Robert Greene's *Groatsworth of Wit* in London in 1592. This angry pamphlet of a dying man contained much railing at his rivals. These include an atheistic gracer of tragedies (probably Marlowe), a ' young juvenal, that biting saturist,' probably Nashe, and one ' driven to extreme shifts,' probably Peele. Then came a reference to:

> an upstart Crow, beautified with our feathers, that with his *Tygers hart wrapt in a Players hyde*, supposes he is as well able to bombast out a blank verse as the best of you: and beeing an absolute *Johannes fac totum*, is in his own conceit the onely Shake-scene in a countrey.

The quotation is a parodied line from 3 *Henry VI*, I. iv, and there can be no doubt to whom the term Shake-scene refers. William Shakespeare was by now a recognised writer as well as an all-round worker in the theatre. At the close of 1592 Henry Chettle, another of the playhouse tribe, apologised in his *Kind-Harts Dreame* for Greene's offensive diatribe on the fraternity of play-makers. In a long and clumsily written sentence there is a tribute to one unnamed but generally taken to be this Shakescene—Shakespeare,

> my selfe haue seene his demeanor no lesse ciuill than he exelent in the qualitie he professes: Besides, diuers of worship haue reported his uprightnes of dealing which argues his

honesty, and his facetious grace in writting, that aprooues his Art.

From this it is plain that by the end of 1592 Shakespeare was an up-and-coming dramatist and theatre-worker, jealously resented by some for his energy and ability, strongly commended by others (and those of rank) for his integrity of life and for his command of wit and grace in composition. The resentment was felt by his rivals: the commendation came from ' divers of worship.' The young man was already climbing socially. The great friendship with the Earl of Southampton had begun.

But what had happened before that? What was his first employment? Why and when did he leave Stratford? Here fancy has vastly enjoyed itself in making Shakespeare schoolmaster, lawyer, soldier, sailor, poacher, tippler, theatrical call-boy and holder of horses for the play-going gentry (as it might be a car-park attendant outside a theatre to-day). We shall have to thread our way through all this forest of conjecture as best we can, remembering that we have no certain facts whatever and that our task is to consider the relative value of later anecdotes and gossip and also of the possible indications in the man's own writings. Sir Edmund Chambers, great, precise, and careful scholar of all things Shakespearean, would take no chances and concluded his first chapter of *William Shakespeare* upon a note of cautionary agnosticism.

The main fact in his earlier career is still that unexplored hiatus, and who shall say what adventures, material and spiritual, six or eight crowded Elizabethan years may have brought him? It is no use guessing. As in so many other historical investigations, after all the careful scrutiny of clues and all the patient balancing of possibilities, the last word for a self-respecting scholarship can only be that of nescience.

' Ah, what a dusty answer gets the soul
When hot for certainties in this our life! '

At the other extreme is William Bliss, who in *The Real Shakespeare* confidently sends William to sea with Drake in the

Golden Hind. This conjecture sets the lad wandering to Milford Haven and taking ship to Plymouth, where he embarked with the adventurous admiral on December 13, 1577, and returned in September, 1580. By that time he would have learned plenty of what the ship-boy suffers ' upon the high and giddy mast ' under the visitation of those winds

> Who take the ruffian billows by the top
> Curling their monstrous heads and hanging them
> With deafening clamour in the slippery shrouds.

Also he had discovered with aching teeth how dry is ' the remainder biscuit ' after a long ship's voyage: which, by the way, is certainly an odd piece of knowledge for Jaques to have come by in Arden.

Bliss then packs off the young man, after marriage, on a Mediterranean voyage in a vessel called *The Tiger*, which gave him views as well as notions of ' Argosies with portly sail like Signiors and rich burghers of the flood.' William was finally shipwrecked off the coast of Bohemia and Illyria at the top of the Adriatic Gulf, made off into Italy, met and was succoured by the young Earl of Southampton then travelling on vacation from St. John's College, Cambridge, and so brought back to London after a stay in France where he met the Countess of Rousillon and picked up the raw material for the plot of *Love's Labour's Lost.* All very neat and tidy!

Bliss has no difficulty in showing, what has been oddly overlooked, that Shakespeare took a vivid interest in shipwrecks and wrote about them with unusual detail. There are at least five shipwrecks in the plays, and in two of them, it is shrewdly observed, the menaced sailors ask for sea-room.

In *Pericles* III, i, the mariners speak thus:

First Sailor Slack the bolins there!—Thou wilt not, wilt thou ? Blow, and split thyself.
Second Sailor But sea-room, and the brine and cloudy billow kiss the moon, I care not.

and in *The Tempest* I, i, the Boatswain also prays for room. Bliss's comment upon this is perfectly fair,

These were no fresh-water sailors or longshoremen. They were proper deep-sea sailors who hated a lee-shore worse than the devil. They were long-voyage men. Landsmen and coast-huggers feel that to keep in sight of land is comforting. Where would Shakespeare have learned the true gospel that bids the sailor cry out for room enough unless he had been for a long voyage himself?

My own conviction is that Shakespeare certainly did have voyages, did talk to sailors, and did see weather at its worst, even perhaps a wreck. But we need not rush to sign him up with Drake or with the Master of the *Tiger*, Aleppo-bound. (Aleppo was not a sea-side entrepôt of Near-Eastern trade, but geography seems scarcely to have been one of the strongest points in the curriculum at Stratford Grammar School—if, indeed, it was ever mentioned.) The poet-actor's sea-going might very well have been a voyage to Italy with one of the ' divers of worship ' (divers in its non-aquarian sense) or with a company of players crossing to the Low Countries on their way to Germany and Scandinavia. After all, one can, to one's cost, be sufficiently acquainted with a ship ' boring the moon with her mainmast, and anon swallowed with yest and froth ' by merely crossing from Dover to Calais. Although the points about sea-room and remainder biscuits are interesting, I shall leave William Bliss to his nautical fancies and return to the more usual interpretation of the hidden years.

The Schoolmaster Theory had an early start. So had the Butcher-boy picture. In fact they begin together. The first biographer of William Shakespeare was John Aubrey who included what we should now call a Profile of the poet in his *Brief Lives*. As many references to that piece of writing will have to be made in this book, I print it in full:

Mr William Shakespeare was borne at Stratford vpon Avon, in the County of Warwick ; his father was a Butcher, & I have been told heretofore by some of the neighbours, that when he was a boy he exercised his father's Trade, but when he kill'd a Calfe, he would doe it in a *high style*, & make a Speech. There was at that time another Butcher's son in this Towne, that was held not at all inferior to him for a naturall witt, his acquaintance and coetanean, but dyed young. This Wm. being inclined naturally to Poetry and acting, came to London I guess about 18 and was an Actor at one of the Play-houses and did act exceedingly well: now B. Johnson was never a good Actor, but an excellent Instructor. He began early to make essayies at Dramatique Poetry, which at that time was very lowe; and his Playes tooke well: He was a handsome well shap't man: very good company, and of a very readie and pleasant smooth Witt. The Humour of . . . the Constable in a Midsomers-night's Dreame, he happened to take at Grendon [In margin, ' I thinke it was Midsomer night that he happened to lye there.'] in Bucks which is the roade from London to Stratford, and there was living that Constable about 1642 when I first came to Oxon. Mr Jos. Howe is of that parish and knew him. Ben Johnson and he did gather Humours of men dayly where ever they came. One time as he was at the Tavern at Stratford super Avon, one Combes an old rich Usurer was to be buryed, he makes there this extemporary Epitaph,

Ten in the Hundred the Devill allowes
But Combes will have twelve, he swears & Vowes:
If any one askes who lies in this Tombe:
Hoh! quoth the Devill, 'Tis my John o'Combe.

He was wont to goe to his native Country once a yeare. I thinke I have been told that he left 2 or 300^{ll}. per annum there and therabout: to a sister. [In margin, ' V. his Epitaph in Dugdales Warwickshire.'] I have heard Sr. Wm. Davenant and Mr. Thomas Shadwell (who is counted the best Co-moedian we have now) say, that he had a most prodigious Witt, and did admire his naturall parts upon all other Dramaticall writers. He was wont to say, That he never blotted out a line in his life: sayd Ben: Johnson, I wish he had blotted out a thousand. [In margin, ' B Johnsons Underwoods.'] His Comoedies will remaine witt, as long as the English tongue is understood; for that he handles mores hominum; now our present writers reflect so much upon particular persons, and coxcombeities, that 20 yeares hence, they will not be understood. Though as Ben: Johnson sayes of him, that he had but little Latine and lesse Greek, He understood Latine pretty well: for he had been in his younger yeares a School-master in the Countrey. [In margin, 'from Mr—Beeston.']

There are two other notes of Aubrey's about Shakespeare which can be considered later on.

The first thing is to establish the value of Aubrey as an informant. John Aubrey (1626-97) was a wandering gossip, wit, and scholar, who picked up information about notable people and jotted it down: his manuscript was ultimately acquired by the Ashmolean Museum at Oxford. It is generally accepted that Aubrey worked as a gatherer of material for Anthony Wood, author of *Athenae Oxonienses*. The *Brief Lives* left by Aubrey are brilliantly written, pungent, concise, witty, and worthy to be put on the shelf beside the diaries of his 'coetanean' Pepys. But they are certainly not reliable. His statements, even about himself, have an air of imaginative fiction, e.g. that he suffered from an ague while still in his mother's womb. His life was odd enough to make for fanciful rather than factual composition. He caught the smallpox at Oxford, had much trouble with the other sex, and continually found all his affairs running 'kim-kam.' That he could write is shown by such a picture as this of one Gwin, the Earl of Oxford's secretary:

A better instance of a squeamish, disobligeing, slighting, insolent, proud fellow perhaps can't be found. . . . No reason satisfies him but he overweenes, and cutts some sower faces that would turn the milke in a fair ladie's breast.

This is as good as anything of its period, the prose of Pepys included.

But to Aubrey's accuracy there are no tributes. Wood, for whom he worked, called him 'a pretender to antiquities. . . . He was a shiftless person, roving and magotie-headed and sometimes little better than crased. And being exceedingly credulous would stuff his many letters sent to A. W. with folliries and misinformation, which sometimes would guide him into the paths of errour.' To begin by calling one's colleague

magotie-headed and well-nigh crazed, and then finish with the
suggestion that he sometimes fell into error, is a considerable
descent in vituperation. Wood was writing, it seems, after a
quarrel. Halliwell Phillips, an early Shakespearean biographer,
also dismissed Aubrey as a collector of tittle-tattle rather than
a sifter of evidence, and Dr. Andrew Clark, a modern editor
of *Brief Lives*, made small claim for their factual value, but
paid a strong (and a justified) compliment to their vivacity.
But with regard to the Shakespeare life, Aubrey was in touch
with William Beeston, of whom he wrote later that Dryden
called him ' the chronicle of the stage.' This Beeston, who
died in 1682, was the son of Christopher Beeston, Shakespeare's
fellow-player. Christopher's name occurs in the list of Lord
Chamberlain's servants who, headed by Will Shakespeare and
including Hen. Condell, Joh. Hemings, Ric. Burbage, and
Will Kempe, were listed by Ben Jonson as the players of *Every
Man in His Humour* (1598). So it is quite likely that what
Aubrey got from William Beeston was of better value than the
local gossip which he may have picked up by travelling in
Warwickshire.

The butcher-boy story, advanced by Aubrey, with the
assertion that John Shakespeare was a butcher and that
William ' exercised his father's trade ' and even did so with
oratorical rites and dramatic ceremonies, may be deemed to
be supported by the first substantial biographer and editor of
Shakespeare, Nicholas Rowe. To his edition of the plays,
published in 1709, Rowe prefixed *Some Account of the Life of
William Shakespear*. Rowe, who is said to have made a special
journey into Warwickshire towards the end of the seventeenth
century to gain local information about the dramatist, relates:

His Father, who was a considerable Dealer in Wool, had so
large a Family, ten Children in all, that tho' he was his eldest
Son, he could give him no better Education than his own
Employment. He had bred him, 'tis true, for some time at a
Free-School, where 'tis probable he acquir'd that little Latin
he was Master of: But the narrowness of his Circumstances,
and the want of assistance at Home, forc'd his Father to

withdraw him from thence, and unhappily prevented his
further Proficiency in that Language. . . . Upon his
leaving School, he seems to have given intirely into that way
of Living which his Father propos'd to him; and in order to
settle in the World after a Family manner, he thought fit to
marry while he was yet very Young. His Wife was the
Daughter of one Hathaway, said to have been a substantial
Yeoman in the Neighbourhood of Stratford.

This supports the view of poverty and social difficulty in
John Shakespeare's household and of the boy's early succession
to his father's trade. But that trade is not stated to be
butchery.

On the other hand, a glover, dealing in wool and hides, may
very well have tapped the stream of supply higher up by
conducting a slaughter-house of his own. Were there such
premises adjacent, William could have known all about the
horrid exercise and may have been, no doubt reluctantly, an
assistant in the despatch of animals. That he gloated rhetori-
cally over the demise of a calf seems extremely unlikely in the
case of one so sensitive to the sufferings of animals hunted or
otherwise attacked.

It is worth noting that Shakespeare drew a number of
metaphors from the butcher's craft, especially in the earlier
plays. Dr. Caroline Spurgeon in *Shakespeare's Imagery* observes:

In 2 and 3 *Henry VI*, outside the symbol of the fruit and flower
garden, already noticed, there is the even more obvious one
of the butcher and slaughter-house, slightly carried on in
Richard III.

King Henry's compassion for the doomed Duke of Gloucester
is thus expressed:

> And as the butcher takes away the calf,
> And binds the wretch, and beats it when it strays,
> Bearing it to the bloody slaughter-house;
> Even so, remorseless, have they borne him hence:
> And as the dam runs lowing up and down,
> Looking the way her harmless young one went,

And can do naught but wail her darling's loss;
Even so myself bewails good Gloster's case
With sad unhelpful tears; and with dimm'd eyes
Look after him, and cannot do him good,—
So mighty are his vowed enemies.

A little later the Earl of Warwick is back in the metaphorical shambles, though such aristocrats would hardly draw their similes from the common trade of the flesher.

Who finds the heifer dead and bleeding fresh,
And sees fast by a butcher with an axe,
But will suspect 'twas he that made the slaughter.

The third part of *Henry VI* intensifies the talk of knives and butchers, as Dr. Spurgeon reminds us:

In 3 *Henry VI*, Clifford, Edward and Clarence are all called ' butchers,' Richard is ' that devil's butcher,' parliament is thought of as a ' shambles ' and the realm as a ' slaughter-house,' Gloucester sees himself hewing his way to the crown with a bloody axe, and Henry, when Gloucester comes to kill him, pictures himself very aptly as a sheep yielding his throat unto the butcher's knife.

William Bliss, with his notions of Shakespeare as a sailor, will be glad to find a further discovery of Dr. Spurgeon's, namely, that in 3 *Henry VI* there is ' an immensely large number of pictures of the sea and ships, more than in any other play.' Moreover, the wind-borne or wrecked ship is prominent.

One thing is certain, that the writer of the plays knew a great deal about leather and gloves. In this same Part III of *Henry VI* there is allusion (III, i, 22) to the deer's skin as the gamekeeper's fee or perquisite, which sounds like rustic knowledge though it does not prove the practice of poaching; furthermore, mention of the various uses of the various leathers abounds. The kid-skin or cheveril was particularly in his mind as a symbol of softness and elasticity. Why should Mercutio say (*Romeo and Juliet*, II, iv, 87) ' Here's a wit of cheveril, that stretches from an inch narrow to an ell broad'? This is trade-talk, an echo of the paternal workshop.

The fact that Shakespeare knew something of the shambles and of the glover's craft which drew its material from the slaughter-house does not prove that he was long, or ever, a worker definitely apprenticed therein. He may have given an occasional hand: or he may have written of what he saw, not of what he practised. It is obvious that a boy so receptive to the beauty of things would rather be away from the blood and guts, the squalor and suffering of the butcher's yard. Whither would he turn? Aubrey says to school-teaching. Later suggestions have favoured the law.

The idea that Shakespeare was for a while a schoolmaster has early authority from Aubrey, but not from Rowe. There is no suggestion in the plays that he had any sympathy with the members of that profession. He laughs at them as fantastical pedants and nowhere shows compassion for the tormented usher who must somehow impose a discipline and instil learning among a noisy and unmannered crowd of reluctant pupils. Was he a lawyer's clerk for a while? There is no early external evidence of that apart from a sneering reference by Thomas Nashe to ' a sort of shifting companions, that runne through every arte and thrive by none, to leave the trade of *Noverint* whereto they were borne, and busie themselves with the indevors of Art, that could scarcelie Latinize their necke-verse if they shoulde have neede.' This refers to a recreant lawyer who practised tragedy: it may or may not refer to Shakespeare.

But a legal training has been quite commonly assumed on the internal basis of Shakespeare's addiction to legal terminology and metaphor. Again he shows no affection for the calling, and, when its members are mentioned, it is as false leaders and sounders of ' quillets,' i.e. quibbles. But then writers are rarely kind to lawyers: an Inns of Court lad may be gay and an advocate may be magnetic in a story or a play, but how often does an office-lawyer or solicitor become the hero of any fiction? He is usually a character-part left to exercise the humours of a cogging quilletmonger and to display the sly knavery of what is habitually called a pettifogging attorney.

The internal evidence for some legal training is certainly strong. The plays are stuffed with fee-simples and the like: the butcher's boy turned strolling player would scarcely have such profound acquaintance with the attorney's technicalities; why should a country lad, when he grew up to be dramatist and sonneteer, so often draw his images from the seal and parchment of the lawyer's office? Being a magician in his own craft Shakespeare could turn the office jargon to majestical purposes and Romeo's heart breaks as he bids his lips

> seal with a righteous kiss
> A dateless bargain to engrossing Death.

'Engrossing Death'! It is a strange epithet for one not legally minded.

Even Shakespeare's women, and not Portia only, are strangely legalist. Mistress Page has fee-simple, fine, and recovery at her lips' ends and the swain-commended Silvia thinks in terms of pawn and fealty. As Fripp points out:

> Parolles, trembling and sweating under the examination of his captors, indulges in this rhetorical pedantry, 'Sir, for a quart d'ecu he will sell the fee-simple of his salvation, the inheritance of it, and cut the entail from all remainders, and a perpetual succession for it perpetually.'

There is no occasion for that rogue Parolles to be acquainted with the phraseology of the deed-box. Shakespeare often took his examples and similes from the stage, from the studying and forgetting of parts, from the ill-graced and boring performance, from the passion-tearing tragedian and the gagging clown. But even more frequently his mind, in quest of imagery, seems to draw on memories of work with an attorney. Indeed, he could build a whole sonnet on the lingo of title and lease. Wherever we turn there is law: even Greeks and Trojans in *Troilus and Cressida* talk in terms of fee-farm and fee-simple. Fee-farm means tenure without limit. Why be so technical about enduring possession ? And why should Hamlet, skull in hand amid the Danish sepulchres, be so extremely precise about the grim relic's possible owner and the details of his past conveyancing ?

Hamlet There's another: why may not that be the skull of a lawyer ? Where be his quiddits now, his quillets, his cases, his tenures, and his tricks ? why does he suffer this rude knave now to knock him about the sconce with a dirty shovel, and will not tell him of his action of battery ? Hum! This fellow might be in's time a great buyer of land, with his statutes, his recognizances, his fines, his double vouchers, his recoveries: Is this the fine of his fines, and the recovery of his recoveries, to have his fine pate full of fine dirt ? will his vouchers vouch him no more of his purchases, and double ones too, than the length and breadth of a pair of indentures ? The very conveyances of his lands will hardly lie in this box; and must the inheritor himself have no more, ha ?

Horatio Not a jot more, my lord.

Hamlet Is not parchment made of sheep-skins ?

Horatio Ay, my lord, and of calf-skins too.

Hamlet They are sheep and calves which seek our assurance in that.

It is almost as though Shakespeare visualised the very bones of some dead master who had ruled his youth. Then, at the end, the leather-lore of the leather-worker's son breaks in upon the prattle of the lawyer's office.

I agree with Fripp's conclusion that law is part of him and ' slips from him unawares.'

We have no reason to believe that he studied at the Inns of Court or practised at the bar. The facts, however, demand professional experience in an attorney's office, and without doubt at Stratford, in or about the years 1579-87.

Such experience was less likely in the service of Thomas Trussell (a kinsman probably of his mother), Walter Roche (his late schoolmaster), or William Court (son of a former steward) than of the town clerk and steward from 1570 to 1586, Henry Rogers.

And I can see him yawning his head off among the vouchers and conveyances on a summer afternoon when the water-meadows of Avon were inviting to fresh air.

None of these conjectures about Shakespeare's hidden years need be exclusive. People argue the case for butcher, peda-gogue, and lawyer as though the young Shakespeare must certainly have been one of these alone. But it was possible for the youngster to drift uneasily from job to job. Why should he not have lent a hand with the gloving, possibly with slaugh-tering too, tried a term as junior usher, and then moved on to legal apprenticeship or at least to helping and copying for one of the Stratford lawyers? The folk of that town were, as the records show, extremely litigious, and there must have been abundant occupation in the transfer of property and the copious disputation thereupon. 'Bright Lad Wanted,' or the Tudor equivalent, may easily have caught his eye outside the lawyer's office when he was weary of dressing leather or exasperated by the whining schoolboy, the horn-books, and the drone of task-work in the drowsy classroom air. It must be remembered that he was married at eighteen, and a parent just after he was nineteen. His wife would naturally prod him to keep moving in search of better salary. Therefore I am ready to accede to all suggestions about Shakespeare's early occupation and bread-winning; there is no reason why one should bar the others.

I see him indulging a considerable vein of melancholy. His plays are rich in eloquent melancholics. To be sad was a prominent part of the mental foppery of the age in London and, as a reader, Shakespeare in Stratford must have caught the modish infection. In any case it is the nature of quick youth to be, like Jaques, 'by often rumination' wrapped in 'a most humorous sadness.' Jaques is entirely a creation of Shakespeare: Lodge who gave him Rosalind had not put this wry philosopher into the Arden greenwood.

He is Warwickshire's own moody contribution to the English scene. So Shakespeare, wandering, mused as Jaques did, purporting, as youth generously will, to ' cleanse the foul body of the infected world,' then finding no easy salve for this great cosmic therapy, ending with a sigh and a laugh, and perhaps a tune. Shakespeare, so quick to harmony, must early have understood ' The musician's melancholy which is fantastical.'

Whether or no he was nursing memories of Anne Whateley, he saw his family in trouble and the pride of the Ardens lowered; he had domestic burdens and he must have felt the frustration natural to young blood mewed up in an office or a schoolroom or a workshop. It is incredible to me that the man who was to empty his heart of such grandeur, such grief and such passion in his after years was in boyhood an ordinary, well-conducted, respectably insensitive member of the country-town bourgeoisie. Some have felt this so strongly that they have denied the possibility of the London Shakespeare and the Stratford one being the same person. I see no impossibility in uniting the two, if we visualise the young man in his teens and early twenties deeply reading, avidly composing his *juvenilia*, watching, dreaming, restless, melancholy. Much has been conjectured about Anne Shakespeare as a shrewish wife; much, too, might be said about her William as a difficult husband. He may or may not have got into trouble by poaching, drinking, and insulting the nobility and gentry. I think it is more likely that, with the happiness of ' boy eternal ' over, he suffered some growing-pains of the spirit and was by no means an ideal employee and diligent bringer-home of the weekly wage.

There is a certain parallel between the boyhoods of the two greatest creators of English character in letters, William Shakespeare and Charles Dickens: everything that Shakespeare may have endured, Dickens certainly suffered more acutely. Both boys witnessed parental decline and humiliating stress of poverty. John Shakespeare was in trouble with his creditors and the authorities: John Dickens muddled himself into a debtors' prison. William Shakespeare, according to Rowe, was withdrawn early from school, owing to the ' narrow circumstances ' of his father, and, according to Aubrey, was put to the slaughter-house or at least the glove-shop. Dickens, too, had a broken schooling and was sent to the dark hell of the blacking-factory, the memory of which was to be always like a scar across his mind. Dickens, after escape from the factory and on leaving school, became clerk to a solicitor, and, after working all day at the law, studied shorthand and reporting most of the night. Both were, when they found their proper task in life, ferociously industrious. Both were self-educated in the sense that both possessed and exercised the greatest gift obtainable by any writer, what Dickens called ' the key of the street.' All the England that was shut off from these boys by social circumstances was open to the darting glance. Dickens felt very bitterly about his boyhood: Shakespeare, obviously, was never lacerated like that until he reached adolescence; but school was a bore to him and there must have been something that burned in the very roots of his being before he left Stratford.

When he did go, there was, inevitably, a ferocious domestic explosion. He may have been forced out as a penalty for young follies, as we shall see later on; in that case what would Anne say of the reckless wretch who was leaving her with three small children and no certainty, not even the probability of quick fame and fortune in London? If he was not driven away, if he of his own free will hitched his star to the players' property-cart, he was taking one of those very gallant plunges to which distraught wives are apt to give a name far less polite than that of ' risk.' For a schoolboy to be apprenticed in his early years to a fellowship of players or to join a boy's company was natural, normal, and economically safe: little Salathiel Pavy we know was quite an old hand at the age of twelve: but for a young husband and parent to be thus up and off into an alien world was to risk a bout with destiny indeed. Only an ambition that nagged him like ' a pugging tooth,' only an ambition supported by an active melancholy about his present work and scope, could have stirred him to take his chance among the University wits, who had twice his scholarship, and among the ' harlotry players,' who had far less of his responsibility. Nor was it likely that his parents, with the Arden name behind them and troubles round about, could possibly have cared to see the eldest son depart for a career, which at the time had little to offer save insecurity and even ill-repute. At least a bourgeois family in a country town was likely to regard with anger and dismay the disappearance of the eldest son, the survivor after two earlier deaths, their ' apple of the eye.'

The story that he left Stratford after disgrace and punishment as a poacher of deer is now generally discredited. Aubrey, the nearest biographer in time to Shakespeare's life, says nothing of this, which is noteworthy: Aubrey's idea is that William came to London at eighteen, i.e. late in 1582 or early in 1583, following his marriage. This would support the idea of a forced, unhappy union with Anne and of a flight from misery. But the arrival of the twins in 1585 is damaging to this view. The poaching legend begins with the Rev. Richard Davies, Rector of Sapperton, in Gloucestershire, who poured out this dribble of gossip to a fellow-parson, the Rev. William Fulman, of Meysey Hampton, in the same shire. (It occurs in Fulman's papers now at Corpus Christi College, Cambridge.)

Much given to all unluckinesse in stealing venison and Rabbits, particularly from Sir—Lucy who had him oft whip[t] and sometimes imprisoned and at last made him fly his native country to his great advancem[t], but his reveng was so great that he is his Justice Clodpate and calls him a great man, and y[t] in allusion to his name bore three lowses rampant for his arms. . . . He dyed a papist.

This was written about the beginning of the eighteenth century. Rowe developed the notion thus:

an extravagance that he was guilty of, forc'd him both out of his country and that way of living which he had taken up; and tho' it seem'd at first to be a blemish upon his good manners, and a misfortune to him, yet it afterwards happily prov'd the occasion of exerting one of the greatest genius's that ever was known in dramatick poetry. He had, by a misfortune common enough to young fellows, fallen into ill company; and amongst them, some that made a frequent practice of deer-stealing, engag'd him with them more than once in robbing a park that belong'd to Sir Thomas Lucy of Cherlecot, near Stratford. For this he was prosecuted by that gentleman, as he thought, somewhat too severely; and in order to revenge that ill usage, he made a ballad upon him. And tho' this, probably the first essay of his poetry, be lost, yet it is said to have been so very bitter, that it redoubled the prosecution against him to that degree, that he was oblig'd to leave his business and family in Warwickshire, for some time, and shelter himself in London. It is at this time, and upon this accident, that he is said to have made his first acquaintance in the play-house. He was receiv'd into the company then in being, at first in a very mean rank; but his admirable wit, and the natural turn of it to the stage, soon distinguish'd him, if not as an extraordinary actor, yet as an excellent writer.

Davies is an inconsiderable witness. He could not even get the name of Justice Shallow correct, confusing him with Shadwell's Clodpate. Rowe put the story more reasonably, but both, it must be remembered, were writing about a century and a quarter after the event. Local gossip can stretch a tale a long way in a year or two: the yarn that spans a hundred years is not much in the way of testimony. Aubrey, drawing on a Warwickshire journey, as well as on Beeston, much earlier, had said not a word of all this: and it was just the colourful stuff to which his gossiping nature was addicted.

The case against the poaching episode depends not only on Aubrey's silence but on the ascertained facts that Charlecote, Sir Thomas Lucy's estate, was not then legally emparked—to keep a deer-park at that time needed a permit of the Crown—and that poachers were not liable to whipping or imprisonment. Shakespeare may, of course, have been involved in some escapade of ' flush youth ' which was built up by rumour into the series of forays for which he was ' oft whipt and sometimes imprisoned,' as Parson Davies told the tale. The story, as it has been handed down, is impossible in its detail: but it is the kind of stuff that is dear to immature romantics; naturally the rhymers of the district played up to it later on by finding (or inventing) the ballad against the squire, which Rowe asserted was lost. It started, twenty years after Rowe and nearly a century and a half after the supposed event, as a jingle:

> Sir Thomas was too covetous
>> To cover so much deer,
> When horns upon his head
>> Most plainly did appear.
> Had not his worship one deer left?
>> What then, he took a wife;
> Took pains enough to find him horns
>> Should last him during life.

This trickle of bawdy quip is not a good effort in simulation of a master's hand, even in boyhood, and the later ballad, traceable to 1750, beginning:

> A Parliament Member, a Justice of Peace,
> At home a poor scarecrow, at London an ass,
> If lousy is Lucy, as some volk miscall it,
> Then Lucy is lousy, whatever befall it

and then rambling on through a page of stanzas, is even poorer stuff. Later in the century the gossips and the romantics had thrown sex in on top of trespass and theft. By that time William had seduced the keeper's daughter! For the legend of 'Local Boy Makes Good' the public does indeed love a startling beginning in which the local boy makes very bad indeed. The Shakespeare Myth shows no exception to this rule.

Sir Thomas Lucy, a Member of Parliament, frequently commissioned by the Privy Council, and a person of very high importance for the execution of State policy in the Midlands, cannot reasonably, or even possibly, be identified as the ludicrous little fribble Shallow, a local justice of no parts or importance and incapable of anything but supply of comedy to Shakespeare's master-hand. Charlecote, the scene of the alleged Warwickshire poaching-party, which may or may not have given London, Britain, and the world its greatest dramatist, was added to the properties owned by the National Trust in 1947 and so made open to the public view, after being held through the centuries by the Lucys and Fairfax-Lucys. When I visited this composite mansion in that year—composite in the sense that it is Tudor, glorious Tudor at the gatehouse, with subsequent additions—I found that the Trust had provided a lively, witty and informed escort who was as cautious about legend as he was learned about works of art: he said nothing of the poaching matter, though most of the tourists must have been waiting for it.

The ancestral home of the Lucys, whose descendants held on until the end of the Second World War, should certainly be seen by Stratford visitors. (It is some four miles out and pleasantly set by the banks of the Avon.) Within it provides an entrancing epitome of the taste shown by the British landed gentry down the ages, admirable and execrable alike. There are Italian and Oriental importations, the latter looking as apt to Warwickshire as the Taj Mahal would look in the Scottish Highlands. There are frolicsome excursions into eighteenth-century baroque and Victorian ornament as well as a solid background of Tudor oak, brick, solidity, and seemliness. In what is now the great park are Spanish piebald sheep and the dappled fallow-deer long so popular with British milords of the park-owning class. The tourist may not, after all, be treading in the footsteps of William the Poacher: but he will see a true piece of the seigneurial English Midlands, an evocative relic of the old regime, and a stretch of Avon whereon, should the sun shine, it will gild a pale stream with heavenly alchemy. Also he will wander among the deer, the fate of whose ancestors at William Shakespeare's hand has been so long a subject for genial anecdote and bitter controversy.

In my opinion Shakespeare left Stratford because he saw and heard the players and fell in love with their rant and mummery, their laughter and bravura, the music that they made, and the beauty-flash that lit the whole proceedings and turned the

D

rough vagrant cavalcade into a service of poetry itself. He had had the chance to see players in plenty. Stratford was almost a ' Number One Date,' as a theatre manager would say nowadays, for the London troupes upon the road. Fripp, the exact student of Stratford records, gives the following list of visitations during Shakespeare's boyhood and early manhood:

> In 1569, in John Shakespeare's bailiwick, came the Queen's Players and the Earl of Worcester's; in 1573 the Earl of Leicester's; in 1575 the Earl of Warwick's, and again the Earl of Worcester's; in 1576, a second time, Leicester's and, a third time, Worcester's; in 1579 Lord Strange's and the Countess of Essex's; in 1580 Earl Derby's; in 1581 Worcester's for the fourth time, and Lord Berkeley's; in 1582, for a fifth time, Worcester's and a second time Berkeley's; in 1583, for a third time Berkeley's (who divided five shillings from the corporation purse with ' a preacher '), and Lord Chandos's (Lord Chandos being Giles Bridges of Sudeley Castle); in 1584 the Earl of Oxford's, Worcester's, their sixth recorded visit, and the Earl of Essex's; in 1586 a company unnamed; in 1587 the Queen's for the second time, Essex's for the third time, Leicester's for the third time, a company unnamed, and the Earl of Stafford's men.

This adds powerful testimony to the fact that Stratford was not then merely a dirty village, with nothing but ignorance and oafs in its houses.

It is especially interesting to read of the visits of Lord Berkeley's ' cry of players,' because these can be linked up with an old tradition that the young Shakespeare lived for a while, perhaps as a tutor, in Gloucestershire. Berkeley Castle, near the Severn, is mentioned with detail in two plays, for no obvious reason, and it is described with something like special knowledge of the South Cotswolds and the terrain beyond ' these high wild hills and rough, uneven ways.' When Richard II asks ' Barkloughly Castle—call they this at hand ? ' was he using some old local pronunciation ? Again, ' There stands the castle by yond tuft of trees.' Why that tuft unless there was some visual memory at work ? Dr. Caroline

Spurgeon, who believes that Shakespeare found his ' temple-haunting martlets ' in the martins that long nested at Berkeley Castle, also points out that the Cotswold names mentioned by Justice Shallow (2 *Henry IV*, v, i), William Visor of Woncot and Clement Perkes o' th' hill, fit into the Berkeley landscape, since there were well-known families of Vizard at Woodmancote (Woncot) and of Perkes at Stinchcombe Hill, known as ' The Hill.' To what does this lead ? To the likelihood that Shakespeare spent that schoolmastering or tutoring period mentioned by Aubrey with or near the Earl of Berkeley, a great patron of the players, and there made young acquaintance with the craft and its witchery. Since this team played several times at Stratford, William may have followed them home—or away.

Perhaps 1587 was the deciding date. The Queen's Men, with Tarleton and Kemp as Chief Clowns, were in Warwickshire at midsummer. This was the company which he was later to serve and to grace. Berkeley's men had given him the taste: the great Alleyn had strengthened it, when Worcester's Men arrived by the Avon: now there came a company of even brighter ' stars,' men royally favoured, glamorous indeed. It is as good a guess as any that at this moment Shakespeare could stand Stratford no longer. He asked for an audition, he showed the Queen's Men his pleasant ' well-shap't ' presence with the hazel eye, he spoke a passage on trial, he showed them—more important—a piece of text. They were short of a ' hired man ': they needed a furbisher of plays: he was too old by then to be a boy-apprentice. An offer was made and snapped up. That is a fair conjecture.

Hired for how much, how long, with what safety, what prospects ? His ears buzzed and burned with such questions when he went back to Anne (and three children), told the news to his father and mother and gave notice to the lawyer or headmaster with whom he was in service, restless, fretful, full of the high notions of a young, aspiring mind. Surely that is a likelier picture of William Shakespeare's break with Stratford than is contained in the ' oft-whipt ' anecdotage of Davies and Rowe. The story that he came unknown to London and held horses' heads outside the playhouse, and organised a service of Shakespeare's Boys for similiar jobs is an eighteenth-century invention. Dr. Johnson gave it his support, but Aubrey and Rowe assert that he became a player at once, first of course in small parts; they make no mention of the horse-holding story, which sounds like a picturesque addition to the poaching legend, with romance at work again.

There was, as I have suggested, a rare family row about the choice. The young man, piqued, desperate, knowing how small was his chance of sending home enough and regular funds, would make reckless promises that he would have them all on the top of the world, if he could only show his mettle. And how could he do so as a home-bound hack, Stratford-limited, in bondage to the quill and quillets of an attorney's office or a dominie's desk ? He pledged himself to become as rich and great as any of the mummers, to restore the coat of arms, to build the family fortunes: only let him go, let him be trusted. He was past any cautious counsel now. Anyhow he was going: certainly he went: certainly he won. In a decade it was John Shakespeare, Armiger: in a decade, too, it was William Shakespeare of New Place. There could be no disputing the speed and fullness of the victory.

Once engaged and at work he could throw off that melancholy: until the Dark Lady broke into his heart and made havoc where she trespassed, there would be no time for young indulgence in a humorous sadness. He might write of these moods, but he would not suffer or practise them. There would be no time, too, for the fantastic gloom and little ecstasies of a young man devising for himself in small-town isolation the harmonies upon a lute or the intricate pattern of words which he so loved. He would be a London man. He would be busy ' in the quick forge and working-house of thought.' He would be the Chamberlain's and the Queen's (and the people's) humble servant. He would work round the clock and revel in the dedication. He had done with mental growing-pains, self-pity, and the pleasures of young introspection: or so he thought. Women would intervene and illness and, in his early forties, some great darkness of spirit. But now he felt himself, already four years a parent, to be fully a man: and hope arrives when boyhood, even youth, depart.

G. K. Chesterton, writing of Dickens' bleak beginnings, has put that point with characteristic skill.   Alleging that a starless outlook is common in the bitterness of boyish distresses, that there seems to be a dreadful finality about any early disaster, and that a lost child can suffer like a lost soul, he added:

> It is currently said that hope goes with youth, and lends to youth its wings of a butterfly: but I fancy that hope is the last gift given to man, and the only gift not given to youth.   Youth is pre-eminently the period in which a man can be lyric, fanatical, poetic; but youth is the period in which a man can be hopeless.   The end of every episode is the end of the world.   But the power of hoping through everything, the knowledge that the soul survives its adventures, this great inspiration comes to the middle-aged; God has kept this good wine until now.   It is from the backs of the elderly gentlemen that the wings of the butterfly should burst. There is nothing that so much mystifies the young as the consistent frivolity of the old.   They have discovered their indestructibility.   They are in their second and clearer childhood, and there is a meaning in the merriment of their eyes.   They have seen the end of the End of the World.

G. K. C. wrote before the atom was split and the End of the World became more than a phrase.   But there is perennial truth in what he said.

At twenty-three Shakespeare was not old.   But he was much older than most men of that age are now, even though they be veterans of wars and hardened to a world of chaos and cruelty.   He was old enough at any rate to see melancholy as a ' humour ' which henceforward would decorate his plays instead of as a blanket with which a lad could shelter his drooping spirits.   And so he left his family and found his task: he gave up the security of a desk for the chances and changes of the motley: and he did so with this great asset, that, like the emerging Dickens, he was old enough to hope.

CHAPTER V

' *In the Quick Forge* '

THE London to which Shakespeare came was given by
him one significant adjective—quick. It was the ' quick
forge and working-house of thought,' and quick meant then
the opposite of dead, something lively as well as rapid. It was
a city with a light in its eyes, a city on its toes. Writers about
Shakespeare have laid great stress on the Warwickshire background and so underrated, perhaps, the influences rained upon
him by the starry firmament of London life. As I have said,
his sporting metaphors and rural images could have been
found within a few minutes' ride of the city. But quite as
precious to the playwright as the liberty of the ancient Forest
of Middlesex and of meadow and marsh in Essex and Surrey
was the key of the London street. He may have found Justice
Shallow in the Cotswold and Dogberry—as Aubrey said—in
Bucks, beside the road to London. But his wits and beauties
were moulded in the city's ' quick forge ': his Cleopatra
played gipsy-wanton on the fringes of the English throne; his
Mercutio came from the Inns of Court by boat to flash a
phrase and a rapier on the Bankside. His Bardolph was in
any tavern of his visitation. For Shakespeare, as for Dickens,
it was all there. They had the key, the wrist to turn it, and
the eyes to see what lay behind the door.

The adjective spacious, applied with Tennyson's authority
to the days of Queen Elizabeth, has always seemed to me
curiously inept. Geographically her London was mostly
cramped within its city walls: it overflowed, of course, to the
' south suburbs by the Elephant ' and the Southwark Bankside,
outside the city's pale, could amply spread itself for the shows
and revels which it offered to the commerce of delight. But,
inside the city, streets were narrow and roofs were low. Clothes

were padded, stuffy, voluminous. Ablution was neither general nor thorough. In hot weather Body Odours must have been rank in the halls of the nobles as well as in the dark, pestiferous, insanitary, jostling places of the people. The Fleet ditch was a main drain: there were copious stenches, as well as music, in the air.

Politically, too, there was a sense of confinement: a man had to watch his words and deeds. Science had not opened his eyes to the world's immensity of age or to our tiny whirling globe's colossal adventure in the chasms of illimitable space. The old astronomy made the firmament move in order, harmony, and pattern round the earth. Such was the decree of global fixity, which man must study and obey in order to achieve a fixed security on earth. The stars in their courses: the classes of men in their proper ranks. That was the decree of Nature. The system was small, tidy, and tight. You looked up to get your social bearings from sun, moon and stars. The sky, astronomically, was the limit. And the sky, politically, was the Crown.

Presumably the spaciousness, of which Tennyson thought, lay in the liberties of the mariners, who were ranging the seas as never before, and came home to Wapping to rest and drink, to cure themselves of scurvy, and to forget the 'remainder biscuit' which had been vexing their teeth and gums. One great difference between London of Elizabeth and that of the nineteenth and twentieth centuries was that it used its river. Only one bridge bestrode the Thames, a stream broader than it is now when our embankments have defined the banks and pressed the current inwards. To bridge the Thames at all had been, for the Middle Ages, a gigantic task: to lace it with bridges was impossible. Hence the ubiquitous watermen, who had their champion and poet in John Taylor, rhymer, oarsman, and defender of the craft.

Here, at any rate, was the Tennysonian spaciousness. On the river one could breathe a cleaner air and add to the whispering wind the strains of lute and lyric: for the ferried gallants took their music with them to any party. John Taylor numbered the London boats at 2000 and the ferrymen, arguing and chaffering over their fares, rivalled the Watch and the Water Carriers among London ' cards ' and characters. The cries ' Eastward Ho! ' and ' Westward Ho! ' were watermen's advertisements of their destination. The Queen, the Archbishop, the Lord Mayor, the City Companies, and the great noblemen, whose family mansions lined the Strand and are now remembered in the names of streets running down to the river, Arundel, Norfolk, Essex, and so on, all had their barges of state: these may not have burned upon the water like a burnished throne, as Cleopatra's barge glowed upon the Cydnus, but the Queen's, we may be sure, was ' bravely pavilioned ' and had some ' pretty, dimpled boys ' for pages. The river was a channel for pomp and procession of all kinds: it offered noble scenery—the ' bricky towers ' of the mansions sung by Spenser—and passage for pageantry, including the rites of solemn funeral.

As far as the Tower the Thames was serviceable and elegant: farther east, too, it had its glories, such as Drake's *Golden Hind* anchored at Deptford, whither the industrious waterman carried sightseers to gaze and feast: for the catering side of the ship's possibilities were not neglected. But there was the sordid aspect as well. Just below Wapping was Execution Dock, of which Stow wrote that it was ' the usual place of execution for hanging of Pirats and Sea Rovers, at the low water marke, there to remain till three tides had overflowed them.' Shakespeare knew of this place and practice and alluded to it in *The Tempest*. Antonio speaks of a rascal who deserved to ' lie drowning the washing of ten tides.' Were the victims really suspended, half-hanged, at the mercy of several immersions ? Considering the brutality of contemporary punishments it is not impossible. Those who took boat to Deptford might see sights as odious as any wayfarer by Tyburn Tree.

Spaciousness for the mind and senses was rapidly arriving. The Reformation had broken one great check on the freedom of thought and had only partially imposed its own discipline which was later on to be a darkening influence. There was far more peace and stability than England had known for centuries, and the religious persecutions, which followed when the bloody quarrels of York and Lancaster were over, had diminished in scope and horror. The hangman was still busy with rope and knife, but it was the alleged traitor, mixing politics with a suspect creed, who stood in greatest danger. Spain, after all, had its Fifth Column among the English Catholics: vigilance was hardly to be blamed, though some of its penal manifestations were revolting.

At the same time something had happened to the English people; they were, in a sense, lit up. That phrase has in our time been applied chiefly to alcoholic illumination. But it aptly describes the alertness of the Tudor world, its relish of new things, its response to all the sights and sounds which the Renaissance had released. It had imported the fashions and notions of ' ingenious Italy ' and was busily blending them with habits and fancies of its own. One result—and an excellent example—of this fusing was the new English language, enormously enriched by importation, yet still native under a Jonson's or a Shakespeare's touch, still racy, still itself. The Court, naturally, and its imitators were more affected by the new noises, new looks, new accents, new tricks and games. It was nearer to Whitehall than to Warwickshire that Shakespeare heard the targets of Mercutio's disdain, the

> antic, lisping, affecting fantasticoes; these new tuners of accents!—' By Jesu, a very good blade!—a very tall man!—a very good whore! '—Why, is not this a lamentable thing, grandsire, that we should be thus afflicted with these strange flies, these fashion-mongers, these *pardonnez-mois*, who stand so much on the new form that they cannot sit at ease on the old bench ? O, their *bons*, their *bons*!

The country might be faithful to its morris: the Court, with its Frenchified talk and its cult of lavolt and pavane, would prefer the new Italian steps. Troilus complains of his disadvantage in sex-appeal when contrasted with the Grecian youths ' swelling o'er with arts and exercise ' ; in doing so he speaks for the simple Englishman against the Europeanised gallants and fantasticoes:

> I cannot sing,
> Nor heel the high lavolt, nor sweeten talk,
> Nor play at subtle games; fair virtues all,
> To which the Grecians are most prompt and pregnant.

In *Troilus and Cressida* the Greeks represent the privileged, courtier class: the Trojans are the simple outsiders. The simpletons saw the fairest ladies joining the new dance and could not be expected to like it. But they too in time were quickened and lit up.

In this spell between the brutish welter of the baronial wars and the coming of the indignant and intolerant Puritans the spirit of England had a chance to play and to make players, and the purse of England was at least sufficient to dress the mummers and adorn the stage. The gentry played the subtle games so detested of poor, anxious Troilus as he foresaw the surrender of his Cressida to the prompt—again that quickness! —and pregnant-witted Greeks. What games were these? Not cards and chequers, bowls, tennis, and billiards only, but the exchange of verbal conceits, rhymes, sonnets, and all the punning, risqué banter which tinkles and twinkles in the courtly comedies of Shakespeare. Berowne and Rosaline in *Love's Labour's Lost* are the essential voices of this kind of erudite flirtation, which darts, quick as a flourish of silk or sword, to the listener's ears. Now we are inevitably baffled by much of its excessive ingenuity. It is not our lingo: it is not our idiom: it is not our kind of fun: it has allusions naturally difficult or even impossible to grasp. What strikes us most, perhaps, is the speed of the riposte: it is like volleying at tennis: the forge of thought is so quick and these Tudor-Grecians are so prompt in its expression, so nimble in this power to ' sweeten talk.'

They are all instructed in music. Again Troilus has his grievance, ' I cannot sing.' He was out of it, indeed, if like poor rustic Bottom he had only a ' reasonable good ear ' for the tongs and bones and was deaf to the ' lascivious pleasing of a lute.' Here again the peace that Elizabeth had brought was fruitful. During the bloody brawling of the greedy

Baronial Houses, dignified with the far too picturesque name of the Wars of the Roses, the musicians and other artists had tended to go abroad and seek their patrons in France or the Netherlands. But the Tudors reclaimed them and the composers, singers, and lutanists returned with their art enriched by new styles of composition. The Reformation did not destroy church music in England, though its influence was a limiting and constraining one. The laymen of the later sixteenth century, led by the great nobles, habitually kept a household musician or were increasingly devoted to glees and madrigals, and it was deemed the normal business of any proper guest to take his place after supper in the family music and to sing his part. In Morley's *Plain and Easie Introduction to Practical Musicke* (1597) one of the characters explains his failure and disgrace in this matter:

> But supper being ended, and Musicke bookes, according to the custome being brought to the table; the mistresse of the house presented mee with a part, earnestly requesting mee to sing. But when, after manie excuses, I protested unfainedly that I could not, everie one began to wonder. Yea, some whispered to others, demaunding how I was brought up.

Shakespeare himself would have suffered no embarrassment in such a situation. For the allusions to music in his plays are as abundant as affectionate. Not only was harmony sweet to his ear: it was for him the guiding principle of all public conduct and affairs. He would have echoed with more art and grammar, but with no more ecstasy, the player Laneham's simple and serene description of music in the air when Queen Elizabeth stood by night on the bridge at Kenilworth in the summer of 1575 and listened to the melody coming off the barges through the tranquil night:

> Noow, Syr, the ditty in mitter so aptly endighted to the matter, and after by voys so deliciously deliver'd . . . every instrument agayn in hiz kind so excellently tunabl; and this in the eeving of the day, resooundung from the calm

waters, whear prezens of her Majesty, and longing to listen, had utterly damped all noyz and dyn: the hole armony conveyd in tyme, tune, and temper thus incomparably melodious; with what pleazure, Master Martyn, with what sharpnes of conceyt, with what lyvely delighte, this moought pears (pierce) into the heerers harts; I pray ye imagin yoorself az ye may; for, so God judge me, by all the wit and cunning I have, I cannot express, I promis yoo. . . . Muzik iz a nobl art!

Laneham's raptures are richly expressive of an age that had suddenly discovered the sensibilities as well as the senses. Life and the arts that are life's decoration were savoured to the full.

Two things especially distinguished the Elizabethan design for living: one was its range of activities, the other was the passion of its devotions, enjoyments and affections. The London to which Shakespeare came had its cliques of fantasticoes, of course, but on the whole it was far more free from the specialist than we are to-day. The young nobleman would be trained to horse and hound: but he would also be expected to play the lute and take his part tunefully in domestic rounds of music: he would be swordsman, horseman, falconer, bowler, as well as showing a palate for food and wine: he would fight as readily in the Navy as the Army, sail to Cadiz, or march into Flanders: at the same time he would not only esteem but practise poetry, not only enjoy the spectacle of masque and play but dance a measure and compose, albeit privately, a comedy for the Twelfth Night or Shrovetide revels in his own mansion or at his Inns of Court. Shakespeare was called Johannes Factotum, Jack of All Trades, but his patrons were themselves no less deserving of the title.

' In the quick forge and working-house of thought ' is indeed a full and accurate description of that London, which was beauty's teeming workshop. The very play-boys were demons of industry. They even found time, amid all their gaieties, for a very serious cult of gloom and they worked at that with a most humorous diligence. Indeed, they seem to have enjoyed their dumps as much as any rapture of them all.

The English milords have been ready in the field of sport or battle often enough. But they have rarely, at least in later centuries, been as ready with a sonnet as with a sabre or a fowling-piece. They have rarely been exquisite in taste as well as admirable in arms. But Shakespeare's London was full of these high-spirited omnicompetents. The very fact that those who wish to deny Shakespeare the authorship of the plays can find seven or eight different grandees with some qualification for the part of author and some report of practice in poetry and theatre is a remarkable tribute to the age. You could hardly pick out of Mayfair and Westminster to-day even a tiny team of men of affairs capable of composing plays and poetry of the first rank, as well as being passable musicians and skilled to scribble a sonnet to their loves of comfort and despair and toss it across a night-club table.

The second point is the emotional temperature at which the Elizabethans lived: they were amateurs in the fullest sense of the word. It is too often forgotten in our time that an amateur is not just someone who plays a game without a fee. He plays it because he loves it: liking is scarcely sufficient to justify the term. The Elizabethans were continually in love with what they saw and heard and fancied. They were always being ' ravished '—that is their strong and favourite word for fascination by beauty: and more often they were ravished by the beauty of man's creation than of Nature's. Nowadays our intellectuals and would-be connoisseurs use such tepid adjectives as amusing and intriguing of things acceptable to their fancy. The Elizabethans were not amused: they were inflamed. They were not intrigued: they were enraptured. Beauty did not toy with their appreciation. It devoured their senses whole.

Poetry and music were the particular sources of this ravishment. The English musicians, Dowland and Byrd, gave far more than mere pleasure to their age: they won praise as though they were distributors of paradisal joy. While the town-taverns were full of fiddlers and dancers—the Puritan Gosson grumbled at the swarms of such light fellows—the hall of the big house was echoing with verses and with madrigals.

This double passion of the time is very well expressed in a sonnet by Richard Barnfield to a friend:

> If Musique and sweet Poetrie agree,
> As they must needes (the Sister and the Brother),
> Then must the Love be great, twixt thee and mee,
> Because thou lov'st the one, and I the other.
> Dowland to thee is deare; whose heavenly tuch
> Upon the Lute, doeth ravish humaine sense;
> Spenser to mee; whose deepe Conceit is such,
> As, passing all Conceit, needs no defence.
> Thou lov'st to heare the sweete melodious sound,
> That Phoebus Lute (the Queen of Musique) makes:
> And I in deepe Delight am chiefly drownd,
> When as himselfe to singing he betakes.
> One God is God of Both (as Poets faigne),
> One Knight loves Both, and Both in thee remaine.

It can be argued that the Elizabethans wrote of a ravishment which they never truly felt, that it was the common form of their society to lay on the terms of devotion until affection was disguised as adoration. But I do not think that this was generally true of the Amateur of that age. There is so much of the rapture that seems to ring absolutely true. The air in the quick forge was warm and gave a glowing ardour to the enjoyment of its products.

In Shakespeare's London they had been singing Green Sleeves, the ' smash-hit ' of balladry, since 1580, with answering verses:

> Green sleeves is worn away,
> Yellow sleeves come to decay,
> Black sleeves I hold in despite,
> But white sleeves is my delight.

It was the fashion to re-write the favourites. (I have heard the suggestion—Mr. Bridges-Adams passed it on to me as a possibility—that dying Falstaff did not babble of green fields but of Green Sleeves.) Dowland's songs went through edition after edition. The playgoers, bound for the Bankside, took their lutes and viols with them on the water: they would have disdained to attend a barber who did not provide a singer for the entertainment of his customers. Such an addition now appears, perhaps, ' unEnglish.' Yet to be acquainted with the fingering of a lute or of a virginal was then the common obligation of a man about town. UnEnglish? In Oxford there is a portrait of the leading organist of that time, Gresham Professor of Music, renowned, and given a royal appointment for his virtuosity. His lightly-bearded face is thin, his nose and forehead long, his hair and eyes very dark: a long-skulled Mediterranean type, you would say, or possibly one of those descendants, obstinately Iberian, of the ancient mariners who left their long barrows and circles on our coasts. Certainly he looks alien, delicate, hyper-sensitive, one given to ' the musician's melancholy which is fantastical.' Yet his name, to one's delight, turns out to be John Bull.

It was a period with an unquenchable appetite for dressing-up. In Shakespeare's earlier comedies the gentry are always ready for a masquerade, and, when this takes place in our modern productions with the donning of false noses by the men and of dominos and vizors by the ladies, followed by a rather half-hearted canter round the stage with noises deemed to be jocund, the result is rarely amusing or enchanting. In the later plays there is careful arrangement made for more formal masques and here again the results for us are usually rather sad. What playgoer at *The Tempest* looks forward with any eagerness to the arrival of Iris and Ceres with their botanical observations and their call to a ' graceful ' dance of ' reapers, properly habited,' and of nymphs with ' sedg'd crowns ' and ' ever-harmless looks'? It sounds most innocent and turns out, as a rule, to be uncommonly dull.

But the fashion of the time was for masquing and still more masquing. Elizabeth herself seems to have put up with and even relished the constancy of nymphs in arbours who greeted her arrival at a country mansion; she enjoyed too the caperings of ' wild-men ' among the groves, such antic fellows being the usual partners of the choral nymphs. The Queen was constantly ' on progress ' through the estates of her loyal and wealthy subjects, who arranged pageants and 'triumphs' and masquerades of all kinds: musical and poetical honours were lavish. Later on Ben Jonson was to utter the natural growl of the poet and dramatist who sees his text over-laid by the producer, 'Painting and Carpentry are the Soul of Masque.' But there would be complimentary verses in plenty and the kind of music Laneham so enjoyed as well as the material trimmings, torch-light processions, and other illuminations, when Her Majesty was on the road or when the nobility and gentry found occasion for a revel, which seems to have been often enough.

The members of the Inns of Court were themselves devoted mummers and masquers and gloried in bedizened charades under presidency of a Lord of Misrule. The capers cut on these occasions by statesmen, lawyers, and philosophers might seem to us tedious or childish now. For example, when Gray's Inn and the Temple quarrelled reconciliation might be effected thus—by masquerade:

When the Prince and the Ambassador of Templaria were seated, they were presented with this device: 'At the side of the Hall, behind a curtain, was erected an altar to the Goddess of Amity; her arch-flamen ready to attend the sacrifice . . . round about the same sate Nymphs and fairies . . . and made very pleasant melody with viols and voices, and sang hymns . . . to her deity.' Then there came from another room three pairs of the famous friends of antiquity. Lastly, were presented *Graius* and *Templarius* . . . but the Goddess did not accept their service until the arch-flamen had performed mystic rites, the nymphs had sung hymns and they had renewed their devotions. Then the arch-flamen pronounced Graius and Templarius perfect friends and cursed any who should attempt to separate them. When the show was ended the Prince made the Ambassador a Knight of the Helmet.

Such performance was a natural part of the unflagging amateurishness of the age. Your lawyer was as ready with voice and viol as with quill and quillet. While the villager was always quick in response to the taborer or drummer and welcomed his summons to a jig or morris, the ladies of the Court were no less eager to be sprites of Olympus, nymphs, Dryads, Naiads, and so forth and to take part in the measure and the madrigals which the classical fancies of the English Renaissance ordained.

Sir Francis Bacon is typical of his time in his equal dedication to affairs of State, law, philosophy, and things ' that take the senses.' His essay *Of Masques and Triumphs* shows that he had time and energy for a close study of scenic effects, lighting, and costume: it reveals both the sumptuous nature of the masquerade at high social levels and the careful artistry devoted to it by the happy amateurs of song, dance, and pageant. For the understanding of this noblemen's world which Shakespeare was to see and serve, through his attachment to the Earl of Southampton, this essay by Bacon is supremely important. It shows how nearly professional in skill and application this amateur world of the courtiers was becoming. Bacon, it is true, would brush the subject aside as being toyshop and nursery stuff: but no sooner has he disparaged the juvenile taste of princes who must be thus amused and the ' petty wonderments ' of the resulting masque than he shows himself a devotee of the art and an enraptured master of its detail. He ends on the dismissive note, but it is obvious to any reader that the future Lord Chancellor of England could be extremely happy, and of wise counsel too, when he was play-boy and director of the play. The essay is so brief and is such a miracle of pregnant dramatic criticism that it is worth quoting in full:

Of Masques and Triumphs

These things are but toys, to come amongst such serious observations. But yet, since princes will have such things, it is better they should be graced with elegancy, than daubed with cost. Dancing to song is a thing of great state and pleasure. I understand it, that the song be in quire, placed aloft, and accompanied with some broken music; and the ditty fitted to the device. Acting in song, especially in dialogues, hath an extreme good grace: I say acting, not dancing (for that is a mean and vulgar thing); and the voices of the dialogue would be strong and manly (a bass and a tenor, no treble); and the ditty high and tragical, not nice or dainty. Several quires, placed one over against another, and taking the voice by catches, anthem-wise, give great pleasure. Turning dances into figure is a childish curiosity. And generally, let it be noted, that those things which I here set down are such as do naturally take the sense, and not respect petty wonderments.

It is true, the alterations of scenes, so it be quietly and without noise, are things of great beauty and pleasure; for they feed and relieve the eye, before it be full of the same object. Let the scenes abound with light, specially coloured and varied; and let the masquers, or any other, that are to come down from the scene, have some motions upon the scene itself before their coming down; for it draws the eye strangely, and makes it with great pleasure to desire to see that it cannot perfectly discern. Let the songs be loud and cheerful, and not chirpings or pulings. Let the music likewise be sharp and loud and well placed.

The colours that shew best by candle-light are white, carnation, and a kind of sea-water-green; and oes, or spangs, as they are of no great cost, so they are of most glory. As for rich embroidery, it is lost and not discerned. Let the suits of the masquers be graceful, and such as become the person when the vizars are off: not after examples of known attires; Turks, soldiers, mariners, and the like. Let antimasques not be long; they have been commonly of fools, satyrs, baboons, wild-men, antics, beasts, sprites, witches, Ethiopes, pigmies, turquets, nymphs, rustics, Cupids, statuas moving, and the like. As for angels, it is not comical enough to put them in antimasques; and any thing that is hideous, as devils, giants, is on the other side as unfit.

But chiefly, let the music of them be recreative, and with some strange changes. Some sweet odours, suddenly coming forth, without any drops falling, are, in such a company as there is steam and heat, things of great pleasure and refreshment. Double masques, one of men, another of ladies, addeth state and variety. But all is nothing, except the room be kept clear and neat.

For justs, tourneys, and barriers; the glories of them are chiefly in the chariots, wherein the challengers make their entry; especially if they be drawn with strange beasts, as lions, bears, camels, and the like; or in the devices of their entrance; or in the bravery of their liveries; or in the goodly furniture of their horses and armour. But enough of these toys.

One sees, hears, and even smells it all, the crowd of noble masquers, with that schoolboy eagerness which gives both naïveté and fascination to the Tudor and Jacobean world, the elaborate face-painting, the dressing-up, the whoops and pirouettes of satyrs, baboons, and wild-men, amid the elegance of the ladies. The whole tumult of colour and sound might vex the critical eye by too rich embroidery or the critical ear by some 'chirping or puling,' antecedent, no doubt, of the modern croon, but these would generate pleasure among those not finical. (Women, denied the public and professional stages, were free to participate in masque and all-women casts were not unknown. In 1617 'Younge Gentlewomen of the Ladies' Hall in Deptford at Greenwich,' some kind of senior school, presented a masque called *Cupid's Banishment* to Anne of Denmark, King James the First's Queen, and followed it with an 'Anti-Maske' of Bacchus's children: this revealed—strange theme for nice young ladies—'the severall humers of drunkards and many pretty figures befitting that vayne'!) Bacon allows for a vast wardrobe and his essay postulates very considerable accomplishment in the various arts. Among a crowded audience in a hot room the heat no doubt would be aggravated by the heavy clothes with ruffs for the men and tight-lacing for the ladies; so the sage counsellor advises action against 'steam and heat' by the atmospheric injection of sweet odours. Here was the 'quick forge' of fancy, as well as the working-house of thought, and forges are apt to be very warm places.

Typical, again, was the mixture of gravity with levity. The 'fantastico' of one day was the philosopher of the next. Bacon had entered Parliament in 1584, published his first Essays in 1597, issued his first great treatise on *The Advancement of Learning* in 1605, was Solicitor General in 1607 and then busily engaged in reconciling High Anglicans and Puritans, Attorney-General in 1613, Keeper of the Great Seal in 1617, and Lord Chancellor in 1618. Then, two years later, he brought out his *Novum Organum or the New Instrument for the Interpretation and Discovery of Truth*, which was received with acclamation in the academies of Europe. He had found time, amid his writings of comedies and masques and essays and his legal and political career, to review, classify, and give method to all aspects of knowledge. He preached Inductive as against *a priori* philosophy, i.e. working up from observed facts to principles and generalities instead of beginning with an assumed truth and then applying it to the data of the senses. He conceived himself to be the dedicated servant of truth. ' It is heaven upon earth,' he wrote, ' to have a man's mind move in charity, rest in providence, and turn upon the poles of truth.' A philosopher of our own day, say Bertrand Russell, might have written that: but he could not have written the essay *Of Masques and Triumphs*. To combine the two capacities was the particular habit of that period, in which the sages were also the soldiers, poets, and play-boys of the town. Bacon, unlike most of his time, was no soldier, but he astonishingly combined the gifts and faculties of a Bertrand Russell, a Lord Haldane, and a C. B. Cochran. In the ' quick forge ' of London life it was no offence to be a dabbler, a factotum, a man both of science and of showmanship. The social stage, to whose fringe or prompt-corner Shakespeare was led by Lord Southampton, was crowded with gay, brilliant, restless figures, immensely young and voracious in their appetite for living, uninhibited in their pursuit of anything so tremendous as political treason or so light as a new notion for a masquerade. The metaphysician would not only tread a measure but be proud to invent one. The Lord Chancellor himself would join the dance. Many of the sciences were as yet no further developed than they had been in the Athens of Pericles, two thousand years before; now that we know what science, unfettered, can achieve we need not condole with Shakespeare's London for its backwardness in this department of the working-house. But quiet reflection, as Bacon showed, was by no means neglected in a city of swift and gaily-tinted pleasures.

Yet this home of delicate music, of sonneteering, and of lyric-writing unsurpassed in the history of English letters, this London in which the language of love was written by the poets and spoken by the actors in terms of such high civility and grace, was also a city of brutish and abominable practices that left these chosen spirits oddly unabashed. It seems that man must ever be a creature of inconstancy and paradox. When he has discovered beauty with one eye of discerning adoration, he is immediately leering at beastliness with the other eye of insensitive barbarism. In Shakespeare's London, squalor jostled splendour and cruelty compassion with an urgency and an ugliness of contrast which it is very difficult for us to understand. Yet the facts are there and we are not immune from censure of this kind, having seen in our time to what perversion of human instinct and what cold horrors of deliberate persecution man may suddenly come even in nations which have at one time achieved a moral and mental stature far beyond the ordinary.

It was no offence against public decency to expose the severed heads of criminals and to let them rot in the sun or crumble beneath the greedy beaks of kites and carrion-crows. Consider Shakespeare on his way about London, murmuring on his lips, perhaps, the rough draft of one of those very passages whose delicate invocations of love or appeals to the quality of mercy have rung their bells in our hearts ever since. Had he been coming back from Stratford or from some visit to the westward houses or estates of the eminent he would pass by Tyburn Tree close to the present site of Marble Arch. This was the scene of public executions, which were events as common as popular: but the execution of the convicted carried with it a ghastly ritual of evisceration and mutilation whose enjoyment by the crowd is one of the filthiest witnesses of Elizabethan sadism.

Dover Wilson in *The Essential Shakespeare* has stressed this gruesome contrast of the close-pent spirituality and animalism of the period. He left us in no doubt as to what went on at Tyburn Tree and, very properly, reminded Shakespearean students of what Shakespeare may have avoided seeing but of which he certainly knew. He warns the reader of that which might often have met his eyes had he been one of Shakespeare's fellow-citizens and theatre patrons at large in the western outskirts of the city:

> Here at no cost except a few hours of waiting to secure a good station, you may see the hangman at his work, of which hanging is the least interesting part. It is a common traitor, we will suppose, some Jesuit caught in his vestments at mass by Master Richard Topcliffe, the head of the government secret police, an expert human ferret, and cunning at devising new tortures. The Popish recusant has been dragged to Tyburn upon a hurdle, and the hangman, you hear, is in good form, having already shown marvels of skill with his knife upon other traitors before your arrival.   For the Elizabethan hangman is an artist, and the knife is his chief instrument; the art consisting in tossing his man off the ladder, hanging him, but cutting him down before he breaks his neck, so that he may be dismembered and disembowelled while still alive.   Indeed there is one recorded instance of a priest who was heard praying while the hangman already had his bleeding palpitating heart in his hand—and skill could hardly go beyond that.   Did Shakespeare ever attend executions of this kind ?   Not often, I think; yet Macbeth's cry, ' As they had seen me with these hangman's hands! ' shows that he could be present at least in imagination.

A mile and a half farther east at the Earl of Southampton's great mansion in Holborn there would be such delicate pursuit of beauty in masque, comedy, and song as the finest wits and talents of the town could provide: but as they went their way to and from his high entertainment Tyburn might have to be passed, offering such spectacle as this.

On his way from lodgings in North London to the theatre at Blackfriars, of which he became part-owner, or to find a waterman who would ferry him to Southwark and his work at the Globe Theatre, Shakespeare would pass the Bridewell prison, outside which the public whipping of women for harlotry was a usual spectacle.   He has left us small comment on the proceedings at Tyburn, but when he poured into

King Lear the cataract of world-hatred and of contempt of mankind—moods which both infected and inspired his art in his early forties—he cried out in vehement protest against the hypocrisy as well as the atrocity of the Bridewell flagellations. There was no occasion for the almost prehistoric Lear to be thus precise about the baser London practices of the author's day, but such considerations never impeded Shakespeare when he wished to unpack his heart of anger at injustice. So it is Lear who cries out, amid his utterance of a whirling mind,

> Thou rascal beadle, hold thy bloody hand!
> Why dost thou lash that whore ? Strip thine own back.
> Thou hotly lusts to use her in that kind
> For which thou whippest her!

And so to the Bankside. As Shakespeare either crossed London Bridge on foot or glided past it in a boat he noted the two main targets available for observation by the bird-watchers of the time. On the water rode the swans that were the symbols of the elegance and the splendour of the riverside city. In the air were the scavenging birds of prey, swooping to perform their sometimes grisly, sometimes useful tasks in streets without sanitation. The playhouse audience would not shrink at severed heads: Shakespeare himself introduces them—one occurs even in so fine a tragedy as *Macbeth*—and they are always an embarrassment to modern producers who either cut the episodes or make the least possible play with them. We can so little respect a tragic hero who returns to our view brandishing a scalp and triumphantly waving a blood-stained package. The result is apt to be laughter. But Shakespeare's own auditors might have seen something similar on London Bridge immediately before entry to the theatre. It was no absurdity to them.

Across the river Shakespeare was outside the jurisdiction of the City and consequently in the headquarters of pleasure, where the Puritanical or otherwise repressive notions of the grave and reverend seniors of the City were ineffective. Here were the brothels and their inmates, the Winchester Geese, ladies so called because the Bishop of Winchester was the resident landlord of that area: here the theatres: here, as great an attraction as any, Paris Garden.

This famous pleasaunce, on the South bank of the river, had been an amphitheatre for sixty years or more when Shakespeare reached London. It throve and expanded until 1642, when the Puritans closed the famous Bear Garden which had been its chief source of profit and delight. The actor-managers who were the ' big shots ' of London entertainment at the time of Shakespeare's arrival were as much interested in the arena as in the stage. Henslowe, the play-broker and playhouse manager, and Edward Alleyn, his son-in-law, the Roscius of his day and supreme ' star ' at Southwark and the London theatres until Burbage dethroned him, were no less concerned with Hunks and Sackerson, the famous bears of the period, than they were with Marlowe's Muse of Fire and all the fine-sounding rhetoric that hungry and thirsty poets would bring them for a pound or two. By December, 1594, these two had complete control of Paris Garden, and ten years later they were, by Royal appointment, made Masters of the Royal Game of Bears, Bulls, and Mastiff dogs.

Newly come to the town, Shakespeare would naturally seek its most trumpeted pleasures. That he enjoyed them is unlikely: the sympathiser with ' Poor Wat,' the hunted hare, who at least had a chance to elude the hounds, can hardly have had a song in his heart or a huzza upon his lips when he watched the baiting of the stake-bound beasts who might inflict savage punishment on their opponents but could never go free: death was their only liberty. Frequently he alludes to this horrid spectacle. Macbeth protests:

> They have tied me to a stake; I cannot fly
> But bear-like I must fight the course.

What sort of spectacle would there be, on a summer afternoon, with the Queen, a frequent patron, present with her ladies and gentlemen and all the fashion of the town, as well as its rogues, harlots, and lawless resolutes, packed round the stifling arena ? Trumpets, of course: then, Item One, the bear tied to a stake, perhaps an old favourite like Harry Hunks, or one of his less-known predecessors. His teeth have been broken short so that he cannot bite deep, but he can still clutch and claw and crush. The mastiffs are loosed, fly at his throat, and are hurled back bleeding and maddened, in a slavering ferocity. At last some of the dogs are killed: the fang-marked bear is considered to have done enough. Another is led out, new mastiffs are tarred on. The shambles, and the popular raptures, are renewed.

No less repulsive to a compassionate onlooker would be Item Two. An old, blinded bear is released to run about the arena while small boys slash it with canes and dodge it as it blunders after them in a frenzy of pain and frustration. The audience, no doubt, is impartial, and will cheer if a lad stumbles, is caught, and mauled and then has to be rescued by the attendants and carried off terrified and screaming. There is allusion to this in *Coriolanus*; the Volscians are said to attack and then run from the Roman hero as ' children from a bear.'

After the bears, the bulls. Item Three, a fine white bull, also stake-bound, is the target for the mastiffs as the bears had been before him. His defence is in his horns and dog after dog may be impaled and tossed by a bull of mettle: the attendants actually stand by with a receptive frame made of pliant sticks, and on it they deftly catch the bodies of the sky-flung dogs and so break their fall. The wounded on both sides can be mended to perform again. Paris Garden was intended to pay and the livestock were a capital investment.

Item Four, a producer's tour-de-force and kept for the red-letter days of royal attendance. An ape, shrieking and gibbering with terror, is set on the back of a stallion, at whose heels are launched a team of barking, ravening dogs. Round and round goes the horse, with the dogs baying and snapping behind him and risking a punitive hoof. The dogs begin to leap at the screaming ape: finally the horse slips and staggers, the ape is thrown off and the dogs fall upon it: perhaps the ape has his brief revenge by gashing the throat of one of his persecutors before he is reduced to the steaming mess which the menials arrive to sweep away. The Queen is bowed out. The crowds disperse to the Bankside taverns. They have seen the alternative to *Romeo and Juliet*.

Therein lies the mystery of this medley that was London life. The Globe Theatre was built next door to Paris Garden. In the animals' quarters, where the bear-wards gingerly patched up their wretched charges for another occasion, there would surely be howling and roaring day and night. The din coming off the arena during performances, din of infuriated beasts and din of applauding men, must have been continual and horrid.

Shakespeare, as we have seen, was revolted by the rascal beadle, whip in hand. The bears, too, touched his pity, as well they might. The dogs had some of his sympathy as the conversation between Rambures, Orleans, and the Constable of France (*Henry V*, III, vii) indicates:

Rambures   That island of England breeds very valiant creatures; their mastiffs are of unmatchable courage.

Orleans   Foolish curs, that run winking into the mouth of a Russian bear, and have their heads crush'd like rotten apples! You may as well say, that's a valiant flea that dare eat his breakfast on the lip of a lion.

Constable   Just, just; and the men do sympathize with the mastiffs in robustious and rough coming-on, leaving their wits with their wives; and then give them great meals of beef, and iron and steel, they will eat like wolves, and fight like devils.

Orleans   Ay, but these English are shrewdly out of beef.

(The last line bears a smack of later larders.)

The implication seems to be that the dogs are too crass for much compassion and that the men's wives are too intelligent to bother with the baiting. It may be almost a form of blasphemy, treason, and heresy to say of England's hero that he was not a dog-lover: but Shakespeare frequently refers with distaste to fawning dogs, who are his symbol for odious flattery, and he might certainly have been more charitable to the foolish curs so vilely misused, not by their own stupidity, but by the crudity and cruelty of man.

For us, at any rate, the strangeness lies in the proximity of the two contrasts. The Londoners who attend nowadays a prize-fight at Harringay arena are most unlikely next night to be found at a Symphony Concert or a production of *Hamlet*. The same building has housed music as well as pugilism, but not for identical company.

There may be a few exceptions to such a general statement: in any case the allure of a prize-fight fought with gloves is far less brutish and sadistic than were the pleasures of Paris Garden. The participants are volunteers, not animal conscripts: and they are paid on the film-star level. But in Southwark the very men and women who sat as models for Orsino and even Viola could be happily entertained with such spectacles as I have described and alternate them with visits to *Romeo and Juliet* and *A Midsummer Night's Dream*. It can be argued that Shakespeare's larger public preferred his more violent and bloodstained plays: certainly the crudities of *Titus Andronicus* and the picturesque and homicidal villainy of *Richard III* were powerful at the box-office. But it is emphasised over and over again that what the students and the courtiers most appreciated was the sweetness of their gentle Shakespeare and the neat fluency of his ' sugre'd ' line.

> When he speaks
> The air, a charter'd libertine, is still
> And the mute wonder lurketh in men's ears
> To hear his sweet and honeyed sentences.

Shakespeare wrote that of Henry V: he had, as we know from the Sonnets, a considerable opinion of his own powers, and he may have had some thought of his own rapidly established fame for verbal mellifluity when he composed those lines. But in the London theatres of his day, if ' mute wonder ' was achieved, it was something of a triumph. For the audiences were noisy and, in Southwark, Paris Garden must have been a far from tranquil neighbour.

This vision of a discerning as well as a thick-eared public ready for anything, from subtlest poetical analysis of the spirit of love to a roaring enjoyment of Harry Hunks and Sackerson as they crushed the heads of mastiffs like rotten apples, may be difficult for us to entertain. But it fits well enough into the general view of Tudor London's quick forge of thought and fancy. We have to remember that the emergence from the Middle Ages was quite recent: the havoc and horrors of the Baronial Wars had not long ceased to form the surroundings and the background of a milord's life. Also, these same milords, who fetched musicians from Italy and poets from the English Universities, who now made it a point to be finely practising artists as well as patrons of the finest arts, these informed and delicate spirits had rough origins and blood-boltered pedigrees. They had grandfathers and sires whose heads had tumbled to the public cheers and whose entrails had reeked in the hangman's hands because of some alleged or proven deviation from the path of loyalty to a monarch they hated or despised. They were themselves living on a stage whose trap-doors might open suddenly to receive them as consignments for the cellarage, the dungeon, and the block.

The rise and fall of the Earl of Essex exemplified the swift glories, hazards, and disasters of the epoch. It was an age, as I have said, of the unquenchable amateurs who could scarcely slake their thirst for adventures of the senses as well as of the mind and of the fancy. They were in love with anything brightly coloured and blood cannot be denied that form of attraction for the eye. They were not men to flinch when their time came, but went, if need there was to go, ' very handsome to the gallows.' Like Shakespeare's Antony, that Roman model of the Tudor or Jacobean nobleman, spendthrift of life and passion, unsparing in the pursuit of beauty, indulging his every faculty in the great enterprise of living amply, the noblemen of Shakespeare's day could claim to be devotees and amateurs even in the art of dying.

> I will be
> A bridegroom in my death and run into 't
> As to a lover's bed.
>
> *Antony & Cleopatra*, IV, xii.

The voice of the era is in its sadness as well as in its raptures. Here, too, are beauty and flowers, linked as the symbols of exquisite transience, as in Shakespeare's question how the frail blossom of beauty could hold a plea against the rage of life. Nashe, coarse and tough of fibre, the Grub Street bravo, could sing thus during the plague of 1593, and plague in his teeming, insanitary London must have been a hideous and terrifying visitation:

> Beauty is but a flower
> Which wrinkles will devour,
> Brightness falls from the air;
> Queens have died young and fair;
> Dust hath closed Helen's eye;
> I am sick, I must die.

There, indeed, was loveliness: rarely did dying fall have a sweeter strain. ' Brightness falls from the air.' It is a line good enough for Shakespeare's own hand of glory. Brightness, the spark and flame of the quick forge, was natural to Shakespeare's world with its snatching at thrills of spectacle and the ecstasy of experiment. When death overtook the Earl of Essex or any grandee of his kind, what was it but the end of that in which they had so often joyed, the last line of a sonnet, the last step of a pavane, the curtain falling on a masquerade ?

CHAPTER VI

'And Working House'

THE theatre into which Shakespeare came was young,
plastic, self-confident and busily experimental. Also it
was commercial. Essentially it was a new thing: drama might
be as old as human nature, but this brisk sale of a mimed story
was comparatively fresh. Drama had become a money-maker.
Moreover, it drew the brain and spirit of the town. Thus it
was the obvious magnet for youth in search of opportunity
and for a quick intelligence whose owner had rapidly to make
a career. Young ravens must be fed: there were three of that
kind as well as a mother in the Stratford nest: parental
criticism must be met and recent personal decisions justified.
For an able young man with a gift of words, a young man in
a hurry, determined to prove the wisdom of that decision to
leave the country town for the capital and to prove, no less,
his ability as a bread-winner, the London theatre of the
fifteen-eighties was the obvious place. There was no Fleet
Street.

Everything was changing. Drama had for centuries been a
social rite ordained and shaped by a tradition mainly religious,
Christian as well as pagan. It was never expected, during
those ages, to show a profit or to provide careers. But when
Shakespeare came to the stage-door and sought his first
employment, he would have no idea of participating in a
ceremony of faith and morals, no wish to celebrate Jack-a-Lent,
the spirit of the Spring, or to bury the Old Year and to welcome
it reborn as the New. Such notions had been the seeding-
ground of English drama in the Middle Ages and of world-
drama long before that. But this playhouse into which he
came was, for the first time in its history, a secular and commercial institution. It was no religious service that it offered,

but a piece of story-telling, a history, a love-affair, a thrilling narrative of villainy, the triumph or the downfall of some mighty hero. It was meant to excite, to please, to pay. So, when people of lofty intention nowadays dismiss the commercial drama with a sneer, it is permissible to retort that one of the first products of the commercial drama in England was the art and career of William Shakespeare.

The fun of it, no doubt, was a large part of the attraction; the magic of it, the glamour—to give that much-abused word its proper, high significance—seized many of the brilliant young careerists of the colleges and Inns of Court. But there was money in it too and there was no shame in going for the rewards as well as for the laurels: and desperately Shakespeare must have needed the weekly visit of the pay-master.

To understand the nature of drama, a word which in truth meant simply ' thing done,' we have to look far back into the mists of time. The first paintings of primitive man, which, incidentally, are far from primitive in technical accomplishment, show a cavalcade of animals on the cave-wall. It is generally supposed that this was a form of sympathetic magic: the hunter thus depicted in the act of killing his prey would be assisted in the chase by the limning of his victory. The more bulls you drew, the more bulls'-eyes would your flint-arrow or spear obtain. The more you poured out your aspirations in art, the better would your larder be filled. Miming had the same origin. Instead of painting what he wanted, the huntsman or the farmer might perform or copy in action what he wanted. (Each, of course, may have used a specialist to do the job for him, perhaps some weakling unfit for the chase; the artist may have arrived in human society as the invalid, just as the early tradition of the blind poet suggests the relegation of one useless in fighting or food-getting to the secondary task of providing relaxation.) So the first acting, like the earliest mural decoration, had really been a form of prayer.

It was an activity with a social and utilitarian purpose. The hunter drew, or obtained a drawing-man, to help to win his trophy: he mimed, or obtained a mummer, in order to ensure a better harvest, or, more ambitiously, to overcome the monster

Death himself. Drama, after all, is scarcely a natural occupation. The cave-man would not have wasted so much effort
and skill on imitation unless there were, in his opinion, great
gains to be won thereby.

If, sitting in a modern theatre, you suddenly lean back,
shake off all memory and knowledge of theatrical history and
tradition and try to see this odd performance as it were afresh
and for the first time with all its laborious dressing-up and
memorising, with all its imitations and recitations, your first
emotion may well be astonishment that the thing should be
done at all. Why should this seeming childishness be enjoyed
by any body of adult persons ? Life is there, we may say; so
why copy it ? Life appears to ask of reasoning man that he
comment upon it in speech, line and colour. But why this
queer ceremony of imitation, which involves so much scene
and costume, so much painting and pretending, so much
labour, worry and expense ?

The answer can only be found by looking backward, as far
back, indeed, as the origins of human society. The earliest
acting, the start of the whole business, was a serious, purposive
activity, like prayer and the prayer-painting of the caves. Man
was mimic of his own desires. Did he want the king-god of
the community to be eternally beside him, strong to save ?
Then he copied in action the legend or narrative of a king's
death and of a supposed resurrection, since that would give
Heaven the hint. To act the renewal of life would actually win
that renewal. The first of the world's great plays, the tale of
the death and resurrection of the Egyptian king-god Osiris, was
one of these resurrection prayer-dramas. It was enormously
long and played by hosts of performers, a truly social and
national effort. When the ancient Athenians, in the sudden
flowering of their rational civilisation, came to ennoble the
rough mimic practice into a fine art of tragedy (while, less
nobly and more bawdily, they were promoting the old fertility
rites into the genial art of comedy), the subject-matter was
frequently the sufferings and escapes, the earthly death and
later immortality and deification, of the tribal hero.

All this performance was arranged for times of holy festival, done to get the king-god on one's side, done to procure, as far as might be, security for the State and to ensure immortality first for the national leader and then, through him, for all. (The distinction between kings and gods is shadowy in primitive times: kings rise to god-head after death and are assisted by the prayers of their people to immortality.) Of course there was no gain sought in such solemn ceremonial nor any thought of professional entertainment.

The whole thing was inextricably bound up with its priestly and ceremonial origins. If, while watching a Greek tragedy, you are mystified by the nature of the story and by the chantings of the chorus which break up the narrative and the action, you must remember that the performance of a Greek tragedy was in essence an occasional religious service and scarcely at all the provision of ' an attraction.' The idea of a Greek tragedy being put on ' for a run ' and with any sort of box-office calculation would have scandalised Aeschylus. The play was for solemn occasions only and the high priests sat in the front row: the chorus-lyrics are hymns and the conclusive speech of a Greek tragedy is often a piece of theological exposition, explaining the origin of some rite, especially rites connected with the tombs of heroes.

That tradition of drama as a public duty was only just dying when Shakespeare was born. The English medieval drama had been Biblical in theme and social in spirit: the craftsmen, organised in their Guilds, celebrated their holy days (and made them into holidays) by performances proper to their function. The shipwrights, for example, would enact the building of the Ark and so forth. There was no thought of a career upon the stage. Later the themes became more abstract and the result probably less attractive: the characters were Virtues and Vices. (Feste knew the old Vice with sword of lath, whom Shakespeare may have seen in his boyhood.) These so-called Mystery Plays partly replaced the Miracle Plays of the Guilds, but both were the occasional work of genuine devotees. Companies of boys began to operate, but the idea of a life-job in a commercial theatre was quite alien to our medieval society.

E

At the same time, in the villages, the old type of Christmas and Spring-tide mummery went on, and this was a direct descendant of the early resurrection plays. The traditional English Christmas Play, that of St. George, Slasher the Turkish Knight, the magical Doctor, and the King of Egypt's daughter, can be traced right back to the dawn of our history and discovered in varying forms all over Europe. (Sir Edmund Chambers in *The English Folk-Play* has charted its origins and forms of development across Europe with his usual exemplary thoroughness.) There is a description of a typical Dorset performance of it in Thomas Hardy's *The Return of the Native*, and it is still kept alive, more by artificial respiration than by surviving spontaneity of social impulse, in some places. The struggle, the calamity of a dying man and the resurrection of a dead one are common to all versions.

In all primitive drama there are always conflict, death, and revival. You can, if you like, say that this symbolises the battle of fruitful summer with barren winter, the passing and burial of summer, and its resurrection in the surging foison of the spring. Or you can see the Tragic Agôn or Conflict as a more personal matter. The mummers are killing and reviving their hero as a suggestion to their own God that He be careful to revive both leader and led. Whichever way you look at it, the spirit is the same. The drama is there for use: there is an urgent purpose behind it. It is a social necessity and making money is no business of the mime, who copies what the people need and pray for, just as the primitive priest will leap beside the crops as an urgent intimation that they should leap likewise from the earth and soar into fertility. I am not suggesting that laughter and excitement were banished by the solemnity of the motive. Jesting, even bawdy jesting, could be admitted to a sacred theme and the farming-folk of the Cotswolds or of Dorset did not gather to see the battle of St. George and the Turkish Knight without readiness to relish the slap-stick and any fun that might be going.

The quips of the English Folk Play, which was still living on strongly and naturally after Shakespeare's time, consist of puns and verbal inversions (' I met a bark and he dogged at me ') and there is much talk of good winter feeding ('We've come to the land of plum puddings, houses thatched with pancakes, and little pigs running about with knives and forks stuck in their backs crying, "Who'll eat me, who'll eat me?"') The quibbling part of the fun and the play on words were probably influential in keeping the professional drama of the Capital at work on the same (to us rather dreary) furrow.

Both in Greece and Rome the drama, which had been created as a form of social supplication, lived on to become a public entertainment: this was naturally more true of comedy than of tragedy. But in both cases some professionalism did at last enter in and the whole mood of drama was changed. But in England, during the static Middle Ages, there was continued acceptance of miming as a mainly social and ceremonial exercise; it might be a Christmas carol, a summons to the loaded table, a lusty jollification before or after Lent, or it might be a vehicle for the expressions of the crop-hunger which is natural to farming folk. Or, later on, when the drama of abstract ideas was succeeding the old drama of fable and legend, it might be a solemn affair like the story of Everyman, with the qualities of man, good and evil, personified by the characters. Whatever it was, it was mainly amateur in its working and also in the best sense of the word: it was the product of amor, amour, of love for the thing and of love for doing it. The Folk-Play company might pass round the hat, seeking Christian charity and proffering the Christmas 'box.' But the idea of regular pay was never in their minds.

After the Reformation and with the influx of Renaissance classicism two tendencies were soon at work. Protestantism was shy of the antics permitted by the older religion and its more ascetic forms of worship could not be accommodated to the mimings which had once been prayer-in-practice. Scholasticism, admitting and studying the old Greek and Roman plays, permitted and even encouraged the performance in schools and colleges of plays from or about the classics. Thus the Holy Day plays of the Guildsmen tended to dwindle, while the University men, the eager young lawyers at the Inns of

Court, and the nobility in their great salons were delighted by the pleasures of masquerade. They used the classic themes and the examples drawn from their educational curriculum as an occasion and as matter for their own play-acting.

The case of Polonius in *Hamlet* is most informative. His observations sum up all the changes from the old mumming to the new, secular and professional theatre. The Danish Chamberlain is obviously a specimen of the universal, and so of the English, Court-Councillor. (We need not necessarily identify him with Burghley or any other individual.) Polonius is simply one type chosen from the elderly gentlemen whom Shakespeare met and with whom he had to bargain when he and his team were commanded to perform at Court: he may have had to listen to their pontifical booming on the subject of drama which he understood considerably better than they did. Such is often the fate of the hired professional among the wealthy and important amateurs.

Polonius had been an undergraduate actor in his day: he knew all about the heaviness of Seneca and the lightness of Plautus, the chief masters of Roman tragedy and comedy and the accepted models of dramatic art in the Universities. He had himself dressed up and performed. ' I did enact Julius Caesar. I was killed i' th' Capitol. Brutus killed me '; to this Hamlet replied with one of his less fortunate and less satisfactory jests about the ' brute deed ' of the killer. Later in life Polonius had come to know all about a new race of people, the professional troupe, the vagabonds who are living by their power to perform to the general satisfaction items from their very extensive repertory of ' tragedy, comedy, history, pastoral, pastoral-comical, historical-tragical, etc., etc.' During the life-time of Polonius, that is to say during the life-time of one of Shakespeare's seniors (if Polonius be taken as a portrait of a Tudor statesman), the whole field of dramatic activity had altered. A New Drama had arrived.

Polonius, though a busy statesman, considered himself, like any Tudor grandee, to be knowledgeable in the arts; he was critical, justly enough, of the Player King's vocabulary and was a man of opinion in these grease-paint matters. Hamlet dismissed him curtly, much as a serious young stage-progressive of to-day dismisses the Tired Business Man, whose guineas are supposed to be the origin and the prop of so many light-hearted and empty-headed entertainments. ' He's for a jig or a tale of bawdry or he sleeps,' says Hamlet contemptuously of the old courtier. The jig was the dance in which the pro-fessional comedians of Shakespeare's own day excelled and with which they terminated the proceedings, sometimes no doubt to the public relief, even after a solemn tragedy: obviously the author of the tragedy could hardly relish such an anti-climax. The tragedian Shakespeare seemed unable to forgive the jigging.

There, then, is an epitome of the change that swept over English theatrical activities during the sixteenth century. A New Drama had arrived. This phrase New Drama was frequently employed in England during the beginning of the twentieth century to describe the realistic play of ideas, the ' social-platform ' writing of the political and economic reformers who followed and drew upon Ibsen, that is to say Shaw, Galsworthy, Granville-Barker and other authors no less intense of purpose but rather less gifted in dramatic sleight-of-hand.

This New Drama of our time was contrasted with the previous Old Drama of romance, spectacle, and actor-managerial personality; the latter had been a larger-than-life, rhetorical, sentimental affair, with its own particular culture of magnificence in acting, the emphasis being on the solo performance rather than on the team-work. The innovators endeavoured to weave the performances of a company more closely to an artistic unity and were unimpressed by ' star ' names and ' star ' exhibitionism. Their New Drama was remarkable for the everyday nature of the theme and for a type of naturalistic, balanced, and truthful presentation suitable to the realism of use and wont. This was contrasted with the old romanticism, with its unusual and, sometimes, incredible contents. The same title of ' New Drama ' could very well have been applied to the plays which Shakespeare saw when he first came to town. What Marlowe, for example, was doing

was no longer stiffly classical or piously religious in theme.
Indeed, Marlowe was accused of atheism and in such lines as

> I count religion but a childish toy
> And hold there is no sin but ignorance

he may well have enjoyed the writing of heretical doctrine.

The New Drama, then, was a young man's opportunity. It
had a lively and eager public. Its social status was low and
the professional actors were classed with rogues and vagabonds.
But this dismissal by that old pedant, the law, was more than
atoned for by the patronage and protection of the young
nobility and of the Court itself. Lord Mayors and peevish
Puritans might grumble: the theatre, they said, collected a
mischievous, thievish, and lecherous crowd of 'tag-rag
people': it spread the fever of sex as well as of plague.
Stephen Gosson, as early as 1579, was especially precise about
this newly arrived form of demoralisation.

> In our assemblies at plays in London, you shall see such
> heaving, and shoving, such itching, and shouldering to sit by
> women: such care for their garments, that they be not trod
> on: such eyes to their laps, that no chips light in them: such
> pillows to their backs, that they take no hurt: such masking in
> their ears, I know not what: such giving them pippins to pass
> the time: such playing at foot-saunt without cards: such
> tickling, such toying, such smiling, such winking, and such
> manning them home, when the sports are ended, that it is a
> right comedy to mark their behaviour. . . . For they
> that lack customers all the week, either because their haunt is
> unknown or the constables and officers of their parish watch
> them so narrowly that they dare not quetch, to celebrate the
> sabbath flock to the theatres, and there keep a general
> market of bawdry. Not that any filthiness in deed is com-
> mitted within the compass of that ground, as was done in
> Rome, but that every wanton and his paramour, every man
> and his mistress, every John and his Joan, every knave and
> his quean, are there first acquainted and cheapen the
> merchandise in that place, which they pay for elsewhere as
> they can agree.

Gosson was no less indignant over the themes.

> The argument of tragedies is wrath, cruelty, incest, injury, murder, either violent by sword or voluntary by poison: the persons, gods, goddesses, furies, fiends, kings, queens, and mighty men. The ground-work of comedies, is love, cozenage, flattery, bawdry, sly conveyance of whoredom; the persons, cooks, queans, knaves, bawds, parasites, courtezans, lecherous old men, amorous young men.

'What schooling is this?' he asks and does not stay for the answer. We have already moved some way indeed from the theatre as a temple of prayer and from the drama as a religious exercise aimed at the fuller life and better destiny of man. We need not be too much impressed by the denunciations of the Puritans and so be driven to conclude that Shakespeare's audience consisted mainly of wenchers, nibblers of apples, crackers of nuts, pickers of purses, and seekers after filthy jesting. The Puritans were stating their case and the righteous are not always right in their presentation of the facts. They can be shrewdly, even wickedly, selective.

The New Drama might be judged by some to be the Academy of Evil, but it was fashionable and rewarding. Moreover it was moving and growing and improving all the time. The theatre could be said by the carping Gosson to have lost its soul: but it had found its genius, which was to unite the new flow of classical lore and language with the native English speech: it created a platform on which the arriving band of writers and players could demonstrate their mastery.

What was the workshop? Enough books have been written about the geography, architecture, and carpentry of Shakespeare's theatre to build an entire playhouse with their own boards and paper. Players in those days were strollers and accustomed to setting up shop and practising their craft anywhere, in a tavern-yard, a gentleman's mansion, a royal palace, a town hall, or on a village green. But there did grow up, in London, the natural headquarters of the new-fangled industry of entertainment, a particular form of playhouse building which was acceptable to the players and the audiences and convenient to the management and its officers, whose important task was to arrange the seating and the prices and to collect the takings. Scholars often write as though the theatres of Shakespeare's time were designed specially for the authors and performers; such a sedulous merchant of the young art as Henslowe was thinking also, and thinking acutely, of receipts. When the fashion moved from half-open theatres like the Globe to the roofed-in, like the Blackfriars, it was the appeal to the audience of the new comfort that was in managerial minds just as much as the more subtle artistry which the acoustics, the scenery and the artificial lighting of a covered house would supply.

The tavern-yard, with its galleries for the good payers and its floor-space for the cheaper stance of the groundlings, was an obvious model for the builders who began to serve the rising industry in the latter half of the sixteenth century. When Shakespeare was twelve years old and having a first taste, perhaps, of the touring drama, as it arrived, bag and baggage, scrip and scrippage, with a parade of motley and a roar of eloquence, ready to act anywhere at any time at command and for reward, James Burbage was just opening The Theatre in Shoreditch, outside the domain of interfering and censorious City magistrates. This provided the old trestle-stage of the inn-yard with a substitute for the inn itself. After all, the ' taverners,' as the early and vagrant troupes could justly be called, were earning a deal of money for the innkeepers, who hired them a yard and thus collected a profitable crowd of hungry and thirsty customers. It was natural for the conductor of a players' troupe to ask himself why he and his men should thus stimulate the trade of others.

To what extent an Elizabethan theatre profited by its catering is not, I think, known. ' The bars ' are a very important element in the finance of the theatre to-day and it is unlikely that the shrewd ' sharers ' in Shakespeare's Company failed to make what they could from the sale of wine to the exalted tenants of the galleries and of small ale (or large) to the groundlings. That ale was ready to hand we know from the sad story of the Globe's destruction. In 1613 the great Globe, having reached the unlucky age of thirteen, was burned down owing to some reckless use of artillery in a sumptuous and realistic performance of *All is True*, 'representing some pieces of the reign of Henry VIII.' Sir Henry Wotton, writing to Sir Edmund Bacon, described the scene thus:

Now, King Henry making a masque at the Cardinal Wolsey's house, and certain cannons being shot off at his entry, some of the paper, or other stuff wherewith one of them was stopped, did light on the thatch, where being thought at first but an idle smoke, and their eyes more attentive to the show, it kindled inwardly, and ran round like a train, consuming within less than an hour the whole house to the very ground. This was the fatal period of that virtuous fabrick; wherein yet nothing did perish but wood and straw, and a few forsaken cloaks; only one man had his breeches set on fire, that would perhaps have broiled him if he had not by the benefit of a provident wit, put it out with a bottle of ale.

So ale was handy, as well as the nuts and pippins to which allusion was frequent. The drama had not altogether ceased to inhabit the inn-yard: but the premises were now its own and the catering profits too.

Before Shakespeare came to London—I am assuming a date of 1587 or thereabouts—there were five chief hostelries functioning as theatres, the Bull, the Bell, the Belle Sauvage, the Cross Keys, and the Boar's Head. The close proximity of food, liquor, music, poetry, mimic, passion, and bed-chambers was noted with alarm by the Puritan Fathers and a London Ordinance of 1574 noted ' the inveigling and alluring of maids, especially orphans and good citizens' children to privy and unmeet contracts.' Fortunately for the theatre-folk there were niches in the town known as Liberties, which, though parts of London, were outside the stern jurisdiction of the City. These were the natural places in which the players could live, work and build. Shoreditch was such a Liberty; so was Blackfriars, where Shakespeare's colleagues acquired a theatre later on; so was the Clink in Southwark, another of their shelters. (The slang word clink for a prison came from a Southwark gaol and there is a Clink Street there to-day.)

In 1576 there occurred an event which was notable indeed and infinitely fruitful for the arts and glory of England. A real playhouse, a building specially devoted to and shaped for the new industry of dramatic entertainment, was opened near Finsbury Fields by one of the professional actors, James Burbage. It was called The Theatre, because it was just that: there was no other. It was the inn-yard minus the inn—or with some of the inn's functions and profits transferred to Burbage. The development was a success and so it led to the opening of the Curtain near by: and that led to further theatrical expansion and construction south of the river, first at Newington Butts and then with the important opening, about 1587, of the Rose, whose governing spirit was Henslowe, father-in-law of the mighty Edward Alleyn. Alleyn became first ' star ' of the new and rising profession, and especially famed for his delivery of ' Marlowe's mighty line ' in the roles of Tamburlaine, Faustus, and the Jew of Malta. In the London to which the defeat of the Armada had just given a great liberation of spirit and cause of rejoicing, the Rose by the riverside must have been the magnet for all the eager spirits and lovers of this brave, new art.

These theatres were circular, or hexagonal, galleried, half-exposed to the sky. They provided a large, uncovered stage projecting into the central standing-space (relic of the old inn-yard) and a smaller stage under a sheltering roof; this was known as the shadow and was supported by pillars. The fore-stage brought the player into close contact with his audience and so gave point to the speaking of soliloquies. Behind the stages was a small, curtained inner-room, set under a gallery used for balconies and battlements, city walls, and other elevated places, such as Cleopatra's ' monument '' and also inhabitable, at need, by musicians. On either side of the platform-stage were doors for the entrances and exits: in plays of military or social conflict each side had its own door, which eased the spectators' comprehension of the 'flourish and alarm' part of the play. The small, curtained back-stage was used for closet scenes, for hidings and discoveries, e.g. for the person, later corpse, of Polonius. It could be employed for Prospero's cell and the discovery of ' Ferdinand and Miranda playing at chess,' assuming that *The Tempest* was being played in one of the open houses of this pattern and not in the ' private ' roofed-in establishments of the later mode.

It is obvious that the architecture and equipment of the Elizabethan theatre was not constant: size of stage, nature of background, amount of scenery (if any), richness of wardrobe, would all vary. What I have outlined provides only a very rough idea of Shakespeare's earliest workshop: over details of carpentry the argument has been immense and sometimes tedious and it is no great concern of ours in our pursuit of the man. Enough has been said to give an impression of the ' working-house ' in which the players were engaged.

Some writers seem always to assume that the plays of the period were composed specially for the architecture of these early theatres; but that can hardly have been so. Of course the shape of the stage did have considerable influence, but the general scheme of writing, production, and performance must have been fluid. It was useless to plan your play and the playing of it with an eye to one species of platform and back-ground only; the players were under constant requisition to appear anywhere and to earn their fee on any kind of dais. Indeed, the most valuable performances of a play were not given in the theatre at all; they were given either at Whitehall, before royalty, or in noblemen's houses before the grandees whose patronage it was vitally important to acquire and to retain. Shakespeare, Burbage, and Kempe, we know for certain, were giving comedies and interludes before Queen Elizabeth in the winter of 1594, and it is certain, too, that the companies played in the halls of the Inns of Court and in the meeting chambers and assembly rooms of the great seigneurial mansions.

John Manningham of the Middle Temple recorded in his diary (Feb. 2, 1602), ' At our feast wee had a play called " Twelve Night, or What You Will," much like the Commedy of Erroes or Menechmi in Plautus, but most like and near to that in Italian called Inganni. A good practice in it to make the Steward believe his Lady Widdowe was in love with him . . .' Then we have the evidence of Sir Walter Cope in a letter to Robert Cecil, Lord Cranborne, which proves not only the use of halls in private houses but the still existing contempt among some of the aristocracy for this upstart and mountebank profession of the actor.

> I have sent and bene all thys morning huntyng for players Juglers & Such kinde of Creaturs, but fynde them hard to find, wherfore Leavinge notes for them to seeke me, Burbage ys come, & Sayes ther ys no new playe that the quene hath not seene, but they have Revyved an olde one, Cawled *Loves Labore lost*, which for wytt & mirthe he sayes will please her excedingly. And Thys ys apointed to be playd to Morowe night at my lord of Sowthamptons, unless yow send a wrytt to Remove the Corpus Cum Causa to your howse in Strande. Burbage ys my messenger Ready attendyng your pleasure.

Love's Labour's Lost may contain some most exquisite writing in Shakespeare's young vein of conceit amid amorous fancy; but still to such as Cope the players of this stuff ranked with ' Juglers and such kinde of Creaturs.' Southampton knew better.

From this it is quite plain that play and production were easily portable from house to house and that theatrical architecture, though important for the safe and profitable accommodation of as large an audience as could be gathered, did not matter greatly to author and actor; the latter had to be ready to go anywhere and do anything. We come back to the players who arrive at Elsinore in *Hamlet*. They are not regarded by Shakespeare as a primitive type of antique ' buskers ': they are made the target of his own strong opinions about the proper rendering of tragedy and the limits of permissible invention in clowning, gagging, and funny business. Hamlet talks to them as Shakespeare wanted to talk, and (through this medium) did talk to his own colleagues. They are not a voice echoing down from the Miracle Plays of the Middle Ages; they are the voice of the Globe Theatre, which

had been opened in 1599 or 1600 as the new public establishment of the Lord Chamberlain's Men. These craftsmen
of entertainment travel light; they make no bother whatever
about shape of premises or nicety of production. If requested
to do their job, they will do it. There would, presumably, be a
hall with a dais. The words, and the way in which they are
spoken, are what matters, not properties, or lighting; the play's
the thing. That, for them, as for Hamlet's stratagem, was the
rule. The players went into action relying on their author
and themselves.

So we may assume that Shakespeare's own colleagues,
though they carried a brand of eloquence less wearisome than
that of the Player King in *Hamlet*, were likewise ready to find
a stage where bidden and, without any fuss or throwing of
temperaments, to ' do their stuff.' In times of plague they
travelled out of town and played under all roofs or none:
their luggage must have been fairly light, since roads were few
and bad and cartage difficult to obtain on a large scale. We
know that one of Shakespeare's Company, Laurence Fletcher,
got as far as Aberdeen in the unbeaten way of professional
adventure, and Shakespeare may have been with him, picking
up material for *Macbeth*. It is hardly to be thought that these
men, with these manifold varieties of workshop from the
simplest platform to their own specially erected Globe, lacked
invention and spontaneity; they were tolerant of all discomforts and disadvantages and ready to body forth a drama as best
they could in any circumstances.

The Great Hall of the day, whether belonging to a corporation or an individual, would be helpful because its architecture
had much in common with the public theatres. The dais at
one end was used by the more august members of the audience:
at the other end was a large screen, with two doors leading to
the kitchens. Over and behind the screen was a minstrels'
gallery. So the players engaged in such places had at least a
likeness to their own building: they would find tiring-rooms
somewhere in the kitchens and servants' quarters and come in
through the doors by which the pantlers had previously arrived
with the victuals—or, in case of a late supper would later on

do so. They had a gallery above them for Juliet's Balcony or the walls of any beleaguered city. But the conditions of lighting were entirely different: here, in the Great Hall, they would depend on candles, torches, and lamps, whereas in the public theatres they played to the weather and the sky and such illumination as the day happened to afford.

The more I see of Shakespeare's plays or of any plays of that period the more obvious it seems to be that they were written for delivery in any space or on any plinth from a milord's lawn to a town hall, from the deck of a ship to the great Globe itself. I mention the deck of a ship because we know of such maritime performance, and since the ships of the time were mere cockleshells by our computation of size, the stage-quarters must have been cramped indeed. The scholars now consent to the authenticity of passages from the journal of William Keeling, captain of the East India ship *Dragon*, which was sailing to the East Indies with two other vessels called *Hector* and *Consent*. Keeling's diary runs as follows:

> 1607, Sept. 5. I sent the interpreter, according to his desier, abord the Hector whear he brooke fast, and after came abord mee, wher we gaue the tragedie of Hamlett.

> 30. Captain Hawkins dined with me, where my companions acted Kinge Richard the Second.

> 1608, Mar. 31. I envited Captain Hawkins to a ffishe dinner, and had Hamlet acted abord me: which I permitt to keepe my people from idleness and unlawful games, or sleepe.

The tribute to drama is not altogether a high one and it is interesting to see that the earliest praise of *Hamlet* of which we have any documented knowledge merely welcomes the tragedy as providing a better time-killer than loafing, snoring, and gaming. But the passage does reveal that the habit of the time was to act plays in any odd corner, even cramming them into such a cupboard as a ship no larger than a modern trawler could find for their bestowal.

The truth is that to make a fuss about staging Shakespeare

is wholly unnecessary. An elaborate production may be fun: it may be clever: it may yield spectacular delight. But it will not assist the actor or the play. This is not to rule elaboration out.

> There are nine and sixty ways of composing tribal lays
> And—every—single—one—of—them—is—right!

There are quite as many methods of devising and presenting Shakespearean productions as of composing tribal lays, and they are all correct. You can give them austerity or sumptuosity, fancy dress, modern dress, historical accuracy perfect to the last figure on a tabard, Royal Academy realism, ' constructivist ' or soap-box scenery, black and white or purple and gold, moonshine, sunshine, or the last contraption of the lighting experts, you can wrap them in raree-show splendour or turn out your troupe in a simulacrum of the old, elementary inn-yard stage, and the thing will be completely satisfactory, *if you can do it well in its own kind*. I should like to revisit Irving and Tree amid all their surroundings, which any young critic would now echo Shaw in describing as fustian, because, if fustian it were, it was certainly first-class fustian: not less would I like to see old William Poel walk again: Poel was the Puritan pastor of the Shakespeare cult and would keep us, in his reverence of text, to bare-bones presentation. His way was the right answer to over-elaboration of the visual element: it, in turn, needed a reply and has received it in our time from what might be called the fanciful-economical style made obligatory by the effort to link rising costs with ' something for the eye.'

As I write it is fashionable to clothe Shakespeare in the garments of any age but his own and to ' fantasticate ' the rougher comedies such as *The Taming of the Shrew*, *The Comedy of Errors*, and even *The Merchant of Venice* out of all recognition. Would Shakespeare have protested ? Does an angry ghost haunt Stratford and, as it peers at some madly bedizened version, not only of the romping comedies but even of *Romeo and Juliet*, does it mutter in impotent protest against the orgy of affectation ? Would William say that we do him wrong, being so majestical, to offer him the show of playfulness ? We know that he hated to see his work fooled about with by ' gagging ' and similar extravagance of the actors; presumably he might have had a similar loathing for arrogant or impudent mishandling of his texts by the modern producer. Yet he would have welcomed, I think, energy, courage, and invention : he was accustomed to writing for any kind of auditorium and for widely different audiences; his patrons' qualities and proclivities ranged from the most cultivated to the least in-formed: he served both the intellectual foppery of the Court and of the great houses and the rough popular appetite for a good murder, a brave revenge, and a view of a severed head. The one inexcusable offence in the production of Shakespeare is to make a mess of whatever effect you are trying to establish: the crime lies not in making the experiment, but in the botching of it.

I have myself witnessed a good example of the plasticity of the Tudor play-structure on a great occasion in Denmark. In the summer of 1937 Laurence Olivier, now Sir Laurence, and Vivien Leigh were to lead the ' Old Vic ' company in per-formances of *Hamlet* in Kronborg, the castle built in Re-naissance style on the site of the early fortress of Elsinore where the Hamlet-story was once played out in reality to its bloody end. There seems to be no suitable indoor hall in Kronborg, or Danish fear of fire-damage was so great that they dared not use the chambers of the castle. So a large platform stage, on several levels, was built in the castle court for open-air sessions and the last rehearsals took place on that. I remember watching one: it was extremely chilly. Castle courtyards, stone-flagged, are not so much theatres as powerful conveyors of foot-freezing draughts. They call rather for rugs and hot-water bottles than for sessions by the blink of the moon.

Then, on the appointed evening, a cold and gusty rain poured steadily down. The stage was made dangerously slippery and the seats in the courtyard were sodden. So there was a wise and swift decision to transfer the operation to the ballroom of the near-by Marienlyst Hotel in which the company were staying. Naturally it could not accommodate as big an audience as had been expected, but the weather had kept many away. So, led by the Crown Prince of Denmark and his friends, what was left of the audience moved off to shelter and was packed into the ballroom. The players took over a tiny stage used for purposes of cabaret and a fore-space on the dancing-floor in front of it was reserved for the overflow of the action; then the public gathered round about that double, but still meagre, place of performance. The players, of course, had to improvise their entrances and exits and fit their prepared moves and ' business ' to the new and strange surroundings. It was all done at a moment's call. Standing at the side, I could hear them rapidly arranging their movements, as for a charade at home. And yet, triumphantly, it worked. What I saw was as good a performance of *Hamlet* as I have ever seen. The words, the story, the driving emotional pressure of the play were clear and compelling. Indeed the very smallness of the stage and the nearness of the audience round about—during the duelling one feared for the nobility and gentry in the front row—seemed to intensify the excitement which *Hamlet* never fails to produce.

Here, then, by a curious and apt occurrence, stage-history seemed to have come full circle. We were at Elsinore, the actors had come hither. ' Masters, you are all welcome ' (a Danish welcome is ever a good one, generous in spirit and at board). ' We'll e'en to it like French falconers, fly at anything we see! ' So, like the falconers, Olivier and his colleagues let fly their art in conditions for which there had been no preparation: indeed there had been something almost worse than no preparation, which is to rehearse for one stage and then to be compelled to act upon another. Yet that is what Shakespeare and his men were continually doing, moving from Globe pillar to Whitehall post, calling in at Lord Southampton's, and then, perhaps, off on the road to all manner of platforms far away.

They wrote for these stringencies of performance, packing their scenery into their words, setting the stage with a few, resounding lines, kindling and extinguishing the sun in a couple of epithets, keeping the action fluid, adaptable to any channel, and generally catering for a troupe who must carry their lines in their heads, their costumes in their knapsacks, and their sounding-boards in their own throats and lungs. When necessity forced the 'Old Vic' company at Elsinore to behave just as the Players did who had called on Prince Hamlet in the play, Olivier and his team rose to the challenge with skill and with victory, partly, of course, because the play rose likewise to the occasion. It was as though one form of drama had come home again: it had been liberated from the trappings which can be oppressive: it soared and swooped on that cabaret stage in a Danish dance-hall like the Frenchman's falcon given its wings. Here, once again, was Shakespeare's work—in Shakespeare's working-house: all the world, and all its architecture, were his stage.

The many productions in schools and colleges lead to the same conclusion—that 'four boards and a passion' are the Tudor theatre still. The excellent habit of linking Shakespeare the curriculum-subject with Shakespeare the playhouse man, a habit far too rare in the past, has given both teachers and taught a chance to discover that the production of the world's greatest tragedies is not overwhelmingly difficult. The words must be learned and spoken with proper relevance to their meaning and not as an essay in 'Eng. Lit.,' not as purple patches of 'Poetese.' Certain speeches, especially in the Histories, demand their flourish and gesture, their mouthing and intoning, to suit the rhodomontade of the lines: but, on the whole, Hamlet's advice holds: temperance gives smoothness and modesty of manner, with the words flowing trippingly on the tongue, will produce the high effect, so long as the speech itself has the right vividness and power. The nature of the place makes no certain or decisive difference. A model theatre will help: but a dusty classroom can become Illyria under shrewd persuasion of the human voice.

Since the Tudor dramatists, and most especially Shakespeare, could well provide the power and fascination, their working-house was wherever the players were ready and the audience assembled. Playing on their home ground, at the Swan or the Globe, they had certain advantages, no doubt. They knew exactly what tricks could be played, what devices could be used to embellish, to excite, and to amuse. But they were equally ready for the stance in front of the screen in a Great Hall, to which they would adjust their moves and measures, as the 'Old Vic' company did upon that stormy night in Elsinore.

There are some who advise the construction and use of an exact model of Shakespeare's Globe or of Henslowe's Fortune (for the latter we have the exact specifications) in order to house modern performances of Tudor plays. (In the Folger Library at Washington there is such an architectural reminder of the Shakespearean working-house, but it is more used for contemplative study than for the hot or merry action of the play.) It is certainly odd that neither in London nor in Stratford-upon-Avon has such a building ever been erected: the addition of complete roofing would mean the use of artificial light and so alter the old conditions, but would greatly add to the structure's convenience and attraction. The cost in the past would have been small enough, and even now would not be prohibitive, and the producing and watching of plays in the exact conditions of Shakespeare's own headquarters would be valuable and entertaining. I have myself seen Poel at work with a platform stage of Elizabethan dimensions run out over the orchestra-pit and stalls of a big music-hall. It seemed enormous: from the dress-circle one could almost have jumped on to it.

The Tudor actors certainly had space, and their battle-scenes, which are always a source of headache to the modern director, had at least more freedom of movement than we enjoy as a rule to-day. It is evident from their frequency that these scenes of scampering combat were much appreciated: to win that appreciation they must have been capably done. (Shakespeare, it is true, apologised for the inadequacy of the stage-warfare in *Henry V*:

And so our scene must to the battle fly;
Where—O for pity!—we shall much disgrace
With four or five most vile and ragged foils,

Right ill-dispos'd in brawl ridiculous,
The name of Agincourt. Yet, sit and see;
Minding true things by what their mockeries be.

To us those lines are now amusing. But were they spoken at
all ? Would not Burbage and the players have insisted on a
cut ? Can a dramatist reasonably and decently say, before the
first performance, that what is coming is going to be a dreadful
mess ? Can he decry his company so ? Might not the four
or five ' vile and ragged ' foils have walked out as a protest ?
It is bad enough to be criticised by the audience, they would
say, and to be pelted with nuts from the gallery and laughter
from the boxes of the supercilious gentry, but must we be
mocked by the author too—and that as a judgment in advance ?)

The fact remains that whether the stage-brawls were or were
not ridiculous, Shakespeare continued to demand them. His
Roman plays, especially, abounded in the clash of armies:
and for such tactical operations his platform stood widely open.
But when the working-house was not a theatre, but part of a
royal chamber or a hall, the disposal of the armies must have
been far more difficult. For that reason we may conclude that
there was no rigid scheme of production of a Shakespeare play
in his own time: the action was not spaced out in detail;
there was no chalk-marking of the stage at rehearsal, because
that stage was only one of many stages, platforms, lawns, or
hall-daises on which the players would have to perform. The
actor learned his lines, his gestures, and some elementary moves.
Granville-Barker, in his Preface to *Coriolanus*, a Preface which,
alas, appeared posthumously, paid special attention to the
author's stage-directions. He noted that

Incidentally, their dramatic value apart, they stand among
the items of evidence of a retirement to Stratford and the
writing of the latest plays in a semi-detachment from the
theatre. Such evidence is, of course, inferential, no better
than guesswork if you will. But *Coriolanus* at least speaks in
this respect pretty plainly of a manuscript to be sent to
London, and of a staging which the author did not expect

to supervise himself. The directions are always expert, devised by someone who has visualised the action very clearly.

But the directions which are mentioned would apply to performances on any kind of stage.

> Draw both the Conspirators and
> kils Martius, who falles,
> Auffidius stands on him.

Granville-Barker adds:

> But the direction to be valued most of all is that given to the actor of Marcius himself. Before he yields to Volumnia he

> Holds her by the hand silent

> —for an appreciable moment, it must be.

The working-house for this could be anywhere.

On the other hand it does seem that workshop conditions did begin to affect Shakespeare's writing at the end of his career. For then a really significant alteration had been made. In 1608, when Shakespeare was forty-four and had his major work behind him, the King's Men (Jacobean successors to the Lord Chamberlain's Men) took over the Blackfriars Playhouse, one of the so-called private theatres, roofed-in, exclusive, a particular resort of the wealthier æsthetes, and for long in the occupation of the Children's Companies, the ' little eyases ' to whose successes Hamlet had made rather bitter allusion. Owing to a bad epidemic there may have been an interval of time before the King's Men were actually working in their new and exalted premises. But they must have been thinking in terms of the new stage and the new audience as soon as the purchase was planned.

When they did get to work on their new model premises the result was profitable. Professor G. E. Bentley has shrewdly made the point that the financial future of the King's Men lay with the Court and the Court party in the private theatres.

Their receipts for performances at court showed them this very clearly. In the last nine years of Elizabeth, 1594-1602, they had received from court performances an average of £35 a year; in the first five years of the reign of the new king, 1603-7, they had averaged £131 per year in addition to their new allowances for liveries as servants of the King. The Blackfriars and not the Globe was the theatre where they could entertain this courtly audience with commercial performances. There is no doubt that in the next few years after 1608 the Blackfriars did become the principal theatre of the company. In 1612 Edward Kirkham said they took £1,000 a winter more at the Blackfriars than they had formerly taken at the Globe. When Sir Henry Herbert listed receipts from the two theatres early in the reign of King Charles, the receipts for single performances at the Globe averaged £6 13s. 8d.; those for single performances at the Blackfriars averaged £15 15s., or about two and one-half times as much.

Bentley stresses the point, against the old, literary type of Shakespearean criticism, that Shakespeare was essentially tied to his workshop and his fellow-workers and thought in terms of saleable drama.

We can be perfectly sure, then, that from the day of the first proposal that the King's Men take over the Blackfriars they had talked among themselves about what they would do with it and had discussed what kinds of plays they would have to have written to exploit it. It is all too often forgotten that in all such discussions among members of the King's company William Shakespeare would have had an important part. He had more kinds of connections with the company than any other man: he was actor, shareholder, patented member, principal playwright, and one of the housekeepers of the Globe; even Burbage did not serve so many functions in the company. Few men in theatrical history have been so completely and inextricably bound up with the affairs of an acting troupe.

If we accept this point of view, we can agree that the change to the new working-house at Blackfriars dictated the change to the type of play written after 1608: these are fanciful, romantic, and vehicles for masque and dance. *Cymbeline*, *The Winter's Tale*, *The Tempest*, and possibly *The Two Noble Kinsmen* and the lost play *Cardenio* (in both of these Shakespeare may have collaborated with John Fletcher), are certainly in a class of their own. The alteration has been commonly attributed to Shakespeare's rediscovered health and serenity in semi-retirement in Stratford. He had done all that was in him—and surely it was sufficient?—for Tragedy on the grand scale. He wished to rest among gentler legends with happy endings, legends into which the increasingly fashionable art of Masquing as well as the increasing use of scenery, which Masque demanded, could be profitably introduced. Beaumont and Fletcher had arrived to serve the new and lighter taste of the courtiers: here, at Blackfriars, was a theatre in which scenic and lighting effects were attained in a way and to a degree never conceivable in the Globe, which, as we saw, was burned to ashes when the new extravagance of showmanship was attempted in the case of *Henry VIII*. So, because of his new workshop, Shakespeare changed his tune and adapted his technique to create drama *à la mode*, dramatic lyrics based on fairy-tale plots and containing a summons to masquerade. He did not let the new workshop dictate to him: but, being a man of commerce as well as a master of craft, he did not disdain to watch the new trend of taste and its relation to the new architecture of the closed-in playhouse.

But we are looking now into his latter days and have not yet analysed his earlier career. How he found his way into the humble theatres of the fifteen-eighties is a problem to be solved, or at least guessed about, before we become entirely stall-bound amid the comparative calm and luxury of the select assembly in Blackfriars.

CHAPTER VII

' The Morning's War '

THE London of the fifteen-eighties had plenty to excite, attract, amuse, and even appal. We have already seen the executioner at work and heard the lash in the rascal beadle's hand, visited the bear-pits and the bull-rings, and smelled and witnessed the squalor of Paris Garden. There were the grandeurs too; and sight-seeing, though not yet to any large extent a cultivated exercise or a source of commerce, was a natural pleasure.

Antipholus of Syracuse, in one of the earliest of Shakespeare's plays, *The Comedy of Errors*, speaks for the new arrival in a noted city, as Shakespeare himself was at some time in London. Having reached Ephesus and taken a room at the Centaur, the Syracusan says,

> Within this hour it will be dinner-time:
> Till that, I'll view the manners of the town,
> Peruse the traders, gaze upon the buildings,
> And then return, and sleep within mine inn.

That he should be interested in people and their habits and especially in the traders was natural enough; but he includes the buildings. Was the Baedeker spirit already born? Were the genuine antique and the on-no-account-to-be-missed already being scheduled? Perhaps the shrewd Antipholus was just looking for likely investments in real estate. Moreover he knew of ' city sharks.'

> They say the town is full of cozenage;
> As, nimble jugglers that deceive the eye,
> Dark-working sorcerers that change the mind,
> Soul-killing witches that deform the body,

> Disguiséd cheaters, posturing mountebanks,
> And many such-like liberties of sin.

Certainly, he had been warned.

Shakespeare may have had similar admonition from the Stratford citizens who knew (or claimed to know) their London before he set out upon his life's adventure. Nor were such counsels unjustified. He was entering a city where civil protection lay with a farcically inept Watch, whose absurdity he was himself to immortalise, a city, too, of constant violence. To seek protection against menaces of force was common practice, though probably it yielded small security. It was not only the scald ruffians of the tavern, the braggarts and bullies of the market-place, and the cast-off soldiery who flashed their blades. The poets as well as the Pistols brandished a weapon and, having applied, no doubt—as Orlando's Adam never did —' hot and rebellious liquors to the blood '—they sought the blood of others.

Shakespeare himself was proceeded against in court for threats of violence. (Sweet Mr. Shakespeare, gentle Mr. Shakespeare, may have been much wronged in this; but the episode does at least reveal the fiery temper of the town in which any young buck or bard might turn to be a Tybalt.) The scholars and the singers, the wits and minstrels of the day, were ready fighters. Ben Jonson duelled and his man was killed. Marlowe we know to have been twice in action with sword and dagger and he died of his second affray: he may have been in many an unrecorded brawl before that end in a rough house at Deptford.

Then there were the thieves who would cut or lift any man's purse, the mountebanks, the sorcerers, the witches. These may sound now like strange bogeys and insubstantial terrors, but even the men of reason in that age had deep-rooted superstitions. The alchemists were there to mystify and cozen: lackwit or frustrated (and so malicious) old women were frequently suspect, seized, and even burned, as witches. The evil eye was not a word only and the Weird Sisters in *Macbeth* were not the problem they are to a modern producer or the bore they may be to a modern audience. They were part of the day's news.

So there was plenty to catch as quick an eye as ever darted here and there upon the various humours of society, noting and relishing the foibles and the qualities of the courtier and the huckster, of the city madam, the ale-wife and the drab. There were countless oddities in the social scene for one who had the eye for them. A line of Marlowe's, frequently attributed to Shakespeare and later on much used, with little alteration, by rival poets,

Infinite riches in a little room

sums up the treasury of mixed experience which waited for the London visitor.

But

Such wind as scatters young men through the world
To seek their fortunes further than at home
Where small experience grows,

(Petruchio's words in another early play) had powerfully seized him. It was a north-wester that carried him down— 'mad nor' nor' west' Anne might have called him—leaving home and duty for a chance, vowing to be a conqueror, pledged to be a bread-winner, ready to set hand and wit to any work that would reward him.

Arriving as an intending or already recruited theatre-worker, with dominie's desk or lawyer's office happily deserted, he gazed, like Antipholus, on men, matters, habits, and houses: especially the playhouses, of which North London had two already, while the Bankside, south of London Bridge, was soon adding 'hencoops of the Muses' to its pens for the baited beast. Inside these theatres were high-pitched voices and minds as volatile as the tempers. A fantastic mixture of the bawdy (some added 'blasphemous') and the beautiful, the childish and the superb was being compounded on the Shore-ditch stages and in the writers' lodgings round about. Ben

Jonson, twenty years later on, was to speak, with all his eloquent gusto, of that madcap, money-hunting, never mealy-mouthed society.

The increase of which lust in liberty, together with the present trade of the stage, in all their miscelline interludes, what learned or liberal soul doth not already abhor ? Where nothing but the filth of the time is uttered, and with such impropriety of phrase, such plenty of solecisms, such dearth of sense, so bold prolepses, so racked metaphors, with brothelry able to violate the ear of a pagan, and blasphemy to turn the blood of a Christian to water.

Talk of blasphemy, in the time of Shakespeare's apprenticeship, would start fingers pointing towards Christopher Marlowe, the audacious, angry, eloquent, conquering, scholar-brawler, who had come by way of Canterbury and Cambridge to make Henslowe's fortunes, to give Alleyn the actor his mighty lines to mouth, and to secure for himself the ear and admiration of the town. In trouble often and in triumph young, he died with half his music in him. But his music had for six years or more been on the lips and in the ears of the City before he was stabbed in a tavern-quarrel by the Thames.

To Shakespeare, getting to work in the London of 1588, there must have been two great events, the emergence of Marlowe and the defeat of the Armada. I surmise that the former mattered most to him, not because he lacked the zeal of an ardent Englishman—his Histories are the sounding-board of his patriotism—but because wars were faraway things and what the navy did—even though it was largely an amateur navy—was a matter of reports and rumours and long intervals, not of evening papers and of wireless news. It is surprising to us that the literature and drama of the time bear so little impress of foreign affairs and of war's immediate alarms. References, of course, there are, but Shakespeare's art was more affected by the magic that he heard in the theatre, with Marlowe as its chief dispenser, than by the world-cinema in which the Spanish king was villain and in which the Spanish galleons provided, by their catastrophe, the ' super thrills ' that such a feature-film demands. Marlowe, whose plays are poorly shaped, overloaded with irrelevant grandiloquence, and far more a young man's fancy than a professional performance, did not make Shakespeare a dramatist: but they powerfully assisted him to be a poet. To a receptive and ambitious youngster, eager and rapid in learning the trick of this new play-writing and poetical game, the glorious tumble of Marlowe's iambics, beating on the ear like the surge and crash of breakers, must have been both challenge and summons. He would do more than imitate; he would surpass.

What plays Shakespeare had seen in boyhood when the players passed through Stratford we shall never know: but we can be sure that *Tamburlaine the Great* was one of his early experiences in London. It is largely trumpet-music, this tale of a world-conqueror, greedy of power, ecstatic in his victories, harnessing the conquered kings to his chariot, craving and possessing the fair Zenocrate. Certainly a tucket sounded when Alleyn in a copper-laced coat with breeches of crimson velvet exulted as Tamburlaine over empires destroyed and monarchs put in cages or when the Soldan of Egypt thus exclaimed:

> Awake ye men of Memphis! hear the clang
> Of Scythian trumpets; hear the basilisks,
> That, roaring, shake Damascus' turrets down!
> The rogue of Volga holds Zenocrate,
> The Soldan's daughter, for his concubine,
> And, with a troop of thieves and vagabonds,
> Hath spread his colours to our high disgrace,
> While you, faint-hearted base Egyptians,
> Lie slumbering on the flowery banks of Nile,
> As crocodiles that unaffrighted rest
> While thundering cannons rattle on their skins.

We can hardly imagine young Shakespeare listening to that, as it went soaring to the galleries, without his fingers itching for a pen.

After the trumpet, the lyre. Tamburlaine is, somewhat oddly, half a plundering Bashaw, half the rapt minstrel and civilised servant of the Muse. Shakespeare, having heard the

Marlovian clarion, heard too the touching of the strings of
love.   Tamburlaine is eloquent of his Zenocrate's face,

> Where Beauty, mother to the Muses, sits,
> And comments volumes with her ivory pen,
> Taking instructions from thy flowing eyes,

and later, in the second part of the play, in his rapture he no
less eloquently explains that

> Now walk the angels on the walls of heaven,
> As sentinels to warn th' immortal souls
> To entertain divine Zenocrate:
> Apollo, Cynthia, and the ceaseless lamps
> That gently look'd upon this loathsome earth,
> Shine downwards now no more, but deck the heavens
> To entertain divine Zenocrate:
> The crystal springs, whose taste illuminates
> Refined eyes with an eternal sight,
> Like tried silver run through Paradise
> To entertain divine Zenocrate:
> The cherubins and holy seraphins,
> That sing and play before the King of Kings,
> Use all their voices and their instruments
> To entertain divine Zenocrate;
> And, in this sweet and curious harmony,
> The god that tunes this music to our souls
> Holds out his hand in highest majesty
> To entertain divine Zenocrate.

Again the ears of Shakespeare tingled and the fingers itched.
A year later came *The Tragical History of Doctor Faustus*, a
broken-backed play by our dramatic standards, with some
comic scenes of childish quality that interrupt the organ-music
of the beginning and the close; the best passages have a lyrical-
rhetorical style of compelling force and beauty.   Here again
was an irresistible noise, another spur to composition by
any rival talent.   For Marlowe's hand in *Faustus* is surer, less
tricky—less of that ' divine Zenocrate ' repetition now—and
the lines have a more delicate flow.

> O, thou art fairer than the evening air
> Clad in the beauty of a thousand stars;
> Brighter art thou than flaming Jupiter
> When he appear'd to hapless Semele;
> More lovely than the monarch of the sky
> In wanton Arethusa's azur'd arms;
> And none but thou shalt be my paramour!

Marlowe's mind, aspiring and perhaps agnostic, was in the stars. His Muse went climbing among planets, orbs, firmaments. Empires on earth and whirling spheres in the sky dominated his fancy: and he could make this new Renaissance English ring with his relish of cosmography—the last a word of his own usage. Tamburlaine speaks more as Marlowe than as an Eastern despot when he proclaims

> Nature, that fram'd us of four elements
> Warring within our breasts for regiment,
> Doth teach us all to have aspiring minds:
> Our souls, whose faculties can comprehend
> The wondrous architecture of the world,
> And measure every wandering planet's course,
> Still climbing after knowledge infinite,
> And always moving as the restless spheres,
> Will us to wear ourselves, and never rest,
> Until we reach the ripest fruit of all,
> That perfect bliss and sole felicity,
> The sweet fruition of an earthly crown.

Shakespeare, with a less aspiring, more domestic mind, at least in his earlier plays, more concerned with the cowslip and the Jenny Wren, and less with the cosmic architecture and the firmaments, brought Marlowe's translunar music down to native earth and so became the speaker for his land and people as Marlowe never could have been. But he had had his lesson and he owed a debt.

A lesson, also, in economics. Two editions of *Tamburlaine* (both parts) were published in 1590 and 1592: and every year until the Civil War the poems and plays of Marlowe were being printed afresh. *Tamburlaine* was drawing audiences after Marlowe's death in 1594, and between September of that year and November of the next Henslowe took at fourteen performances sums ranging from eighteen to forty-five shillings, which meant in the money of those days good houses for a play that had lost its early appeal.

Both *Faustus* and *The Jew of Malta* drew well and remained in Henslowe's repertory till the end of the century. *Faustus* was continually revived after that. It was not only a glorious play, Shakespeare felt, to dabble with the ' heavenly Quintessence that poets still ' and to fashion

> One thought, one grace, one wonder at the least
> Which into words no virtue can digest

but it was a man's life too, a bread-winning business, something you could mix with the playing of parts, the refurbishing of scripts, the observation of the public taste, the study of actions and reactions in the playhouse industry, the counting of box-office returns, the planning of new schemes and the winning of victories for his fellowship of players.

Other influences were plentiful. Music, his delight, music whose harmonies proclaimed for him the principle of public life and private happiness, was to be heard everywhere in finest quality. Dowland, a master of Tudor composition, was in London and aged twenty-five (a year older than Shakespeare) in 1588. William Byrd, now recognised as the supreme musical genius of the time, was then in his maturity. Sir Edward Dyer's well-known poem proclaiming ' My mind to me a kingdom is ' was printed as a ballad in Byrd's *Psalms, Sonets,* and *Songs* in the significant year of 1587.

Another model was John Lyly, the modish author of *Euphues, the Anatomy of Wit,* and of a sequel, *Euphues, His England.* These books popularised, at least among the literary fops of the day, a trick of mixing balanced, antithetical sentences with much aid of alliteration. Lyly wrote comedies whose lyrics are far better than their dialogue, which was streaked with elaborate conceits. Every young writer with a quick, ingenious hand enjoys playing with words, and Shakespeare never wholly tired of this juggling, for which he had an infinite aptitude. The earliest plays are full of puns and Lylyan patterning of words. But his common sense discarded before long the excessive use of them, and that wise decision is voiced in Berowne's disclaimer of the quibbling vein,

> Taffeta phrases, silken terms precise,
>   Three-piled hyperboles, spruce affectation,
> Figures pedantical; these summer-flies
>   Have blown me full of maggot ostentation:
> I do forswear them; and I here protest,
>   By this white glove,—how white the hand, God knows !—
> Henceforth my wooing mind shall be exprest
>   In russet yeas and honest kersey noes.

Marlowe, before him, had disclaimed, in his prologue to *Tamburlaine*, the ' jigging veins of rhyming mother-wits.' Shakespeare besported himself rather longer with this gay verbosity, which never altogether lost its fascination for him. But he mastered his facility in Lylyan pun and conceit, just as he broke the dominion which Marlovian and sky-aspiring bombast had exercised upon him when he wrote *Richard III*. There was a saving sanity about the new recruit. He could see the ruin that lay in mimic brilliance and reject the methods of other men in which he could so easily have excelled.

Now we have to follow Marlowe's devotee into Marlowe's working-house and later on into the rival establishments.

What were the nature, time, and place of Shakespeare's apprenticeship in the theatre in which he was to be both prosperous in his profession and supreme in his art? The indisputable facts are scanty enough. In March of 1591 a play of *Henry VI* (*henery vj*) is mentioned in Henslowe's diary. We cannot certainly say that this is a section of the Shakespearean or partly Shakespearean trilogy admitted to the First Folio by its editors, who knew their man and his handiwork. But the probabilities point that way. Nobody can tell how many hands co-operated in these early plays; points of style and verbal usage do not certainly prove that a passage was written by any one person: it may have been written by his admirer who was copying his tricks or by a jealous plagiarist lifting thievishly.

A book entered in the Stationers' Register in August, 1592, *Pierce Pennilesse*, by Thomas Nashe, contains this,

> How would it have joy'd brave Talbot (the terror of the French) to thinke that after he had lyne two hundred yeare in his tombe, hee should triumphe againe on the Stage, and have his bones new embalmed with the teares of ten thousand spectators at least (at severall times) who, in the tragedian that represents his person, imagine they behold him fresh bleeding.

In Shakespeare's *Henry VI*, Part I, Act IV, scene vii, ' brave Talbot,' dying beside his dead son, says of his boy,

> Dizzy-eyed fury and great rage of heart
> Suddenly made him from my side to start
> Into the clustering battle of the French;
> And in that sea of blood my boy did drench
> His over-mounting spirit; and there died
> My Icarus, my blossom, in his pride.

Then he utters a conventional defiance of death, using the adjective ' antic ' so dear to Shakespeare (we remember Richard II's soliloquy,

> Within the hollow crown
> That rounds the mortal temples of a king
> Keeps Death his court: and there the antic sits
> Scoffing his state and grinning at his pomp:
> Allowing him a breath, a little scene,
> To monarchize):

Talbot, far less beautifully than Richard, but with one or two hints of the hand of glory that was now holding the 'prentice pen, departs orating thus, mingling conceits with eloquence :

F

Thou antic death, which laugh'st us here to scorn,
Anon, from thy insulting tyranny,
Coupled in bonds of perpetuity,
Two Talbots, winged through the lither sky,
In thy despite, shall scape mortality.
O thou whose wounds become hard-favour'd death,
Speak to thy father, ere thou yield thy breath!
Brave death by speaking, whether he will or no;
Imagine him a Frenchman and thy foe.—
Poor boy! he smiles, methinks, as who should say,
Had death been French, then death had died to-day.

The last line surely declares the true Shakespearean hand.

There can be little doubt that Nashe was alluding to this stage episode and his allusion makes it certain that the young author of the play had already hit the fancy of the town; both the size and the number, as well as the emotion, of his audiences are stressed: a triumph, then, for Shakespeare, if, as seems most probable, it were indeed Shakespeare, the new Johannes Factotum, who had done so well for Talbot, Earl of Shrewsbury. He, who was soon to set the town in a roar of laughter, had already made it cry. Less than a month later comes the famous Factotum reference made by Robert Greene,

Yes, trust them not; for there is an upstart crow, beautified with our feathers, that, with his tyger's heart, wrapt in a Player's hide, supposes he is as well able to bombast out a blanke verse, as the best of you; and being an absolute Johannes Factotum, is in his own conceit, the only Shake-scene in a countrie.

Few dispute that this refers to William Shakespeare. Evidently then, by September, 1592, Shakespeare was worth attacking: his raid upon London was showing good results: disappointed seniors do not bother to sneer at young failures or obscure nobodies. Marlowe's chief rival and successor was already a marked man.

Venus and Adonis, a long narrative poem, Ovidian and

sensuous, was an immediate favourite. It was entered at Stationers' Hall in April, 1593. Then *Titus Andronicus* and ' A Booke intituled the firste parte of the Contention of the famous houses of York and Lancaster' (probably *Henry VI*, Part 2) were entered in February and March of 1594.

In the *Titus Andronicus* Quarto there is no mention of Shakespeare's name or of any author's. Francis Meres attributed *Titus* to Shakespeare and that, followed by the verdict of Heminge and Condell, who admitted the play to the First Folio, is strong testimony to set against the many doubts caused by the undeniable crudity of this blood-boltered melodrama. Probably it was a piece which Shakespeare took over from some rougher hand in order to do what he could with it for his company's advantage. He left his mark amid the carnage. There are hints of ' Sweet Mr. Shakespeare's ' authentic hand in the trick and rhythm of

> She is a woman, therefore may be woo'd;
> She is a woman, therefore may be won;
> She is Lavinia, therefore must be loved.

This is surely by the author of *Richard III*, with its

> Was ever woman in this humour woo'd ?
> Was ever woman in this humour won ?

Again

> What fool hath added water to the sea,
> Or brought a faggot to bright, burning Troy ?

And

> Come and take choice of all my library
> And so beguile thy sorrow

are surely the real thing. The latter has a smack of the riper Shakespeare in one of his enchanting moods of dulcet melancholy. Such lines almost anticipate Prospero.

Titus Andronicus, whatever its origin, was much and long beloved by the public and was kept in print by several new editions, even after the Folio; this is no evidence of good public taste, but proof only that Johannes Factotum knew his box-office.

It is late in December, 1594, that we reach the vitally important information left in the Accounts of the Treasurer of the Chamber. This records payments to William Kempe, William Shakespeare, and Richard Burbage,

> servauntes to the Lord Chamberleyne, upon the Councelle's warrant dated at Whitehall xv Marcij 1594, for twoe severall comedies or enterludes shewed by them before her majestie in Christmas tyme laste paste viz upon St. Stephen's daye and Innocentes daye . . .

Here is conclusive evidence that Shakespeare was in the winter of 1594, aged thirty, established and important. He is one of his company's triumvirate and that company was the Lord Chamberlain's own and therefore especially connected with the Court. This, at least, is not conjecture: it is one of our few pieces of certain knowledge concerning his early conquest of the town.

Both strenuous research and amusing guesswork have abundantly gone to tracing the steps in Shakespeare's progress in the years before 1594. The eighteenth century filled up the gaps according to its fancy and developed, as we have seen, the kind of legend that people like: no popular millionaire ever began with more than half a crown in his pocket, and Shakespeare's tips as a horse-warden serving the playgoers are in that class of mythology. Which company he first joined and in what playhouse he first worked are subjects with a vast and inconclusive literature of their own. The ordinary reader, playgoer, and enjoyer of Shakespeare need not worry over the secrets of the first seven years, seven, that is, if we give 1587 as the date of his leaving Stratford; the period contains some, but not much, of that for which we love him most. The emerging fact is that in 1594, still in the flush of youth, he had come through, had made himself by *Venus and Adonis* into the darling singer of the town and was heading a team of players. He would be meeting through one patron, Southampton, and through another, Lord Hunsdon, the royal Chamberlain, such members of the Court and aristocracy as cared to exercise their wits with those of the poets and players and, to do so, invited them to their mansions as well as frequenting the salons or the taverns where such company was kept. He had arrived.

CHAPTER VIII

Seven Ages of the Man

IT is no part of this book's purpose to follow Shakespeare's output year by year, analysing and assessing the growth of his genius and the scope of his performance. That has been done a thousand times. Nor shall I try to date the plays. In order to date them scholars have incessantly worked away at the internal allusions, tricks of style, verbal usage, metrical tests and so on. From this a certain rough agreement as to the age-groups of the plays has been reached, but there is not, and cannot be without new evidence, certainty as to the exact year in which the plays were thought out, worked upon, and produced upon the stage. The plays were, in some cases, rewritings of older pieces and they were themselves revised for later appearances. Hence a possible allusion to a historical event proves nothing much: it may have found its way into the First Folio text, issued seven years after Shakespeare's death, many years after the first draft of the piece: it may, for example, have been put in for topical effect during a revival.

But it is important for the understanding of the man's life, the change of his outlook, and the working of his mind that we should have a general time-table of his achievement during the three decades lying between his arrival in London and his death in Stratford. I shall therefore attempt a brief summary of his work, setting it out in seven divisions. This grouping can indicate and express the forces that shaped his mood and method, his sway of happiness and suffering, his changing valuations—for he had no simple, single, easily defined creed of first and last things—and his response to the charms and terrors which life in the city and countryside held out to him from time to time.

In examining and classifying an author's work we have to remember the several factors which may determine it. First of all, Shakespeare was building a career. He had chosen a profession and he had to succeed in it. He had his natural pride. There were also a wife and three children: two parents, furthermore, and some brothers and a sister were keeping a hopeful watch on him. He had a natural instinct for ownership and property, as his behaviour after achieving some prosperity conclusively proves. Later on, speaking through Hamlet, he might disparage the inability of 'the general' to appreciate the caviare of authorship, but in his youth he had to note ' the general ' closely. It was their applause that would make him; it was their money that he wanted. It was profitable, no doubt, as well as flattering, to get commissions from royalty and nobility and to act in palaces and mansions: but the majority vote had also to be remembered. Such a box-office piece as *Titus Andronicus* was kept in performance and in print by public demand: tiresome, perhaps, but the drama's laws the drama's patrons gave, then as ever.

The second consideration is that Shakespeare was one of a fellowship. The fact has been much forgotten by the Olympian school of commentators, who are always probing the mind ' out-topping knowledge ': it has also been so well remembered by Professor G. E. Bentley that I cannot refrain from quoting at some length his trenchant observations in *Shakespeare Survey*, 1948, on this point:

Shakespeare was more completely and continuously involved with theatres and acting companies than any other Elizabethan dramatist whose life we know. Most Elizabethan dramatists had only their writing connection with the theatres, but Shakespeare belonged to the small group which both wrote and acted. In this small group of actor-dramatists, the best-known names are those of Heywood, Rowley, Field and Shakespeare. Of this thoroughly professionalized band, Shakespeare is the one most closely bound to his company and his theatre, for he is the only one of the four who did not shift about from company to company but maintained his close association with a single acting troupe for more than twenty years. Besides this, he was bound to theatres and actors in still another fashion which makes him unique among all Elizabethan dramatists: he is the only dramatist we know who owned stock in theatre buildings over an extended period. His income was derived from acting, from writing plays, from shares in dramatic enterprises, and from theatre rents. From the beginning to the end of his writing career we must see him in a theatrical context if we are not to do violence to the recorded facts. At the beginning is our first reference to him in Greene's allusion to the ' Tygers hart wrapt in a Players hyde '; at the end are his own last words, so far as we know them, in his will. This will is mostly concerned with Stratford affairs, but when he does turn to the years of his London life and his many London associates, he singles out only three for a last remembrance. These men are John Heminges, Henry Condell, and Richard Burbage—all three actors, all three fellow-sharers in the acting company of the King's Men, all three fellow-stockholders in the Globe and the Blackfriars. If Shakespeare's proper context is not the London commercial theatres and the professional troupes, then evidence has no meaning . . .

So Shakespeare had to write with his eye on his fellows and with an ear to their suggestion of themes, parts, and profit-making possibilities. It does not demean his genius to say this: rather does it emphasise the man's uncanny dominion over his medium that he could both serve his colleagues and his art with such unparalleled performance.

There is a third point. Both Shakespeare and his fellowship were under patronage. They had to please the public and bring in the gate-money: at the same time they dare not offend the Crown, its chief servant in this matter, the Lord Chamberlain, and such noblemen as showed them a particular favour, e.g. the Earl of Southampton. The first systematic biographer of Shakespeare, Rowe, says that ' he had many great and uncommon marks of friendship from the Earl of Southampton, famous in the histories of that time for his friendship to the unfortunate Earl of Essex. . . . There is one instance so singular in the munificence of this patron of Shakespeare's that if I had not been assured that the story was handed down by Sir William Davenant, who was probably very well acquainted with his affairs, I should not have ventured to have inserted that my Lord Southampton, at one time, gave him a thousand pounds to enable him to carry through a purchase which he heard he had a mind to.' There may be something wrong here. A thousand pounds would have been a colossal gift in those days. New Place, after all, the chief house in Stratford, only cost Shakespeare sixty pounds. But the story, though its arithmetic may be faulty, comes from one of the earlier and better sources and is significant. In asking the why and wherefore of Shakespearean work we cannot leave such a lavish patron out of account.

Also, Shakespeare was a man of intense sensibility. (The stodgy insensitive bust in the church at Stratford and the dreary, constipated dullard of the Droeshout portrait cannot be true either to Shakespeare the actor or Shakespeare the author.) We may not with certainty find him in his work, but we can with some confidence look for him. I, for one, absolutely refuse to believe that he kept himself out of his writing, that his Sonnets are a formal exercise, and that his plays are examples of abstract and remote dramaturgy, from whose themes and persons and language he carefully withdrew all personal feeling and opinion. Only the dullest of study-bound professors could pretend that authorship so vibrant as Shakespeare's is possible on those lines. My own opinion (and certainly not mine alone) is that he portrayed and betrayed himself continually. The state of any author's sub-conscious self, at the time any play or book is written, must emerge to some extent in the language and similes which he employs. We can tell, fairly surely, what was vexing or delighting him, if we note his choice of epithets, his use of metaphor, and his selection of vocabulary.

So here are three factors governing the development of Shakespeare's work. The first is economic, the second is professional, the third is personal. He wrote for himself, as a professional theatre-worker with an eye to a competence: he wrote for a ' cry of players ' with whom he was associated, in friendship and finance, from first to last: and he wrote as a man of feeling, intensely susceptible to beauty, to passion and to Nature, easily and overwhelmingly horrified by the bestiality of man, and yet easily restored to calm and happiness by ' a fancy from a flower-bell.' If we bear these three traits and conditions in mind, we shall better understand the various ages of the man.

Variety is the keynote of the first Shakespearean phrase. His early role, we have seen, was that of Johannes Factotum, Jack-of-all-trades. He was actor and mender of plays, soon an author on his own account. Greene's sneer at the ' upstart Crow, beautified with our feathers ' suggests a charge of plagiarism and an unknown poet ' R. B.' added to this a general accusation that robbery was common; this he did in a poem called *Greene's Funeralls*. Here is the accusation,

> Greene, gave the ground, to all that wrote upon him,
> Nay more the men, that so Eclipst his fame:
> Purloynde his Plumes, can they deny the same ?

' R. B.'s ' plural, ' the men,' was presumably meant to include ' Shake-scene.'

This business of playhouse feather-plucking has to be seen in the light of the contemporary theatre practice. The play-wrights sold their plays to the company of players, whose property they became: they retained, at least in the early period of Shakespeare's working life, no private rights: the manager or leaders of the company could thus order repairs or a new version of an old script to be undertaken by another person. There was constant rehandling of old pieces with attempted ' modernisation,' as we might say. Naturally the original author would not appreciate this: he would be proud of his plumes of speech and to see them trimmed away by one hand or adopted by another would be extremely exasperating.

The situation in an Elizabethan theatre seems closely to have resembled that in a newspaper office to-day. The reporter reports on paper or by telephone; the special correspondent files his cable. But both messages have to be ' sub-edited ' and that for very good reasons. The copy sent in will probably be too long for the allotted space. (Plays often suffer from the same prolixity and need a visit to the barber.) Cutting is naturally most likely to occur when journals are severely truncated by lack of their raw material, the species of paper called newsprint. The incoming ' story ' may cut across or repeat or conflict with news already received and so will have to be carefully considered from that angle. It may need improvement of grammar, style, and manners; possible errors of fact and judgment must be removed and the danger of libel avoided. Attractive and intelligent headlines and introductory paragraphs have to be prepared. Thus the sub-editor's many functions are always important to the editor and usually odious to the correspondent and the reporter; they see their plumes disappearing or rearranged, not in order to falsify reports, but to improve their presentation and to fit them into the pattern of the day's paper. And who enjoys being ' improved ' by another's hand ? Self-pity is the natural temper of all who see their handiwork amended.

Plays in the modern theatre are considerably sub-edited by managers and producers or directors before and during the course of rehearsal; not always for the better. (The newspaper reporter, too, may be badly sub-edited and have a just complaint that the cutting of his words has cut out the sense of them too.) It is reasonable to suppose that, in the rough workshop of the Elizabethan theatre, a young man's first task would be amending rather than creating; Shakespeare would be, as Greene and ' R. B.' indicated, a sub-editor, a plucker and rearranger of other men's wordy plumage. He would also be a small-part actor and to that, again, Greene testified by his quotation from *Henry VI*, Part 3, Act I, scene iv, where the Duke of York upbraids Queen Margaret with these words,

O tiger's heart wrapt in a woman's hide!
How couldst thou drain the life-blood of the child,
To bid the father wipe his eyes withal,
And yet be seen to bear a woman's face ?
Women are soft, mild, pitiful, and flexible;
Thou stern, obdurate, flinty, rough, remorseless.

The passage must have been powerfully delivered in the theatre and left its mark on the memory of audiences. Otherwise there would have been no point in pulling out the first line quoted, altering one word, and so talking of ' Shakescene's ' possession of a ' tyger's hart wrapt in a player's hide.' Nor would there have been any point in the taunt if Shakespeare had not been known as an actor.

In 1592 a disaster befell the London theatres: there had been a riot of apprentices, which involved closing as a security measure. Then a severe epidemic of plague swept over the town, and such places of congregation as playhouses had, prudently, to be closed. The actors on these occasions went on tour and Shakespeare may have travelled: one thing is certain. He found time to write *Venus and Adonis* and was in touch with Southampton and his circle. The publication of that poem marks the beginning of his second phase, the lyrical.

What, then, had been the characteristics and accomplishments of the Johannes Factotum period, which I date from 1587 to the closing of the playhouses in the summer of 1592 ? In 1693 a visitor to Stratford, Edward Dowdall, recorded the information given by the ' clarke of the Church,' an old man of ' above 80 ' and therefore born just before Shakespeare's death, that ' Shakespear was formerly in this Towne bound apprentice to a butcher: but that he Run from his master to London and there was Received Into the play-house as a serviture and by this means had an oppertunity to be what he afterwards prov'd.' Leaving aside the butcher's boy tradition, that implies the acquisition of a hired man's place. Adult theatre companies then had three ranks, share-holding members, boy apprentices and hired men. It depended on the skill and tact of these last whether they worked their way up from journeyman's status to be a ' sharer,' and as such a governing member, of the team. Shakespeare's ' very readie and pleasant smooth Witt ' (Aubrey) must have carried him rapidly upwards. For the statement in the Accounts of the Treasurer of the Chamber, linking him with Burbage and with Kempe as a payee for Court performances, makes it certain that he had ceased, as early as 1594, to be ' a serviture ' and was now a person holding authority.

The work generally attributed to this period is

> *Henry VI*, Parts 1, 2, 3
> *Titus Andronicus*
> *The Comedy of Errors*
> *Richard III*
> *The Two Gentlemen of Verona*

The marks of the period are an increasing mastery of rhetorical force (this culminates in *Richard III*), decreasing crudity (*The Two Gentlemen of Verona* offers more polished, if less exciting, company than do the two pairs of twins in *The Comedy of Errors*), and a slowly growing realisation of the author's lyrical genius. *The Two Gentlemen* is a transition play.

> O how this spring of love resembleth
> The uncertain glory of an April day.

There is a change here from the sounding of Marlovian trumpets. The wood-notes are beginning. The ' Who is Silvia ?' song is an early piping of the supreme lyricist of the English language. It is in this play that Shakespeare observes:

> Much is the force of heaven-bred poesy.

Much indeed. When he got a rest from playing and play-writing (owing to the plague which closed the theatres) there was time to write the two long pieces in a narrative-lyrical style; this ' poesy,' whether bred of heaven or more sensual earth, had force enough to give the writer fame and to turn his pen upon new courses.

So to Age Two. This was the Lyrical Period. It ran from 1592-3 to 1596. Its principal products were

> *Venus and Adonis*
> *Lucrece*

The Early Sonnets
Love's Labour's Lost
Romeo and Juliet
A Midsummer Night's Dream
The Merchant of Venice

The first two might have been called by Browning dramatic lyrics. They gave the poet assurance and brought in reward. *Love's Labour's Lost*, of which there was a reshaped version in 1598, is a Frenchified play compounded of sonnets, song, conceits and courtly banter, the whole being humanised and naturalised by some rough native drollery. I surmise that it was a radical redrafting and rewriting of some nobleman's attempt at drama, which, being found dull, was brought to Johannes Factotum for repairs. Shakespeare added the ' amateur theatrical ' fun, which he repeated in *A Midsummer Night's Dream*, poured himself into the part of Berowne, gave us a glimpse of his Dark Lady, and especially through Berowne, pronounced his own judgment on that aristocracy's darling, the Euphuistic style with its 'spruce affectation,' in which the play had first been written. The original author may have been Southampton or any of his set, but he had good reason to remain proud of it when such a hand had made alterations and laid on the charm. It was at Southampton's house, we saw, that the piece was to be given for Queen Elizabeth's entertainment, according to Sir Walter Cope's message to Lord Cranborne.

Next come the lyric tragedy of *Romeo and Juliet* and the lyric comedy of *A Midsummer Night's Dream*. *The Merchant of Venice* is the transition play of this phase: it has a song in its heart and Portia's Belmont is a palace of poetry; this last is scarcely essential to the drama, but it is exquisite in its own lyrical right. The story of Shylock links the play to larger matters and the next phase.

Common to all the work of Age Two is a new pursuit of beauty in words: the influence of Marlowe is less: the rhetoric is reduced: where once was crackling fire, there is now radiant light as well; loveliness continually breaks in. The author, one feels, is a happy man, self-confident, conscious of increasing powers and of a firm hold upon his public, sure of his expanding career. His country memories give him his comedy and prompt the bird-song in the woods of Athens and the park of Navarre: his reading and his new acquaintance with the big houses and their scholarship give him plots, allusions, a Renaissance touch.

Yet his stage-craft was not yet beyond criticism. *Romeo and Juliet* contains as much of sheer verbal beauty as anything he ever wrote, but it never wholly succeeds upon the stage, partly through technical inexperience (the end is disappointingly contrived) and partly because the poet was himself still too young, blithe and happy in success to pour a full heart into his tragedy as well as to exercise head and hand upon it. Why is it that an actor so rarely makes his name as Romeo ? (Indeed most actors of renown find it difficult even to maintain their reputation in that role.) It is not merely that Mercutio is bound to steal the first half of the play: the technical accomplishment which was to make Hamlet a part in which none fails was not yet ripe enough to make Romeo an equally safe role. Juliet, too, is notoriously difficult; her portrayer must look like a child, and yet, in the later scenes, have the acting range and capacity of an experienced ' star.' The Lyrical Age of Shakespeare has its peculiar fascination. It is the sweet of the Shakespearean year, the proud-pied April, the flush of May, the cowslip-time. The rose of his achievement, with ' blood-drops burning in the heart of June ', was soon to come. But there was an interval.

Age Three of William Shakespeare is Historical. It lasts from 1596 to 1599. It contains

> *King John*
> *Richard II*
> *Henry IV*, Parts 1, 2
> *Henry V*

There may have been some political urgency behind this work. That gift of a thousand pounds (if there really was so vast a subsidy) may have come for services rendered, through the Chamberlain's Company, to the Crown. The moral of all Shakespeare's histories is that of national solidarity under a monarch. The ' troublesome reign ' of King John and the baronial wars provide march and counter-march, plot and counter-plot, all emphasising the general damage caused by the schismatic caterpillars of the realm. Good gardening needs a master gardener.

The service of the Crown certainly did not exclude the service of the public and, while *Henry IV* was striking down rebellion, Falstaff was putting up receipts. Falstaff, in short, was demonstrating the author's full discovery of his own wit and proving that historical-comical could be a ' mixed mode ' of delicious quality. The tremendous effort of composing the two *Henry IV* plays was evidently exhausting. For the comedy in *Henry V* is strained and Pistol misfires, at least on our stages. For Harry turned Hero Shakespeare had to rely mainly on his old mastery of rhetoric and so he used the clarion to the full and triumphantly.

On the whole it is a happy period. But there had been the bitter loss, in August, 1596, of Shakespeare's only boy, Hamnet, now aged 11. Since 1596 is the date generally given to the writing of *King John* (Chambers says ' the winter of 1596-7 is not unlikely '), it is more than probable that deep personal feeling strengthened the anguish of the lines in which Constance laments the fate of the young Prince Arthur.

> There was not such a gracious creature born.
> But now will canker-sorrow eat my bud,
> And chase the native beauty from his cheek,
> And he will look as hollow as a ghost,
> As dim and meagre as an ague's fit;
> And so he'll die; and, rising so again,
> When I shall meet him in the court of heaven,
> I shall not know him: therefore never, never
> Must I behold my pretty Arthur more.

Pandulph   You hold too heinous a respect of grief.

Constance   He talks to me that never had a son.

King Philip	You are as fond of grief as of your child.
Constance	Grief fills the room up of my absent child,
	Lies in his bed, walks up and down with me,
	Puts on his pretty looks, repeats his words,
	Remembers me of all his gracious parts,
	Stuffs out his vacant garments with his form;
	Then have I reason to be fond of grief.

' As dim and meagre as an ague's fit.' There is an authentic death-bed vision in those words. The language of Paul Dombey's passing becomes pure theatre when matched with those brief epithets from a theatrical speech, dim and meagre, which drive into the very heart of sick-room actuality, of young decay and bitter parental desolation. Immediately after these lines come two others, widely known, but rarely attributed to their proper source,

> Life is as tedious as a twice-told tale,
> Vexing the dull ear of a drowsy man.

Most would give *Macbeth*, *Hamlet* or *King Lear* as the text in which that poignant cry of world-weariness occurs. But it happens to be an anticipation, not an amplification, of

> ' Life's but a walking shadow . . . . a tale
> Told by an idiot, full of sound and fury,
> Signifying nothing.'

The historian-comedian was finding his mastery of pathos and the minor key. *Richard II* was further proof of that development. That king is a supreme, as well as an early, example of the contemplative, self-pitying failure-type which was especially to fascinate Shakespeare and to evoke some of his greatest penetration of character and felicity of phrase in the presentment of an aching heart beneath a restless mind.

Age Four may be described in Duke Orsino's word as ' high-fantastical.' It is a period as superb as short, lasting for about two years after 1598. Its products were:

Much Ado About Nothing
The Merry Wives of Windsor
As You Like It
Twelfth Night

Here are the summits of Shakespearean Comedy, the work of happy hours, the lyrical indulgence of romantic dreaming, the marriage of music and of wit, incredibly rich in charm of phrase; the master of craft is glorying now in his own assured fertility. There is a glorious abundance of verbal and metaphorical invention. ' So full of shapes is fancy.'

The Merry Wives, it can be protested, hardly merits such praise. The tradition that it was a sequel to the Falstaff historical plays commanded by Queen Elizabeth, who wished to see the fat knight in love, goes back even beyond Rowe's biography of 1709. The same statement had occurred a few years earlier in the writings both of Charles Gildon, dramatist and bookseller (1665-1724), and of John Dennis, dramatist and critic (1657-1734). Gildon said that the royal command was executed within a fortnight, while Dennis reduces the time of composition to ten days. The play shows signs of haste, is mostly in prose, and offers a Falstaff of more gross humours than of nimble wit. Sir John has his gleam of phrase still, but, on the whole, this Falstaff is unworthy of the grand original: but the piece acted, and still acts, well: it has usually been ' good box-office.' Shakespeare's fellowship of players had nothing to complain about when the parts of Mistress Ford and Mistress Page were handed to the boys or young gentlemen who played the maturer ladies.

The other three ' high-fantastical ' comedies are radiant with sheer joy in achievement. Arriving within so short a period and providing rich parts for a boy-actor who could glitter in highly elegant, conceited dialogue as well as in the poetry of fancy, they suggest composition with a close eye on the casting. If the Lord Chamberlain's men had a young star who was drawing the town, it was obvious policy to follow up ' sweet Beatrice ' with ' heavenly Rosalind ' and Rosalind with Viola's smooth, rubious lip and maiden-pipe of amorous messages.

Such a lad would help to follow victory with victory. He had to be fed with the right roles. But how to make one magic fade into the next? Fortunately the recruit of 1590 was already the master of 1600. There was nothing that could defy his contrivance now. The students were crying his praise at Cambridge while Viola was on embassage to Olivia and Rosalind was sprinkling Arden's forest with the cascade of her wit.

Shakespeare was only thirty-six when all this was accomplished. The last decade's work had been astounding in its grasp of human character and growth of theatrical method, in its blending of copious flow with mental quality, in its speedy absorption of life's comedy observed and in the no less speedy knack of putting the essential follies, humours, and beauties back on to paper and into ' the wooden O ' of the player's working-house. It was surely, on the whole, a happy decade. Clouds there had been: Hamnet's death left grief to fill the room up of the absent child; there had been infatuation with some dark, false charmer whose story, told in the Sonnets, haunts some at least of the plays. There was the increasing fear that his friend and patron, Southampton, with his evil genius, the spoilt, brilliant, wayward Earl of Essex, was embarked upon dangerous courses. The town had its menaces as well as its shining hours, its cruelties and corruptions as well as its enchantments for the eye and ear. But the latter were still more dominant than the former. The scent of life was yet delicate in his nostrils.

Then, with the turn of the century, there was a turn of temper too. The ugliness of things leaped up at Shakespeare: like assassins surrounding a man from all quarters the deadly sins of envy, lust, jealousy and tyrannical ambition sprang out from behind the arras of his happy high-fantastical imaginings; they stabbed at his ecstasy in living.

Shaw has maintained that Shakespeare had begun by now to distrust his art, sneer at his own successes and despise his public. The titles of *Much Ado About Nothing*, *As You Like It*, and of *Twelfth Night or What You Will* are, he thinks, contemptuous. There may have been a sardonic smile as Burbage

and the team commanded another box-office part for that
triumphant boy-player with a rare talent for sweet heroines
or when they insisted that an Illyria must have another
fairy-land to follow and so created Arden (or vice versa). But
these plays, whether labelled with a sour smile or not, are
certainly not sour in themselves. Does anybody feel, as he
sees or reads the high-fantastical comedies, that Shakespeare
was hesitant or ashamed of what he was doing ? He never
bothered much about his plots; he can hardly have cared
much about Don John, Duke Frederick, or how he straightened
out the tangle of *Twelfth Night*. But he was more than knee-
deep in love with Beatrice, Rosalind, and Viola; they were
by no means negative causes of much ado: they were fashioned
as he liked them; they spoke as he willed.

However that may be, the sun sank sharply in his sky. The
pettiness of man and the frailty of woman began to obsess his
meditation and obscure his laughing outlook on the glittering,
turbulent panorama of the town. Nor was there the old
comfort in the country. The earth which had been so fair a
frame for meadows painted with delight became a pestilent
congregation of vapours.

So we pass from the Fourth Age of High-fantastical to the
Fifth Age, that of Bitter Comedy. This Fifth overlaps the
sixth, the long, the strenuous, and yet superbly inspiring Age
of the Dark Vision. *Hamlet* had been written before the Bitter
Comedies were over; but after the Bitter there was no comedy
at all for half a dozen years, and then there came not comedy
renewed but fresh search for romantic escape.

The Bitter Comedies are

> *All's Well that Ends Well*
> *Troilus and Cressida*
> *Measure for Measure*

They are generally dated, between *Hamlet* and *Othello*, in the
opening years of the seventeenth century. *Troilus and Cressida*
was entered at Stationers' Hall in Feb., 1603. Although these
plays cannot be classed as tragedy they have little of comedy's

essential laughter. Their humour is often squalid; the brothel and its ailments are on Shakespeare's mind, as is the injustice of society and the abuse of authority. *Measure for Measure* contains meditations on death, both accepting it as an escape into rest, sleep, nothingness, and shrinking from it as a form of tortured exile for eternity. We cannot imagine Claudio's speech beginning

> Aye, but to die and go we know not where,
> To lie in cold obstruction and to rot

occurring on Duke Orsino's lips. It strikes to the icy core of pessimism, like much in the tragedies of the Dark Vision, the tragedies which were just beginning to take form.

Various things are noticeable in the Bitter Comedies. They lack zest for life and they are anti-authoritarian. The great ones are seen in their smallness; the classic Greeks are robbed of their dignity. These classroom heroes, these pets of the dominie, Shakespeare seems to say, were no more than lechers and brawlers, just as the frigid Angelo was no better than a burning debauchee, indeed worse because of his snow-broth of hypocrisy. There is much reference, also, to physical distresses. ' The gout, serpigo, and the rheums ' begin, along with boils, blains, and imposthumes (or abscesses), to pepper the text. It is no extravagance to suppose that Shakespeare was undergoing bodily trouble and was seeing something of the doctor; when he was in Stratford there was his future son-in-law, John Hall, to treat him and to talk with him of maladies and remedies. Lastly, and certainly not least, there were the political danger and personal loss occasioned by the revolt of Lord Essex in which Southampton was implicated.

The Essex Rebellion occurred in 1601. Essex himself was executed, Southampton sent to the Tower. Whether there was still a deep attachment between the patron and the poet we cannot tell; but there were certainly close acquaintance and theatrical association. *Richard II*, a play disliked at the Court by reason of its deposition scene, had been given at the Globe by the Lord Chamberlain's Men at the request of the Essex faction on the day before Essex began his insurrection; naturally this episode was much discussed. Fortunately for the players the Chamberlain, Lord Hunsdon, was a loyal supporter of Elizabeth and had no entangling alliance of any kind with Essex. The actors were not punished, but they retired, tactfully, for a tour. It must have been a terrifying episode for Shakespeare as the author of a play so much in question at so perilous a time. Essex went to his death, Southampton to his cell. There was reason enough why Shakespeare's own laughter, coming from a mind so disturbed by calamity and possibly from a body afflicted by a severe ailment, should have turned to bitterness as he toiled away to keep his company supplied with fresh material.

The Sixth Age of Shakespeare records the Dark Vision amid which comedy at last becomes impossible and only the blackest tragedy will suffice for his beating mind. This phase begins with *Hamlet*. I have so far made no mention of *Julius Caesar*, which seems to mark the transition to the sombre view of life. Some high-fantastical comedy did follow it and it does not fit easily into any grouping of the plays. But it is plain that Brutus foreshadows Prince Hamlet in the Shakespearean studies of self-analysis and indecision: he is noble without the resolution that is needed to confirm nobility. ' His life was gentle ' and Hamlet might have echoed Brutus when the latter said of himself,

> Oh Cassius, you are yoked with a lamb
> That carries anger, as the flint bears fire;
> Who, much enforced, shows a hasty spark
> And straight is cold again.

This Age of the Dark Vision lasted (with some overlapping of other phases) nearly ten years. But for the tremendous tragedies which it yielded the pace was necessarily slower and the facility, which had yielded two or even three plays a year amid all the other theatrical responsibilities of management as well as the labours of acting, now suffered some abatement.

The pieces of this Age are:

Julius Caesar
Hamlet
Othello
Macbeth
King Lear
Timon of Athens
Coriolanus
Antony and Cleopatra

The last of these is a transition play: its magnificent study of human extravagance, and of power squandered for passion's sake, ends with a kind of serenity not to be discovered in *Timon*, *Lear*, or *Othello*.

The great tragedies from *Othello* onwards take the major vices in turn, jealousy, lust of power, vanity and cruelty, ingratitude, pride, and lust of sex, and put them under the magnifying glass that Shakespeare's genius provided. Into them he poured some speeches of world-hatred that are almost without parallel in the whole history of pessimism. The author of *King Lear* and *Timon of Athens*—the latter is probably not all Shakespeare's, but, when Shakespearean, overwhelmingly so— was living in a world of darkness unqualified. Comedy is left to the Fool who is either more piteous than any figure of supposed sanity or is briefly inserted to keep the company's comedians at least tolerably quiet, in the fragmentary, episodic scenes for gravedigger, porter, fig-seller and so on.

At this period the King's Men were saved at the box-office by a willingness of the public to accept high tragedy and by the enormous prestige and drawing power of their principal player, Richard Burbage. But after a decade the first of these conditions began to dwindle; what Macbeth called ' a dismal treatise ' and a supper of hair-raising horror had been too constantly supplied. Hair no longer rose and so pretty romances were designed to please a lighter fancy. The wonder is that the company endured this black mood of Shakespeare's so long since the comedians got nothing out of it but five-minute episodes. What sighs of relief must have been heard in a certain quarter when he once more began to turn in full-scale 'comics' like Autolycus, with Clowns as well, and to write the old robust, horse-play, word-play, boozy stuff for Trinculo and Stephano! Meanwhile the tragedians had such scope as never before or since and Burbage was there.

Throughout the dark period of Shakespeare's life his company seemed to have retained the favour of King James I. After his enthronement the King made a signal demonstration of his regard for the players, and he did, in fact, give them much more practical encouragement than Queen Elizabeth had ever done. Between 1594 and 1602 the Lord Chamberlain's Men averaged about £35 a year as payment for Court performances; and that was in the cheerful age of the Histories and the High-fantastical. Between 1603-7, when the blackest tragedies were the new offerings, the average annual taking of the King's Men, as they now were, was, for Court productions, £131.

Of course old and lighter plays were revived, but *King Lear* was actually the Christmas play at the palace of Whitehall in 1606, a strange choice, as we would think, of suitable holiday entertainment. King James has been a target for many criticisms, and his Court was certainly no school of morals: but it was an academy of drama at its highest and he did not withdraw his patronage when Shakespeare piled horror upon horror in his plays and railed against authority whose ' robes and furr'd gowns ' hide all iniquity. If the plays were not discreetly cut for command performances, then James could ' take it,' as we say, and is the more to be honoured. Elizabeth gave Shakespeare and his fellows some support when they were writing smooth things: James gave far more support when their word was harsh and the mood austere.

So we reach the last phase of all, which may be described as Fancy Free. It yielded from 1608-13,

Pericles
Cymbeline
The Winter's Tale
The Tempest
Henry VIII

Shakespeare is slacking off. *Pericles* and *Henry VIII* are generally admitted to be co-operative writing, the former perhaps having the hand of Wilkins in it, the latter, most probably, the hand of Fletcher. *Henry VIII*, as we have seen, helped to demolish the Globe Theatre by an accident in a spectacular production. But the King's Men had for some years owned and controlled the Blackfriars and that was now their headquarters.

This indoor house had long been fashionable as the working-house of a Boys' Company; the King's Men were ousting a once powerful rival, on whose ' little eyases ' and the publicity and support which they received there is some rather acid comment in *Hamlet*. Ben Jonson had been one of the boys' chief authors. It was a distinguished house, frequented by the nobility and gentry: also by the literary figures and the modish Osrics of the day. What was most important was the opportunity it gave, with its roofed-in premises, for quieter acting, subtler production, and more lavish decoration than the open stage of the Globe had ever done or could ever do. Accordingly rhetorical writing would be less in demand: the great roarings and trumpetings in the Marlovian style, so apt to the open platform, would be regarded as ' ham ' by the cognoscenti of the Blackfriars. Furthermore, this audience was accustomed to the pleasures of Masque, the libretti for which Jonson could quickly supply and which Inigo Jones could so elegantly decorate. Jonson did not like this new service of the pen, but the fashion was established and Shakespeare himself began to comply with it.

Cymbeline contains a Masque with apparitions, a Masque in which ' Jupiter descends in thunder and lightning, sitting upon an eagle: he throws a thunderbolt.' This sort of thing belongs to what Bacon in his Essay *Of Masques and Triumphs* had called ' petty wonderments.' It was also, one would think, a stage manager's headache, but the Blackfriars stage-craft evidently allowed for gods on flying eagles. *The Tempest*, as every schoolchild knows, demands storms, a magical banquet, and a masquerade with classic goddesses appearing.

The stage was set, then, for something less than high tragedy.

The success of Beaumont and Fletcher with romantic comedies was creating a vogue in lighter entertainment. Shakespeare complied. He was in the mood for it, with his darkness of outlook eased. It is absurd to say that the last plays are purely serene: Leontes is a figure of fretful jealousy, speaking in the old, tortured way of sex and its ferocities. There is some of the old Shakespeare in Posthumus too: but Shakespeare gave neither of these men the whole play; there was room for youth, romance, revels, masquerade. He was in a mood for fairy-tale, for fancy free. All the last plays, except *Henry VIII*, have far-fetched plots: Shakespearean plots, it is true, never were remarkable for plausibility, but in *The Winter's Tale* and *The Tempest* the events are fairy-tale matters. Some of the sweetest and noblest of Shakespeare's poetry was attached to themes of magic and of let's-pretend. The actors presumably were happy enough. The theatre is always a changeable place and their theatre was, being so young, a quicker mover than most. Their master-hand was tiring, but it knew its business still, and Stratford would send up texts which gave the stage manager, as well as the actor, the chance to operate as best he could and meet the new demand.

Early in this chapter it was said that a dramatist's work must be related to his own mind, to the craft and working-house of his colleagues, and to the world about him. So for the sake of the reader's convenience I have tried to work out a scheme of Shakespearean chronology, from his arrival in London onwards. The dates of the plays can only be approximate on the evidence we possess. This pattern of his play-writing is set out in Appendix II.

CHAPTER IX

' My Lovely Boy '

SO much for the outline of the output. I have said that I do not intend to examine in detail the chronology, style, and artistic success of each of Shakespeare's plays and poems. This has been done hundreds of times in hundreds of ways with myriads of conflicting results. My purpose, certainly bold and perhaps impossible, is to discover the man behind the writing and to extract his motives, passions, frustrations, despairs, triumphs, and delights from the ravelled sleave of contemporary allusion and of such personal portrayal as his legacy of writing and its verbal images contains. So I shall not busy myself or afflict readers with a count, for example, of weak line-endings and the like in order to date a play or contradict the dating of it by others. Surely no other author has commanded more statistical devotion and more arithmetical application than William Shakespeare. He has provided material of the most attractive kind to the well-intentioned weevils of research: these have been delighted to go digging for victory with results, inevitably, somewhat dry.

The first certain record of Shakespeare's career as an actor occurs only at the end of 1594. The accounts of the Treasurer of the Chamber, as we saw, recorded sundry payments to Kempe, Shakespeare, and Burbage, servants to the Lord Chamberlain, upon the Council's Warrant, for ' twoe severall comedies or enterludes shewed by them before her majestie in Christmas tyme.' That Shakespeare's function was becoming more that of the script-writer than the actor, perhaps against his will, seems obvious from his output of plays and the rather scrappy gossip about the roles he performed. Kempe for comedy, Burbage for tragedy, and Shakespeare for authorship, for the patching up of plays, and for general aid with production. Is not that what Greene's Factotum sneer would signify ?

But before those command performances at Whitehall's Christmas revels much had happened. There had been the approval of ' worshipful persons.' Shakespeare had published his first book and with it scored a first, and a striking, victory. He had asserted himself as a narrative poet with a rich lyrical strain, he had hit the fancy of the town, and he had endeared himself to the young gallants who liked to have a volume in their hands and a line upon their lips. He was on the way to being Sweet Mr. Shakespeare, with his portrait in the studies of the University and Inns of Court wits. All this was over and above any reputation that he had so far established in the playhouse. Moreover, among ' divers of worship ' who gave him their support, was one brilliant and influential figure, that of Henry Wriothesley, Third Earl of Southampton.

The conquering poem, *Venus and Adonis*, was entered at Stationers' Hall on April 18, 1593. The publisher was Richard Field, a member of a Stratford-upon-Avon family and another of ' the lads from the regions ' who had come up to capture London. Field was already doing well in book production. Four years earlier he had issued a volume much liked by the cultivated Elizabethans and well used as a source of instruction by William Shakespeare himself. This was Puttenham's *Arte of English Poesie*. Then Field would also have delighted his fellow-Avonian and fellow-Ovidian by his publication of Ovid in translation as well as of *Orlando Furioso*. Field's ' list ' was representative of the vogue for ' classical-romantic ' which the English form of the Renaissance particularly favoured and *Venus and Adonis* was perfectly in tune with that taste.

It had a carnal, Titianesque richness of beauty: it had neatness of touch: it had the cleverness of phrase which an age, so conscious of ' conceits,' particularly relished. The story of Venus's assault upon the virtue of the handsome Adonis can scarcely be called popular now: after all, Shakespeare's first readers did not know what he could do when he was a matured genius working at full height and at full stretch. We, knowing all that, and having all the later work available, are the less impressed by his 'prentice' hand. Furthermore, there is a certain sickly nastiness, a mixture of sugar and cantharides, about the attempted seduction which we find distinctly oppressive: at times the Anglo-Ovidian writing has even a crude vulgarity. Venus, for example, complains to her reluctant Adonis,

> Were I hard-favour'd, foul, or wrinkled-old,
> Ill-nurtured, crooked, churlish, harsh in voice,
> O'erworn, despised, rheumatic, and cold,
> Thick-sighted, barren, lean, and lacking juice,
>> Then mightst thou pause, for then I were not for thee,
>> But having no defects, why dost abhor me ?

It is scarcely inspired. Or shall we say that juice is to our taste too much of the larder for a song of love ?

But that is the low ebb of it, and much of the country stuff, description of the perfect horse or of poor Wat, the hunted hare, the dew-bedabbled wretch, cunningly but vainly making his labyrinthing 'cranks and crosses' as he runs, are true and essential Shakespeare, early imprints of the hand of glory. Dover Wilson has compared the emergence of *Venus and Adonis* with the way in which Swinburne's *Poems and Ballads* burst upon London in 1866. He might have added Cambridge too; for there the undergraduates, with linked arms, chanted the new rhythms upon King's Parade.

It is at times laboured and at others a little stuffy, but in its defects as in its merits, in its pictorial quality and in its loading of every rift with ore, it reminds us more of the young Keats, the Keats of *Endymion*, than of any other poet.

As with Keats too, the passion for Beauty, less explicit than the fleshly passion, is so all-pervading as to remain our abiding impression when the book is closed and the details fade from the memory. It comes out most in those references to country life and animals in which the poem abounds. These glimpses of Stratford are indeed so much happier than the descriptions of the efforts by amorous Venus to awaken passion in her Adonis, that it is not difficult to see where Shakespeare's heart lay.

But Shakespeare cannot be wholly excused in that way for sensuousness and even sensuality. He had been ten years married and was a man of experience: it is hardly to be supposed that his lip had 'virgined it' during his London years: he obviously delighted in physical sensation when young: a year or two later he was as much appalled by the power of physical desire and by the aftermath of self-indulgence as he was drawn by the appeal of sexual beauty. His first, and rejoicing, public was not, I think, much interested in the morals of the matter when Adonis answered the temptress,

> Call it not love, for Love to heaven is fled,
> Since sweating Lust on earth usurp'd his name;
> Under whose simple semblance he hath fed
> Upon fresh beauty, blotting it with blame;
>   Which the hot tyrant stains and soon bereaves,
>   As caterpillars do the tender leaves.

> Love comforteth like sunshine after rain,
> But Lust's effect is tempest after sun;
> Love's gentle spring doth always fresh remain,
> Lust's winter comes ere summer half be done;
>   Love surfeits not, Lust like a glutton dies;
>   Love is all truth, Lust full of forged lies.

His readers liked the rich sound of it and they gleefully found it to be what Gilbert's Bunthorne called 'a wild weird fleshly thing, very tender, very yearning, very precious.' Here, as for Bunthorne, was a chance to sing.

> What time the poet hath hymned
> The writhing maid, lithe-limbed,
> Quivering on amaranthine asphodel.

A writhing maid, indeed, was Shakespeare's Venus, and she quivered her way from classic asphodel into Field's publishing house to the general satisfaction of the town.

The dedication of *Venus and Adonis* ran thus:

I know not how I shall offend in dedicating my unpolished
lines to your lordship, nor how the world will censure me for
choosing so strong a prop to support so weak a burden: only,
if your honour seem but pleased, I account myself highly
praised, and vow to take advantage of all idle hours, till I
have honoured you with some graver labour. But if the
first heir of my invention prove deformed, I shall be sorry it
had so noble a god-father, and never after ear so barren a
land, for fear it yield me still so bad a harvest. I leave it to
your honourable survey, and your honour to your heart's
content; which I wish may always answer your own wish
and the world's hopeful expectation.

When Shakespeare spoke of the first heir of his invention
he meant not his first piece of writing, since he had been
play-making for some years, but his first published book. The
dedication is in humble terms: but it is not servile, as dedications went in those days. It is also a sign of literary and
social ambition. Thomas Nashe, in similar buoyant spirit,
offered a book to the same Earl and was snubbed for his
pains. This volume was the picaresque novel *The Unfortunate
Traveller* or *The Life of Jack Wilton*. ' Long have I desired to
approve my art unto you,' wrote Nashe. But in vain: the wit
was not approved by the judge whose favour was in request,
though it proved to be popular enough elsewhere. The
dedication to Southampton vanished from the second edition,
proof of a rebuff in one quarter, as of success in another. But
no such intimation of disfavour came to Shakespeare: the
editions of *Venus and Adonis* poured out to meet the clamorous
demand. Ten printings were required in ten years and the
dedication was not withdrawn.

Just over a year later a second long Shakespearean poem of
similar type, *Lucrece*, was published by Field. The dedication
this time was to the same high personage, but written in a far
more confident and even cordial style. The piece is actually
described as ' assured of acceptance ' and the note of friendship
warms the expressions of devotion:

The love I dedicate to your lordship is without end; whereof this pamphlet, without beginning, is but a superfluous moiety. The warrant I have of your honourable disposition, not the worth of my untutored lines, makes it assured of acceptance. What I have done is yours; what I have to do is yours; being part in all I have, devoted yours. Were my worth greater, my duty would show greater; meantime, as it is, it is bound to your lordship, to whom I wish long life, still lengthened with all happiness.

Not only is a poet writing to a patron; a friend is writing to a friend.

The success this time was, perhaps, not so remarkable. By 1616 only five new editions had been called for. But of course a far larger first print may have been made, based on the previous success. At any rate contemporary allusion to the poem suggests wide public acceptance for this second adventure in the lush pastures of amatory verse. Here again the immediate world of Shakespeare's experience was not forgotten. I have already alluded to the passage of *Lucrece* about the backward flowing eddy which Dr. Caroline Spurgeon has traced to the Clopton Bridge over the Avon at Stratford. *Lucrece* is more rhetorical than *Venus and Adonis* and there are set-pieces on favourite themes of Shakespeare's, Time and Night, beginning thus,

> Mis-shapen Time, copesmate of ugly Night,
> Swift subtle post, carrier of grisly care,
> Eater of youth, false slave to false delight,
> Base watch of woes, sin's pack-horse, virtue's snare;
> Thou nursest all, and murder'st all that are:
> O, hear me, then, injurious, shifting Time!
> Be guilty of my death, since of my crime.
>
> O comfort-killing Night, image of hell!
> Dim register and notary of shame!
> Black stage for tragedies and murders fell!
> Vast sin-concealing chaos! nurse of blame!
> Blind muffled bawd! dark harbour for defame!

One sees here the first stirrings of the hand that wrote *Macbeth*.

'Dim register and notary of shame' is actually in the style of Shakespeare's high maturity. But it was the sugary quality of the descriptive verse, with its fleshly images, its luscious vocabulary, and neat conceits that chiefly took the town.

> Her lily hand her rosy cheek lies under,
> Cozening the pillow of a lawful kiss;
> Who, therefore angry, seems to part in sunder,
> Swelling on either side to want his bliss;
> Between whose hills her head entombed is:
>   Where, like a virtuous monument, she lies,
>   To be admired of lewd unhallow'd eyes.
>
> Without the bed her other fair hand was,
> On the green coverlet; whose perfect white
> Show'd like an April daisy on the grass,
> With pearly sweat, resembling dew of night.
> Her eyes, like marigolds, had sheath'd their light,
>   And canopied in darkness sweetly lay,
>   Till they might open to adorn the day.
>
> Her hair, like golden threads, play'd with her breath;
> O modest wantons! wanton modesty!
> Showing life's triumph in the map of death,
> And death's dim look in life's mortality:
> Each in her sleep themselves so beautify,
>   As if between them twain there were no strife,
>   But that life liv'd in death, and death in life.

Contemporary comment harps especially on this succulence of the English Ovid's style, 'All praiseworthy, Lucrecia Sweet Shakespeare . . . Wanton Adonis,' is one gentleman's jotting in 1595. In 1598 Richard Barnfield testified thus:

> And *Shakespeare* thou, whose hony-flowing Vaine,
> (Pleasing the world) thy Praise doth obtaine.
> Whose *Venus*, and whose *Lucrece* (sweete, and chaste)
> Thy Name in fames immortall Booke have plac't.
>   Live ever you, at least in Fame live ever:
>   Well may the Bodye dye, but Fame dies never.

Francis Meres, schoolmaster and clergyman, who went to Rutland from Pembroke College, Cambridge, but kept an eye and an ear for London events and had a relish for estimating London reputations, paid his well-known tribute in the same year.

As the soule of *Euphorbus* was thought to live in *Pythagoras*: so the sweete wittie soule of *Ovid* lives in mellifluous and hony-tongued *Shakespeare*, witnes his *Venus* and *Adonis*, his *Lucrece*, his sugred Sonnets among his private friends, etc.

Undoubtedly the first heirs of Shakespeare's invention had, with their copious, sensuous, sometimes even sickly quality, gratified a world in which a sweet tooth seems to have been a common possession. As has been pointed out, there was continual use of the word ' honey ' in describing Sweet Mr. Shakespeare's compositions. In 1599 John Weever, an antiquary, also chimed in with a ring of bells saluting ' honie-tongued ' Shakespeare:

Rose-checkt *Adonis* with his amber tresses,
Faire fire-hot *Venus* charming him to love her,
Chaste *Lucretia* virgine-like her dresses,
Prowd lust-stung *Tarquine* seeking still to prove her:
Romea Richard; more whose names I know not . . .

The Earl of Southampton had good reason, as soon as *Venus and Adonis* had been issued, to be proud of his discovery. Nashe could be shrugged aside. But Shakespeare was ' a hit,' patronised by the ' quality,' and now the delight of the quantity of readers too. So the man from Stratford, eager to justify his breach with home and with security, was by 1593 well on his way not only to a powerful patron but to an exalted friend. If Southampton was indeed the recipient of the first century of Sonnets, then the mutual attachment had passed well beyond the giving and receipt of protection and of favour. When all allowance has been made for changes in social and literary fashions and terms of personal address, a commoner belonging to an ' outcast ' profession, that of stage-player—'outcast' is his own choice of adjective—would certainly not address one of the brightest and loftiest stars of young nobility with such phrase as ' my lovely Boy' unless he had been very sure of his ground.

Henry Wriothesley, the young Earl of Southampton, was in 1593—on indisputable record, where so much is disputable— the poet's patron. He was notable by reason of his talents and attainments as well as of his wealth and power. He had been born at Cowdray in Sussex in October, 1573, being thus nine and a half years younger than the poet whom he was to champion. He came of the highest blood in the land and could claim John of Gaunt and Warwick the King-Maker among his ancestors. His grandfather was a Viscount Montague, a point which may have occurred to Shakespeare while considering the finer qualities of his Romeo. His father, who had been a Catholic recusant and penalised on that account, died young, when his son Henry was only eight. Nothing could have been more distinguished than the wardship arranged for the boy. The great Lord Treasurer, Lord Burghley, took charge of him. He went to Cambridge (St. John's College) at the age of twelve and duly wrote essays in Latin: the sentiments were those proper to a Tudor gentleman and made the ' hope of glory ' one of the major motives of good living. Glory there was to be, but more from his choice of a dependant than from any action of his own. He became M.A. of Cambridge at sixteen: a year before that he had been admitted to Gray's Inn, which was Bacon's Inn and noted for its miming, masques and revels as well as for its learning in the law.

Marriages were arranged early in that period and Burghley was eager to make a match between young Henry Wriothesley and Lady Elizabeth Vere, daughter of the Earl of Oxford: Henry's mother too was eager for the arrangement. But the boy, in 1590, was only seventeen and he had his eye on a larger glory and romance than lay in the hand of Oxford's fifteen-year-old daughter. He wanted to be a soldier and to serve in the foreign wars. He esteemed all the pleasures of the playhouse, where he was early a connoisseur, and of the countryside, where he was skilled as horseman and hawker.

> Some glory in their birth, some in their skill,
> Some in their wealth, some in their bodies' force;
> Some in their garments, though new-fangled ill;
> Some in their hawks and hounds, some in their horse;
> And every humour hath his adjunct pleasure,
> Wherein it finds a joy above the rest:
> But these particulars are not my measure;

Not the measure of young Southampton's sonneteering friend, but very much the measure of the Earl himself, who could glory—how often, how significantly that word reappears—in horse and hound as well as in wealth and birth.

The first twenty-five of Shakespeare's Sonnets, followed by an Envoi, beginning

> Lord of my love, to whom in vassalage
> Thy merit hath my duty strongly knit

are an appeal to a handsome young man, son of a handsome mother, to marry and so, by passing on his qualities to futurity, to defy that general tyrant, devouring Time. Lady Southampton, Henry's mother, then forty, an age deemed in that period to be autumnal, if not wintry, must have been agreeably confronted by the lines of her son's protégé, when he wrote to his patron,

> Thou art thy mother's glass and she in thee
> Calls back the lovely April of her prime.

Perhaps she had already paid the clever young man, now rising to renown, to compose these appeals on behalf of Lady Elizabeth Vere. Lord Burghley, a careful man, might have thought such fees wasted: as, indeed, they were. The young Earl did not respond. But later it was reported that he was courting, with too much familiarity, Mistress Elizabeth Vernon, a royal Maid of Honour and a relative of his dear friend the Earl of Essex. Like Shakespeare, Southampton was on his way to fatherhood before he was married.

At the end of August, 1598, a gossiping letter-writer, John Chamberlain, wrote:

.I came up from Oxfordshire to see the funeral. . . . Mistress Vernon is from the Court and lies in Essex House. Some say she hath taken a *venue* under the girdle and swells upon it; yet she complains not of foul play but says the Earl will justify it. *And it is bruited underhand that he was lately here four days in great secret of purpose to marry her and effected it accordingly.*

The funeral here mentioned was that of the great Burghley. Elizabeth, mourning her Elder Statesman, was in no mood to be merciful to the waywardness of youth. Southampton justified the rumours by marrying Mistress Vernon—their daughter was born legitimate rather over two months later. The Queen was furious at his conduct; being jealous for the honour of her Maids and dubious about any close friend of her sometimes darling, but often distrusted, Earl of Essex. Southampton had his first taste of royal rage and went to the Fleet Prison: but not for long. There was bad news from Ireland and Essex was soon in commission to ' bring rebellion broached on his sword ': keen young soldiers could not be wasted in the cells. So Southampton was released for the wars. His mother had just married for the third time, the new husband being Sir William Harvey.

We know of the adolescent Southampton that he was regarded by contemporaries as ' a little wild ': the young and wealthy Tudor nobles were spoiled children of fortune and the society of which Essex and Southampton were leaders was rich in flares of temper and of pride. They quarrelled amply while they slaked their ample thirst for living. South-ampton was handsome, generous, ambitious, a constant play-goer, devoted to ' masques and triumphs ': his epitaphs, thirty years later, stressed not only his zeal for sport and arms, but his ' acting all parts of goodnesse on the world's faire Stage ' (Pettie). Whether Shakespeare had Southampton in mind when he claimed, somewhat boldly, but in the end accurately, that his Sonnets would give their subject im-mortality, cannot be proved and has been much disputed. The Sonnet Mystery remains and will remain. Unless new facts are discovered, which is unlikely, there can be nothing but conjecture as to the persons and events behind these uneven but often superb outpourings of a spirit more often tormented than at peace.

Shakespeare's ' sugred Sonnets ' among his private friends were known to Meres in 1598, but they were not published until, eleven years later, one Thomas Thorpe, an adventurous bookseller, brought out his famous Quarto of 1609. This included a poem called *The Lover's Complaint*, which may or may not be Shakespeare's, and one or two Sonnets probably not his. The feature which has particularly baffled all subsequent scholarship and elicited endless conjecture is a prefatory note by the Publisher. The Sonnets were announced thus,

> Shake-speares Sonnets.   Never before Imprinted.
> At London.   By G. Eld for T. T. and are to be
> solde by John Wright, dwelling at Christ Church
> gate, 1609.

Prefixed by this dedication:

> To . the . Onlie . Begetter . of .
> These . Insving . Sonnets .
> Mr . W . H . All . Happinesse .
> and . that . Eternitie .
> Promised . by .
> Ovr . Ever-Living . Poet .
> Wisheth .
> The . Well-Wishing .
> Adventvrer . in .
> Setting .
> Forth .
>
> **T.T.**

Had the acquisitive Thorpe been more frankly communicative he would have spared the students of Shakespeare thousands of books and articles.

The Sonnets consist of twenty-five appeals to the handsome

young man to marry, a 'century' more in which the poet complains that the friend has played false with his (the poet's) mistress and that a rival poet is winning the friend's favour and admiration. Many are full of abstract meditation on the ravages of time and the nature of love. The writer is ashamed of his public position. But he later forgives, with rather surprising nonchalance, the friend's offence and even admits some guilt of his own. Finally, after the break at Number 126, which is not really a Sonnet but a dozen lines of rhymed verse, he applies himself to the Dark Lady who had been the cause of so much trouble and to musing upon the havoc wrought by lust in the affairs of men. These Dark Lady Sonnets have been brushed aside as 'a disordered appendix' to the larger body, but they voice intensely experienced suffering. The Lady, with her 'mourning' eyes of raven black, the Lady, 'black as hell, as dark as night,' is not to be elbowed aside. She has greater reality for the reader than the 'man right fair,' who is the poet's comfort. The finest sonnets do occur before No. 126. But some at least of the later 'Dark Lady' series burn fiercely and linger like embers in the mind.

Two of the Sonnets, 138 and 144 in the Quarto Edition, had already been printed and used by the printer Jaggard in a volume called *The Passionate Pilgrim* in 1599. The other 152 were now, in 1609, in type and on public view for the first time. It is noteworthy that only one edition was printed. Sonnet-sequences may then have passed their highest vogue, but since the day of Sidney they had been very successful, and one by so popular a hand as Sweet Mr. Shakespeare's would be expected to sell well and run through one printing after another, as his longer poems had done sixteen years earlier. It is reasonable to suspect disapproval and withdrawal of the book. For, after Thorpe's single printing, it was not to appear again until 1640 when J. Benson published an edition of these 'excellent and sweetly composed poems of Master William Shakespeare.' Benson said that they had lacked 'the due accommodation of proportionable glory' because of 'their infancie' in the poet's death and added that the lines would invite public 'allowance.' He further stated that the poems appeared ' of the same purity as the author himself then living avouched.' But the poet survived the printing of the Sonnets by nearly seven years, so there is little sense in attributing failure to his immediate death.

Plainly there is some smell of scandal here. The first edition is snuffed out—or at least kept small. Then the author has to avouch the ' purity ' of the poems. Purity of text ? Scarcely, for the Thorpe Quarto is not a good text, but full of difficulties. Purity of conduct ? Traducers could well have seized on the Sonnets, and have done so ever since, in order to suggest that the poet had loved Mr. W. H. more than wisely; that view is, I think, easily refuted, but it has strongly attracted those with a predisposition to think and feel in that way.

The whole affair has become so voluminous in research and, still more, in speculation, that it is quite impossible, within reasonable limits of space, to do more than summarise the various schools of opinion and trends of surmise. There is, in the first place, a fundamental dispute as to the meaning of Thorpe's words ' onlie begetter.' Mr. W. H. is so described, certainly: but what does that imply ? Was he then the object of the Sonnets, the lovely boy, or was he the man who ' begot ' the volume by somehow acquiring the manuscript ? Obviously if Mr. W. H. is the poet's beloved friend, then he must fulfil certain conditions. His initials, for example, must be or closely resemble W. H. He must have been a marriageable lad, unwilling to marry. He must have been the sole hope of his house, with his father dead. If, on the other hand, the ' onlie begetter ' was the purloiner or betrayer of the manuscript, then we have to look for somebody with those initials who might have done the job; after that the lovely boy can be looked for without regard to his name. But it seems strange to me, as it does to Chambers, that a dedication would use this phrase, ' onlie begetter,' of any but the subject, the author's friend. Would the ' all happinesse ' and the ' eternitie ' promised in the poems be desired for the book-broker and not the lovely boy ? Still, unlikeliness is not impossibility.

Let us start then with the possible W. H.'s of the first order. Henry Wriothesley seems the most obvious choice. But you have to stand his initials on their head to get that part of the puzzle right. And why should an Earl be reduced to a Mr. and his initials be turned round? Wriothesley, however, must stand in the forefront of probability, because of the indisputable dedications of the long poems. He was not only Shakespeare's patron but his friend in the 1590's when the Sonnets, or most of them, must have been written. (The *Lucrece* dedication is proof of that cordiality.) At the time of that gesture Southampton was twenty-two years old and the tone of the Sonnets is in tune with the dedication.

He was the only son of a great house and a handsome mother: his father was dead: he was being pressed to marry. He was the kind of youth to stir warm friendship in a poet and dramatist who was immensely responsive to beauty and to the élan of a radiant personality. He was ' a little wild ' and devoted to the world of poets and plays. He wore long curling locks, was fair, and esteemed handsome: tastes in appearance vary with the generations and many of the romantic heroes and heroines of the world of ancient glamour look ordinary and prosaic enough on canvas, Nell Gwynne, for example, and Bonnie Prince Charlie. So we need not be deterred by the rather foxy look of Southampton in the two Welbeck Abbey portraits, one of a white-coated youth, the other of a sombre-suited prisoner in the Tower. It is enough that the world of his time took him to be all April and May and that his poet found him more lovely than a summer day. All this fits in with the Sonnets.

The second strong candidate has the right initials, but several other things about him are wrong. He is Lord William Herbert, later Earl of Pembroke, one of the ' most noble and incomparable pair of brethren ' to whom Heminge and Condell dedicated the First Folio of Shakespeare's plays seven years after the poet's death. Their preface establishes the fact that William Herbert, Earl of Pembroke, as Lord Chamberlain, and his brother, Philip Herbert, Earl of Montgomery, as Gentleman of His Majestie's Bed Chamber, had ' prosecuted ' both plays and author with much favour. So, after pledging that the best had been done for the text, the editors ' humbly consecrate ' to these two ' the remains of your servant Shakespeare.'

Pembroke, then, like Southampton, had shown warm favour, but his, of course, was later. It has been remarked as odd that Southampton, who had received cordial dedications from the poet's own hand, did not get the honour of the Folio dedication from its editors. But more than twenty years had elapsed, Shakespeare himself was dead, and the theatre-men would naturally turn to the Lord Chamberlain as protector and patron of the King's Men in particular. There are strong points against Pembroke's claim: the dates are difficult: he was only fifteen in 1595. He was not the sole hope of his great house, having both a father and a brother: he was not an owner of long, fair locks, comparable to marjoram, but dark of hue.

Those who read the preface to Bernard Shaw's *The Dark Lady of the Sonnets* are introduced to the strange, goitred presence of one Thomas Tyler, who from a desk in the British Museum reading-room, promulgated the once fashionable theory that Pembroke stole a wanton lady of the court called Mistress Mary Fitton from Shakespeare's embraces: Pembroke is thus the Man, M. F. is the Dark Lady and the Sonnets are explained. That makes a nice simple pattern. But since the Sonnets were out and about among ' private friends ' before Meres wrote of them in 1598, then William Herbert cannot be the man. He was born in 1580 and did not come to London till 1598. Moreover, it has since been inconveniently discovered that Mistress Fitton had light-brown hair and grey eyes; if the Sonnets assert anything it is the ebon colour of the lady's eyes and hair. The pitch-black orbs are unforgettably described.

Then there is the casting of the Man as Willie Hughes, a supposed actor; a real ship's cook of that name was found by Samuel Butler, but a ship's cook seems an odd target for the reverential tone of some of the Sonnets. The name of Hughes appealed both to Butler and to Oscar Wilde, as

well as to others, because of a punning line in the famous
Sonnet 20,

> A woman's face, with Nature's own hand painted,
> Hast thou, the master-mistress of my passion,
> A woman's gentle heart, but not acquainted
> With shifting change, as is false women's fashion;
> An eye more bright than theirs, less false in rolling,
> Gilding the object whereupon it gazeth;
> A man in hew all *Hews* in his controlling,
> Which steals men's eyes, and women's souls amazeth.
> And for a woman wert thou first created;
> Till Nature, as she wrought thee, fell a-doting,
> And by addition me of thee defeated,
> By adding one thing to my purpose nothing.
> But since she prickt thee out for women's pleasure,
> Mine be thy love, and thy love's use their treasure.

Of course this kind of pun on names and words is Shakespearean and the Sonnets themselves pun on the name-word
Will on several occasions. But all the seventh line need mean
was that the lovely boy was in the habit of flushing and changing
colour very easily. This quick change of colour in the face is a
quality of which Shakespeare spoke frequently, so much so
that Dr. Caroline Spurgeon has suggested, in a passage already
quoted, that he himself was quick to flush and blush. It seems
likely, on the evidence of this Sonnet, that Mr. W. H. was the
owner of that volatility of tint. The fact that Hews was printed
in italics in Thorpe's Quarto proves nothing, for italics occur, for
no obvious reason, more than twenty times in the short volume.
There is no trace in any records of any actor or boy-player
called Will or Willie Hughes.

So now we turn back to the supposition that the 'onlie
begetter' means procurer of the manuscript. As I said, this
does not seem to be a likely usage, especially as it is linked
with extravagant promises of 'eternitie.' On the other hand
there is a likely candidate for office in William Harvey;
admittedly he was *Sir* William Harvey, in 1609, but at least
he was not an Earl who has been degraded to 'Mr' in the

ever-baffling note by Thorpe. If anybody is coming down to ' Mr ' it might be a knight who had been one in his youth, not an Earl who had previously been a Lord. Mrs. Carmichael Stopes has put the point plainly.

There is no objection in the use of ' *Mr* W. H.' ' Sir ' was not a title in the same way as Earl or Baron. Lady Southampton always called her husbands in correspondence, ' Master Heneage,' and ' Master Harvey,' though both of them were knights. The late Dr Furnivall was argued into agreeing that though the Harvey theory was not absolutely certified, it was the best which had ever appeared.

There has also been hunted out a William Hall, a relative of Shakespeare's son-in-law, Dr. Hall, who acted as a printer and literary jobber in London. It has even been argued that the words ' Mr. W. H. All Happinesse ' include a pun on his name. Of these two I prefer Harvey, a man of literary as well as military interests, who became Lady Southampton's third husband and would certainly have looked with curiosity and pleasure through the family papers and so might have found the Sonnets to his step son; he might also have judged that the Sonnets were too good to be lost to the world, in which case we are all very much in his debt for taking them to the printers. Lady Southampton had died in 1607, leaving ' the most part of her stuff ' to her husband: in one way or another he must have known about the Sonnets and wondered whether their secrecy need be longer kept. William Hall may have got them from Shakespeare or, more probably, Harvey may have got them from the Southamptons. The possibility has been suggested by Mr. Walter Thomson that W. H. stands for William and Henry (i.e. Shakespeare and Wriothesley). Some of the Sonnets, he urges, are Southampton's replies to the appeals and occasionally to the scoldings of his friend and protégé. This notion he backs by quotations from the mysterious, metaphysical, and supposedly Shakespearean poem *The Phoenix and the Turtle*, which he relates to Southampton.

So they loved as love in twain,
Had the essence but in one,
Two distincts, division none,
Number there in love was slain.

Property was thus appalled,
That the self was not the same:
Single nature's double name,
Neither two nor one was called.

Reason in itself confounded,
Saw division grow together,
To themselves yet either neither,
Simple were so well compounded.

Hence the telescoping of the ' onlie begetters,' William and Henry, into Mr. W. H. It is a fanciful but just tenable theory.

It is, I think, indisputable that some of the Sonnets are more intelligible if taken as replies, especially if we find that the feebler in style—and there are a number of poor Sonnets—may be the answers. Take, for example, No. 77, typically Shakespearean with its emphasis on ' Time's thievish progress ' and the ' dial's shady stealth.' It obviously accompanies the present of a diary or a commonplace book which the recipient is to fill with his reflections or jottings.

Thy glass will show thee how thy beauties wear,
Thy dial how thy precious minutes waste;
The vacant leaves thy mind's imprint will bear,
And of this book this learning mayst thou taste.

Thomson sets beside this No. 122, in which the writer excuses himself for having given away a book of ' tables ' recently sent to him, because he had no need of them. It is a poor, limping Sonnet and might very well have been written by someone seeking to sustain the idiom of the Sonnet correspondence but lacking the full power to do so.

It will be evident by now that to reading about the Sonnets there is no end: nor, of course, can there be any end to speculation either. In an effort to see Shakespeare's career as a whole, and that within some reasonable limits of space, there is room only to summarise the suggestions and the arguments. The reader's best course is simply to read: to read, that is, the Sonnets themselves and to read them as though he or she had heard nothing of them previously. It will surely be decided that the Sonnets are varied in quality, ranging from the perfect to the trivial: that they are often obscure, alluding to matters of of which we have, and can have, no full cognisance: and that they are intensely personal. It has been argued that they are formal essays in a convention of amorous and tributary writing, which had its own common currency of sonneteering phrase ' and conceit. But that seems to me a view wholly incredible. The best of the Sonnets are pulsing with passions of affection, devotion, resentment, despair, even loathing. The author has taken Sidney's advice to look in his heart and write. Here is no prize competition for a Tudor 'Newdigate,' no verbal trifling for the pleasing of a lord.

It has been contended that Shakespeare's affection for the lovely boy outsteps propriety. That, I think, is no more than wishful thinking on the part of those who reject conventional sexual morality. Sonnet No. 20, already quoted, certainly has an opening couplet which may be called self-accusation, even self-condemnation. But when it is remarked that the word passion could mean—and often did mean—to an Elizabethan no more than an emotional poem, the line is less remarkable. Such passions were a literary vogue of the time; Shakespeare gives the word quite lightly in *A Midsummer Night's Dream* to Duke Theseus when he alludes to the passion or love-story of Pyramus and Thisbe. In any case the final lines of this Sonnet are an explicit denial of guilt. The affirmation is crystal-clear. Shakespeare is devoted, in all innocence, to a friend, who is much sought after by women: so much so, indeed, that one of those women made him play the poet false. That is all that can be gathered from the poet's own assertion. So those who, like Hallam, are embarrassed by this performance of a genius who has become a national hero and, to preserve his good name, wish the Sonnets had never been written, are needlessly disturbed.

We live in an age when it is unusual and impolitic to express intense emotion in describing masculine friendship: Shakespeare was under less restraint. His period did not make it prudent to smother his praises of the patron, the lovely boy, who had enriched his life and enabled his talents to be shown. Who this was, we may not with confidence say. My own guess is that Mr. W. H. is Sir William Harvey, Southampton's stepfather, who procured the MSS., and that the lovely boy is not W.H., but the young Earl of Southampton. If Harvey accounts for the initials, there is no need to stand Henry Wriothesley on his head. There are fewer difficulties in accepting this explanation than in crediting any other of the countless conjectures.

Whatever the factual solution of the 'Mr. W. H.' problem may be, the Sonnets are an incomparable outpouring of emotion. Moreover they have the unique quality of personal statement: Thorpe probably did not have the poet's own *imprimatur*, but the very fact that the lines were written for privacy gives them a particular fascination and importance. In his plays Shakespeare may or may not be speaking his own mind through his characters: in many of his Sonnets he speaks, as nowhere else, for himself, vehemently, masterfully, frankly.

What emerges most clearly is, as in the two long poems, the total dedication to beauty of a nature quickly responsive to every line, hue, and harmony that takes the sense. The poet thrills to each petal of ' Beauty's Rose '; but leaves must fall, so he laments the transience of things. Again and again he rails at Time, whose cold hand touches all fresh and vivid growth. While he glories now in the rich spectacle of young manhood, he none the less sees that Life is defiled by its own excess, which is Age, just as Love is defiled by its own corruption, which is Lust. The lovely boy, the ' man right fair ' is the symbol of life and loveliness: he is Beauty's Rose, pattern of that flower to praise whose hue in language worthy of its splendour was the poet's special faculty and pleasure. (The word hue often recurs, but I cannot accept it as a pun on the name Hugh or Hew as it was then spelled.) The ' woman colour'd ill ' has, in the poet's eye, let her own heritage of beauty become stained by that overplus of loving, that decay of sensuous ecstasy into sensual excess which is Lust. And Lust becomes for Shakespeare a personal monster, ' murd'rous, bloody, full of blame.' That anybody should find the Sonnets immoral is astounding. The garland of their sentiments could be hung in the most austere of Puritan chapels, where the other garland of their verbal graces might certainly do good.

The value of the Sonnets is uneven and that has encouraged commentators to allot the failures to other hands; but genius can nod and Shakespeare's genius was still young and experimental. In any case he nodded sufficiently later on; who would expect *All's Well That Ends Well* from Mr. W. S. at the height of his power ? He was never a man for constancy of form. Accordingly we meet in the Sonnets what may be sighed over as sadly mawkish alongside what is undeniably magnificent. Let us take, for example, No. 97 in the Quarto:

> How like a winter hath my absence been
> From thee, the pleasure of the fleeting year!
> What freezings have I felt, what dark days seen!
> What old December's bareness every where!
> And yet this time remov'd was summer's time;
> The teeming autumn, big with rich increase,
> Bearing the wanton burden of the prime,
> Like widow'd wombs after their lords' decease:
> Yet this abundant issue seem'd to me
> But hope of orphans and unfather'd fruit;
> For summer and his pleasures wait on thee,
> And, thou away, the very birds are mute;
>   Or, if they sing, 'tis with so full a cheer,
>   That leaves look pale, dreading the winter's near.

And this follows, No. 98.

> From you have I been absent in the spring,
> When proud-pied April, drest in all his trim,
> Hath put a spirit of youth in every thing,
> That heavy Saturn laught and leapt with him.
> Yet nor the lays of birds, nor the sweet smell
> Of different flowers in odour and in hue,

Could make me any summer's story tell,
Or from their proud lap pluck them where they grew:
Nor did I wonder at the lily's white,
Nor praise the deep vermilion in the rose;
They were but sweet, but figures of delight,
Drawn after you,—you pattern of all those.
    Yet seem'd it winter still, and, you away,
    As with your shadow I with these did play.

They are flattering: but they are fine.   Dignity is not lost in
the comparison of the poet's adoration of the lovely boy with
the emotions called up by natural beauty.   They contain lines
that are simple, and tremendous.

        Nor did I wonder at the lily's white,
        Nor praise the deep vermilion in the rose.

There is a typically Shakespearean couplet; he instinctively
but not obtrusively practises the alliteration W—L—W and
turns back to L in vermilion: then comes the majestic roll of
' rose ' at the finish.   It was the kind of trick that Shakespeare
was to go on playing—no doubt unconsciously—for the rest
of his life.   In the Sonnets there is early and delicious taste of it.
  Then turn to 99:

    The forward violet thus did I chide:
    Sweet thief, whence didst thou steal thy sweet that smells,
    If not from my love's breath ?   The purple pride
    Which on thy soft cheek for complexion dwells
    In my love's veins thou hast too grossly dyed.
    The lily I condemnèd for thy hand;
    And buds of marjoram had stoln thy hair:
    The roses fearfully on thorns did stand,
    One blushing shame, another white despair;
    A third, nor red nor white, had stoln of both,
    And to his robbery had annext thy breath;
    But, for his theft, in pride of all his growth
    A vengeful canker eat him up to death.
        More flow'rs I noted, yet I none could see
        But sweet or colour it had stoln from thee.

The sentimental conceit that the flowers have stolen all their beauty and fragrance from the boy is tiresome and sickly: there is no memorable line. (But the Southamptonites, viewing their hero's locks in the early portrait, can throw in marjoram as an argument on their side.) The common trouble about deep affection between susceptible young men is not corruption of morals. It is corruption of taste. How could the author of No. 116, beginning

> Let me not to the marriage of true minds
> Admit impediments. Love is not love
> Which alters when it alteration finds,
> Or bends with the remover to remove:

have stooped to this rubbish about the violet purloining a young man's breath! The answer is that, as Ophelia said of another matter, young men will do it.

The Sonnets are rarely a source of strikingly original opinion or emotion. But thought and feeling, at least in the best of them, have been delivered with such vehemence of spirit as well with such virtuosity of phrase that the reader, mystery or no mystery, must hang on every line, rapt by the splendour of the words and music. A volume which contained only Nos. 18, 87, 94, 97, 98, 116 and 129 would stand on the peak of English poetry.

It is surely idle to worry overmuch about the identity of the persons: it is enough that they were cause of writing which raises language to a higher power: if Southampton was indeed the fountain of this noble torrent, the more blessed he. But we need not rack our brains over the problem of identification in order to enjoy the magnificent result. George Saintsbury put it thus. Of the theories about the characters,

> None is proved: and for the literary purpose, none is really important. What is important is that Shakespeare has here caught up the sum of love and uttered it as no poet has before or since, and that in so doing he carried poetry—that is to say, the passionate expression in verse of the sensual and intel-

lectual facts of life—to a pitch which it had never previously reached in English, and which it has never outstepped since. The coast line of humanity must be wholly altered, the sea must change its nature, the moon must draw it in different ways, before that tidemark is passed.

People will never cease to argue about the Sonnet Story: but, as a verdict on the poetry, Saintsbury's words are final.

CHAPTER X

'Woman Colour'd Ill'

S O, for a while, we may leave the lovely boy, a glow-worm presence in a night of conjecture. With the Sonnets he passes out of Shakespeare's work, having played his part, which was to enrich English poetry for all time. The 'man right fair,' if he be Southampton, disappears, after 1598, into politics, conspiracy, the fatal association with Essex, and the Tower. But there was also she, the dark woman, with whom the fair man played Shakespeare false. It is not plain whether he was supposed to have seduced her or she him. Sonnet 144 says the latter: but that was written before Shakespeare was certain of the victory.

> Two loves I have of comfort and despair,
> Which like two spirits do suggest me still:
> The better angel is a man right fair,
> The worser spirit a woman colour'd ill.
> To win me soon to hell, my female evil
> Tempteth my better angel from my side,
> And would corrupt my saint to be a devil,
> Wooing his purity with her foul pride.
> And whether that my angel be turn'd fiend
> Suspect I may, yet not directly tell;
> But being both from me, both to each friend,
> I guess one angel in another's hell:
>   Yet this shall I ne'er know, but live in doubt,
>   Till my bad angel fire my good one out.

On the other hand Sonnets 40 and 42 suggest that Shakespeare is forgiving the man who took the woman.

But whereas the man seems to fade out of Shakespeare's affection and resentment, the woman does not. She is there, in his heart's core, certainly until he had written *Troilus and Cressida*, *Timon of Athens*, and *Antony and Cleopatra*. For years the Dark Lady, in my opinion, kept him on edge, a figure adored and loathed, a memory that shone and scorched and tormented. It is fashionable now to dismiss the Dark Lady with a smile. Is she not half a century out of date among the myriad Shakespeare fancies?

Bernard Shaw's preface to his one-act jest, *The Dark Lady of the Sonnets*, has given a certain immortality to Thomas Tyler, that top-hatted, frock-coated frequenter of the British Museum reading-room, the misshapen scholar with whom G. B. S. struck up a cordial acquaintance and discussed not only Shakespeare but the Higher Pessimism. Tyler cosseted a prodigious gloom about the fate of man; it seems odd now that even one so physically plagued as Tyler was should have been so sorry for us all in that period of plenty and security. Tyler fell under the baleful fascination of Mistress Mary Fitton, whom he chased as far as her tomb in Cheshire. Shaw reviewed Tyler's book on the Sonnets, which identified Pembroke and Fitton as the ' man right fair ' and ' woman colour'd ill ' in the *Pall Mall Gazette* of January 7, 1886. This, Shaw thinks, introduced Mary Fitton to Frank Harris, who wrote a play about that charmer and subsequently made her a principal character in his book on *The Man Shakespeare and His Tragic Life Story*. Harris, in short, became a leading Public Relations Officer for the Earl of Pembroke and a very voluble Chairman of the Old Fittonians. When Harris espoused a cause it was his and nobody else's. Shaw pointed out that the ' onlie begetter ' of this theory was Tyler. The G. B. S. Preface reminds us of that.

Therefore I make it clear that I had and have personal reasons for remembering Tyler, and for regarding myself as in some sort charged with the duty of reminding the world of his work. I am sorry for his sake that Mary's portrait is fair, and that Mr W. H. has veered round again from Pembroke to Southampton; but even so his work was not wasted: it is by exhausting all the hypotheses that we reach the verifiable one: and after all, the wrong road always leads somewhere.

So there, as they say, the matter rests. Pembroke, in the role of Mr. W. H., is out of favour: the dates are against him and so are some of the qualities attributed in the Sonnets, such as lack of father and brother. But while Southampton has tended to take his place, there is no new name put forward for the Dark Lady. Mistress Fitton goes out with her known lover, Pembroke. And no one else is cited.

But she is there, Lady Anon, indubitably there. She is, as I said, out of fashion and criticism now tends to pass her by as Frank Harris's fad. Nobody can deny that Harris was a vulgar and a wayward 'card.' But he was also—I would add—a man with singular flair for a good thing. The *Saturday Review* under his editorship had G. B. S. as dramatic critic and later on ' the spritely, the incomparable Max.' It is useless to pretend, after this piece of evidence in his favour, that Harris was no more than a flamboyant bounder.

I was myself introduced to Shakespeare by Harris's book, to which in turn I had been brought by Arnold Bennett. Like most schoolboys I had been sickened of Shakespeare by education. I was wearied almost to revolt by this examination business of commenting and annotating. All too well did I know and was able to repeat on paper what the Rialto was: I could define an argosy to any teacher's delight and could be profound about Arden, Ducdame, and the Symbolic value of Ariel and Caliban. Hour after hour I had estimated Significances, contrasted Characters, explained Allusions. By the age of eighteen I was allergic to Shakespeare almost beyond hope of therapy.

But cure did come. It came by way of a weekly paper called *The New Age* in which, under the signature of Jacob Tonson, Arnold Bennett commented on books of the day with a frankness and liveliness unusual at the time. When Harris's book appeared in 1909 Bennett cried its merits high. It was praised as an admirable alternative to Dry-as-dust and the professional or pedagogue's Shakespeare of those days who ' out-topp'd knowledge ' and bored young people into a total hatred of ' Eng. Lit.' Fortunately we have improved our instruction in Shakespeare: some teachers of ' Eng. Lit.' are now discovered working in

theatres and producing his plays with gusto and with excellent
results.

Harris's point was that Shakespeare was neither perfect
ratepayer nor dreary, correct, impersonal genius. He was a
man of like passions with ourselves who declared his frailties in
his plays, his melancholy, his sex-hunger, his infatuation for
Mary Fitton, his remorse, and his tendency to expose a broken
heart and blubber all over the place. Harris, being essentially
an excessive man, as his personal use of jewellery showed, was
excessive in his notion of Shakespeare as an outsize among
inspired cry-babies. Shaw, naturally, retorts to this.

Frank conceives Shakespear to have been a broken-hearted,
melancholy, enormously sentimental person, whereas I am
convinced that he was very like himself; in fact, if I had been
born in 1556 instead of in 1856, I should have taken to blank
verse and given Shakespear a harder run for his money than
all the other Elizabethans put together. Yet the success of
Frank Harris's book on Shakespear gave me great delight.

It also delighted Bennett-Tonson and a completely unimportant
student-reader, myself. Here, at last, was a Shakespeare in
whom I could begin to believe. After the Droeshout portrait
and the Stratford Church bust, after the life by Sir Sidney Lee
and all the solemn buzz-buzz of the Victorian scholars, here was
neither a prosperous careerist nor a great mind condescending
to write plays. Here was a credible, likeable man. Here too
was his weakness, here both the flame of his heart and the kindler
of some magnificent passages, a Dark Lady who haunted him
from *Love's Labour's Lost* and the Sonnets to the last superb,
breath-taking scene of *Antony and Cleopatra*, whose ' lass unparallel'd ' is her finest and her final portrait.

Shaw, who knew Harris well and has always retained the
proper loyalty of a contributor to an editor who has given him
space and liberty, wrote of his ' range of sympathy and understanding that extends from the ribaldry of a buccaneer to the
shyest tenderness of the most exquisite poetry.' He thus

justified, fairly, Harris's right to speak about Shakespeare. One must be, at least to some extent, a fellow-traveller of the scamps and the sensualists to be a complete Shakespearean—and how many of the learned have been that?

Where so much is uncertain, two things in Shakespeare's life were unquestionably set down in writing by himself, his dedications to Southampton and his descriptions of the Dark Lady. The latter occur both in the Sonnets and the Plays and we must, inevitably, I think, agree that the same charming and cruel one is being described in both. These descriptions of hair, eyes, and habits are the more remarkable because Shakespeare did not as a rule give particulars of his characters. We know sometimes that they were small or large, bearded or unbearded. Master Slender in *The Merry Wives of Windsor* has ' a little wee face with a little yellow beard, a cane-coloured beard.' Sir Andrew Aguecheek's hair hangs ' like flax on a distaff.' Hotspur's speech is thick: Maria is very small: and so forth. But these are single and occasional details. In the case of the ' woman colour'd ill ' there is a definite and recurring delineation unique in Shakespeare's writing.

The first of the Dark Lady Sonnets (127) proclaims her. The eyes of his mistress, the poet proclaims, are ' raven black ' and seem like mourners. In Sonnet 130 her hair is likened to black wire—this is a sonnet of derisive insult and the Lady is even accused of halitosis. But we must remember that breath was one of Shakespeare's obsessions. To an intensely sensitive man the grease, sweat, and heavy breathing of the Elizabethan mob were a continual offence, and the ladies and gentlemen did not escape his censure when they displayed like symptoms of uncleanliness; they had the less excuse.

Again in Sonnet 132 he reverts to the fascination of those eyes, and to the dominion of the colour black: this was an unconventional opinion at the time, since Queen Elizabeth had put fair, which included red, into fashion.

> Thine eyes I love, and they, as pitying me,
> Knowing thy heart torments me with disdain,
> Have put on black, and loving mourners be,

Looking with pretty ruth upon my pain.
And truly not the morning sun of heaven
Better becomes the gray cheeks of the east,
Nor that full star that ushers in the even
Doth half that glory to the sober west,
As those two mourning eyes become thy face:
O, let it, then, as well beseem thy heart
To mourn for me, since mourning doth thee grace,
And suit thy pity like in every part.
    Then will I swear Beauty herself is black,
    And all they foul that thy complexion lack.

In Sonnet 137 he attacks the dark one's freedom and licence
of conduct. She is shameless in her relations with men; she
is ' the bay where all men ride ' and ' the wide world's common
place.' In the immediately following Sonnets there is more
talk of her eyes, her painted lips, her tuneful tongue, her base
touches inviting to a sensual feast. In No. 147 the poet's own
infatuation is a fever past cure; he is ' frantic-mad with ever-
more unrest.'

    For I have sworn thee fair, and thought thee bright,
    Who art as black as hell, as dark as night.

The Sonnets, in short, give a precise picture of a pale-skinned,
red-lipped, black-haired woman, with eyes of gleaming black,
witty, fond of music, alluring, maddening, magical, utterly
wanton. She has broken her ' bed-vow ' with her husband and
betrays lovers no less lightly. The later Sonnets were mostly
written in resentment and in contrite loathing of the weakness
that enslaves men and keeps them vassals to such ' daughters
of the game.' No. 129 drives into the very heart of a lover's
self-contempt.

    The expense of spirit in a waste of shame
    Is lust in action; and till action, lust
    Is perjur'd, murd'rous, bloody, full of blame,
    Savage, extreme, rude, cruel, not to trust;
    Enjoy'd no sooner but despisèd straight;

Past reason hunted; and no sooner had,
Past reason hated, as a swallow'd bait,
On purpose laid to make the taker mad:
Mad in pursuit, and in possession so;
Had, having, and in quest to have, extreme;
A bliss in proof, and prov'd, a very woe;
Before, a joy propos'd; behind, a dream.
  All this the world well knows; yet none knows well
  To shun the heaven that leads men to this hell.

With that picture in mind let us turn to the plays.

Frank Harris, who owed much to the Danish scholar Georg Brandes, has traced the Dark Lady's image as it appears and reappears, gleaming and merciless, under various names. It is indeed astonishing how clearly She of the Sonnets re-emerges, feature by feature, in *Romeo and Juliet*. She is, of course, not Juliet; she is Romeo's first and never seen but closely pictured love, Rosaline. The word madness is soon upon his lip. True, she is holding Romeo off at first on plea of chastity, a habit common enough in feminine tormentors. So she maddens her man. Mercutio uses the following adjectives and phrases to describe this Rosaline. ' She has Dian's wit.' Then

I conjure thee by Rosaline's bright eyes,
By her high forehead and her scarlet lip,
By her fine foot, straight leg, and quivering thigh.

He next indulges in considerable grossness of wit; Mercutio evidently does not take Rosaline's chastity very seriously. Later he condoles with ' poor Romeo . „ . stabb'd with a white wench's black eye, shot through the ear with a love-song.'

Ah that same pale, hard-hearted wench, that Rosaline,
Torments him so that he will sure run mad.

There is no good reason for this little flow of detail, no dramatic cause for recording the facial items, the pallor, the high fore-head, the jet-black eyes, the alluring foot (we shall meet

that foot again in Cressida). The only explanation is that
Shakespeare was himself haunted by such a mask. Rosaline
never enters the play and soon fades from the mind of the
audience; Romeo has to be the sad hero of another and a
larger romance. It is the more astonishing, therefore, that
Rosaline, who is nothing in the story compared with Juliet,
should be drawn with such definition, almost with a catalogue
of features. ' Stabb'd with a white wench's black eye.' That
is not only the very language of the Sonnets, it is the very
Lady.

When we turn to *Love's Labour's Lost* the same vision of
black-and-white astonishingly reappears, as it were a half-
timbered cottage gleaming with its magpie brilliance across a
sunny landscape in Mistress Fitton's own beautiful corner of
Cheshire. The dating of the Sonnets, *Romeo and Juliet*, and
Love's Labour's Lost can be infinitely disputed. Various Sonnets
have been attributed to any and every year between 1588 and
1608. I have assumed them to be mainly work of the early
1590's. The two plays are both on Meres's list and therefore
were written before 1598. *Love's Labour's Lost* is generally
supposed to have been an early play, redrafted for publication
in 1598. *Romeo and Juliet*, the first tragedy, is generally assigned
to 1595 or thereabouts. The exact years do not concern us.
What is evident is that from three types of work of this ' pre-
Meres ' period, a tragedy, a courtly comedy, and the Dark
Lady Sonnets, the same pair of eyes looks out, the ebon-dark,
pitch-ball 'mourners' which Shakespeare could never escape.
I can hear in advance a complaining murmur that this is a
sentimental, melodramatic, Frank-Harrisian, unscholarly view
to hold. But the words of Shakespeare are there to read, and
Frank Harris, though he was always ready to overplay his hand
and over-write a case, was this time, assisted by Brandes,
Tyler, and possibly others, incontestably ' on to something.'

Surely it is remarkable that the same name of Rosaline, the
same white face, the same black eyes, should suddenly move
from Verona to Navarre—or *vice versa* according to the dates
of the two plays' composition. We have seen her in Italy:
now she bobs up, sparkling as ever, in France. *Love's Labour's*

Lost is a highly artificial comedy, its iambics interspersed with Sonnets, its country humours of the English village mingled with the punning ripostes and equivocal conceits so dear to the young Tudor milords. Much of it now is difficult for us and too allusive to be widely popular. It has to be produced with the fantastic graces of a ballet-masque to be attractive. But it is especially interesting as containing a self-portrait of the poet in the character of Berowne, one of the young lords who hastily forswears for study's sake the society of women, and, having sworn in haste, repents with no less speed. He is described there, by no other than Rosaline, a dark-eyed beauty, one of three attending the Princess of France.

> Berowne they call him; but a merrier man,
> Within the limit of becoming mirth,
> I never spent an hour's talk withal:
> His eye begets occasion for his wit;
> For every object that the one doth catch,
> The other turns to a mirth-moving jest,
> Which his fair tongue—conceit's expositor—
> Delivers in such apt and gracious words,
> That aged ears play truant at his tales,
> And younger hearings are quite ravished;
> So sweet and voluble is his discourse.

Shakespeare, whose Sonnets boasted the ability of his ' powerful rhyme ' to confer immortality and outlive marble and the gilded monuments of princes, did not suffer from excess of modesty. As Shaw puts it,

The timid cough of the minor poet was never heard from him.

He had a good conceit of himself and this picture of Berowne not only would gratify the self-painter but exactly fits in with all the contemporary tributes to Sweet Mr. Shakespeare, affable, well-spoken, and quick in writing, and with Aubrey's attribution of ' prodigious Witt.'

This witty, all-compelling charmer Shakespeare-Berowne is immediately engaged in flirtatious combat with Rosaline. It is not the kind of combat we relish nowadays because it is full of tricks of speech particular to the wits of that epoch. Their world is very much of the Sonnets—this play, as I said, has Sonneteering embedded in the text—and Frank Harris justifiably drew attention to the reply made by the courtier Boyet to Berowne's question whether Rosaline is wedded or no. ' To her will or so,' comes the answer, and it is a singularly pointless answer unless there is a pun on the name Will. Married to her own resolve? Why say it unless there is a link with Sonnets 135 and 136 with their elaborate punning on Shakespeare's first and familiar Christian name? Of course the Dark Lady was not wedded to Will; but she may well have described their partnership with a light evasion by describing her own state as being wedded ' or so.'

Then comes the most curious part of the whole very curious characterisation of Rosaline. The three girls attending on the Princess of France are presumably such nice and attractive young persons as would naturally grace an artificial comedy and take the fancy, even the hearts, of young men deliberately and vainly pretending to hold off. But suddenly Berowne announces that she is ' the worst ' of the Princess's trio and that she is perjured and wanton; then he adds that vivid, almost livid description which links her, beyond any possibility of doubt, with the other Rosaline and with Her of the Sonnets.

> A whitely wanton with a velvet brow,
> With two pitch-balls stuck in her face for eyes;
> Ay, and, by Heaven, one that will do the deed,
> Though Argus were her eunuch and her guard:
> And I to sigh for her! to watch for her!
> To pray for her! Go to; it is a plague
> That Cupid will impose for my neglect
> Of his almighty dreadful little might.

These few lines might have come straight out of *Troilus and Cressida*, when, in the depths of his embitterment, Shakespeare is raging and snarling at that frailty of women which turns them into ' sluttish spoils of opportunity.' Why should Berowne know so much about the wantonness of Rosaline?

He had ' danced with her in Brabant once,' but there is no evidence of further knowledge. Yet suddenly he breaks out with this vicious condemnation of Rosaline as being one who would somehow escape the hundred eyes of Argus if there were a chance of a man and of misconduct in the offing. This violent insult he combines with another reference to whiteness of skin and blackness of eyes. There is no dramatic need for this description and Harris is well justified in his comment. (He uses the spelling Biron for Berowne.)

It is, of course, a blot upon the play for Biron to declare that his love is a wanton of the worst. It is not merely unexpected and uncalled-for; it diminishes our sympathy with Biron and his love, and also with the play. But we have already found the rule trustworthy that whenever Shakespeare makes a mistake in art it is because of some strong personal feeling and not for want of wit, and this rule evidently holds good here. Shakespeare-Biron is picturing the woman he himself loves; for not only does he describe her as a wanton to the detriment of the play; but he pictures her precisely, and this Rosaline is the only person in the play of whom we have any physical description at all.

It could be argued that there was a boy-player with eyes like sloes set in a parchment face and that the lines were written in for him. But that will not make sense. Rosaline is an unacted and unseen character in *Romeo and Juliet* and the Dark Lady of the Sonnets is, of course, unseen too. The boy-player can have nothing to do with the pitch-ball eyes, the whitely brow, the wantonness, which are common to them all. Shakespeare was here writing from a passion-ghosted memory or after a recent half-blissful, half-tormented anchorage in a ' bay where all men ride.'

The Dark Lady makes later and obvious reappearances. She is both person and symbol. At the turn of the century, on the evidence of the plays written about or after 1600, Shakespeare began to be acutely disgusted by sex: the expense of spirit in a waste of shame obsessed his mind as it worked on the great tragedies. Such disgust is naturally accompanied by a morbid fascination. Lust is like an ulcerous sore: that is a recurrent theme of the Middle Period plays. Woman, whose name is frailty, both provokes and feeds the pestilence: the infection has seized the poet; he must contemplate what he loathes, rail and rail again at what he would most gladly forget and overlook.

There is the case of Hamlet,

> The expectancy and rose of the fair State,
> The glass of fashion and the mould of form.

Might not we expect from such an one an example of clean speaking and good manners ? Yet Hamlet is intermittently and unpardonably coarse, and in his interview with his mother he harps with quite unnecessary force and crudity on the physical details of her offence. There are times in the play when one feels that Hamlet is more distressed by his mother's sensual surrender to the ' bloat king ' and his ' reechy kisses ' enjoyed ' in the rank sweat of an enseam'd bed ' than by the murder of his father.

When mocking and taunting Ophelia he delivers the famous attack on women,

> I have heard of your paintings too, well enough; God has given you one face, and you make yourselves another: you jig, you amble, and you lisp, and nickname God's creatures, and make your wantonness your ignorance. Go to, I'll no more on 't; it hath made me mad. I say, we will have no more marriages: those that are married already, all but one, shall live; the rest shall keep as they are. To a nunnery, go.

Why these particulars ? Women do not habitually jig, amble, and lisp or nickname God's creatures. (Jig, it is true, is on Hamlet's mind. He grumbles at Polonius's senile-puerile taste in entertainment. ' He's for a jig or a tale of bawdry or he sleeps.' He is out of temper with the theatrical practice of the time, as he shows in his rebuke of the too robustious tragedian and the gagging clowns. There was habitually a jig at the end of a Tudor tragedy and the man who had just written the world's masterpiece in this kind might reasonably feel sore with the sequel. When Hamlet has said ' The rest is silence ' the taborers will strike up and the drolls start their antics and their jigs. A little later he exclaims, ' Oh God, your only jig-maker! '—for no very good reason except that jigs were ' biting ' him.)

But, apart from this general dislike of jiggery, it is surely plain that Hamlet has some special woman in mind, a wanton, with special tricks of speech, with a habit of using mocking names, and with a tendency to some kind of fidgety or skipping gait.

Now, of Shakespeare's Cressida, a creation of the same period and a notorious example of fascination, frailty, and treachery, there are some physical details. She is ' fair Cressid,' but the adjective does not apply to colour apparently, for her hair is later described as something darker than Helen's: she herself calls it ' bright ' (IV, i), which might refer to any gleaming tint, from ebon to platinum. Troilus praises especially the whiteness of her hand and her ' gait.' Does she jig and amble ? One might not think so until the wicked old love-broker Pandarus meets ' the giddy expectation ' of Troilus with the odd statement that

She's making her ready, she'll come straight: you must be witty now. She does so blush, and fetches her wind so short, as if she were fray'd with a sprite: I'll fetch her. It is the prettiest villain: she fetches her breath as short as a new-ta'en sparrow.

Twice comes that emphasis on shortness of wind. Young people do not pant like this unless they suffer from asthma or have been running, dancing, or jigging. And it is part of Troilus's jealous complaint that he cannot dance, while the Grecians, who are skilled heelers of ' the high lavolt,' can. This nimbleness, this alacrity in jigging, is on his mind, as it was on Hamlet's.

There remains still stronger evidence that this ' gambol faculty,' this ambling and jigging until breath be lost, was the characteristic of one individual. Cleopatra, last and loveliest of the Dark Lady's stage-shadows, is given exactly this same habit of skipping and then fetching her breath short, a habit evidently bewitching to her infatuated observer who, no doubt, enjoyed restoring her to calm and quiet. Enobarbus actually enumerated the exact number of paces over which the breathless and exquisite Cleopatra skipped to the common delight.

> I saw her once
> Hop forty paces through the public street;
> And having lost her breath, she spoke, and panted,
> That she did make defect perfection,
> And, breathless, power breathe forth.

This is the sparrowy Cressida over again. Gasping or wheezing is not, for most people, a sex-appealing exercise or malady. But Shakespeare seems to have found it so. When Antony meets Cleopatra after a fleeting victory he strangely bids her

> leap thou, attires and all,
> Through proof of harness to my heart, and there
> Ride on the pants triumphing.

Most of the points have been noted by hunters of the Dark Lady. There is another which I believe I am mentioning for the first time. Shakespeare was much attracted by the tracery of veins, especially of veins showing brightly blue upon an ivory-white surface. As early as the poem on *Lucrece* we find the addiction to this willow-pattern of vein and skin. That Roman beauty's breasts, we learn, were ' like ivory globes circled with blue ' and the ravisher Tarquin especially doted over

> Her azure veins and alabaster skin,
> Her coral lips, her snow-white dimpled chin.

In *Troilus and Cressida* Diomed cannot be scathing about Helen without allusion to her ' bawdy veins.'

H

When Shakespeare was writing *Cymbeline* and working on the scene in which Iachimo has invaded Imogen's chamber in order to win his wager, Tarquin came back to mind and so did veins: this time the tiny veining of the eye. What an astonishing passage is this which begins like an echo from *Macbeth* and suddenly is transformed into a Sleeping Beauty lyric! It is indeed one of the loveliest of Shakespeare's lyrics, although written in iambics, and those the somewhat irregular iambics of his later work; irregular but still exquisite in pattern:

> The crickets sing, and man's o'er-labour'd sense
> Repairs itself by rest. Our Tarquin thus
> Did softly press the rushes, ere he waken'd
> The chastity he wounded.—Cytherea,
> How bravely thou becomest thy bed! fresh lily!
> And whiter than the sheets! That I might touch!
> But kiss; one kiss!—Rubies unparagon'd,
> How dearly they do't!—'Tis her breathing that
> Perfumes the chamber thus: the flame o' the taper
> Bows towards her; and would under-peep her lids,
> To see the enclosed lights, now canopied
> Under these windows, white and azure, laced
> With blue of heaven's own tint.

The features which continually appealed to Shakespeare's ' æsthetic of women,' white skin, the veins' blue tracery, and the motion of a bosom stirring as it breathes, are here again. This might not amount to much, were it not for one significant line, which occurs in *Antony and Cleopatra*. Now there is no doubt at all about the ' tint ' of the Egyptian Queen, Antony's delight and ruin. Whatever the actual colouring of this daughter of the Ptolemies may have been in historical fact, to Shakespeare she was certainly dark and once spoken of as black. In the first ten lines of the play she is called a tawny gipsy. Later ' with Phœbus' amorous pinches black ' is Cleopatra's own description of herself. There can certainly be no question here of a white skin and obviously black skin would not emphasise blue veins; certainly it would not emphasise the fascination of their tint. Yet when Cleopatra is talking to the Messenger from Italy (II, v) this is how she speaks.

Antony's dead!—if thou say so, villain,
Thou kill'st thy mistress: but well and free,
If thou so yield him, there is gold, and here
My bluest veins to kiss,—a hand that kings
Have lipp'd, and trembled kissing.

My bluest veins to kiss! What a cry! And what nonsense if the writer is thinking of a blackamoor! But he is not, he is thinking of an ivory-skinned beauty, of the whitely wanton with a velvet brow, of her to whom his thoughts and remembrance continually danced their saraband of ecstasy and disenchantment.

Before Shakespeare came to write *Antony and Cleopatra* he had passed through a period of devouring pessimism, a pessimism laced with sex-obsession. In eight or nine years at the beginning of the seventeenth century he wrote no comedy with the exception of *Measure for Measure*, which is not, by our standards, a comedy at all, and has its own hard core of bitterness: as Shakespeare-Berowne had cried ' Now step I forth to whip hypocrisy,' so Shakespeare stepped into Angelo's Vienna to perform the same office and he could not journey thither without making most searing comments concerning the abuses of authority on high and on the way of all flesh in the brothels below.

During that black period a conspicuous feature of Shakespeare's workmanship is not only the continuous majesty of the writing but also the constant surrender to disgust with the physical side of love. The outbursts have their own splendour of phrase, their burning, blazing vehemence. But they are often irrelevant. Just when tragic genius appears to be climbing most happily to the very peaks of Parnassus, the Satyr jostles his way in among the Muses and interrupts Melpomene with the lickerish language of Priapus. Shakespeare almost relishes the bawdy, while he scolds it; Hamlet cannot rebuke his mother without seeming to gloat over the physical defects of her passion, and Lear cannot curse an ingrate world without some reference to the stench of sex and to the riotous appetite of women. The maddened old king must, ' in the country near Dover,' stop thus to rail upon the manifestations of the flesh.

> When I do stare, see how the subject quakes!
> I pardon that man's life.—What was thy cause ?—
> Adultery ?
> Thou shalt not die: die for adultery! No;
> The wren goes to 't, and the small gilded fly
> Does lecher in my sight.
> Let copulation thrive: for Gloster's bastard son
> Was kinder to his father than my daughters
> Got 'tween the lawful sheets.
> To't, luxury, pell-mell! for I lack soldiers.—
> Behold yond simpering dame,
> Whose face between her forks presages snow,
> That minces virtue, and does shake the head
> To hear of pleasure's name,—
> The fitchew nor the soiled horse goes to't
> With a more riotous appetite,
> Down from the waist they are Centaurs,
> Though women all above:
> But to the girdle do the gods inherit,
> Beneath is all the fiends';
> There's hell, there's darkness, there's the sulphurous pit,
> Burning, scalding, stench, consumption;—fie, fie, fie!, pah,
> pah! Give me an ounce of civet, good apothecary, to
> sweeten my imagination: there's money for thee.

What has all this to do with a drama of hasty temper and ingratitude ? Dover Wilson, hardly to be accused of being a wayward or irresponsible biographer or a fanciful successor to Frank Harris, puts it thus, in *The Essential Shakespeare*.

> Another personal clue, also with a close parallel in the literature of to-day, is the strain of sex-nausea which runs through almost everything he wrote after 1600. ' Sweet Desire ' has turned sour! It has become ferocious also; Venus and the boar have changed roles; and Shakespeare was to have no security until the beast is fast chained to the rock beneath Prospero's cell. Whatever the cause, whether it

had something to do, as many think, with the dark-eyed mistress of the Sonnets, though that episode must have been long past in 1601, or simply to the general morbidity of the age, certain it is the change is there. And that it was not a mere trick found useful to a practising dramatist is, I think, proved by its presence in the ravings of Lear, where there is no dramatic reason for it at all. Further, it is difficult to avoid associating it with personal jealousy of some kind. Jealousy is the mainspring of no less than four plays, *Troilus and Cressida*, *Othello*, *Winter's Tale*, and *Cymbeline*, while there are traces of it in *Antony and Cleopatra*, and one may suspect that it furnished material for the scene between Hamlet and his mother. That ' couch for luxury and damned incest,' which, unseen, is ever present to the mind both of Hamlet and of the audience, is, I think, symbolic. Far more than the murder, it is this which transforms the Prince's imagination into something ' as foul as Vulcan's stithy ' . . .

Young Love, which had once been the meaning of the universe, a triumphant deity, upon whose altar, decked out in all the pomp and splendour of poetry, boy Romeo and girl Juliet delight to die upon a kiss, goes out a bedraggled cupid with the sad youth Troilus, and does not re-enter Shakespeare's world until Florizel, led by his falcon, discovers Perdita. Its place, however, is not left vacant; Lust has it.

Dover Wilson also mentions, inevitably, *Timon of Athens*. This is an uneven play, of which Chambers says ' There is little to fix the date.' To its making went a second-rate collaborator, by many thought to be George Wilkins; it has an air of being unfinished. So soaked is it in misanthropy, so embittered with sex-obsession, that it may have been started, or worked upon, by Shakespeare in a mood verging upon nervous breakdown. His hand in it is manifest, apart altogether from the fact that the editors of the First Folio vouch for it as Shakespearean. It is the story of an Athenian whose lavish generosity was his ruin. Having squandered his wealth in benefactions, Timon finds what an ingrate world is this: the beneficiaries of his bounty are in no mood to rescue a sinking man. That Timon should inveigh against ingratitude is natural; but why must he turn his frantic rhetoric upon the

frailty of woman ?   There is no reason, except the anguish to
which Shakespeare had been reduced by some overwhelming
personal experience in which a faithless woman had played a
devastating part.

In Act IV, Scene 3 of *Timon of Athens*, Timon, changed by
fate and man's ill-doing from Lord Bountiful to raging misanthrope, heaps curses on humanity, and even on nature,
' to whom all sores lay siege.'   Throughout the plays of this
period, especially in *Hamlet, Troilus and Cressida*, and the later
Timon, the amount of medical reference is large.   Whenever
there is railing, the air is made loathsome with sores, imposthumes, and ulcers.   Thersites, the vile-mouthed outcast of
the Greeks, is a medical dictionary in his own person as well
as a master of invective.   In his vocabulary are not only leprosy
and dry serpigo but such a catalogue as this.

> The rotten diseases of the south, the guts-griping, ruptures,
> catarrhs, loads o' gravel i' th' back, lethargies, cold palsies,
> raw eyes, dirt-rotten livers, wheezing lungs, bladders full of
> imposthume, sciaticas, limekilns i' th' palm, incurable
> bone-ache, and the rivell'd fee-simple of the tetter.

(Note the legal phrase, fee-simple, working its way into a
schedule of maladies.)   Timon is soon hurling ' siege of sores
and hoar leprosy ' in the face of the world.   He curses ' yellow
gold,' of which, incidentally, Shakespeare's whole career shows
that in his cooler moments he was reasonably fond.   This is
how Timon sets about it.

> This Yellow slave
> Will knit and break religions; bless th' accurst;
> Make the hoar leprosy ador'd; place thieves,
> And give them title, knee, and approbation,
> With senators on the bench: this is it
> That makes the wappen'd widow wed again;
> She, whom the spital-house and ulcerous sores
> Would cast the gorge at, this embalms and spices
> To th' April day again.

Wappened is an unknown word. Commentators can give it what ugly meaning they please: the usual interpretation is stale. Before this Timon has dismissed society thus.

> Who dares, who dares,
> In purity of manhood stand upright,
> And say, ' This man's a flatterer ' ? if one be
> So are they all; for every grise of fortune
> Is smooth'd by that below: the learned pate
> Ducks to the golden fool: all is oblique;
> There's nothing level in our cursed natures
> But direct villainy. Therefore, be abhorred
> All feasts, societies, and throngs of men!
> His semblable, yea, himself, Timon disdains
> Destruction fang mankind!

That, for a misanthrope, is all in the way of business, except that the constant return to diseases makes one inevitably wonder whether the poet was not himself in some extreme of physical distress. Conversations with his son-in-law at Stratford would give him the lazar-house lexicon which he used so freely, and Dr. Hall, possibly less scrupulous about professional confidences than such a man would be now, may have revealed to his wife's father some of his *Select Observations On English Bodies*.

But then Alcibiades arrives in the woods, bringing with him, for no good reason, two harlots. They are there to provide targets for Timon's loathing of sex, for which there is no particular justification in the play. Timon loses no time in calling Alcibiades' company by the name of whore, though there is no cause for him to know anything of the ladies' morals. To this Phrynia replies, curtly but not without provocation, ' Thy lips rot off.' Then Timon turns to the other, Timandra, and becomes almost unprintably offensive on the subject of sex and disease.

Next follow passage after passage of ferocious declamation against greed and lust, passage after passage so urgent in their agony, so winged with flesh-hatred, that one cannot believe this to be dramatic writing only; a broken heart, and very nearly a broken mind, were surely above the pen that splashed this venom on to paper. For my part, I can only interpret such spasms of anti-eroticism so. And still the disease-images cluster thick: within a column or so come plague, poison, shudders, agues, birth-pains, miscarriages, pox of wrinkles, consumption, rotting of bones, and falling of hair. Ghastly as this rhetoric appears, it is, in its own macabre way, superb. For its torrents of world-loathing and summoning of doom there can be nothing like it in English literature, not even in Shakespeare's masterpieces. Apemantus, too, Timon's churlish philosopher, with a part obviously written for a specialist in blunt roles who had played Kent in *King Lear* and was to play Enobarbus in *Antony and Cleopatra*, speaks no less eloquently at times.

> What, think'st
> That the bleak air, thy boisterous chamberlain,
> Will put thy shirt on warm? Will these moss'd trees,
> That have outliv'd the eagle, page thy heels,
> And skip when thou point'st out? Will the cold brook,
> Candied with ice, caudle thy morning taste,
> To cure thy o'er-night's surfeit? Call the creatures
> Whose naked natures live in all the spite
> Of wreakful heaven, whose bare unhoused trunks,
> To the conflicting elements expos'd,
> Answer mere nature, bid them flatter thee;
> O, thou shalt find—

This is on the level of Lear, higher even—and handed to a second-part actor! But we know that spendthrift dramatist who tossed to a First Murderer

> The west yet glimmers with some streaks of day:
> Now spurs the lated traveller apace
> To gain the timely inn

while the wonderful speech beginning

> All furnish'd, all in arms;
> All plum'd like estridges that wing the wind;

> Bated like eagles having lately bathed;
> Glittering in golden coats, like images;
> As full of spirit as the month of May,
> And gorgeous as the sun at Midsummer,

went to the tiny part of Vernon. When Shakespeare was in flood, he did not stay to mark the destination of a runnel.

Timon, in his fury, tells Apemantus that if he had been born to high estate and its pleasures

> thou wouldst have plung'd thyself
> In general riot; melted down thy youth
> In different beds of lust; and never learn'd
> Thy icy precepts of respect, but follow'd
> The sugar'd game before thee.

The game again, whose ' daughter ' Cressida had been. Shakespeare at a certain period was haunted by it. The ' Sugar'd Game ' has become his obsession. Like Catullus of old, but with a hundred times the eloquence, he has proclaimed ' Odi et amo,' I love and loathe. Then love fades out. In *Timon of Athens* there is no affection left for man or woman, fair or dark. There is the familiar cursing of painted faces; there is a new and general condemnation of sex and even of natural fertility. Timon calls on Earth.

> Ensear thy fertile and conceptious womb;
> Let it no more bring out ingrateful man!
> Go great with tigers, dragons, wolves, and bears;
> Teem with new monsters, whom thy upward face
> Hath to the marbled mansion all above
> Never presented!

He prays for the end of all human breeding and for the odious disruption of all humanity.

> And may diseases lick up all their bloods

is the squalid end of it. That long, sex-haunted, disease-scarred scene, in a play which is fundamentally about ingratitude, not about lust and lazar-houses, is signed in every phrase as Shakespeare's. His handiwork quivers in each line; each fantastic, scarifying image and metaphor comes from the quick forge of one brain only and that in a red-hot frenzy of composition.

Dover Wilson thinks that the Dark Lady episode was over long before 1601 and that *Timon of Athens* was probably written much later than that. An episode over, perhaps. But more episodes could follow and something had brought Shakespeare, in Dover Wilson's own phrase, to the razor's edge when he was pouring this stuff out. What something but a woman or a woman's memory? She is implicit in the writing of several plays, most of all in the great Commination Service that is *Timon of Athens*. The woman colour'd ill had achieved her worst: she had well-nigh cracked a great heart and she had driven to wild ravings a hand unparallel'd. But the battle of the two was not over. In *Antony and Cleopatra* Shakespeare was to paint her for the last time and almost to forgive her. Why this change of mind? Because, I believe, she was by that time dead.

CHAPTER XI

' Lass Unparallel'd '

SHE was dead: or she had moved altogether away from the humble sphere of a player-poet. That would have meant that she had left London, for the English capital of Shakespeare's day—no larger than Oxford in our time—was no easy place in which to miss or to avoid people of note or notoriety. Had she moved onwards and upwards in her conquering progress the player-poet would hardly have forgiven her: and *Antony and Cleopatra* is essentially a hymn of forgiveness. By the time that Shakespeare had finished with the Dark Lady in this tremendous tragedy, she had declared her immortal longings and made Death proud to take her. Almost one might say that the ' daughter of the game ' was now a royal spirit, soaring, on the wings of her own beauty, into an empyrean; the whitely wanton, and at other times gipsy wanton, had, through sheer integrity of wantonness and complete concentration upon passion, somehow become in tune with the infinite.

The last two acts of *Antony and Cleopatra*, acts which contain the most heart-searching poetry that Shakespeare ever wrote, cannot be interpreted in any other way than as a salute to love which tolerates no mitigation, to a lavishness and a luxury which count the world well lost if love be satisfied. They are also a farewell. The Dark Lady may or may not have been dead. But something had snapped. The ecstasy and the agony were over.

There is an absolute break between the mood of *Timon of Athens* and the mood of *Antony and Cleopatra*. Where sex is concerned, the former play carries railing to a point where it becomes revolting: some of the speeches have the stench of a casualty clearing station in the lists of love. Shakespeare pours out maledictions upon the breed of man and warns him

235

against further breeding. But, in the case of *Antony and Cleopatra*, the sulphurous clouds have cleared away. There is no longer the clinical vocabulary, the harping on physical corruption, and the sexual obsession in all its ugliness. The Dark Lady is still her old self in Cleopatra's person: she is lecherous, wanton and fickle: she beguiles her man ' into the very heart of loss,' and yet she is now sublime, as she never was in the Sonnets or in any of the plays in which she had reared the velvet brow, the mourning eyes of ebon black, the blue-veined whitely skin, the hair like coal-black wire, the panting bosom and the jigging feet.

There is no means of certainly dating *Timon of Athens* and no Jacobean performance is recorded; many have placed it later than *Antony and Cleopatra*; Chambers gives *Timon* to 1608, while putting the Roman play back to 1607. The arguments for this are trifling compared with the general feeling of the two plays. *Timon* marks the climax of the enraged, darkened, and even frenzied period of Shakespeare's life: it continues the sourness and the anti-feminine invective of *Troilus and Cressida*: it has the fang'd pessimism that snarls and snaps in the world defiance and raging misanthropy of *King Lear*. But from *Antony and Cleopatra*, although the woman remains in unmistakable form, the hatred and contempt have suddenly vanished.

Nor were they ever to return. For though in two of the subsequent plays, *Cymbeline* and *The Winter's Tale*, there are, in the characters of Posthumus and Leontes, vigorous and lurid studies of masculine jealousy, reminiscent of the earlier temper, there is also a complete and significant alteration of feminine portraiture. The innocent maids, as flower-like as the buds and blossoms which increasingly begin to dapple the plays' dialogue with their beauty, are the new model of Shakespearean womanhood. Imogen, Perdita, and Miranda move in a different universe from that of Cressida and Cleopatra: they are beyond the range of Hamlet's harsh misogyny. The foul stithy of Shakespeare's overwrought mind is replaced by that palace of innocence and nest of natural goodness, Belarius's cave, where life is

Richer than doing nothing for a bribe,
Prouder than rustling in unpaid-for silk

and replaced, no less, by the library and liberal arts of Prospero. The world still begets sinners, dark minds, and vile suspicions: but the girls are not the offenders; they are no longer gipsy wantons: they are good examples.

Antony and Cleopatra superbly marks the transition between the middle and the end of Shakespeare's work, between possession by devils and the achievement of serenity. It is the crisis in Cleopatra's career and her subsequent suicide, celebrated by the noblest flight of Shakespeare's poetry, that signify the end of a mental and emotional fever.

The word fever reminds one that insight may be gained into the working of Shakespeare's mind by simple recourse to a Concordance, that is to say a volume which records his use of terminology by ascribing to each word the various passages in which it occurs. The absorption in and exploitation of medical detail begin with *Hamlet* and abound especially in *Troilus and Cressida*. The only Shakespearean use of ulcer and of imposthume (abscess) occurs in those plays and the adjective ulcerous occurs in *Hamlet*, *Macbeth* and *Troilus and Cressida*, all work of the same period. Boils and plague-sores appear in *King Lear*, *Coriolanus* and *Troilus and Cressida*: the same is true of fever and feverous. Leprosy and lazar-house are mainly to be found in *Hamlet* and *Troilus and Cressida* (leprosy is once used in *Antony and Cleopatra*, but merely as part of a conventional curse). The word plague occurs thirteen times in *Troilus and Cressida* and eight times in *King Lear*: not once in *Antony and Cleopatra*, whose text is almost entirely free of the sick-room and the surgery lingo, free of the boils and blains, the tetter, the serpigo, and the bone-ache, which are so hideously prominent in the plays written immediately before it. After Troy, Denmark, and the cliffs of Dover, the Near East, where Antony and his queen live their luxurious hours, has an astonishingly clean bill of health.

One may, of course, surmise from this that in the early years of the century Shakespeare himself suffered from a severe attack of staphylococcic infection and was plagued with recurrent boils and even worse distresses of the blood and skin, and that by the time he was writing of Cleopatra's passion he had recovered from such torturing and weakening maladies. There are incontestable and ubiquitous signs in the Roman-Egyptian tragedy that it was written in a far calmer state of mind and probably in a far healthier state of body than were the plays immediately preceding. That easing of nerve and that relief of mind came just in time. Shakespeare was still in his most powerful period as a writer: his fertility of phrase was not yet clogging up and confusing his lines with a flood of intricate and involved similes and metaphors. So we get *Antony and Cleopatra*, the work of a hand restored and a mind refreshed, written when both hand and mind were capable of their highest, grandest composition. There is plentiful reason, I think, for holding that this, or at least some of this, masterpiece was worked upon during the convalescence that followed the frenzy of bitterness and the physical distress which had been the birth-pains of the great tragedies. The boils and ulcers fade out of the poet's dictionary; the allusions to bodily afflictions cease and the metaphors undergo considerable disinfection. ' Out of the west a wind that blows ' has healthily mingled with the Mediterranean siroccos of the play. One has a whiff of the hedgerow, a welcome bouquet of English country. Although the themes and images prominent in *Antony and Cleopatra* are imperial, even cosmic, confronting us with the orb of the world, with vast dominions below, and with the rolling spheres above, the text is strangely permeated by native and farmyard smells and details; the acrid richness of the dungy earth and the aroma of meadows painted with delight are mixed with the perfumes of the scented East. There are touches which suggest that Shakespeare was on a visit to his home, or at least to the country, when he was pouring his heart into this old romance of ' all for love.'

It was one of his habits—theatrically, of course, an inconsistency and a weakness, but likeable in its own way—to introduce country matters where they are least likely. The most striking example, perhaps, of this occurs in Queen Gertrude's speech about Ophelia's death. Here is the Majesty of Denmark, overwhelmed with grief, yet pausing in an account of the pitiful tragedy, to drag in a reference which would certainly have won a laugh from Christopher Sly and his fellow-sots in a rustic alehouse. I refer to the famous speech beginning

> There is a willow grows aslant a brook,
> That shows his hoar leaves in the glassy stream;
> There with fantastic garlands did she come
> Of crow-flowers, nettles, daises, and long purples
> That liberal shepherds give a grosser name,
> But our cold maids do dead men's fingers call them:

What on earth has the herdsmen's bawdy word for long purples to do with the Queen's mourning for Ophelia's muddy death? The lines are remarkable for this vital irrelevance. In just the same way when Cleopatra's navy has betrayed Antony and cost him defeat at sea by the treachery and cowardice of its command, Scarus, one of Antony's officers, describes the disaster thus.

> The greater cantle of the world is lost
> With very ignorance; we have kist away
> Kingdoms and provinces.

Enobarbus   How appears the fight?
Scarus   On our side like the token'd pestilence,
> Where death is sure. Yon ribaudred nag of
> Egypt,
> Whom leprosy o'ertake!—i' the midst o' the fight,
> When vantage like a pair of twins appear'd,
> Both as the same, or rather ours the elder,—
> The breese upon her, like a cow in June,—
> Hoists sails and flies.
Enobarbus That I beheld:
> Mine eyes did sicken at the sight, and could not
> Endure a further view.
Scarus   She once being looft,
> The noble ruin of her magic, Antony,

Claps on his sea-wing, and, like a doting mallard,
Leaving the fight in height, flies after her:
I never saw an action of such shame;
Experience, manhood, honour, ne'er before
Did violate so itself.

Within a few lines this classical general of Rome, busily warring
in the Near East, has referred to the farmyard, to the biological
phenomena of the stockyard, and to the doting mallard whose
love-flights go whirring over our rivers and marshes in the
spring. Ribaudred, a rare word, is generally supposed to
mean lustful and the breese or gadfly is another term of sexual
application. The frisking of a heated cow in June is certainly
a very odd simile to apply to Egypt's delicate and perfumed
queen. But such practice of writing, such upthrust of rural
sights and memories, is exactly parallelled by the rude nickname for long purples which occurs so oddly in Queen Gertrude's speech.

One finds, too, in *Antony and Cleopatra*, the description of the
flag or iris, moving to and fro on the river's surface, so that
it ' lackeys the varying tide ' until it ' rots itself with motion.'
Such a sight is common in eddies under bridges or beside the
millrace. Images of this kind are naturally put to paper after
a walk by a river on a summer afternoon. Indeed this soaring
play of Eastern opulence and self-indulgence, this tale of
Alexandria and Nile, this crash of empires, has a very English
and even a humble quality in its range of reference and metaphors. We meet milk-maids and chare-women, roses and
spaniels, as well as livestock, mallard and such country matters:
there are damp, disponging mists about, which are more
reminiscent of the stolchy water-meadows of our shires than
of burning acres of Egyptian sand. Even with all its surging
poetry of sensual rapture, its proclamation that ' the beds i'
the East are soft,' its honeyings and dalliance that kiss a world
away, it has far more fresh air about it than have the preceding
tragedies. It not only excites; it exhilarates.

Why, it can fairly be asked, should we identify this later
Cleopatra with the earlier manifestations of a whitely wanton ?

Her darkness, it is true, is not only of the hair but of the skin, which is described as tawny or even black. Yet Shakespeare, as I pointed out, forgot about that and thought of veins conspicuously blue, which implied a mind's-eye vision of a fair skin. Cleopatra, too, is a dancer (' if you find him sad, say I am dancing '). She is ready for any jigging or ambling, even in the public streets, and after such exercise she fetches her breath charmingly, ' making defect perfection,' as Cressida had done. Like the Dark Lady of the Sonnets she is keenly musical; music for her is the ' moody food of us that trade in love.' She joins in all such sports as a Jacobean court lady might choose to follow when in an antic disposition and she must have music with them. ' Let us to billiards.' No, her arm is sore. She suggests fishing (would that be easier for a sore arm?). She cannot ply a rod without orchestral accompaniment. Consider this dialogue with her maid of honour, Charmian.

> Give me mine angle,—we'll to the river : there,
> My music playing far off, I will betray
> Tawny-finn'd fishes ; my bended hook shall pierce
> Their slimy jaws ; and, as I draw them up,
> I'll think them every one an Antony,
> And say, ' Ah, ha ! y'are caught.'
>
> *Charmian*   'Twas merry when
> You wager'd on your angling ; when your diver
> Did hang a salt-fish on his hook, which he
> With fervency drew up.
>
> *Cleopatra*   That time,—O times !—
> I laught him out of patience ; and that night
> I laught him into patience ; and next morn,
> Ere the ninth hour, I drunk him to his bed ;
> Then put my tires and mantles on him, whilst
> I wore his sword Philippan.

To say that this has the strong stamp of personal reminiscence will be disputed: to assert as much will be dismissed as ' fictionised biography.' But to me that wagering and wantoning, that gaming and laughing and wining point back to the

Lady of the Sonnets—to the dark Rosaline who had appeared more than a decade earlier and was at once so vividly described as one who would do the deed though the hundred eyes of Argus were working to spy on her incontinence. And is she not, this volatile and teasing beauty of Egypt whose allurements will corrupt the very piety of priesthood, completely fore-shadowed by Ulysses when Cressida, forsaking Troilus, is bestowing her kisses with alacrity on the entire General Staff of the Greek army ?   Ulysses snaps out,

> Fie, fie upon her !
> There's language in her eye, her cheek, her lip,
> Nay, her foot speaks ; her wanton spirits look out
> At every joint and motive of her body.
> O, these encounterers, so glib of tongue,
> That give accosting welcome ere it comes,
> And wide unclasp the tables of their thoughts
> To every ticklish reader ! set them down
> For sluttish spoils of opportunity
> And daughters of the game.

So there, upon Nile, she is seen again, but she is twice herself, greater, far greater than ever before. Cleopatra is a figure seen in perspective, with all her faults upon her and all her fascinations too, seen with infatuation, with devotion, with amazement, and at last with compassion. She is the Wanton Absolute, but just because of her absolute, unconditional, un-hesitating pursuit of heart's desire, because of her courage in her quality, because of the very bigness in her pettiness, she is almost shriven before death in Shakespeare's fancy. Lust has ceased now to be the dominant part of her loving. Early in the play, amid all the charges of sensuality brought by the Romans against the Egyptian beauty, Antony's henchman Enobarbus gives a tingling description of her mischievous play-acting and then proceeds to make it plain that she is no ordinary strumpet: her passions contain ' the finest part of pure love.'

It is Enobarbus who gives us with insight as well as with eloquence our picture of Cleopatra: he relates the scene upon the river Cydnus, where she was seen by Antony for the first time. Her beauty ' beggar'd all description ' and at once ' pursed up his heart.' The passage about the Queen's barge with poop of beaten gold, with purple sails drenched in perfume, and with music streaming on the water, is so familiar as not to need further quotation. It leads on to the famous judgment, also by Enobarbus,

> Age cannot wither her, nor custom stale
> Her infinite variety ; other women cloy
> The appetites they feed ; but she makes hungry
> Where most she satisfies : for vilest things
> Become themselves in her ; that the holy priests
> Bless her when she is riggish.

A sensual tribute is there: but perception of the subtler qualities emerges in a notable assessment from the same lips. Enobarbus talks thus of her throwing of temperamental tricks and her mimicry of swooning and even of death to make the right effect.

> Cleopatra, catching but the least noise of this, dies instantly ; I have seen her die twenty minutes upon far poorer moment : I do think there is mettle in death, which commits some loving act upon her, she hath such a celerity in dying.
> *Mark Antony* She is cunning past man's thought.
> *Enobarbus* Alack, sir, no; her passions are made of nothing but the finest part of pure love: we cannot call her winds and waters sighs and tears; they are greater storms and tempests than almanacs can report: this cannot be cunning in her; if it be, she makes a shower of rain as well as Jove.
> *Mark Antony* Would I had never seen her!
> *Enobarbus* O, sir, you had then left unseen a wonderful piece of work; which not to have been blest withal would have discredited your travel.

Could homage be justified with more persuasion ?

The burden of the play is succinctly and immediately proclaimed. Philo, one of Antony's men, is thus explicit:

> Nay, but this dotage of our general's
> O'erflows the measure: those his goodly eyes
> That o'er the files and musters of the war
> Have glow'd like plated Mars, now bend, now turn,
> The office and devotion of their view
> Upon a tawny front: his captain's heart,
> Which in the scuffles of great fights hath burst
> The buckles on his breast, reneges all temper,
> And is become the bellows and the fan
> To cool a gipsy's lust.   Look where they come:
> Take but good note, and you shall see in him
> The triple pillar of the world transformed
> Into a strumpet's fool: behold and see.

Antony, Octavius Caesar and Lepidus are the three possessive pillars of the world. Antony has crowns for the giving, treasure for the spending: but what does he care for these enormities of power and purse ? Egypt, with Cleopatra, is all. Here, too, the declaration of theme and purpose is immediate. Antony's first line is

> There's beggary in the love that can be reckoned,

and his first speech of any length is a disclaimer of political ambition, since the summit of life is to be discovered in the map of love and not in any chart of earthly kingdoms.

> Let Rome in Tiber melt, and the wide arch
> Of the ranged empire fall! Here is my space.
> Kingdoms are clay: our dungy earth alike
> Feeds beast as man: the nobleness of life
> Is to do thus: when such a mutual pair,
> And such a twain can do't, in which I bind,
> On pain of punishment, the world to weet
> We stand up peerless.

'The nobleness of life.' To that ideal of love-over-all Antony is true: he tosses away his universe for a woman: and the very size of that sacrifice, the strength of the decision, seem to fire Shakespeare's keenest admiration.   It is impossible to read or see this play without conviction as to where the playwright's sympathy is placed. He no longer rails at the tyranny of passion; he accepts it, even reveres it, so it be tyrannical enough. It has been well said that gambling is only contemptible if carried on within your means. For Shakespeare, in the mood of this play, this view holds of wenching as well as of wagering. Sexual surrender can lose its shabbiness by loyalty to its own excess.

Time and again Shakespeare, in Sonnet and in play, had cried out against this excess, the expense of spirit in a waste of shame. But now he has lost that careful temper: the lurking Puritan within him has been ousted for a season by the forthright hedonist. So the play moves through its early and not easily staged acts with their abundance of classical history, vexatious to a modern audience, and their manifold changes of scene, as it were a film unfolding. For these reasons and because it needs almost superhuman performance and is lost without the best in casts and direction, *Antony and Cleopatra* will rarely, if ever, be ' good box-office.' The action scrambles forward until it reaches the peaks of the last two acts, peaks not only of the play's own composition but of the Shakespearean workmanship which gives to every word a higher power. It is in the closing passages of this tragedy that we come, in my opinion, closer to Shakespeare's heart than anywhere else, even in *Hamlet*. The temper and opinion there revealed are certainly not characteristic: Shakespeare was, on the whole, a temperate man, careful of his money, nervous that his sensibility might betray him, afraid of his passions. But upon this occasion, he stripped moderation from his mind and paid salutation to a man who would keep nothing.

> His legs bestrid the ocean: his rear'd arm
> Crested the world; his voice was propertied
> As all the tuned spheres, and that to friends;
> But when he meant to quail and shake the orb,
> He was as rattling thunder. For his bounty,
> There was no winter in't; an autumn 'twas
> That grew the more by reaping: his delights

> Were dolphin-like; they show'd his back above
> The element they lived in: in his livery
> Walkt crowns and crownets; realms and islands were
> As plates dropt from his pocket.

He paid salutation no less to the woman who would take all.
Half-measures, prudent courses, on the part of either of them
would have lost the creator's enraptured obeisance. To find
nobleness in such squandering of property and power was not
his enduring philosophy; far from it. But when the vision
of such bounty did blaze upon his eyes, he wrote with an
intensity, even with a sublimity, not elsewhere equalled in the
canon. Cleopatra has the phrase ' lass unparallel'd ' dropped
upon her dying body: it is this concept of supremacy, of
uniqueness (' we stand up peerless ') and of absolute dedication
to love which upon this occasion evoked from him those breath-
taking achievements, the death-scenes of Antony and Cleopatra: self-slaughtered both, they die in the high Roman way
and make death their proud partners on the last of all the
Orient's soft beds.

Under Shakespeare's hand the two undeviating sensualists
are dowered with nobility—as was promised in the first speech
—shown as fine spirits touched to the finest issues, and thus
made vehicles for a delicacy of poetry which leaps out from
their physical beauty into rare loveliness of thought and fancy.
Consider Antony's farewell to amorous life and his glimpse of
amorous eternity. ' I come, my queen,' he cries and then this is
thrown in among his talk to Eros, his page,

>   Eros!—Stay for me:
> Where souls do couch on flowers, we'll hand in hand,
> And with our sprightly port make the ghosts gaze:
> Dido and her Aeneas shall want troops,
> And all the haunt be ours.—Come, Eros, Eros!

The vanity of it is no less victorious than the beauty of it.
' Where souls do couch on flowers ' these two, the peerless, will
march like film stars on a gala night and rob even Queen

Dido of her fanciers. Sprightly too! Had that dancing motion come back to mind? Would the Dark Lady go jigging and ambling into the Elysian Fields?

Cleopatra's lament, after Antony's death, when ' the case of that huge spirit now is cold,' again makes magical beauty while it stresses the familiar note of the ' peerless, the unparallel'd, the unique.'

> The crown o' the earth doth melt.—My lord!
> O, wither'd is the garland of the war,
> The soldiers' pole is faln: young boys and girls
> Are level now with men; the odds is gone,
> And there is nothing left remarkable
> Beneath the visiting moon.

Their union must never be broken.

>   It were for me
> To throw my sceptre at the injurious gods;
> To tell them that this world did equal theirs
> Till they had stoln our jewel.   All's but naught;
> Patience is sottish, and impatience does
> Become a dog that's mad; then is it sin
> To rush into the secret house of death,
> Ere death dare come to us?

And so to that end in which the gipsy-wanton has been almost forgotten and Cleopatra becomes far more than a heroine of harlotry; she is indeed a figure of splendour as she defies the world of Caesar and follows Antony to where the ghosts gaze.   Womanly still, she must dress the part.   ' My best attires, I am again for Cydnus, To meet Mark Antony.' Yet a moment later femininity is spurned.

>   I have nothing
> Of woman in me; now, from head to foot,
> I am marble-constant: now the fleeting morn
> No planet is of mine.

Then she arranges for the little venomous snake that is to help her,

> To do the deed which ends all other deeds,
> Which shackles accident and bolts up change.

The final moment comes and here is the farewell, the last farewell to all her greatness. The passage and the passing of the Queen have a magnificence that would justify quotation and quotation again. How can the ear be surfeited with such glory?

> Give me my robe, put on my crown; I have
> Immortal longings in me: now no more
> The juice of Egypt's grape shall moist this lip:—
> Yare, yare, good Iras; quick.—Methinks I hear
> Antony call: I see him rouse himself
> To praise my noble act; I hear him mock
> The luck of Caesar, which the gods give men
> To excuse their after wrath:—husband, I come:
> Now to that name my courage prove my title!
> I am fire and air; my other elements
> I give to baser life.—So,—have you done?
> Come then, and take the last warmth of my lips.
> Farewell, kind Charmian;—Iras, long farewell.
> Have I the aspic in my lips? Dost fall?
> If thou and nature can so gently part,
> The stroke of death is as a lover's pinch,
> Which hurts, and is desired.   Dost thou lie still?
> If thus thou vanishest, thou tell'st the world
> It is not worth leave-taking.
> *Charmian*   Dissolve, thick cloud, and rain; that I may say
> The gods themselves do weep!
> *Cleopatra*   This proves me base:
> If she first meet the curled Antony,
> He'll make demand of her, and spend that kiss
> Which is my heaven to have.—Come, thou mortal wretch,
> With thy sharp teeth this knot intrinsicate
> Of life at once untie: poor venomous fool,
> Be angry, and dispatch.   O, couldst thou speak,
> That I might hear thee call great Caesar ass
> Unpolicied!
> *Charmian*   O eastern star!

Cleopatra   Peace, peace!
 Dost thou not see my baby at my breast,
 That sucks the nurse asleep ?
Charmian   O, break! O, break!
Cleopatra As sweet as balm, as soft as air, as gentle,—
 O Antony!—Nay, I will take thee too:—
 What should I stay—
Charmian In this vile world ?—So, fare thee well.—
 Now boast thee, death, in thy possession lies
 A lass unparallel'd.—Downy windows, close;
 And golden Phoebus never be beheld
 Of eyes again so royal!—Your crown's awry;
 I'll mend it, and then play.

So dies the woman of whom Antony had said,

> I found you as a morsel cold upon
> Dead Caesar's trencher; nay, you were a fragment
> Of Gneius Pompey's; besides what hotter hours,
> Unregister'd in vulgar fame, you have
> Luxuriously pickt out: for, I am sure,
> Though you can guess what temperance should be,
> You know not what it is.

From a king's morsel, incapable of chastity, she has become marble-constant; when the body wilts, she is turned to fire and air. Strange metamorphosis!

We shall never know, it seems, who the Dark Lady was. The Pembroke-Fitton theory of man right fair and woman colour'd ill has been discredited. The certainties are few; the later Sonnets are indubitably haunted by an ebon-haired and dark-eyed mistress and she seems to reappear vividly in the plays, especially in those plays where love is the main theme. She may, in her final and most glorious embodiment as Cleopatra, have been more of a remembered fancy than a woman of fact; but one feels so powerfully in this play the presence of intensely personal feeling. There is no ' false fire ' about the blaze of admiration for the self-doomed but yet indomitable pair. With the end of the tragedies—*Coriolanus* is usually put later than *Antony and Cleopatra*, but may have been worked upon earlier—the vision passes. Sour masculine suspicion of the frailty that is woman remains to be portrayed with quivering vitality, but there is no further glimpse of the arch-wanton who has been, as Ben Jonson's Alchemist might have said, so ' sublimed and dulcified ' as to become a lass unparallel'd, radiant as fire, cold and constant as marble, no more a minion of the fleeting and the fickle moon.

The underlying philosophy of *Antony and Cleopatra* is, as I have said, at odds with what we know of Shakespeare's life, which was diligent and thrifty, a well-calculated essay in the restoration of bourgeois fortunes for a country family. Antony tosses ' realms and islands ' from his pocket: Shakespeare, carefully amassing property in land, houses, tithes, dropped not a rod, pole or perch. He was never accused of meanness: Aubrey's record speaks of an ' open and free nature,' which may refer to his readiness in spending as well as to his sociability in conversation. But he was certainly no wastrel and yet of waste upon a mighty scale he became, in fancy, the rapt, enthusiastic celebrant. The dominion of his sympathies included all; he noted and revelled in the smallest things; the minutiae of Nature were his darlings. But *Antony and Cleopatra* is conceived in terms of vastness, by whose allurements he is on this occasion totally infected. The text of the play is full of orbs, spheres, planets, sun and moon, compared with which the Earth is but ' a little O ': kingdoms and empires are as the plates which a juggler throws and catches in his play-boy occupation. In this temper, in this surrender to size and size again, in this reverence for a colossal love which inflicts as well as endures colossal damage, Shakespeare is well away from his usual route of steady progress towards a shrewd investor's stake in the country and a sound professional career in town.

It can be argued, of course, that this is only another proof of wrong ascription: that Shakespeare, the prudent actor-manager, could never have written such lyrical praise of imprudence practised on a monstrous scale and that *Antony and Cleopatra* is essentially the work of a grandee, free of all shopkeeper's calculation and town councillor's environment. But there is no proof in the general history of art that men's public work is always the true mirror of their private feelings or capacities. The passions and performance of the actual Algernon Charles Swinburne cannot be fairly derived from the melodious and delighted eroticism of his earlier poems. An artist can work outside himself and work at his best none the less; he may be pouring on to paper or canvas what he would like to have thought of him or what he would, in certain moods or moments, most eagerly choose to be, which is something very different from what he is. The novels of Charles Dickens seem to present a full declaration of what the author believed, enjoyed, and hated. But the real Dickens was quite a different man from that image of Dickens which a reader may derive from the books. There are days, no doubt, perhaps months and years, too, in which an austere and even arid Professor of Moral Philosophy views himself, and would like to be viewed, as the devil of a fellow. Sinners in prose have been grave pietists in fact and the righteous have written with glee and conviction of loves profane as well as sacred. Shakespeare under influence of a mood or, as I think, of a definite person, wrote *Antony and Cleopatra* in a temper and with a mastery which he was never to recover. The best had gone out of him when he was, in one sense, being far from himself. It is interesting to speculate on the number of artists whose most applauded and triumphant work has been least typical of their own way and purpose in the organisation of their lives.

For my part, I read the great finale of *Antony and Cleopatra* as a valediction. Something had ended in Shakespeare's life. His health was better, his grip upon himself far more assured than when he was pouring out—one might almost say retching up—the lazar-house cursings of *Timon*. My submission is that because the Dark Lady would neither entrance nor madden him again, he could look back and withhold the stinging phrase with which he had scourged the ebon hair and eyes, the white and blue-veined skin of that exquisite but ' jigging ' wantonness. He would do more than spare, since now, being released, he was free to praise, and because she would not hurt him again, he would forgive, he would adore. For certainly both Antony and Cleopatra die ennobled and esteemed. The world first bidden to ' weet ' that they stand up peerless sees them lie down no less supreme in their own reckless, lavish, superbly improvident kind.

> Now boast thee, death, in thy possession lies
> A lass unparallel'd.

The brief, affectionate ' lass,' the weighty rolling ' unparallel'd'—they are typical Shakespearean magic. They are also a proclamation of pardon, a statement of forgiveness as well as of farewell—to the wanton Cleopatra certainly, and, as I think, to another also, the poet's own love of ecstasy and despair. This, at least, is beyond dispute: that, if we owe some of the Sonnets and all of *Antony and Cleopatra* to a Lady Anon, Tudor-Jacobean beauty of her day, then our debt to the unnamed, elusive creature outranges calculation.

CHAPTER XII

In the Motley

SHAKESPEARE the poet and Shakespeare the lover was also (or had been) Shakespeare the actor. It has been denied that he ever was an actor; the assertion has been made that his connection with the playhouse was never more than that of author, sharer, and manager. But the evidence of the time and the weight of tradition are against this view, which has been argued by William Bliss in *The Real Shakespeare*, and I can see no reason at all for holding any such opinion. The astonishing thing is how Shakespeare found time, after the Johannes Factotum period, to study and perform parts: he was turning out two or three plays a year: he was composing sonnets and poems: he had an eye on property in Stratford: he had leading managerial and commercial interests with the Lord Chamberlain's (later King's) Men. And yet, in 1603, when he was fully established in authorship and had some of his finest work (including *Hamlet*) behind him, he was still acting, according to the list of the cast given in the Folio Works of Ben Jonson. The play was *Sejanus* and the ' principall Tragodeians ' are given thus,

Ric. Burbage.	Will. Shake-Speare.
Aug. Philips.	Ioh. Hemings.
Will. Sly.	Hen. Condel.
Ioh. Lowin.	Alex. Cooke.

I have seen the tragedy of *Sejanus* produced by William Poel upon a platform stage. It is good solemn Jonson, which is far less than good Shakespeare, whether the latter was in solemn or in playful mood. Was it worth while for one who was

just setting out to write *Othello*, *Lear* and *Macbeth* to be memorising in private and regurgitating on the stage the Jonsonian
eloquence ?   How big was his part ?   The numbering suggests
the fifth largest; and there was much ' doubling ' in those days.

The anti-Stratfordians will here intervene briskly.   Does not
this continued preoccupation with playing, they will urge,
prove that there was no time for the Oaf, Clown or Mummer
from ignorant Stratford, to be also the Immortal Bard ?   I
think there was time: but it is obvious that, if in 1603 Shakespeare was still being a Factotum and busy in the tiring-room
as well as at his desk, he was an uncommonly quick mover.
But then the world does from time to time throw up uncommonly quick movers.   They are unusual; and slow-movers,
the ' continual plodders,' despised by Shakespeare, are unable
to believe in them at all.   But there they are.   Charles
Dickens found time to indulge his passion for amateur acting
on the grand scale and for addressing audiences of all kinds,
at dinners, meetings, and at ' Readings,' while he was pouring
out his immense novels, along with articles and short stories,
editing, quarrelling, travelling and generally conducting a life
for which the word full is wholly inadequate.   Shakespeare was
a man of that nimbleness: to his speed with a pen his colleagues
attested; he may also have learned a part as quickly as he
wrote one.

As to the quality of his performance, there is no contemporary
evidence; tradition slights it and limits him to smallish roles
and specialisation in old men.   But the tradition is a long way
subsequent to Shakespeare's own life and much may have been
forgotten, something invented.   It is a pity that contemporary
evidence is so slight: we must make the best of what there is.

Greene's Factotum reference and the sneer at the Upstart
Crow with a Player's hide have already been discussed.   When
Chettle answered Greene he called the man referred to, ' excellent in the qualitie he professes.'   That probably means
acting as well as writing, but nobody can prove that it does.
It is reasonable to assume that a Stage Factotum would include
acting in his work, especially as the Player's hide was set upon
his shoulders.

Some have identified William Shakespeare with a William Shakeshafte who was named in 1581 as belonging to a troupe of players maintained by a Lancashire gentleman, Alexander Houghton of Lea. This Shakeshafte later on transferred to another north country fancier of the stage, Sir Thomas Hesketh. Since Hesketh was associated with the Stanleys, the Earls of Derby then as now, this lad Shakeshafte may have found his way to London as one of Ferdinando Stanley's 'cry of players.' The name Shakeshafte was, it is true, a Warwickshire alternative to Shakespeare at a time when names were extremely fluid in their composition. Moreover, it appears in the records of Snitterfield, which was Shakespeare's father's village.

But this identification implies that William had left Stratford before he was seventeen: then he must have returned to Avonside to beget Susanna, to marry Anne Hathaway (and possibly to be parted from Anne Whateley), and to beget his twins two years later. His plays show no particular interest in or knowledge of Lancashire, whereas they do reveal some close understanding of Gloucestershire. It is much more likely, in my opinion, that he made his acquaintance with stage-plays nearer home than in Lancashire. It has already been pointed out that just across the ' high wild hills and rough, uneven ways ' of Gloucestershire, of which he wrote feelingly in *Richard II*, stood Berkeley Castle, where Lord Berkeley kept a troupe, sending them on tours as well as enjoying their works on the premises. On the whole I think this is a much likelier place for Shakespeare's apprenticeship in the quality of acting. I find it hard to believe in the Lancashire sojourn and the taking of the name of Shakeshafte.

The already cited warrant for payment for Court performances at Christmas, 1594, links Kempe, Shakespeare, and Burbage, in that order, as servants of the Lord Chamberlain, and there is really more reason to suppose that Shakespeare's name is there as one of the actor-sharers than as a sharer only.

In 1598, according to the Ben Jonson Folio, he was one of the ' principall Comoedians ' in *Every Man in His Humour*. This time his name comes first. Did he play the lead ? If so, he may have disappointed. Either because he had done poorly and was not wanted a second time or because he was too busy, he was not mentioned as acting with Burbage, Phillips, Sly, Heminge, Condell, and Pope in Jonson's sequel, *Every Man out of His Humour*. Considering that 1599 must have been as busy a writing year as Shakespeare ever had, the absence is not surprising. For with *Henry V* probably just over, he had *Julius Caesar*, *As You Like It*, *Hamlet* and *Twelfth Night*, all, as the modern advertisements say, ' in active preparation.' But, as we have seen, he came back to be tragedian in *Sejanus* in 1603.

He is named in the same year among the King's Men licensed and authorised by James I, on his accession,

> freely to vse and exercise the Arte and faculty of playing Comedies, Tragedies, histories, Enterludes, moralls, pastoralls, Stageplaies and Suche others like as theie haue alreadie studied or hereafter shall vse or studie as well for the recreation of our lovinge Subiectes as for our Solace and pleasure when wee shall thincke good to see them duringe our pleasure.

In this roll he is second: the head name is that of Lawrence Fletcher. Shakespeare's name comes first on the list of the King's Men, as they now were, who received for the Coronation ceremonial,

> Red Clothe bought of sondrie persons and giuen by his Maiestie to diuerse persons against his Maiesties sayd royall proceeding through the Citie of London.

A year later he stands first in the list of King's Men to whom their dead comrade Augustine Phillips assigned sums of money in his will. He had left to the juniors (hired men) of the Fellowship ' five pounds of lawfull money of England to be equally distributed amongeste them,' and he made personal as well as cash bequests to these youngsters,

> Item, I geve to Samuell Gilborne my late apprentice, the some of fortye shillings, and my mouse colloured velvet hose,

and a white taffety dublet, a blacke taffety sute, my purple
cloke, sword and dagger, and my base viall. Item I geve
to James Sands my Apprentice the some of fortye shillings
and a citterne a bandore and a lute, to be paid and delivered
unto him at the expiracion of his terms of yeres in his in-
denture of apprenticehood.

The wardrobe would be valuable financially and professionally
as well as for reasons of sentiment: so, too, the musical instruments which, with his cash, Master Sands was not to get
until he had earned them.

Shakespeare, Condell, and Beeston—the Beeston whose son
was to be Aubrey's source of gossip—received thirty shillings
in gold: Fletcher and some others twenty shillings. Burbage
was left out. So was Heminge, whom, owing to the joint
editorship of the First Folio, we inevitably associate with Condell. Actors do quarrel. There may have been disagreements.

It is plain that Shakespeare did now back out of the tiring-
room. After *Sejanus* there is no more mention of him in the
casts of the Jonson plays given by the King's Men. (If only
Shakespeare's Folio had preserved the cast-lists, as Jonson's
did, what a deal of conjecture would have been saved, especially
if the actors had been named with their particular parts, which
information Jonson stupidly omitted to give!) Burbage and
the others in greater or less number were mentioned as cast
in Jonson's *Volpone*, *The Alchemist* and *Catiline*, and the Second
Folio of Beaumont and Fletcher's works discovers Burbage and
some of the others in *The Captain*, *Bonduca* and *Valentinian*, all
given before Shakespeare's death: but William was not among
them. Nor was he in the cast of Webster's *Duchess of Malfi*
when Burbage played Ferdinand and Master R. Sharpe the
Duchess. Burbage died in March, 1619.

Finally, Shakespeare is put first among the 'principall
Actors in all these Playes' by Heminge and Condell in the
Shakespeare First Folio of 1623. It is very difficult to see why,
if he was only author, producer, and sharer, he was so consistently named among the actors, at least up to 1603 and
then again, retrospectively, in 1623.

J

He was, most luckily for the world, more author than actor; so contemporary allusion is much more to sweet Mr. Shakespeare of *Venus* and of *Romeo* than to greasepaint William of the player's cloak and periwig. But in 1610 John Davies of Hereford, who had previously scribbled ' W. S.' ' R. B.' (we may conjecture William Shakespeare, Richard Burbage) in the margin of a book where actors and acting are mentioned, wrote the following rather cryptic lines,

> Some say (good Will) which I, in sport, do sing,
> Had'st thou not plaid some Kingly parts in sport,
> Thou hadst bin a companion for a King;
> And, beene a King among the meaner sort.
> Some others raile; but, raile as they thinke fit,
> Thou hast no rayling, but, a raigning Wit:
> And honesty thou sow'st which they do reape;
> So, to increase their Stocke which they do keepe.

One can scratch away for ever as to the exact meaning of all this; what distinctly emerges is that Will had at some time played kingly parts.

The well-known sonnet of an Oxford student, William Basse, on Shakespeare's Death, beginning

> Renowned Spencer, lye a thought more nye
> To learned Chaucer, and rare Beaumont lye
> A little neerer Spenser to make roome
> For Shakespeare in your threefold fowerfold Tombe.

calls him ' rare Tragoedian ' later on. Nowadays the word tragedian is applied more to the player than to the author: but we cannot assume that the sonneteer was complimenting the dramatist on his histrionics, though Basse, who was twenty when Shakespeare gave his last known performance (in *Sejanus*), might well have seen him on the stage.

Heminge and Condell, when they collected and edited Shakespeare's plays in the First Folio seven years after his death, made no direct reference to his acting: Shakespeare was their ' friend and fellow,' as he had shown in his will when these two 'fellows' were selected with Burbage for a bequest of 26s. 8d. apiece to 'buy them rings,' rings being the memorial tokens of the day. Ben Jonson's famous Folio tribute is to the poet: it was his book, line, and scene that moved the other complimentary contributors, but there are two separate references to Shakespeare's departure to 'the grave's tiring-house' (in the verses by Hugh Holland and 'I.M.'), and these do suggest that the writers remembered their Will as a man of the motley and the dressing-room as well as of the book and the study.

So much for contemporary evidence. There is no reason to believe on this showing that Shakespeare was a 'star': the fact that he sometimes headed a list of the King's Men may well be based on his status as sharer, guiding genius, and author-in-chief, rather than on the precedence of his roles. Certainly we may thank his fellows if they dissuaded him from too much performance and forced him back to his pens and paper.

Later tradition about his place upon the stage is slender and, on the whole, 'the notices' are inconclusive. Aubrey, however, being the first to speak (1681) and having the authority of William Beeston, son of Shakespeare's acting-colleague Christopher Beeston, must be considered. He says bluntly that Shakespeare 'was an Actor at one of the playhouses and did act exceedingly well: now B. Jonson was never a good Actor, but an excellent Instructor.' This statement suggests that Jonson ably 'produced' or 'directed,' as we should say, his own plays, and there is here no hesitation about the allotment of good marks to Shakespeare's performance. In 1699 an antiquary called James Wright stated in a dialogue that Shakespeare was a much better poet than player. Then Nicholas Rowe, in his much fuller biography (1709), which drew on the talk of the great actor of the day, Betterton, gave some support to that view.

It is at this Time, and upon this Accident, that he is said to have made his first Acquaintance in the Playhouse. He was receiv'd into the Company then in being, at first in a very mean

Rank; but his admirable Wit, and the natural Turn of it to the Stage, soon distinguish'd him, if not as an extraordinary Actor, yet as an excellent Writer. His name is Printed, as the Custom was in those Times, amongst those of the other Players, before some old Plays, but without any particular Account of what sort of Parts he us'd to play; and tho' I have inquir'd, I could never meet with any further Account of him this way, than that the top of his Performance was the Ghost in his own *Hamlet*.

In the middle of the eighteenth century William Oldys, antiquarian and biographer and Norroy King of Arms at the Heralds' College, collected materials for a life of Shakespeare (never completed) in which is some gossip about Sir William Davenant being Shakespeare's natural son and there is also a strange story to the effect that,

One of Shakespeare's younger brothers, who lived to a good old age, even some years, as I compute, after the restoration of K. Charles II, would in his younger days come to London to visit his brother Will, as he called him, and be a spectator of him as an actor in some of his own plays.

This looks like nonsense: Shakespeare's younger brothers died in 1607 (Edmund, the actor), 1612 (Gilbert) and 1613 (Richard). Had any of them survived the Restoration they would have been anything from 80 to 100 years old. In any case, if this narrator, who is described as having such an impaired memory as to be almost weak of intellect, were a descendant of one of the brothers, he had little enough to tell,

and all that could be recollected from him of his brother Will in that station was, the faint, general, and almost lost idea he had of having once seen him act a part in one of his own comedies, wherein being to personate a decrepit old man, he wore a long beard, and appeared so weak and drooping and unable to walk, that he was forced to be supported and carried by another person to a table, at which he was seated among some company, who were eating, and one of them sung a song.

This obviously refers to Adam in *As You Like It*; the part is small. It might well, however, have been allotted to the player of the Ghost in *Hamlet*. If Shakespeare took such minor assignments he could then have given time to the general direction or ' instruction ' of rehearsals, assuming that Burbage allowed him to do so and did not resent the guidance. There must have been ' production ' of a sort and Aubrey, as we saw, cited Jonson as an able ' instructor ' of this kind. It has been argued by Dr. Flatter in *Shakespeare's Producing Hand* that the punctuation of the First Folio represents the poet's ideas, as a producer, of timing and stressing the lines.

So we have little enough on which to form a view; certainly, I think, he acted, but decreasingly (and fortunately) in view of his supreme gift for creating the lively scene that others would enact and in shaping the exquisite words that others would deliver. It is likely enough that ghosts and seniors were his line; the parts would not be too exacting and would provide leisure to watch and shape the greater part of the rehearsal.

The actors of the time were an increasingly prosperous fellowship. But their legal status was still that of protected outcasts. When Shakespeare was eight years old an Act of Parliament was passed which designated as ' Roges, Vaca-boundes, and Sturdye Beggers all Fencers, Bearewardes, and Comon Players in Enterludes and Minstrels.' All these types and manners of life were deemed by the Act to be ' lewd ' and such folk were to be ' taken and adjudged ' for the aforesaid roguery and vagabondage, unless ' belonging to any Baron of the Realme or Towardes any other honourable Person of Greater Degree.' In short, the player, however exalted his theme and his author, was on the windy side of the law unless sheltered by some nobleman's cloak; fortunately such cloaks were fairly plentiful and the Tudor Lords, by shielding the players, not only saved the Commoners of England from deprivation of pleasure by their Puritanical legislators; they also made Shakespeare possible, thus rendering an unique service to England and the world.

So, by patronage, the letter of a foolish law was kept while the public mind was engaged, amused, exhilarated and occasionally, no doubt, bored, by the entertainments thus provided. It is a general habit to pass laws so stupidly tyrannical that they cannot be enforced; loopholes have to be found and in this case the Lord Patron was the loophole. The Crown itself was at the head of the rolls of patron protectors. Yet Shakespeare, coming from a bourgeois home with that proud Arden blood in him, was never wholly happy in his profession, although it brought him wealth, status in Stratford and a large house, and won his family a coat of arms. He had made himself ' a motley to the view ' and he intermittently expressed his feeling of the player's outcast state and social insignificance. As a poet he felt confident of abiding fame, and he blithely, almost blatantly, promised himself and his subjects some enjoyment of perpetuity. But as an actor he often felt himself to be a creature of a frail and insubstantial nature. ' The best in this kind are but shadows,' says Duke Theseus in *A Midsummer Night's Dream*. He speaks for William Shakespeare's occasional distrust of plays and players when these are matched with the great actualities of public life and of real action in the forum of the world. He cannot always have thought so; but he had queer pangs of shame about his playhouse occupations.

These are given most expression in the Sonnets, since there he is addressing a nobleman and, sometimes rather mawkishly, dwelling on his own humility and on the limitations of theatre life wherein he has ' sold cheap what is most dear.'

' With what I most enjoy contented least ' he rebukes Fortune.

> O, for my sake do you with Fortune chide,
> The guilty goddess of my harmful deeds,
> That did not better for my life provide
> Than public means which public manners breeds.
> Thence comes it that my name receives a brand;
> And almost thence my nature is subdu'd
> To what it works in, like the dyer's hand:
> Pity me, then, and wish I were renew'd;

> Whilst, like a willing patient, I will drink
> Potions of eisel 'gainst my strong infection;
> No bitterness that I will bitter think,
> Nor double penance, to correct correction.
>   Pity me, then, dear friend, and I assure ye
>   Even that your pity is enough to cure me.

Yet one does not feel that the Fellowship of the Lord Chamberlain's Men suffered much from ' branded names.' And there are times when Shakespeare glories in the actor's power over his fellows and even over the cormorant Time.

>   How many ages hence
>   Shall this our lofty scene be acted o'er
>   In states unborn and accents yet unknown!

cries Cassius after the murder of Caesar. Cleopatra's fear of ' the quick comedians ' is at least an acknowledgment of their power, and there could be no greater salute to the profession than to call them ' the abstract and brief chronicles of the time.' They are thus elevated to be the true servants of History, which, in fact, they often are. But very soon Shakespeare is smiling ruefully at the irony of things. The actor's passions are false, his problems shadows. He works himself up, ' tears in his eyes, distraction in's aspect '—and all for nothing, all for Hecuba. Life is real, life is earnest, but not for actors!

Shakespeare, as so often occurred, was in two minds. His name was branded, his hand was stained, his stage inadequate, but still ' the Muse of fire ' could ' ascend the brightest heaven of invention ' and bestow ' imaginary puissance.' He might be in the motley; he was also in command.

The conditions of performance for which Shakespeare wrote and amid which he directed rehearsals and undertook ' supporting roles,' some of them, it seems, of a minor character, were vastly different from our own. Not merely did the physical structure of the public theatres dictate the description of scenery rather than the use of it; it also determined the style of acting, which had to be louder and broader in the open air than it would be in the private and roofed-in houses. Most important was the complete absence of women from the cast, which affected the writing and rendering of love-scenes. The ladies of the Court might enjoy a masquerade, and there were women of all ranks in Shakespeare's audience, but the Boy-Player alone was allowed to perform in women's parts along with those professionals who were still potentially ' roges and vacaboundes ' in the eyes of the law.

Women were freely admitted to perform in masques, both in and out of Court in the ' Jacobethan ' world. Bacon recommended ' double masques,' one of men, another of ladies, to add ' state and variety.' The ladies by masquing did not mingle with the professional actor, except in so far as Ben Jonson or another of the theatre-men might be standing by as author and director, with Inigo Jones as decorator. The Queen herself might be a masquer and that in robes of unusual cut. In *The Vision of the Twelve Goddesses*, given at Hampton Court, Pallas, impersonated by James I's Queen Anne, is reported by Carleton

> To have had a trick by herself, for her clothes were not so much below the knee, but what we might see a woman had both feete and legs which I never knew before.

No woman appeared on the English public stage until December, 1660, when Killigrew presented Mrs. Hughes as Desdemona and Mrs. Rutter as Emilia.

The boys who had hitherto played the parts of young women in the English professional drama were certainly not incompetent. After all, they had a far longer tradition of acting than their seniors possessed. The acting of plays was a regular part of the curriculum in a Tudor boys' school and was a well-established habit. The boys of St. Paul's had been acting miracle plays as early as 1378 and in the time of Henry VIII they were taught to act interludes by their chief author, Heywood. The Children of the Chapel Royal were also trained for dramatic performances at that period and in 1576 they were publicly performing at a theatre in Blackfriars, while the St. Paul's boys were soon working professionally under Lyly. How the children's companies became strong enough to worry Shakespeare is common knowledge. According to Dr. Sisson,

> In the early history of the Elizabethan stage the literary quality of the boys' plays, as well as the weight of custom, gave them advantage. They could furnish the grace of music, too. But the men's companies, as they developed, allied to themselves scholar-writers and produced their own dramatists of genius. Moreover, they attracted into their ranks the best boy-actors as they grew up, and trained their own boy apprentices. So they could offer to the Court as to the public all the qualities of the boys' performances and in addition the deeper passion, realism, and humanity of adult acting. But there is no doubt that the Blackfriars Children were formidable rivals even to Shakespeare's company at the Globe at the end of the sixteenth century.

The conditions of the boys' service involved apprenticeship at a very early age. Promotion and success came speedily. Salathiel Pavy, of the Queen's Chapel, whose epitaph by Ben Jonson is familiar, died at thirteen after being for three years, in Ben's opinion, ' the stage's jewel.' This poem suggests a genuine admiration and not a mere formal ' obituary notice.'

> Weep with me, all you that read
>   This little story;
> And know, for whom a tear you shed
>   Death's self is sorry.
> 'Twas a child that so did thrive
>   In grace and feature,
> As Heaven and Nature seem'd to strive
>   Which own'd the creature.
> Years he number'd scarce thirteen
>   When Fates turn'd cruel,
> Yet three fill'd zodiacs had he been
>   The stage's jewel;
>
> And did act (what now we moan)
>   Old men so duly,

> As sooth the Parcae thought him one,
> He play'd so truly.

The training must have been constant and severe, for there was plenty of work to be done. In November, 1606, the manager of the Queen's Revels took Abel Cooke 'to be practised and exercised in the sayde qualitye of playinge,' but only on condition that Mrs. Cooke pledged her son to serve and abide with his master for three years. In the adult companies the boys, who were needed for the music, the dancing, and the playing of women's parts, were bound to one of the sharers. There is no reason to suppose that the system did not work equably. The boys could acquire property as well as training. In the will of Augustine Phillips, as we saw, ' my late apprentice Gilborne ' and ' my apprentice Sands ' get not only more money than the fellows of the company but hose, clothes, swords, doublets, and musical instruments.

The boys were not employed for women's parts only. We know that in a revival of *The Duchess of Malfi* one R. Pallant trebled the parts of Cariola, the Doctor, and Court Officer.

The main question is the manner in which the employment of boys affected the composition and performance of the plays at this period of singular dramatic genius. Children memorise easily; the size of their parts was presumably no hindrance to their mastery of the words. That the voice could be so shrill or childish as to ruin a part is suggested by Cleopatra's apprehension lest the quick comedians extemporally should stage her tale and so the world should see

> Some squeaking Cleopatra boy my greatness
> I' the posture of a whore.

That was a most audacious remark. For if Shakespeare's Cleopatra had not got the audience well in hand, the words, which had to be spoken by a boy, could have been turned upon him and so would have raised a most embarrassing laugh.

However, Shakespeare, like the other dramatists of his time, trusted his boys. At times he wrote them exacting as well as exquisite parts; he continually gave them of his best in beauty and in wit. But he could not parade femininity. Even in that kind of drama where all is lost for love he had to be exceedingly careful not to present physical affection in such a way that the pretended passion of a man for a woman who was in fact a boy should appear either ludicrous or offensive. What could not be permitted was embarrassing proximities and caresses of man and boy upon the stage.

Nowadays we are accustomed on the stage and still more on the screen to view prolonged and profuse displays of physical passion, which, even if the embraces had been bisexual, might have astonished and horrified an Elizabethan audience. It is a matter of convention. The Elizabethans relished displays of carnage which we find unpleasant or unexciting; their battle-scenes only embarrass the modern director and seem dull or comic to the modern spectator; they could be thrilled by the display of a severed head, which to us is nastily absurd. On the other hand they might have been shocked to the core had they seen the kind of kisses to which Hollywood at one time accustomed the men, women, children, and even the clergy of the English-speaking nations. (Producers have been compelled to use the stop-watch for lovers more recently.) We may suppose the Elizabethans to have been highly sexed, but to be highly sexed is the very reverse of being highly sex-conscious, which is what we are to-day.

The continual harping on sex-appeal in entertainment is typical of a public which is sexually unsatisfied. Our billing and boosting of cosmic sweethearts was impossible and un-thinkable in their world, even had they been vulgar enough to want it. Their managers could not feature as vastly seductive the Juliet of Master Goffe or the Cleopatra of Master Edmans. (These are Professor Baldwin's attribution of the parts in his book on *The Organisation and Personnel of the Shakespearean Company*.) Probably these lads relied mainly upon recitation and suppressed the mimicry of feminine allurements. There appears to be no evidence in the social records of the time that the boys were the heroes or the darlings of the day, as Master

Betty became later on when he had plenty of feminine competitors.

The remarkable thing is that the names of the boys who took the chief parts are largely a matter of guesswork now. They were not featured. They were not the darlings of the town. The gossips, diarists, and foreign visitors might have been expected to discuss with eagerness the relative merits of this Juliet or that Rosalind, or so-and-so's Viola and so-and-so's Cleopatra. We hear high praise of the great tragedians, Alleyn and Burbage. But about the boys there is a surprising silence.

To the Elizabethan it was not necessary that Romeo should frequently rain kisses on Juliet or that Antony and Cleopatra should be lip to lip and languish in each other's arms. If their dramatist told the public about the lovers' devotion with sufficient skill they would accept this, just as they accepted a Danish ' dawn in russet-mantle clad ' on a summer afternoon in Southwark. The poet provided the scenery and atmosphere of passion as of nature; the display of it was therefore the less necessary.

The first ten lines of *Antony and Cleopatra* establish the dotage of the Roman who has become the bellows and the fan to cool a gipsy's lust, ' the triple pillar of the world transformed into a strumpet's fool.' In modern texts of this play it is announced that the famous couple embrace on Antony's line,

> The nobleness of life
> Is to do thus.

But there is no authority for this in the Folio, which is our only text of the play. Some sort of salute there may have been ; possibly no more was intended than a bow and a kiss on the hand. As Granville-Barker put it,

> Here is a tragedy of sex without one single scene of sexual appeal. . . . The play opens with Cleopatra's parting from Antony and in their two short encounters we see her swaying him by wit, malice, and with the moods of her mind. Not till the story takes its tragic plunge and sex is drowned in

deeper passion are they ever intimately together; till he is brought to her dying there has been occasion for but one embrace. Contrast this with a Cleopatra planned to the advantage of the actress of to-day.

I would add, more especially, ' to the advantage of the screen-actress of to-day.' Of Romeo and Juliet, Granville-Barker reminds us,

> Romeo and Juliet are seldom alone together; never for long, but in the balcony scene; and in this, the most famous of all love scenes, they are kept from all contact with each other.

Antony and Cleopatra, at least for a modern audience, is continually haunted by the ghost of the boy-player whose presence forbade a closer showing of the passionate actualities. Put this play on the stage to-day and one always has a sense of frost upon the Nile. To some extent this may be due to the fact that it is more than usually difficult to find the actress for the part. But, if we had the actress, could she not say with justice, ' This may be grand stuff to recite and I can create a show of passionate temperament by venting my naughty and imperial temper on the women and the slaves. But, after all, the play is about empires tossed away for self-indulgence. A lord of men has become a strumpet's fool; the reason that " crowns and crownets are as plates dropped from his pocket " is that he has his eyes on the royal bed of Egypt, and how do I put this over without a bedroom scene ? ' In a world that is increasingly accustomed to bedroom scenes *Antony and Cleopatra* becomes increasingly difficult to act. There is certainly more show of coquetry in the difficult and more rarely performed *Troilus and Cressida* and the scene where Cressida kisses the Greek generals in turn is hard to equate with Mr. Granville-Barker's view of the boy-player. On the other hand the introduction to the play in the revised Quarto edition definitely says it was ' never staled by the stage.' This must refer to public performance. Perhaps the queer piece was done once at the Inns of Court, or at a nobleman's house, found unsatisfactory, and so not repeated in public.

So Shakespeare tactfully accepted the limitation and wrote girl-into-page or other breeches parts for the boy-players of the company; he equipped them with mischief, wit, poetry, everything but the physical coquettishness which must have been artistically fatal. He laid on the mental caprice to his Beatrice, his Portia, his Rosalind, who are feminine chiefly for the purposes of the plot. The girl who is playing Shakespeare to-day soon realises that sex-appeal is of no importance or even downright dangerous. I make no apology for quoting Mr. Granville-Barker again, for nobody could put better the challenge to the modern actress:

Shakespeare makes no such demands, has left no blank spaces for her to fill with her charm. He asks instead for self-forgetful clarity of perception, and for a sensitive, spirited, athletic beauty of speech and conduct, which will leave prettiness and its lures at a loss, and the crudities of a more Circean appeal looking very crude indeed.

In an interesting essay on *Shakespeare's Actors* Dr. G. B. Harrison has pointed out that in the Romantic Comedy or High-fantastical period the two boys playing the chief girls' parts must have been strongly differentiated in height and colouring. Hero, Celia, and Maria were low and brown, Rosalind, Beatrice, and Viola were probably tall and fair by contrast; Rosalind, we know, was of considerable height. We may assume that contrasting the girls' parts was then a matter of tactics as it is now, when it is customary to set fair and dark together in contrasted feminine roles.

I have often wondered who played the mature women, Gertrude in *Hamlet*, for example. A baritone voice, almost pardonable in Lady Macbeth, would emerge embarrassingly from this far weaker vessel. Yet this could hardly be a young boy's role, as Ophelia obviously was. Were there some full-grown but sexually neutral types specially sought out and retained for parts of this kind? In Mr. Emlyn Williams's play, *Spring, 1600*, which concerned the back-stage life of that period, there was in the first London production a delightful performance by Mr. Frank Pettingell of the player Pope, which suggested, humorously but without offence, that Pope was a soft, tabby-cattish sort of creature and usually cast in the Gertrude type of part. (This is all wrong according to Professor Baldwin, who sees Pope as a heavy comic and the original Falstaff; he has the authority of Samuel Rowlands (1600) who wrote of ' Pope the Clowne ' who ' speaks so Boorish ' in such roles.) It seems probable that far greater difficulties were involved in casting the mature women than in finding the right boy for a girl's part. We may surmise that Cordelia was better played than her sisters and Ophelia better impersonated than the Queen.

An interesting point arises here. Just before and around the turn of the century, that is to say in the High-fantastical period and before the great tragedies, Shakespeare was writing long and exacting parts for his leading boy. Beatrice and Rosalind have to go far towards carrying the play in *Much Ado* and (more especially) in *As You Like It*. Malvolio is the real prop of *Twelfth Night*, as the men of Shakespeare's time knew. They spoke, significantly, of *Much Ado* by the names of Benedick and Beatrice, while *Twelfth Night* they called, simply, *Malvolio*. But Viola is the genius of the piece, if not its pillar. Any young actress would snatch at the part.

Then, with the end of this period, comes a complete change. Three of the great tragedies ask only for a boy who can be softly the cause of tears. ('Sweet invocation of a child—most pretty and pathetical,' Armado had said of another matter.) That would suffice for Ophelia, Desdemona, and Cordelia. All these you may say, or two of them conspicuously, did something which showed strong character. But the roles themselves, as written, are not a great challenge and bestow no great opportunity. One remembers an Ophelia—who that saw Fay Compton has forgotten hers ?—but whoever made or enhanced a reputation as Desdemona or Cordelia, however well the renderings were contrived—or produced ? Cressida, too, is not really a big part, though the play hangs upon her falsity.

One has to assume that the boy-star, the top of whose performance was Rosalind, had grown to maturity: his voice had gone: he had begun to croak as fatally as any raven. So it was resolved to design the ensuing tragedies in a way to make no impossible demands on the company. Burbage would carry them. Hamlet, Othello, Macbeth, Lear—they and the men about them are the play. But Lady Macbeth? However impressive at times, it is not a big part, and the main reason why such a fuss has been made about it is that our stage has so long been populated and dominated by 'Star actresses' for whom Shakespeare had catered inadequately in the Tragedies. So Lady Macbeth, being much more makeable than Desdemona or Ophelia, was later seized upon with avidity and producers had to give the star every chance of using her limited scenes and lines. There is tremendous stuff there, of course, but no copiousness. The play was for Burbage, not the boy—or was it a young adult who tackled the wives?

Then, suddenly, we come to *Antony and Cleopatra* and Shakespeare writes his greatest woman's part of all, the teasing and tremendous role of one who must be royal in her looks, common in her lusts, speaking in exquisite poetry, behaving like a treacherous wanton, now commanding, now kittenish: she is contradictory as ever at the end, first behaving with her generous conqueror, Octavius Caesar, like somebody who is trying to cheat the Customs, then dying to immortal music, and at last vanishing to Elysium as it were the very genius of all selfless passion. Either Shakespeare had found the boy-actor of his lifetime or he had misjudged both part and player. I fancy the player may have failed him, for we hear nothing of the play in performance. Was this, his supreme achievement in poetry, after all ' a flop '?

Whatever happened to Cleopatra, Shakespeare made no more such challenges to youth. He went back to safer country: the breeches part of Imogen is a lovely role but not an exacting one, not at least on Cleopatra's scale of histrionic demand. Marina, Perdita, and Miranda ask for some new arrival in the team, another nice exponent of the ' pretty and pathetical.' They enchant us before they are acted and they are kept to a size with which the junior branch of the King's Men could adequately cope. Did those cruel lines about a squeaking

Cleopatra boying the Queen's greatness in the posture of a whore prove all too prophetic ? Or were they—a possibility—written in later in a fit of chagrin after the ruin had been wrought ? The last of Shakespeare's boy-stars may have been Richard Robinson, first mentioned in the company in 1611 and listed with the complete team of old and new Shakespeareans by Heminge and Condell in the First Folio. Dick was not above a practical joke, if we are to believe Ben Jonson, who wrote expressly of him in *The Devil Is an Ass*.

> But there be some of 'em
> Are very honest lads: there's Dickey Robinson,
> A very pretty fellow, and comes often
> To a gentleman's chamber, a friend of mine. We had
> The merriest supper of it there, one night,
> The gentleman's landlady invited him
> To a gossip's feast: now he, sir, brought Dick Robinson,
> Drest like a lawyer's wife, amongst 'em all:
> I lent him clothes.—But to see him behave it,
> And lay the law, and carve, and drink unto them
> And then talk bawdy, and send frolics! O
> It would have burst your buttons, or not left you
> A seam.
> *Meer*   They say he's an ingenious youth.
> *Eng.*   O sir! and dresses himself the best, beyond
> Forty of your very ladies; did you never see him ?

Who played Cleopatra ? Was it young Gilborne, the favourite and legatee of Augustine Phillips ? He would have been about the right age—and he disappeared from the company; there is no further mention of him in the Ben Jonson lists of King's Men casts and he is not in the great roll-call along with Dickey Robinson in the First Folio. He may have failed on some big occasion and gone elsewhere—or chosen another calling.

There is no doubt about Burbage's supremacy in Shakespeare's company or of his hold upon the town. He inherited theatrical instincts, he was a leading spirit of his team, he fought the rivalry of Alleyn as the virile, full-throated thunderer

of his day, and he ' created ' many of the great Shakespearean
roles. He specialised, claim Pollard and Dover Wilson (in an
essay on Shakespeare in *The Great Tudors*), in bluff soldiers and
whimsical rudesby roles: they allotted him the Bastard in
King John, Berowne, Petruchio, Benedick and Henry V, all
rough wooers: they also think that he ' probably ' was
Bottom and Sir Toby, but surely the Clowns or the Irregular
Humorists, as the semi-clowns were called, would have laid
strong hands on these fat parts. There were naturally various
grades of droll: those of the Tarlton-Kempe-Armin type
actually played the typical Fool parts, jigged and gagged,
while the heavy comedians, such as Pope, who may or may
not have had a Queen Gertrude vein as well, took on the gross
and liquorish knights, rotund and orotund.

Burbage died in 1619, aged 52, which was also the fatal age
for Shakespeare: they burned themselves out quickly in the
Fellowship. A friend wrote an elegy which confirms three of
his Shakespearean roles.

> He's gone and with him what a world indeed!
> Which he revived, to be revivèd so
> No more! Young Hamlet, old Hieronymo,
> Kind Lear, the grievèd Moor, and more beside
> That lived in him have now forever died.

Kind may be a curious adjective for Lear: it was perhaps a
misprint for King, but the facts of the rhyme are useful. (Old
Hieronymo appeared in *The Spanish Tragedy* by Kyd.)

Another tribute ran:

> Astrologers and Stargazers this year
> Write out of four eclipses: five appear.
> Death interposing Burbage and Time staying
> Hath made a visible eclipse of playing.

While a salute in prose describes him as

> never failing in his part when he had done speaking but with
> his looks and gesture maintaining still into the height.

No doubt that description was well intended: but an actor who gestures and calls attention to himself even into the height while his fellow is speaking is a poor and selfish colleague. If he did indeed carry on so, was Burbage always as much loved in the company as he was outside it ? Here is another tribute to this vehemence and versatility:

> His stature small, but every thought and mood
> Might thoroughly from the face be understood
> And his whole action he could change with ease
> From ancient Lear to youthful Pericles.

Sir Nigel Playfair, in an essay on Burbage in the same volume on *The Great Tudors*, gives him Shylock, Richard III, Prince Hal, Romeo, Henry V and Brutus: then Hamlet, Othello, Lear, Macbeth, Pericles and Coriolanus. Playfair gives no authority for this list and I know of none. And who played Antony to the boy-player's Cleopatra ? Surely that was a role for the then maturing Burbage.

We know the names of the Chamberlain's and King's Men down the years, but we must guess the parts which they played. Who was the small, antic boy for whom there are chances in the History and High-fantastical Periods, e.g. Maria, ' the youngest wren of nine,' Falstaff's page in *Henry IV* and *The Merry Wives of Windsor*, and possibly Celia. There was plainly also a very thin man for lean and hungry comedy roles. Was he the Bastard's brother in *King John*, with legs like riding-rods, the meagre Apothecary in *Romeo and Juliet* (' sharp misery had worn him to the bones '), Holofernes, Slander, Aguecheek? But such speculation, however pleasant to indulge in, leads to no certain casting.

After the play, even the most tragical, there was a jig. (The later but similar tradition of a short farce after the long tragedy lasted well into the middle of the nineteenth century.) It may seem outrageous to us that after Hamlet had been carried from the stage, Clown Armin—for Kempe had left the company by 1599—would come jigging on to it. He had had a small day's work as First Gravedigger and he and his kind had been well snubbed by Hamlet in the speech about the naughty gagging of the drolls—if that speech was not left unspoken, as I suspect that it prudently may have been. So he would be ready for his opportunity and would take it to the full.

The jig was more than a clown's double shuffle: it was 'a lyrical farce written in rhyme and sung and danced to ballad measure': it involved, generally, two or more players and some dancers and lasted twenty minutes. Kempe's 'New Jygge between a Souldiour and a Miser and Sym the Clown' was entered at Stationers' Hall in 1595; there were regular jig-scripts and we have that of 'Mr Attowels Jigge between Francis a Gentleman, Richard a Farmer, and their Wives.' This one had four scenes and various tunes of the day were introduced. Moth in *Love's Labour's Lost* gives the recipe for 'jigging off a tune at the tongue's end.'

> Canary to it with your feet, humour it with turning up your eyelids, sigh a note, and sing a note . . . and keep not too long in one tune, but snip and away.

An observant tourist, Thomas Platter of Basle, has left us an idea of the termination of a Shakespearean tragedy with jiggery and clowning: he was impressed by the skill of all the elements. He wrote in German and I quote from Clare Williams's translation.

> On Sept. 21st (1599) after lunch, about two o'clock, I and my party crossed the water and there, in the house with the thatched roof, witnessed an excellent performance of the tragedy of the First Emperor Julius Caesar with a cast of some fifteen people: when the play was over they danced very marvellously and gracefully, as is their wont, two dressed as men and two as women.

Platter also thought highly of the actors' wardrobe and gave a reason for their resources.

> The actors are most expensively and elaborately costumed: for it is the English usage for eminent lords or knights at their decease to bequeath and leave almost the best of their clothes to their serving men, which it is unseemly for the latter

wear, so that they offer them for sale for a small sum to the actors.

Shakespeare cannot have cared much about jigs. Did he ever write the script for one? In his Factotum days, no doubt. However, it was better to have the clowns performing their antics outside the limits of a tragedy instead of improvising and grimacing beyond measure in the middle of it.

The actors' vocabulary has remained curiously constant. In Shakespeare's day parts were ' studied ' and there was a ' prompter ' who held ' the book ' in case an actor was ' imperfect ' with his lines. The available clothes and costumes were called the 'wardrobe.' We cannot, of course, say how the acting of Shakespeare's day would compare with that of our own. There were evidently considerable changes in style and technique during Shakespeare's own lifetime; he himself was an advocate of realism and in the well-known passages in *Hamlet* he commanded fidelity to nature: nothing was to be overdone or to ' come tardy off.' He knew how a conscienceless actor will drag out his own ' business ' in order to wring laughter from the crowd or pause upon an exit in order to get 'a round.' He was for ' tripping ' as against ' mouthing ' speech: he wanted ' temperance ' instead of passion-tearing and uproarious noise. He would have the clowns respect the text which they were given instead of adding lines and drolleries of their own. In short he was banging the desk and asserting his rights.

The speeches inserted in *Hamlet* must have followed some trouble in the Fellowship. There is no justification for these speeches in the play and it seems to me incredible that they were, in fact, spoken in the actual performances. Everyone in the audience would ask at which actor the author was pointing his criticism and the actor, ordered to speak what would be deemed a condemnation of himself or a colleague, would have good reason to refuse. If the chief author of the Fellowship had some grievances against the team, he could have aired them privately instead of asking the poor wretches to denounce their own faults before a tittering audience: at least, so the scolded mummers would say.

It can be suggested that Hamlet's censure of the periwig-pated ranters, roarers, and out-Heroders of Herod was aimed at Alleyn and at rival players. Certainly part of this disquisition is directed specifically to the Boy Players at Blackfriars, who were prospering too well to please the Chamberlain's Men. But the attack on the too heavy tragedian and too intensive clowns was patently double-edged. If Burbage as Hamlet delivered all this outburst against the over-vehement kind of acting, it was open to the audience to bid the great Richard first try his physic on himself, and to advise Clown Armin also to take his master's medicine.

When Shakespeare first came to London the plays were rhetorical in style; the thunderings of Marlowe asked for might of chest and lungs. The audience then was crude and less experienced: its conduct might be rowdy. The actor, to get command of his hearers, would need every trick of the trade and, to deliver the eloquence effectively, would employ a far lustier attack than was necessary later on. As Shakespeare made both the rhythm of speech more subtle and the drawing of character more detailed and precise, he would, of course, need a reform in the actor's elocution and in his methods of impersonation. The move to the closed-in stage of the elegant and aristocratic Blackfriars inevitably affected the technique of the players yet again; in the new conditions ' the modesty of nature ' could be still more accurately pursued. The old bravura methods, the acting that has its drums beating and banners flying, was less necessary than ever. But Shakespeare's idea of modesty and of naturalism may have been much broader than our own. What we nowadays call greasy ' ham ' he might have taken for the good lean meat of acting.

It is odd that the part in *Hamlet* which Shakespeare himself is supposed to have acted—admittedly we have no news of this until a whole century later—is the ' hammiest' thing in the play. A ghost, to begin with, is not within the modesty of nature; and a ghost who describes the process of hair-raising as making

Thy knotted and combined locks to part
And each particular hair to stand on end

Like quills upon the fretful porpentine

is not to be satisfied with a tripping or a gentle speech.   When
the same ghost comes to moan his earlier doom,

> Cut off even in the blossoms of my sin,
> Unhousel'd, disappointed, unaneled

and adds

> Oh horrible, Oh horrible, Most horrible

the player has not only a chance, but a necessity, to ' get
something off the chest.' I do not doubt that if Shakespeare did play the part, he let the audience, from groundlings to galleries, have it good and hard. You could not
' lift the roof' at the Globe, there being no roof to lift. But
you could shiver some timbers: and, if timbers were duly
shivered by this eloquent spook, then one can imagine Burbage's fury when *he* was handed a passage to speak in which
the vehement actor was sharply caned for this very practice
of timber-shivering.

My own supposition is that Shakespeare enjoyed acting,
despite his sighs in the Sonnets concerning the nature of his
career.   Once in the motley, he had to be edged out of it by his
fellows who knew what he could do best; they must have seen
that, while many could powerfully open their lungs, none could
hold a pen like their Will.   One ground for holding this view is
Shakespeare's persistence in performance.   By 1603 he was a
most successful as well as a very busy dramatist.   He was on the
verge of his supreme period of productivity; with *Hamlet* behind
him, he had at least four master-tragedies ahead and already,
perhaps, in mind.   And there he was, mumming away in
Jonson's *Sejanus*, which he must have known to be quite inferior
to his own work.   This suggests an obstinate clinging-on to the
motley, a blank refusal to be evicted from the tiring-house.
What actor, after all, ever managed to retire with but a single
farewell performance ?

He knew the pains of it.   He had ' dried ' in his time, groped
for a prompt, and suffered hell.

With

> As an imperfect actor on the stage
> Who with his fear is put besides his part
>
> *Sonnet XXIII*

and

> Like a dull actor now
> I have forgot my part and I am out
> Even to a full disgrace
>
> *Coriolanus*, v, iii

he proclaims his sympathy with such failure, and his compassion for the

> poor player
> That struts and frets his hour upon the stage
> And then is heard no more.
>
> *Macbeth*, v, v

On the other hand he had seen, and on occasion felt, the thrill
of mastery.

> As in a theatre the eyes of men,
> After a well-graced actor leaves the stage,
> Are idly bent on him that enters next,
> Thinking his prattle to be tedious
>
> *Richard II*, v, ii

It has been suggested that the second line was a tribute to
Burbage, while the third and fourth voice Shakespeare's modesty
about his own achievement in this kind. I wonder. As a
sonneteer Shakespeare showed no bashfulness; he even claimed
to have the power to immortalise the subjects of his pen. He
may reasonably have fancied himself as ' well-graced.'   There
is reference enough to the charms of this ' handsome, well-shap't

man.' He may have been, in his own eyes, the fascinating creature whose successor was bound to seem a prattler and a bore.

The truth is that good actors are bad resigners: and even bad actors may be no readier to quit. Once assurance has been gained it is pleasant to be seen and heard, pleasant to ' get laughs,' pleasant to play upon an audience so expertly that, by timing and emphasis, emotion can be stirred and applause evoked exactly as intended. That Shakespeare was not discouraged by the ' supporting roles ' for which he was cast is shown by his plodding on as an actor long after he was established in the other quality which he professed, that of writing. Amateurs are as stubborn as professionals. When Charles Dickens ought to have been writing or resting and getting his blood-pressure down, he was stumping the country as an amateur actor, storming the stages, overworking the box-offices, and lifting the roof.

In the end they got Shakespeare back to his desk. Perhaps that failure of health, which I have suspected in the early years of the new century, had more to do with it than comradely persuasion. At any rate we see no more of him on the players' lists. But that he itched for it now and again, I strongly suspect. As he saw one of the new ' hired men ' bungle a part or as he watched one of the experienced seniors of the company set the house in a tremble or in a roar, the longing to be up and trying his hand again must have been acute. How many people, who have once got any distance on the stage, are converted to the view that they really are no good at the job and should give it up ? Even if we agree with the eighteenth-century tradition that Shakespeare was but a moderate performer, that is no reason for believing that he withdrew with relief. Old actors, like old soldiers, never die, and it takes them a long, long time to fade away.

Still, vanish he did. And the world is the beneficiary of that retirement. We must thank the stars that Shakespeare was never in his early days a star, that Burbage stole (or rightfully collected) all the thunder that was going, and that Shakespeare, having only short roles to study, had time to write plays and parts, instead of fiddling his life away in the plays and parts of lesser men. If Burbage or any other member of the Fellowship took Shakespeare by the scruff of the neck from time to time and at last bundled him out of the tiring-house for ever with a violent command to waste himself no longer but to go home and scribble, scribble, scribble, then that man has earned, through three and a half succeeding centuries, the unqualified gratitude of all mankind.

CHAPTER XIII

As They Liked It

SHAKESPEARE has qualified to be the Librarian's Pest. Multitudes of shelves are loaded with Shakespeareana: and still they come. (I know my own offence in the addition thereto.) Shakespeare's knowledge of the law, of birds and beasts and flowers, of fowling and the chase, his reading, his religion, his library (or lack of it—as the anti-Stratfordians insist), his investments, his health—all these and much more have become matters of profound, incessant, occasionally fertile, often barren, sometimes exciting and sometimes boring research and scholarship. But his working life, after all, was in the tiring-room, on the platform, at the author's desk, and in the managerial office. Not only was the play the thing; the reception of the play and the finance of the play were also things of primary importance. What was the public liking? What could it be made to like? Which of Shakespeare's plays, as a modern showman might phrase it, was ' a winner ' and which ' a flop '? And why did plays please or displease?

Questions like this have stimulated strangely little inquiry: the evidence, it is true, is scanty, but absence of attested fact has never deterred the lovers and students of Shakespeare from indulging in the pleasure of a good guess. The true reason is, I think, that most of the inquirers have approached Shakespeare as a Poet, as a Mind, as a Thinker, and as a Dramatic Artist. But he was also a Manager-Artist. They do not relate drama to gate-money and to the romances and disasters of the box-office. Yet, without a box-office, there can be no professional theatre, unless, of course, some beneficent State or private ' angel ' is prepared to do all the paying out, an unlikely occurrence.

Were Shakespeare a modern or a recent dramatist we should continually be turning to some such reference book as *Who's*

Who in the Theatre, a contemporary record of the English stage, compiled by that unwearying devotee of theatrical statistics, John Parker. From columns such as these we discover that Shaw scored highest in London with *Fanny's First Play*, which first appeared without his name (624 performances), and next with *Saint Joan* (565 performances), while Galsworthy scored 407 with *Loyalties* and 349 with *The Skin Game*. We feel that in the case of the Elizabethans there ought to be similar knowledge. The theatre of Shakespeare's day was the scene of a true repertory system, whereby plays were produced in series and kept alive by recurrent performances, the most popular recurring most often. The staging of a single play for ' a run,' as we say, was certainly unusual and may never have happened at all. New plays were grafted onto the existing schedule. Favourites reappeared at intervals of about a week. Henslowe's play-lists show, for example, that in the summer of 1594, at Newington Butts, *Titus Andronicus* and *The Jew of Malta* were given twice each between June 3 and June 13.

Unfortunately there were no stage statisticians at work then and the available evidence for estimating the relative popularity of Shakespeare's plays is small. The Chamberlain's Men (later King's Men) have not left such complete lists of productions and receipts as Henslowe did. But we have a few figures, we have some record of Command Performances at Court or in noblemen's houses, we have contemporary allusion (all too scarce), and we have also the list of Play Quartos published. These last may have been derived from ' stolen and surreptitious copies,' as Heminge and Condell related, but none the less they bear witness to public interest in the plays concerned. The texts of the Quarto Editions may often be the faulty work of piratical hands, but pirates do not steal except where there is value. Plays would only be printed by thieves if the thieves could rely on a ready sale. So the number of Quarto Editions of a play is at least some help in judging its impact on the public.

We begin with the undoubted success of *Harey the VI*. This is presumably the play featuring ' brave Talbot,' the play to which Nashe attributed 10,000 spectators at least (at several times), the play printed in the First Folio as *Henry VI*, Part I.

Professor Harbage, in his admirable book on *Shakespeare's Audience*, records the success thus:

> On March 3, 1592, *Henry VI*, Part I, had its opening at the Rose, and brought in as gallery receipts the all-time record of 1,840d. previously noted in the present study. In the following three months, it was performed thirteen additional times. During the first nine of these, the receipts on five different occasions equalled those normally taken on opening days. The four remaining performances show average receipts, the last, June 20, 1592, coming three days before a summer intermission . . . the fourteen performances 'grossed' in the galleries 14,156d.—a record surpassed by only one other play mentioned in Henslowe's *Diary*. When Strange's Men left the Rose, the *Diary* had no more to say of *Henry VI*, Part I, but more would be needless. Henslowe and Nashe, earliest recorders of a Shakespearean play, agree on its power to draw an audience.

The roll of performances and allusions to performances given by Chambers (Vol. 2, pp. 303-353) is also a help to students of Shakespeare's box-office. Of the early period we also know that *The Comedy of Errors* was still sufficiently liked to be given at Gray's Inn among the Christmas revels of 1594 (Dec. 28). A year later *King Richard* (presumably *Richard III*) was part of the supper-time attractions offered by Sir Edward Hoby to Sir Robert Cecil. In 1599 Platter, as we noted, visited *Julius Caesar* and its following Jig. But the information on the whole mocks our curiosity by its meagreness of fact.

Richard II had gone out of favour by 1601, the time of the Essex revolt: it was alleged against the players concerned in that risky performance before the rebellion that they had fished out a piece 'so old—so long out of use' and had been given 40s. more than 'their ordinary' for doing so. Evidently the piece had ceased to attract; a political motive for its revival could therefore be assigned. In 1602 *Twelfth Night* was performed in the Middle Temple Hall at a feast. In 1603 *As You Like It* was being given at the Pembrokes' home, Wilton House, near Salisbury, probably with James I attending. (The evidence for this, including the statement ' we have the man Shakespeare with us ', is in a letter, now lost, but definitely believed to exist by William Cory in 1865; Cory was a careful historian as well as a poet. His hostess, Lady Herbert, spoke of the letter—and the Court was at Wilton at this period.) *A Midsummer Night's Dream* was still being given at Whitehall in this year.

Then we have the Court Revels Account for 1604-5. This document has been suspect as a forgery, but is now generally accepted as useful evidence. The Shakespearean plays seen at Court during the midwinter of 1604-5 include *Othello*, *The Merry Wives of Windsor*, *Measure for Measure*, *The Comedy of Errors*, *Love's Labour's Lost*, *Henry V* and *The Merchant of Venice*, which might be called a good mixed bag.

I have already alluded to the performances of *Hamlet* and *Richard the Second* given at sea to keep the crew of the East India Company's ship *Dragon* from idleness, unlawful games, and sleep. This was in 1607 and 1608. The performances may have been trifling and amateurish, but the choice is important. It shows that the two plays were well established in a wide popularity and were not just Court favourites. Quarto texts of both were available. *King Lear* was the Christmas play at Whitehall in 1606. This is definitely stated in the title-page of the First Quarto.

And so it goes on. *Pericles* was visited by foreign ambassadors in 1608 and the *More de Venise* was mentioned by distinguished strangers as seen at the Globe in April, 1610. The Globe was described in this instance, rather oddly, as ' lieu ordinaire ou l'on joue les Commedies.' This after the superb and sombre output of Shakespeare's Tragic Period. In 1611 comes Simon Forman's fairly well-known description of playgoing at the ' Glob ' where he saw a non-Shakespearean play on Richard II, and *Macbeth*, *Cymbeline* and *The Winter's Tale*.

Returning to the Revels Accounts we find *The Tempest* at Whitehall, the King attending, in Nov., 1611; also *The Winter's Tale*, but by this time John Fletcher is edging his way in to great liking and esteem.

May, 1613, was a great theatrical occasion. At the wedding of Princess Elizabeth to the ' Prince Pallatyne Elector ' fourteen plays were given by the King's Men, of which six or seven were Shakespeare's; the six or seven were *Much Ado*, *The Tempest*, *The Winter's Tale*, *Sir John Falstaffe* (was this one or both of the *Henry IV's* ?), *The Moore of Venice* and *Caesar's Tragedye*. It is worth noting a reference to production of *The Hotspur*, which suggests that the Part of *Henry IV* selected was the First. Also there is mention of *Benedick and Betteris*, obviously *Much Ado*. There was no fixity of title in Shakespeare's time. Plays began to be known more and more by the chief or the conspicuous parts, such as Benedick and Beatrice, for *Much Ado About Nothing*, Malvolio, for *Twelfth Night*, and Parolles, for *All's Well that Ends Well*. A new favourite now was *Cardenio*, whose text has been lost: some believe that Shakespeare had a hand in it.

After Shakespeare's death in 1616 we have a certain amount of Court Records to demonstrate the taste of James I and later of King Charles I. *The Winter's Tale* remained consistently popular. The Falstaff plays (*Henry IV*) were kept going. So were *Othello*, *Pericles*, and *Richard the Second*. If this was Shakespeare's and not the piece that Forman saw, it is odd that the Court should have retained its affection for a play with a deposition scene and linked with an anti-monarchical outbreak. Up till 1640 the royal taste was loyal to *Hamlet*, *Othello* and *Julius Caesar*. *The Taming of the Shrew* turns up again and is marked as ' liked.' So does *Cymbeline*, ' well liked.' These facts, of course, say nothing as to the taste of ' the general,' but they give some indication, especially by their omissions, as to the fate of Shakespeare's plays at the Stuart court; our favourites were not theirs. *As You Like It* drops out. So do *Romeo and Juliet* and *A Midsummer Night's Dream*. *Macbeth* dwindles. *Antony and Cleopatra* gets no mention. *King John* is never spoken of. With regard to this last our taste mainly agrees with theirs, but it had its vogue, when Mrs. Siddons set the audience a-fainting with the ferocity of her outbursts as Queen Constance. *Timon of Athens*, *Coriolanus*, and *Antony and Cleopatra* appear to have been failures all along. They were tragedies and they came when the taste was changing. Shakespeare saw that, altered his tune, and once more scored successes, even with ' mouldy Pericles.'

One play of Shakespeare never liked at any time has been *The*

Two Gentlemen of Verona. Augustin Daly, however, tried to commend the new Daly's theatre to the London public with this piece in 1895; but he took care to avoid Shakespeare's text. G. B. S. described the result as ' not exactly a comic opera ' and said of Daly's short way with Shakespeare's words that he resembled Mrs. Todger at table ' a dodgin' among the tender bits with a fork and an eatin' of 'em.' The artful Todgers had set to work without mercy on Shakespeare at the time of the Restoration and for the next three centuries the selective fork was busily at work; so, too, was the knife for cutting. We have no knowledge of what Shakespeare's fellows did to his scripts. No doubt they saw what went over well and what did not and operated accordingly. But at least he was there till 1616 to put up the age-long playhouse fight of the author against the actor who thinks he knows better.

Next we can look at the evidence of publishing. Eighteen of Shakespeare's plays were put into print in Quarto volumes by various hands and by various methods of acquisition during his lifetime; separate Quartos of individual plays, usually costing sixpence, were still in demand after the inclusive and expensive First Folio had provided an ' Omnibus ' of all the pieces accepted as genuine Shakespeare by his close friends and colleagues Heminge and Condell. As to the way in which these texts were obtained and their degree of authenticity a separate literature has grown up and we need not, for purposes of our present inquiry, sort out the so-called Good and Bad Quartos or discuss the deeds of the literary pirates. But we do want to know what was deemed worth printing, whether it was got honestly or by stealth. Towards the end of his career Shakespeare and his Company acquired more control over the texts and the Quartos were not so frequent. But, while the printing was going on, it did provide evidence of public taste: for the printers were not there to do honour to a genius, but to meet, profitably, a public demand.

The Quarto issues began in 1594 with *Titus Andronicus*, and this gory old favourite was still in demand in 1611 when its third Quarto emerged. The second and third parts of *Henry VI* were early printed, too, and this confirms the testimony of

Henslowe that the sixth ' Harey ' was a winner. Then came, in 1597, *Richard II* and *Richard III* and both remained favourites. In 1622 they were still issuing *Richard III* (sixth imprint); *Richard II* had four printings. The continued demand for Crookback, as for the *Henry VI* plays and for *Titus Andronicus*, indicates clearly that ' the strong stuff,' with murder and rhetoric boiled up in a good blood-pudding, was always an easy seller. Another piece which reached six Quartos was *Henry IV*, Part I: Falstaff was the broad base of this esteem, with Hotspur as an important part of popularity's plinth. *Hamlet* achieved Four Quartos: so did *Romeo and Juliet*, which had sold quickly at the start. *Othello* had one Quarto, *King Lear* had two, and *Pericles* three. The comedies were less requested. *The Merry Wives of Windsor, The Merchant of Venice*, and *A Midsummer Night's Dream* had two Quartos each. *Macbeth* was never in Quarto form: nor were *Antony and Cleopatra* and *Coriolanus*. The final plays of the Romantic period were never in print before the Folio. But we cannot take this as a sign of unpopularity: *The Winter's Tale* seems to have been long a favourite, but the author or the Company or both had evidently determined to hold back the texts, since publication may have been interfering with theatre business at ' the doors.'

What is puzzling is that, while the Quartos were briskly appearing, neither *Twelfth Night* nor *As You Like It* was printed. It is plain that the former was liked. Malvolio was always an attraction. But *As You Like It* seems to have disappointed. There is no mention of any performance in the sixteenth or seventeenth centuries, except the one at Wilton said to have been mentioned in a letter no longer existing. This fact, coupled with the absence of a Quarto, is a strong sign that Touchstone did not amuse then: and now he seems to many to be the least agreeable company among Shakespeare's punning clowns. But we have surrendered to Rosalind and to Arden: did the Elizabethan worshippers of Falstaff and Malvolio find Jaques a bore and Touchstone a sorry substitute for Sir Toby's party ? *As You Like It* has been handicapped with us by being turned into ' curriculum Shakespeare.' So it has, with dull teaching, sent boys and girls unwillingly to school. Yet it is still ' box-

K

office.' But then it had no such disadvantage through the dominie's attention. *Much Ado About Nothing* had one Quarto; so did *Troilus and Cressida*; so did *Love's Labour's Lost*.

In 1619 the printer of the First Folio of 1623, Jaggard, had run out a volume of ten plays all labelled Shakespeare: only three of them had good texts. The rest were pirated stuff or works by other hands. Jaggard desperately wanted sales—otherwise why stoop to these tricks?—and so he would obviously choose what he believed to be strong attractions. He selected *Lear* and *Pericles* among the tragedies: all the *Henries* among the histories: and the *Merry Wives*, the *Merchant* and the *Dream* among the comedies. Presumably he could only use what was in print already, but his choices are some indication of the trend of opinion.

On the whole the evidence of the Quartos supports that of the listed performances. At least on the negative side there is proof that *The Two Gentlemen of Verona* and *King John* of the early plays and *Coriolanus* and *Antony and Cleopatra* of the later were not in demand either on the stage or at the bookshop.

The causes of theatrical success or failure are many and various. In Shakespeare's time, as now, luck must have had much to do with it. The script which the company deemed a certain victor may have missed fire: Burbage, perhaps, was out of form or not suited by his part: the boy-player of the day muffed it; the clown was too slow, too obtrusive, too much pleased with himself. Stage-effects may have gone wrong and actors ' dried ' in a nervous muddle. So the author suffered. Or the taste of the audience was moving on to new things. Perhaps both *Antony and Cleopatra* and *Coriolanus* came too late. Had tragedy on the grand scale been overdone? Fletcher and others were setting a new example of lighter themes, mingling fantasy, romance, and masquerade. Shakespeare by 1608 had said his sombre say: if I have been right in my assumption about his affairs of heart he had got the gipsy wanton finally out of his system: he was always a quick mover, could take a hint, and so he moved on to please the new public at the Blackfriars with his happily fanciful excursions into the cavern of Belarius, the sheep-cotes of Bohemia, and the cell of Prospero.

Contemporary allusion helps us a little to discover what was most enjoyed. At the beginning of his career the narrative poems *Venus and Adonis* and *Lucrece* are chiefly mentioned amid praises for their ' honey-flowing ' vein. In 1598 Francis Meres, a Cambridge man and a student of letters and urban pleasures before he became a country parson, praised Shakespeare ' as most excellent ' in both Comedy and Tragedy, alluded to his ' sugred sonnets ' and also set him among those ' most passionate among us to bewaile and bemoane the perplexities of Love.' He mentions as witness of success all the pre-1598 plays except the *Henry VI* trilogy and *The Taming of the Shrew* (unless that is covered by the allusion to *Love Labours Wonne*, a title strange to us). It is odd that the much-applauded ' Harey ' plays are left out: Meres may have thought them to be not purely by Shakespeare or to contain the work of too many other hands. Heminge and Condell differed on this point. In the same year John Marston wrote of a stage-struck gentleman

> that ne'er of ought did speak
> But when of plays or players he would treat.

Of this worshipper, Marston said that

> from his lips did flow
> Naught but pure Juliet and Romeo.

The antiquary John Weever (1599) selected *Romeo* and *Richard* (whether II or III is unspecified). In the Cambridge ' Parnassus ' plays of about 1600 *Romeo and Juliet* is again mentioned (with the inevitable *Venus and Adonis*); so is *Richard III*, which is also quoted. There is another curious piece of bookman's evidence for the abiding popularity of *Romeo and Juliet*. The copy of the First Folio in the Bodleian has been much worn and thumbed in the section containing this play, especially at the Balcony Scene.

Ben Jonson's prologues have a few references to the rival's vogue. He smiles, even sneers, at the Histories and their verbosity and at their small allowance of ' vile and ragged foils.'

It is odd that Jonson should echo Shakespeare's own criticism in this matter of production. In the Prologue to *Every Man in His Humour* he mentioned those who

> with three rusty swords
> And help of some few foot-and-half-foote words
> Fight over York and Lancaster's long jars
> And in the tiring-house bring wounds to scars.

Much later, in the Prologue to *Bartholomew Fair*, he mentioned *Andronicus*—that old shocker is always turning up!—and a popular Servant-Monster, obviously Caliban, since it precedes an allusion to ' Tales, Tempests, and such-like Drolleries.'

Jonson also, after a failure, jeered at ' Some mouldy tale, like Pericles,' as being what the public wanted. Certainly *Pericles*, now generally agreed to be only partly Shakespearean and a rarity on our stage, was a great favourite; it keeps reappearing in the references. Round about 1600 Gabriel Harvey observed that ' the younger sort takes much delight in Shakespeare's *Venus and Adonis*: but his *Lucrece* and his tragedy of *Hamlet, Prince of Denmark* have it in them to please the wiser sort.' Why *Hamlet* should be linked with *Lucrece*, as opposed to *Venus and Adonis*, is difficult to understand. What is important is that *Hamlet* was a play quickly established.

Allusions of particular value occur in the verses contributed by Leonard Digges to the First Folio. Ben Jonson's tribute in that volume was a general salute to the charm, wit, art and permanence of Shakespeare's poetry with its ' well turnèd and true filèd lines.' Digges, of University College, Oxford, was associated with Shakespeare as the stepson of Sir Thomas Russell, who was one of the overseers of Shakespeare's will.

Digges contributed to both First and Second Folios (1623 and 1640). In the first he alluded only to two plays in particular, holding that nothing could outdo ' Passions of Juliet and her Romeo ' or the scene where the ' half-sword parlying Romans spake '; the later reference proves this to be *Julius Caesar*. In 1640 he states that still by Shakespeare ' the King's Men live.' Upstart writers, needy Poetasters, and other ' vermin ' are

bidden to forbear or else go take their lame, blank verse to the
Bull or Cockpit. Then Digges proceeds to recount his special
favourites, contrasting them with the products of Jonson's heavier
hand. (As Jonson was by this time dead, there was the less
offence in the denigration of one who had given Shakespeare
immortal praise in the First Folio as well as a sneer or two at
other times.)

Digges's delight ran thus,

So have I seene, when Cesar would appeare,
And on the Stage at halfe-sword parley were,
Brutus and *Cassius*: oh how the Audience
Were ravish'd, with what wonder they went thence,
When some new day they would not brooke a line,
Of tedious (though well laboured) *Catiline*;
Sejanus too was irksome, they priz'de more
Honest *Iago*, or the jealous Moore.
And though the Fox and subtill Alchimist,
Long intermitted could not quite be mist,
Though these have sham'd all the Ancients, and might raise,
Their Authors merit with a crowne of Bayes.
Yet these sometimes, even at a friend's desire
Acted, have scarce defraied the Seacoale fire
And doore-keepers: when let but *Falstaffe* come,
Hall, *Poines*, the rest you scarce shall have a roome
All is so pestered: let but *Beatrice*
And *Benedicke* be seene, loe in a trice
The Cockpit Galleries, Boxes, all are full
To heare *Maluoglio* that crosse garter'd Gull.

This gives *Julius Caesar*, *Othello*, the two *Henry IV's*, *Much Ado
About Nothing* and *Twelfth Night* as plays that had been most
enjoyed. Digges's choice is fairly close to the general verdict
of the Court records, the printers' preferences, and the common
trend of allusion. At least the silences are instructive: we
know what failed to please and we have sufficient indication
that first the ' bloods ' (*Titus Andronicus* and *Richard III*), then the
great star-parts of Falstaff, Benedick and Beatrice, Malvolio and
Hamlet especially took the town. Later came the appetite for
sweeter, more fantastical things, for ' Cymbeline well-lik't,' for

Perdita, for Ariel and Caliban. This taste survived at the Stuart Court—Charles I was a devout Shakespearean—and survived, too, the death of Shakespeare and Burbage and the dissolution of the great Fellowship that had been in action, to the glory and reward of English writing and performance, since 1594.

On the side of omission, there is less reference than one would expect to *The Merchant of Venice*. It is curious that this piece, the value of whose plot depends upon a surprise which ceased to be a surprise in the fifteen-nineties, has continued to delight millions: Shylock bestrode the stages of the eighteenth, nineteenth and twentieth centuries, making continual reappearances with various ' readings,' as the great actor-managers succeeded one another in the sovereignty of the more serious stage. But Digges remembered chiefly Brutus, Cassius, Iago and ' the jealous Moore,' and the tributes to Burbage stress rather Hamlet, Othello, and Lear than the livid figure of the tormented and tormenting Jew with which Shakespeare had taught the Marlovians how to give majesty to melodrama on this theme of race and rancour.

The male parts were obviously the magnets. Beatrice is the only feminine role which is given particular mention in the allusions. As I said in the previous chapter, the boys' hold on the town may have been great when they acted as a team on their own. The ' little eyases ' speech in *Hamlet* is proof of that. But they were not starred individually as ' Infant Phenomena ': the gossip of the day passes them over; despite Jonson's reference to Robinson they did not become conspicuous figures in the city's life; and among the King's Men they seem to have been firmly kept in their place. Burbage and his senior friends might have taken it very ill if Masters Gilborne, Sharpe, Robinson and the others had been able ' to steal the notices,' the notices, that is, of the town's talk and of the whispering at Court. *Twelfth Night* was Malvolio's, not Viola's occasion, and drew as such. Yet Shakespeare, by the exquisite parts which he wrote for the boys, gave them every chance to score personal successes.

Rosalind had to wait for centuries to pass before she charmed audiences to accept her spritely dominion. Probably she came too soon. *As You Like It* might have fared much better if it had gone, with a suitable masque attached, to the Blackfriars about 1610 instead of to the Globe about 1600. *King John*, another piece which got no Quarto printing and no contemporary mention, certainly gave Burbage a rich part if he played the Bastard, but it is a part which fades out; his best scenes come early, always a danger in the theatre, and the familiar trumpet voluntary of patriotic sentiment on which he ends the play hardly makes up for his eclipse during the previous scenes. The boy or youth who played Constance may have been a failure: it was Mrs. Siddons who put this play back upon a map where it now only holds a position by occasional revival. I like nearly all of it myself, but am aware of my loneliness in that regard.

The question, ' What was Shakespeare's audience like ? ' is natural, but not easily answered. The Chamberlain's and the King's Men were at the beck of the Court and were more and more called upon to perform in Whitehall during the dramatist's later years: they were also called to the noblemen's houses or to the Inns of Court. There, then, are two or three different types of ' caviare ' audience before we come to meet the general. The public theatre crowds which Shakespeare and his fellows strove to please were at the Curtain, Swan, and Globe in the course of their normal seasons: then, after 1608, there was the Blackfriars audience, whose members were more ' select ' and paid more than did the penny groundlings and threepenny or sixpenny gallery folk of the upper tiers at the Globe and similar popular houses.

The private audiences would evoke and reward a special kind of writing and a less vehement performance. *Love's Labour's Lost* is mentioned as a ' mansion ' favourite and it has all the marks of being written for that kind of taste. Its play upon words, its tennis-rally of elaborate and audacious conceits, were for the ears of Southampton and his friends. Much that baffles us would be sharply pointed for them. (Imagine a London audience of three hundred years hence offered the text of an intimate revue which had set the town laughing to-day!) Such a piece is certainly full of personal allusion and the Dark

Lady herself may have been present to hear about the whitely wanton with a velvet brow who would do the deed though the hundred eyes of Argus were upon her. The same is true, I am sure, of *Troilus and Cressida*, whose Greek-and-Trojan broils must be symbolic of certain political and artistic rivalries at the end of the sixteenth century. The play is full of essential Shakespeare in phrase and feeling, the Shakespeare afflicted in body and mood, but it can hardly please more people now than the pious observers of every Shakespearean revival, the Stratford pilgrims, and the University scholars. Moreover, it was never given publicly in Shakespeare's own time.

The preface to the Quarto of 1609 written ' by an ever writer to an ever reader ' states definitely that *Troilus and Cressida* was ' never staled with the Stage, never clapper-clawed with the palms of the vulgar.' The play is recommended for all-surpassing wit that would make the buyer think his ' testerne ' (sixpence) well bestowed. The buyer is advised not to refuse the play nor to like it the less for not being ' sullied with the smoaky breath of the multitude ' and to thank fortune for ' the scape it hath made.'

What are we to make of this ? Did Shakespeare write, under special commission, for a special audience ? Did the Fellowship turn it down as being impossible for the Globe and bid him try the stuff on his courtiers or his lawyer friends ? We cannot know. But one thing the play and its preface do prove: that is the immense disparity between the refined and the rougher elements in Elizabethan and Jacobean audiences. It is therefore absurd to generalise about them, as do those who assume that Shakespeare was continually pouring pearls before ' stinkards ' and that Burbage was acting most of his time to an accompaniment of banter and bottle-opening. No doubt the actors could run into a rough house, but the criticisms of the Elizabethan audience do need some sifting before they are accepted.

Much of the attack on the prostitution, thieving and ruffianism attracted by ' the harlotry players ' comes from Puritanical attacks on the theatre and on all the pleasures of the town. Gosson and Stubbes, so often quoted for their description of the young male ravens—they would be called wolves to-day—who went spying for fair feminine ' carrion ' through every gallery, were preachers who preferred a fine flourish to accurate reporting: kill-joys on the rampage usually do. Others of a like eloquence joined in to denounce ' that chapel of Satan, the Theatre.'

The Bankside was no kindergarten. Of course a certain amount of mischief went on. It was mixed company with a good deal of what Thackeray's Yellowplush called ' easy pleasantry and lacy ally.' Chaplain Busino, of the Venetian Embassy, attended the Fortune Theatre in 1617 and left an account of the effort to ' vamp ' him made by a lady of the audience. She was a creature of the utmost elegance and even magnificence in costume and she tried her allure in French as well as in English. Also, of course, where there were great crowds there was bound to be some cutting of purses. This happened at church as well as at the play; in all congregations the ' nips ' and ' foists ' would take their chance. Occasionally one such would be caught in a theatre and hoisted on to the stage as a target for abuse and apples before going to his punishment. But that is the kind of picturesque and scandalous event that naturally is singled out for record. No doubt it happened. But did it happen often ?

Professor Harbage has subjected to some statistical analysis the crimes alleged in the rabid anti-theatre campaigning of the Puritans. The results are interesting. One would gather from much of the outcry against Satan's chapel that it was impossible to sit there unrobbed, unseduced, or even unstabbed. But Harbage justly urges,

The least we can do is to view playhouse disorders against the general background. In 1600 a recognizance was taken for the cutting of a purse at the Curtain. If a true bill were found, this would be a capital felony. In the year 1600 the Middlesex justices must have taken many recognizances because 118 true bills were found, all for offences committed elsewhere than in playhouses. In 1610 a purse was cut at the Red Bull. In this year, in the jurisdiction of the Middlesex justices, true bills were found for 15 larcenies from the person

besides 47 other larcenies (none committed in playhouses), not
to mention house breakings, burglaries, and horse-stealings.
In 1613 there was a stabbing at the Fortune, but elsewhere
than at the Fortune there were 11 murders, 12 cases of
manslaughter, 28 cases of assault and battery, 3 assaults with
a sword, and 7 attacks upon officers.   Seventy-two males and
four females were sentenced to be hanged.   Evidently the
playhouses were relatively safe.

It was an age of free conduct and the manners of the gentry
were often rough and callous, as Shakespeare himself shows.
The treatment of the amateur actors by their august audience in
Love's Labour's Lost and *A Midsummer Night's Dream* seems boorish
to us, and Ben Jonson inveighed against ' caprichious gallants '
at the play who approve of nothing, sit dispersed, make faces and
spit, and then ' wagging their upright ears cry, " Filthy, filthy." '
But the angry dramatist, writing after a failure, or the social
satirist, seeking matter for his scolding wit, naturally picks on the
extreme type and the occasional event.   The bulk of the
audience, at any entertainment where they have paid for their
seats, naturally wish to get their money's worth and to see and
hear properly that for which they have put down their coins.
Dekker described brilliantly the young fop or ' Gull ' who makes
a fool and a public nuisance of himself in the theatre: but
Dekker adds that ' the rabble ' were very eager to throw him out.
If the playgoers were bored by the play, they may have shown
their resentment.   But their chief purpose was pleasure not
boredom.   The able dramatist and ' the well-graced player '
could hold the stage by their efficiency.   The public was as
ready to be charmed as to be churlish.

At any rate there was, in an Elizabethan audience, no chilly
calm, none of the smug indifference, which can be so infuriating
to author and players.   There was a tremendous theatrical
appetite in all classes; indeed the enemies of the theatre
denounced its hold upon the poor much as the race-tracks are
denounced in our time.   Harbage quotes from a text of 1603
(Crosse's *Vertues Common-Wealth*):

Nay many poore pincht, needie creatures, that liue of

almes, and that haue scarce neither cloath to their backe, nor
foode for the belley, yet wil make hard shift but they will see
a Play, let wife & children begge, languish in penurie, and all
they can rappe and rend, is little enough to lay vpon such
vanitie.

People who have made such efforts to get into a playhouse are
not going to chatter and eat walnuts all through the play if it
has any merit at all.   The idea that the incidental music of, say,
the first production of *Hamlet* was a nutcracker suite is based on
scattered indictments of the unmannerly. 'The tag-rag
people' might hiss and mew at the end and youths might
'thunder' and fight for bitten apples in a playhouse (Shakespeare mentions both occurrences), but the thunder may have
been applause and we know that the applause was as hearty as
the hissing.   Dekker described how the mob would mightily
clap that which seem'd above their intelligence, standing

> On tip-toe to reach up
> And (from rare silence) clap their brawny hands
> T' applaud what their charmed soul scarce understands.

There were two sides to the violent feeling which the play could
stir.   What the dramatist lost by 'mewing' and cries of
'Filthy, filthy' one day, he could recover by the violence of the
acclamation on the next occasion.

Aggravated dramatists would rail against the 'stinkards' and
'the rout of niffles' who turned down their plays.   In those days
there were no professional critics to be accused of ignorance,
malice, and the scoring of cheap, irrelevant points.   (It may vex
the vainer specimen of dramatic critic to be reminded that
Shakespeare managed to exist, succeed, and flourish without
either press publicity or the counsel of the supposed savants who
write the critical columns.)   So the wrath of the rejected was
turned always on the audience and not, as now, on those
supposed to mislead audiences.

It is an interesting fact that none of the foreign visitors of
Shakespeare's time alludes to unruliness or bad manners in the
auditorium.   Platter of Basle commented on the excellence of

what he saw, and on the comfort of the galleries with their cushioned seats for threepence. Busino, of the Venetian Embassy, although once accosted as I described, was impressed by the good manners as well as the good clothes of the theatre public, whose members, he wrote, ' looked like so many princes listening as soberly and silently as possible.' He also wrote of the virtuous and handsome ladies who went to the play, in the public theatres, among the men without the slightest hesitation. If the theatre had regularly been the bear-garden which some of the satirists described and which piqued playwrights de-nounced, the authorities would have intervened. The theatres were indeed once closed because the overflow from a riot of apprentices invaded them: had they been habitually disorderly houses they could hardly have carried on with so many enemies in authority round about them.

Out of all this conflicting evidence I derive that Shakespeare wrote for a public quicker to demonstrate for or against a play than we are now, a public more gusty of manner and far less inhibited than a modern theatre audience, but by no means frequently or intolerably rowdy. He had to give them what they liked and he generally managed to do so. His few allusions to the hissing and mewing of the ' tag-rag ' people are countered by his tributes to the hold of the well-graced actor on the rapt, attentive auditors. In the private theatres the conduct was naturally suitable to the quality of those attending and the dramatist was sure of what John Marston called

> Gentle presence and the scenes sucked up
> By calm attendance of choice audience.

At the public theatres there would be less tranquil absorption of the banquet provided, but lustier cheers, as well as louder moans. Along with all the denunciations of the noisy ' niffles ' we must remember the ' joy in widest commonalty spread ' to which Digges paid tribute.

> Oh how the Audience
> Were ravish'd, with what wonder they went thence!

This links up with Busino's tribute to a splendid silence when silence had been duly earned.

One point remains for discussion, the bawdiness of the Tudor and Jacobean stage and Shakespeare's part in it. Of the fact that Shakespeare jested often and grossly on sexual matters and pursued with seeming relish words of sexual application there can be no denial. Mr. Eric Partridge has even composed a whole book, mainly in Glossary form, on *Shakespeare's Bawdy*: he has overplayed his hand, I think, and occasionally found more sexual suggestion than Shakespeare had ever intended when he chose a phrase or framed a metaphor. But the persistence of what is usually considered to be ' dirt ' in the texts is there for all to see, not only in the brothel and tavern scenes, but in the exchanges of courtly wit. In the banter of *Love's Labour's Lost* and of Mercutio and his comrades there is no reluctance among the lords and ladies to pun with industrious ingenuity on phallic matters, just as Shakespeare in his Sonnets employed this same type of word-play which is now generally called ' smutty.' Indeed Bernard Shaw, in his preface to *The Dark Lady of the Sonnets*, has written of Shakespeare's 'incorrigible addiction to smutty jokes,' denies that coarseness was part of the manners of the time, and adds ' there was nothing whatever to prevent Shakespeare from being as decent as More was before him and Bunyan after him and as self-respecting as Sidney or Raleigh, except the tradition of his class.'

There can be various reactions to this. One is to cry ' the less Shakespeare he ' and frankly to deplore his weakness in yielding to the theatre practice of the times. A Poet Laureate, Robert Bridges, representing the moral sensibility of the Victorian-Edwardian respectability amid which he so gracefully lived on the genteel fringe of academic Oxford, came out in a white heat of indignation on this subject. But, since Shakespeare had been well-nigh canonised by this time, Bridges carefully put the blame on the audience, an audience, incidentally, which contained royalty as well as all the chosen spirits of the age.

Shakespeare should not be put into the hands of the young without the warning that the foolish things in his plays are for the foolish, the filthy for the filthy, and the brutal for the brutal ; and that, if out of veneration for his genius we are led to admire or even tolerate such things, we may be thereby not conforming ourselves to him, but only degrading ourselves to the level of his audience, and learning contamination from those wretched beings who can never be forgiven their share in preventing the greatest poet and dramatist of the world from being the best artist.

That sort of criticism not only gives ' Eliza and our James ' a good caning; it entirely omits the practical consideration that More, Spenser, Sidney, Raleigh and Bunyan were never working as Johannes Factotum in a Fellowship of Players, were never professional servants of the pleasure-seeking public, and never had to satisfy the drama's patrons who give the drama's laws. It can be argued that Shakespeare ought to have resisted the temptation and should not have given the public his plentiful tit-bits of grossness with an ' As You Like It ' or a ' What You Will ' shrug of the shoulders.   But surely it is foolish and unfair to match him with those who never shared the temptation.

Shaw then proceeds to give the most astonishing explanation of all, while defining his phrase about Shakespeare's class-tradition.   Shakespeare, it seems, dealt in bawdy because ' he conceived himself as belonging to the upper class from which our public schoolboys are now drawn.'   The Arden blood in him and the Arden background, thinks Shaw, drove him to covet gentlemanly status and with it the tradition of his class

in which education or statesmanship may no doubt be acquired by those who have a turn for them, but in which insolence, derision, profligacy, obscene jesting, debt contracting, and rowdy mischievousness, give continual scandal to the pious, serious, industrious, solvent bourgeois.   No other class is infatuated enough to believe that gentlemen are born and not made by a very elaborate process of culture. Even kings are taught and coached and drilled from their earliest boyhood to play their part.   But the man of family (I am convinced that Shakespear took that view of himself) will plunge into society without a lesson in table manners, into politics without a lesson in history, into the city without a lesson in business, and into the army without a lesson in honor.

Shaw pillories the English public schools because their gentlemanly products are ' rowdy, ill-mannered, abusive, mischievous and fond of quoting obscene schoolboy anecdotes ' and sees Shakespeare's weakness in his eagerness to belong to the gentlemanly (and foul-mouthed) set of his time. This would seem to suggest that errand-boys never are or were salacious and that the pupils or former pupils of the free National Schools never scribble obscenities in lavatories. As a matter of noticeable fact it is not only at Eton but everywhere that the spread of education results in obscene words and drawings being observed upon the walls more often (and lower down) than they used to be.

Whereas Robert Bridges put the blame for Shakespeare's bawdy on the audience and Shaw upon the odious habits of the English nobility and gentry, the modern habit is rather to accept the so much criticised jesting as the normal sex-expression of an easily stimulated individual. Mr. Partridge, for example, explains that Shakespeare was ' filled with the joy and sap of life,' ' physically a pagan ' and a ' deliberate sater of that desirous, sex-hungry body, yet merciless contemner of his own yielding.' He was also an ' intellectual voluptuary ' and ' moved by an irresistible need to cleanse, not merely his bosom, but his entire system, of this most perilous stuff.' Probably most young people of to-day, accustomed to the fashionable psychological doctrines of our time, take Shakespearean grossness much more easily than did the generation in which Robert Bridges matured. They are more frankly and more sensibly, as well as more punctually, instructed in sex-matters, with the result that they are far less inclined to browse and snigger over the ' dirty ' passages to which some gloating senior has introduced them.

My own guess is that both views contain part of the truth. Shakespeare was a man of ' sap,' intensely sensitive to beauty, highly sexed and with plenty to get out of his system : he was also a working dramatist who had to serve his public ' as they liked it,' at least to a point. He was among colleagues and rivals who had no squeamishness as to what they wrote, even for the boy-players to utter. Comparisons with More and Bunyan are absurd. Matched with Jonson or Beaumont and Fletcher, Shakespeare was working, with no excessive licence, in the ordinary convention of the time. The private theatre audience was just as ready for loose talk and innuendo as were the groundlings. (Witness *Troilus and Cressida*, 'never clapper-clawed' by the gross mechanicals, but with plenty of obscene allusion to gratify the 'termers' of the Inns of Court if, as is commonly supposed, they were the target of that play.)

I am sure that our, or rather the Victorian, attitude to physical jesting about sex, the attitude typified by Bridges and Shaw, would have bewildered the Elizabethans. Did they think in terms of 'smut and dirt'? To pun cleverly was for them a matter of practice and a cause of approbation. To be frank about the flesh was normal too. The union of play upon words and laughter or delight in carnalities begat with natural ease their kind of theatre fun: surely they did not fuss or titter over it in the way that a repressed product of the Victorian discipline used to gloat and giggle out of school over his discoveries of 'smut.'

So, with the sap in his system and with the actors consenting, or even—especially the clowns—encouraging, Shakespeare wrote as he did. One thing is rarely mentioned, but does deserve notice, namely that no one ever censured him for gross-ness in his own day: quite the reverse. The sensualities of *Venus and Adonis*, as we see them, only provoked copious tributes to the 'sweetness' of his pen: honey, not ordure, provided the imagery applied to his Muse by the instructed opinion of the time. In all the admiration and the com-plimentary verses to this 'pattern of all wit' there was continual emphasis on this dulcet quality of 'gentle Shakespeare.' He was certainly not regarded as especially lewd or lascivious in his time.

Naturally tributes do not dwell on defects. But Shakespeare had his critics too, critics of his supposed ignorance, of his too easy fecundity of composition. Can any contemporary criticism be found which singles him out as a purveyor of filth and arraigns him on a charge of lewdness, of debasing the theatre, or of corrupting the morals of the age ? Could all the outcry about Shakespeare's bawdy be brought now to his attention, he would, I think, be much astonished. He would merely say that he wrote as he liked it for those that so liked it in circumstances where these things were normal, popular, and permissible. To become so excited about these inessentials, these bawdy kick-shaws added to the comedies and these occasional trimmings of his tragedies, is surely to make much ado now about something which was then very little.

CHAPTER XIV

The Man of Property

THE amount of documented contemporary fact about Shakespeare is small; in what there is of such record his activities as an investor are prominent. That is natural, and may be misleading, natural because deals in land and houses were set down on paper or parchment and lingered on securely in office files and cupboards: the accounts and chronicles, the programmes and the scripts of the players were carelessly kept or less esteemed. The fiery end of the Globe Theatre may have incinerated writings that would have been worth hundreds of thousands of pounds to-day; but if they had not been burned on that occasion some other conflagration or mere negligence would probably have destroyed them. Players are less methodical than lawyers.

So, when we contrast what we know of Shakespeare's property in Stratford and London with what we know of his professional career in and around playhouses, and find that our acquaintance with his estate is considerable, we must not immediately assume that Shakespeare was primarily an acquisitive bourgeois. Nor need we accuse him of hypocrisy because he so often, in his plays, seems to lavish sympathetic praise on those most lavish with their gold. The careless spender certainly appears to catch his fancy: he is kinder to Bassanio than most in a modern audience feel themselves to be and he altogether loses his heart to Antony because that great lover is ready to lose the world for his heart. When Cleopatra praises the prodigal quality of her reckless Roman lover, one feels convinced by the intensity of the writing that Shakespeare too is fascinated by such readiness to throw away kingdoms for a kiss. Yet he himself kept and placed his money carefully. Antony might hurl away an Empire; his creator went out and bought another acre.

Having just dealt firmly with a small debtor in Stratford, Shakespeare could none the less revel in the largesse and luxury of the spendthrift Roman who tossed away thrones to his favourites and his allies as others throw lollipops and toys to children.

> For his bounty
> There was no winter in't ; an autumn 'twas
> That grew the more by reaping . . . in his livery
> Walked crowns and crownets, realms and islands were
> As plates dropped from his pocket.

There is no essential humbug in the writing of such lines with such gusto by an essentially careful man. Those who maintain that the actor Shakespeare could never have been the author of Shakespeare's poetry seize happily upon his readiness to praise profligacy and on the absence from the poetry of a philosophy of prudence. Let us admit that the Shakespeare of Stratford does emerge as a cool and calculating type. But artists have often contradicted in their art the even tenor of their lives or the caution of their financial practices. An artist may very well idealise in his work exactly those qualities which he privately knows to be lacking, or at least not abundant, in himself. Just as ugly men write with yearning of handsome heroes, so timid men may glory, artistically, in the deeds of audacity; so, too, may the thrifty pay enthusiastic tribute to those who find saving impossible and spending all too easy. Cyril Connolly has shrewdly observed that inside every fat man there is a thin man screaming for release: in the same way the wise investor may be concealing within him some inhibited genius for extravagance, whose only escape is through poetry. The writer who screams most loudly about sex is often suspect of sexual impotence; he who most glories in denouncing the power of gold may be busily acquiring a fair store of it; Shakespeare's Timon, railing against gold, went well beyond the ordinary poetic commonplaces on the corrupting power of wealth. And many another Shakespeare character said much the same. But the creator of those characters and the author of those screams against the plague of wealth was, like many great artists before or since, well able to look after himself in the market-place. The association of great art with great imprudence is no more common than the ability of the supreme artist to watch his affairs with affectionate discretion and so to leave behind him a fair piece of property as well as an honoured name.

Shaw's idea that Shakespeare conceived himself to be the scion of profligate aristocrats and that he liked to live up to this tradition of shocking the bourgeois with debts and indecency is not at all confirmed by what we know of the Stratford atmosphere. The sense of property ran high, as it usually does in small country towns and in the market centres of the farmer. Litigation was constant and the cause of it was usually some question of ownership. There was a good deal of borrowing and debts were not easily remitted. Almost as soon as we begin to hear of John Shakespeare, the poet's father, he is the victim of a suit of recovery brought by Thomas Syche (for eight pounds). This was in 1556 and in 1558 he was visited with an order for distraint, the prosecutors being ' Adrian Quiney and Thomas Knight.' In 1556 John was himself proceeding against Henry Field for the unjust detention of eighteen quarters of barley.

When the Stratford baker, Roger Saddeler, died in 1578, the will showed that money was owed to him by John Shakespeare, who none the less was an investor in house property, having bought in 1575 for the sum of £40 two houses with gardens and orchards in addition to the houses and gardens in Greenhill Street and Henley Street purchased in October, 1556.

William Shakespeare's boyhood was spent, it is abundantly plain, in a litigious and acquisitive society, where small sums of money mattered much and small parcels of land were jealously coveted: the fact that his father went down the financial slope in his later years would impress upon him all the more the advantages of driving a good bargain and of having money in his purse. When he left Stratford, with a wife and three children to support, one fact must have been painfully apparent to the young man in search of a future; that was the importance of being solvent.

He was before long to meet and to be patronised—in the

true sense of that word—by rich men who were more ready to quarrel over a point of honour or a lady's favour than over a rod of land or a few quarters of grain. But boyhood's environment of petty commerce, the bickering and chaffering of Stratford farmers and tradesmen, the smart purchase, the holding for a rise, the recourse to the town lawyers (for one of whom he himself probably worked after leaving school), the borrowings, with or without ' usance '—all this had been so familiar that he could not easily, even on the fringe of Lord Southampton's household or as a favoured writer and player of the Court, expel them from his system.

In London he passed through his many moods of infatuation, passion, ecstasy, humiliation, despair, and calm. But all the time he was a man of property; ' the tenement or pelting farm ' (pelting means paltry), mentioned by John of Gaunt in his famous swan-song, had been the prize of those who went with him unwillingly to school and stayed by the Avon to plough, crop, and sell the harvest. He was never separated from those men, not even by his lordly friends, by his haunting ladies, by royal favours, by the recognition of the wits, and by success in his profession; and he went back to them to share their talk, their table, and their little vanities of property achieved and expanded. So it is worth our while to follow his commercial, as well as his poetic, career. An examination of his various dealings can, I hope, be informative without being long or tiresome.

Nicholas Rowe believed that Sir William Davenant, who liked to boast that he was Shakespeare's natural son, handed down the tradition that ' Lord Southampton at one time gave him a thousand pounds to go through with a purchase which he heard he had a mind to.' Rowe called this ' a bounty very great and very rare at any time and almost equal to that profuse generosity the present age has shown to French dancers and Italian eunuchs.' The gift, if it ran to that amount, was certainly a large one. It has been suggested that it really was a sum of £100 that Shakespeare received in order to buy himself into a housekeeper's and sharer's position in the Lord Chamberlain's Company, in our language to 'go into management.'

By 1596 Shakespeare was in a position to press for both status and estate. As has been recounted, in the former year John Shakespeare was raised (or restored, as John preferred to think) to the rank of gentleman with a coat of arms, and in 1597 William paid William Underhill £60 for the principal house in Stratford, New Place, built by Sir Hugh Clopton more than a century before. It was not ' a nobleman's seat,' but a considerable country-town house; John Leland, in his Itinerary of 1540, singled it out for mention as ' a praty howse of brike and tymbar.' To this august but not unwieldy establishment Shakespeare returned later in life; it remained in the family until the death of his granddaughter, Lady Barnard, in 1670. It was rebuilt at the beginning of the next century and wickedly demolished by its owner, the Rev. Francis Gastrell, in 1759. Shakespeare managed to recover a little of his not excessive expenditure on this deal by selling to the Corporation of the town a load of stone. At the same time he was pressing on with his career in ownership, and it must have been with his aid and counsel that his parents filed a Bill in Chancery for the recovery of the Arden estate of Asbies.

During the following year there were several transactions to record. Shakespeare, though this was a period of high output in writing, was obviously keeping his eye on his local interests. A letter from Abraham Sturley, who had been Chamberlain of Stratford and could write to his friend Quiney equally well in Latin or English—a point worth noting by those who revile Stratford as a nest of ignorant yokels only—mentioned that in the opinion of Quiney's father their countryman, Master Shakespeare, was ' willing to disburse some money upon some odd yard-land or other at Shottery or near about us.' Tithes were suggested as a better investment. Fripp interprets the affair thus:

Shakespeare, apparently, had written to his wife that he was willing to buy her old home at Shottery, her stepmother having recently died. Old Quyney has heard of this, and suggests a more attractive investment, in keeping with a coat of arms. He was aware of the Poet's desire to stand well in the neighbourhood. He knew also, as did everybody else, his honesty, and the credit he would be as a regular payer, unlike his predecessor at New Place, of the Tithe Rent. Neither ' disbursement ' came off at the time ; but in 1605 Shakespeare made a big purchase of the Tithes, and in 1610, probably with his assistance, Bartholomew Hathaway bought the Shottery farm.

Then comes the affair of the stored grain. Stratford was having a difficult time. There had been a visitation of plague; there had been fires; there had been bad harvests; there was a slump, too, in the price of wool. Bread was scanty for the sufferers everywhere, and the Privy Council commanded local authorities to hold an inquiry into stocks of corn so that hoarding should be put down. In the Stratford Corporation records it is set down that William Shakespeare was the holder of ten quarters of corn in Chapel Street Ward, in which lies New Place. This was by no means the largest holding in Stratford and many leading citizens had stocks.

Shakespeare was by now regarded in Stratford as the man to whom to turn for a little capital. Enterprising people in those days would not have the ear of bank managers or insurance companies; they looked to their friends. So, on October 25, 1598, Richard Quiney, being in London at the Bell in Carter Lane beside St. Paul's, wrote to his ' loving good friend and countryman Mr. William Shakespeare ' asking for a loan of thirty pounds on the security of some mutual acquisitions. What speculation was planned, in addition to meeting Quiney's immediate needs, is not known. It is not known even whether Shakespeare ever got the letter. But it is the only letter to Shakespeare that is preserved, and it is remarkable evidence of the magnitude of the Shakespeare Cult that a plaque was actually erected on the site of the Bell Inn merely because a letter to the Bard had been written from that spot. So far can Bardolatry proceed.

Further evidence of Shakespeare's keen concern with petty local commerce is found in a letter written by Adrian Quiney in November, 1598, to his son Richard in London to the effect that, if he bargained with William Shakespeare and received money, he was to bring it home since there was a fine opportunity for investing money in ' knit stockings,' which were selling very well at Evesham market. It was presumed that Shakespeare would be attentive to this proposition. Perhaps he was—and profitably. Financing an affable ' barrow-boy ' to ask the Avon Valley farming folk ' Can I interest you in a few knit stockings ?' may have been a happy idea. Nor do I see any reason why a great poet should not back the sale of hose as a side-line to his iambics. Man does not walk by verse alone. Those, however, who feel that genius should have no concern with hose and haberdashery may comfort themselves with our ignorance about what occurred in the end. Shakespeare may have had no relish at all for this placing of his funds in the drapery business.

During 1598 Shakespeare was managing, acting (in *Every Man in His Humour*), and turning out plays (two or three a year was his pace at this time) and yet keeping an eye on malt and Stratford matters. But was it his own eye all the time ? It is possible to deal through an agent, and we do know that in one of his next (and larger) purchases, that of 107 acres of arable land from the ' tough,' money-lending family of Combe in 1602 for a payment of £320, the conveyance was ' sealed and delivered to Gilbert Shakespeare to the use of the within named William Shakespeare.' Gilbert, the next of the Shakespeare children to him and two years his junior, may well have been his representative at local sales before this transaction with the Combes. In 1602 William also purchased from Walter Getley a small copy-hold property in Chapel Lane. The minuteness of a deal was no hindrance to the Shakespearean attention, but, as I said, it need not have been William's attention. When Philip Rogers, the Stratford apothecary, was sued in 1604 for the balance of an account for malt (just under two pounds) and for a debt of two shillings in cash, it may have been Mrs. Anne Shakespeare who forced this into court or it may have been Gilbert: Shakespeare himself was then at the top of his performance in the tragedy period and was beginning work on *King Lear*, if we assume that he had finished *Othello*. Of course it is possible to think of small silver even when one is pouring out great verse, but it seems more likely that his family in Stratford were his agents in these matters.

But he would have paid personal attention to so large an investment as that of 1605. Then he purchased, for £440, from Ralph Huband, a thirty-one years' lease of tithes in Stratford and neighbouring villages. The money seems not to have been paid all at once, but by instalments; twenty pounds were still owing in 1606. In 1608 Shakespeare sued a gentleman of Stratford called John Addenbroke for a debt of six pounds: a precept for the £6 plus 24s. costs and damages was issued, but Addenbroke had vanished. So the precept was issued against Thomas Hornby, blacksmith, who had stood surety for the debtor. Shakespeare (or his Stratford representatives) can be said to have shown some rigour in the calling in of loans, but as we do not know the circumstances we cannot pass judgment. The quality of mercy is precious, no doubt, but there is no virtue is allowing those who can pay what they owe to bilk their creditors.

In 1614 certain local landowners, Mainwaring, Replyngham, and William Combe, endeavoured to increase their holdings by a threat to enclose common lands in the neighbourhood of Welcombe. Shakespeare's interests as a tithe-owner were menaced and the enclosers sought to buy him off: his response is uncertain and the dispute—for the local people promptly and properly resisted the enclosures—dragged on until after Shakespeare's death, when judgment was given in favour of the commoners by Chief Justice Coke at Warwick Assizes. Our view of Shakespeare's attitude depends on the reading of a disputed passage in the diary of Thomas Greene, Town Clerk of Stratford, who had lived or lodged at New Place. Fripp believes this to mean that Shakespeare could not tolerate the enclosures, and most people will hope that this is the correct interpretation.

So much for Stratford. Shakespeare's London property was for a long time in theatrical shares. He never set up house there: at least we have no indication of his living in any great style and he was certainly still in lodgings (with Christopher

Mountjoy of Silver Street) in 1604. As a lodger he moved several times. In 1597 he was assessed for ' a subsidy ' of five shillings on goods valued at five pounds in Bishopsgate (St. Helen's Ward): he did not pay, was assessed again, and still did not pay. The matter was then referred to the Bishop of Winchester's court in Southwark, which showed that he had gone across the river. This fits in with the trouble he had, late in 1596, with William Gardiner, a corrupt Surrey justice, and his weak young crony, William Waite. Shakespeare was associated with Francis Langley, the owner of the Swan Theatre on the Bankside, and two otherwise unknown women, Dorothy Soer and Anne Lee, in a violent dispute with Gardiner and Waite. The curious incident was discovered by Professor Leslie Hotson and explained in his book, *Shakespeare versus Shallow*. As Gardiner had Surrey jurisdiction and hated plays and players, strife was likely enough in that area and Waite's demand for ' sureties of the place ' was balanced by Langley's demand for the same. (Those who feared bodily injury told the justice of this menace and the menacing party was then ordered to give surety against carrying out his threat.) These events prove nothing to our purpose, except that Shakespeare was lodging for a period in the rowdy, licentious Bankside, where tempers were hot and hasty, and that his companions there were not all as lofty as the Earl of Southampton.

Then he moved north again and lived with a Huguenot tire-maker called Mountjoy, who was subsequently sued by his son-in-law Belott for failure to carry out the financial settlement alleged to have been made when Belott married Mary Mountjoy. Eight years after the marriage Belott went to court for his money and Shakespeare was cited as a lodger who would know the facts and also as a party who had helped to arrange the match. Perhaps he had taken a friendly interest in the affair, but he could not help the court by remembering clearly the monetary detail. All that concerns us is the comparative humility of his London ' digs ' at a time when he had been owner for some years of the chief house in Stratford. The maker of wigs and head-dresses, doubtless a theatrical acquaintance with a side-line of catering for players, lived in the Cripplegate Ward at the corner of Silver and Monkwell Streets. Ben Jonson refers in jest to a woman who got her teeth in Blackfriars, her eyebrows in the Strand, and her hair in Silver Street: a customer of Mountjoy's, perhaps.

Apart from his shares in theatres Shakespeare's only investment in London was the purchase in 1613 from Henry Walker of the Gatehouse, Blackfriars, near the playhouse in which he was then much interested. The premises, in a street leading down to Puddle Wharf, cost him £140, but were then mortgaged to the seller to the amount of £60. The conveyance was made to Shakespeare and three others, Hemmyng, Johnson, and Jackson. 'Hemmyng' is presumably Heminge of the King's Men. Shakespeare put up the money and leased the house to John Robinson, who must have travelled down to Stratford during Shakespeare's last illness, since he was one of the witnesses of the will. Chambers has shown that the Gatehouse had been associated with Catholic conspiracy, but there is no reason to suppose that it attracted Shakespeare for that reason. Doubtless Robinson wanted the house, and Shakespeare, his friend, thought it a good investment. It went to his daughter Susanna in his will.

Shakespeare was able to save and to invest because he lived thriftily; his lodging with such families as the Mountjoys cannot have been expensive. Nor was he easily dragged out to parties. Our evidence for that is Aubrey's statement, not in his Brief Life of Shakespeare, but made in an additional note, ' The more to be admired because he was not a company keeper: lived in Shoreditch: would not be debauched, and, if invited to, writ; he was in pain.'

Aubrey, as we noted, is a much stronger authority than the eighteenth-century gossips who have given us the Stratford legends of his capacity as a drinker amid the rivalry of village toss-pots. His authority was the son of one of Shakespeare's fellow-players; the Shoreditch lodging may well have been occupied in the early years when Shakespeare was working at theatres in that district. What exactly did Aubrey mean by debauched? Not more, perhaps, than is involved in long nights of hard drinking. Aubrey had previously written that Shakespeare was ready-witted and 'very good company.' There is no essential contradiction here: a man can be a very good companion in ordinary conversation and chosen fellowship without 'keeping company' in the sense of going out readily on any invitation. For a man who was writing as hard as Shakespeare was, especially at the turn of the century, memorising and acting parts, though not the greatest, helping to manage a theatre, and turning out a steady flow of masterpieces, invitations to debauchery, with waste of nights in drinking and of mornings in recovery, could hardly have held much allurement.

He was said by Thomas Fuller (*History of the Worthies of England*) to have been nimbly engaged in wit-combats with Ben Jonson, but this was scarcely dissipation. Much romance has been built round the toping and tattling at the Mermaid, but we have no contemporary evidence that Shakespeare himself was ever inside the place. This is not to say that he was never a patron of ' the local ' or of the more exalted Mermaid, Devil, and Apollo taverns where the wits collected and the ' fiery particles ' gave off their radiation. But we have no reason to suppose that Shakespeare ever kept Anne and the children short in order to enrich the publicans. Nor have we cause to believe that he was talked of in London as a sponge of sherris-sack, brilliantly as he could describe (through Falstaff) the mental stimulation which that liquor could bestow. A pamphlet of 1605 called *Ratsey's Ghost* described some adventures of a highwayman called Gamaliel Ratsey who was executed at Bedford; the writer paid an incidental tribute to the frugality of the players. Ratsey was a critic as well as a cut-purse and he was made by the pamphleteers to observe of the actors whom he met:

Let me hear your music, for I have often gone to plays more for music's sake than for action ; for some of you not content to do well, but striving to overdo and go beyond yourselves often times, by St. George, mar all : yet your poets take great pains to make your parts fit for your mouths, though you gape never so wide.   Othersome, I must needs confess, are very well deserving, both for true action and fair delivery of speech ; and yet, I warrant you, the very best have sometimes been content to go home at night with fifteen pence share apiece.   Others there are whom fortune has so well favored that, what by penny-sparing and long practice of playing, are grown so wealthy that they have expected to be knighted, or at least to be conjunct in authority and to sit with men of great worship on the bench of justice.

Later on Ratsey addresses the First Player, and the allusions strongly indicate that he was talking to Burbage of the King's Men:

thou hast a good presence upon a stage ; methinks thou darkenest thy merit by playing in the country.   Get thee to London, for, if one man were dead, they will have much need for such a one as thou art.   There would be none in my opinion fitter than thyself to play his parts.   My concept is such of thee that I durst venture all the money in my purse on thy head, to play Hamlet with him for a wager.   There thou shalt learn to be frugal—for players were never so thrifty as they are now about London—and to feed upon all men, to let none feed upon thee ; to make thy hand a stranger to thy pocket, thy heart slow to perform thy tongue's promise ; and when thou feelest thy purse well lined, buy thee some place or lordship in the country, that growing weary of playing, thy money may bring there thee to dignity and reputation ; then thou needest care for no man, nor for them that before made thee proud with speaking their words upon the stage.

The unnamed rival may have been Alleyn.

Ratsey bestows a mock-knighthood on the player and exclaims ' Kneel down—rise up Sir Timon Two Shares and a Half.' Among the King's Men both the Burbages owned two and a half shares: so did Shakespeare after some years.   The interest of the passages quoted lies in their tribute to prudence and austerity in a profession more commonly associated with fleeting the time carelessly and spending money freely. The pamphlet fits in with the evidence that Shakespeare was sensible both in his industry and with regard to the fruits of it.

It is very difficult to assess Shakespeare's income. When the Globe Theatre was constructed the two Burbages, who were responsible for the building, held five shares between them, and five players had one share each. They were called the ' housekeepers,' and took in return for keeping up the theatre and as rent for the company, half the money charged for the better places, i.e. in the galleries. The other half, plus the groundlings' pence for admission to the floor of the house, went to the sharer actors. These paid the hired men and the boys their salaries and then divided up the rest according to agreement. Special fees, usually ten pounds, were paid for special performances at Court or Inns or private mansions. Those interested in the finance and seating of the Shakespearean theatre should read Harbage on *Shakespeare's Audience*. Harbage works it out that the average receipts at a public performance were eight or nine pounds. Successes would draw more. The players could give a public performance in the afternoon and a private one at night.

As housekeeper, actor, sharer and author Shakespeare would be drawing money from various sources. He also had income from his books—*Venus and Adonis* and *Lucrece* must have paid well—and his interest on investments in addition. The Rev. John Ward, who became Vicar of Stratford in 1662, recorded a report that Shakespeare ' spent at the rate of £1000 a year ': this would have been a gigantic sum in those days. The Ratsey pamphlet suggests that the players took little in the country; but London rewards would have been much greater. One thing seems to be certain. Shakespeare lived below his income, avoided constant carousal, and was ready to be indisposed when invitations to make ' canakin clink ' were too numerous.

Finally there is Shakespeare's will: it is, in its last form, a complete document, a revised version of an earlier testament. It is the product of a full life. It reveals the bequests of a satisfied and successful man, who is being just to his family while remembering his old friends and colleagues. His widow was provided for by right of dower. Of the actors, Heminge, Condell, and Burbage alone are mentioned, not for large bequests but for money to buy memorial rings in the manner of the time. Many of his comrades had gone earlier; the clown Armin died in the year before Shakespeare's end. The Bankside life took its toll rapidly, and in an age which had little or no preventive medicine and only the crudest form of barber's chair dentistry the expectation of life was very much less than our own. Shakespeare's own stock, apart from his father and mother, were not powerful in the art of survival.

The will has a ghost, that of young Hamnet, dead for twenty years. Shakespeare had hopes of a grandson by Susanna, the elder daughter, now married to the esteemed and prosperous Dr. Hall. She already had a daughter, Elizabeth. The bulk of the property, whose valuation we do not know, was to go to Susanna under entail. She was to get and her hoped-for son was to inherit New Place, the two houses in Henley Street, and the house in Blackfriars and ' all my other landes and tenementes and hereditamentes whatsoever.' After Susanna's death all this was to go to her eldest son or, if there was no son, to her daughter Elizabeth and to her male issue, if any. William Shakespeare dearly wanted to have survival on the male side; but he was disappointed. Susanna had no more children and her daughter Elizabeth was barren, though she had two marriages, first to Thomas Nash, who died in 1647, and later to Sir John Barnard (sometimes spelled Bernard) of Abington.

The other daughter, Judith, married Thomas Quiney, vintner, just before Shakespeare's death in the spring of 1616. There was trouble about the date of their marriage; this was in February, a month not licensed for weddings: there was also ill-feeling over Quiney's failure to find his share of the marriage settlement, one hundred pounds in land. Shakespeare, as a man of property who was treating his daughter well, strongly disliked omissions and unpunctualities of this kind.

Judith's first boy was born in November and given the

Christian name of Shakespeare: but he died in infancy. She also lost her other two boys in their early manhood at the ages of 20 and 19. So Hamnet's place was never filled. The most fertile of the Shakespeares was the poet's sister Joan, who married a local hatter called Hart and founded a long line of Harts who were boasting, naturally and justly, of the Shakespearean connection even into the twentieth century. One of the earlier Harts followed in the trail so gloriously blazed by his grand-uncle William; this was Charles Hart, a leading actor and manager under Killigrew at Drury Lane in 1663.

Of the two sons-in-law Dr. Hall had the greater substance. He lived till 1635. It is generally supposed that he and Susanna acquired among the ' hereditamentes ' Shakespeare's books and papers. The anti-Stratfordians always point out the absence from the will of any mention of such things. It does seem odd to us nowadays that objects of such affection as some of Shakespeare's books must have been to their owner were not specified but left to go in with the rest of his personal belongings; his Ovid and his history-books, Hall, Holinshed, and North's Plutarch, went along with his cloaks and shoes, tables and chairs. But if he was confident that the doctor would appreciate his books, there was no reason to be precise about them. Susanna survived her husband by fourteen years. She was praised in her epitaph as ' witty ' and ' wise to salvation,' i.e. sensible and good.

The Shakespearean goods, chattels and relics must then have passed, if the will was observed, to Elizabeth Hall, William's last lineal descendant. She died, as Madam Elizabeth Bernard or Barnard, wife of Sir John Bernard or Barnard, at Abington in Northamptonshire, her husband having been knighted at the Restoration. She divided her property between the Hathaways and Harts. Sir John outlived her by four years and we have an inventory of his goods: they include books in the study, value £29 11s. Would the books and their provenance had been mentioned by name!

Shakespeare's plays became the property of the Company: his housekeeper's share in the Globe and Blackfriars theatres may have been sold or may have lapsed when he retired to

Stratford and served the King's Men only as an author. For that reason these rights are not mentioned in the will.

The story that Shakespeare died of drinking too hard at a ' merrie meeting ' with Michael Drayton and Ben Jonson came from the Rev. John Ward's notebooks (1661-3). Drayton used to visit the district to stay with Sir Henry and Lady Rainsford at Clifford Chambers, to reach which is an easy walk from Stratford. Jonson is not known to have visited Stratford but may have done so. Fripp, always eager to keep Shakespeare in the close path of virtue, dismisses the ' worthless legend ' and claims for Shakespeare a strict sobriety. But even those who decline company on the score of ' pain ' can make exceptions, and an ailing and rather lonely man, thirsty for talk of the town, may have been gratified and tempted, in his rustication, by the chance of discussing once more in a convivial way the old campaigns of the theatre with some of his fellow-campaigners. We can believe the report or not: I see no reason for dismissing it in the summary way favoured by most scholars. Mrs. Quiney, Shakespeare's second daughter, was alive (and no doubt talking) in Stratford when Parson Ward arrived there. We need not visualise a wildly riotous night; but we can reasonably surmise that Shakespeare may have gone out to dine when he would have been better in bed.

Had he a male heir in William Davenant, the theatrical author and manager of Caroline and Restoration theatres ? It was certainly Davenant's pleasure to claim William Shakespeare as his father. The story is told by Aubrey, who says of Davenant:

A very grave and discreet Citizen : his mother was a very beautiful woman & of a very good witt and of conversation extremely agreeable. . . . Mr. William Shakespeare was wont to goe into Warwickshire once a yeare, and did commonly in his journey lye at this house in Oxon : where he was exceedingly respected. Now Sr. Wm would sometimes when he was pleasant over a glasse of wine with his most intimate friends e.g. Sam : Butler (author of Hudibras) &c. say, that it seemed to him that he writt with the very spirit that Shakespeare, and was seemed contented enough to be

L

thought his Son : he would tell them the story as above. (In which way his mother had a very light report, whereby she was called a whore.)

Hearne, an Oxford antiquarian, repeated the story in 1709, made Shakespeare Davenant's godfather, and added, ' In all probability he got him.' Then he gave this piece of Common Room anecdotage about the young Davenant:

'Tis further said that one day going from school a grave Doctor in Divinity met him, and ask'd him, Child whither art thou going in such hast ? to wch the child reply'd, O sir my Godfather is come to Town, & I am going to ask his blessing. To wch the Dr. said, Hold Child, you must not take the name of God in vaine.

Certainly Shakespeare may have passed through Oxford, if he preferred the Woodstock and High Wycombe to the Banbury and Aylesbury route from Stratford to London. (If it is true that he picked up the character of Dogberry at Grendon in Bucks, as suggested by Aubrey—together with a muddle about the play in which the comic constable appears—then he used the latter road, but he may very well have used both: and of course he may have visited Oxford quite apart from his Stratford journeys.) There are other yarns of Shakespeare's success as a lady's man. John Manningham, of the Middle Temple, told in 1602 the story of the woman who, seeing Burbage as Richard III, made an assignation for the same night with the star of the day; he was to announce himself at her door in the name of his part.

Shakespeare overhearing their conclusion went before, was intertained, and at his game ere Burbage came. Then message being brought that Rich. the 3.^{d} was at the dore, Shakespeare caused returne to be made that William the Conqueror was before Rich. the 3. Shakespeare's name William.

This jest has the strength of being contemporary, unlike most of the Shakespeare legends: but it has the ring of a good Inns of Court story rather than of actual fact.

Here again it is a case of ' believe it or not.' Some have so far believed in Davenant's unfilial report of his mother's ' lightness ' as to see in Mrs. Davenant of the Crown the Dark Lady of the Sonnets.

Whether or not Shakespeare had his affairs (and the mysterious poem of *Willobie His Avisa*, with its reference to a previous amour of ' Mr. W. S.' with the poet's own dear one, is further, but insubstantial, witness) he was a family man at Stratford and a thrifty man in London. He loved his garden (the flowers dance especially in his later plays) and he loved his acres; he was (or was made to seem so by his family acting for him) ready to lend and then to be firm with his debtors; despite a minor tiff with his second son-in-law, Quiney, he was at peace with the world when he died. Had he, in the company of his ' steady,' quoted the happy words of his own Sly in the last months at Stratford:

> Come, madam wife, sit by my side and let the world slip,
> We shall ne'er be younger.

It would probably have pleased this son of the Ardens and of John Shakespeare, Armiger, to know that his granddaughter married a title: it would certainly have gratified him to learn that the inheritance was still solidly there for the Harts and Hathaways to share when his own line ran out. But he would have dearly liked his daughter or granddaughter to have been another Hamnet to carry on the name and take over a property so industriously earned. Parents then were more accustomed to ' losing ' children than they are now. But Shakespeare carried a long sorrow for his son.

> With fairest flowers,
> While summer lasts, and I live here, Fidele,
> I'll sweeten thy sad grave: thou shalt not lack
> The flower that's like thy face, pale primrose ; nor

> The azur'd harebell, like thy veins; no, nor
> The leaf of eglantine, whom not to slander,
> Out-sweeten'd not thy breath:

Is it culpably sentimental to imagine that Shakespeare wrote this exquisite piece of poignancy during a summer residence in Stratford and after a walk to the churchyard by the river ? The pale primrose links with ' as dim and meagre as an ague's fit,' written about little Arthur in *King John* just about the time of Hamnet's death; and once more the delicate blueness of veins has taken his fancy and lingers in the mind.

CHAPTER XV

The Hand of Glory

ON one of the bleakest and bravest English roads I know, the Roman road which breasts the Pennines at Scotch Corner and soars over the noble waste of Stainmore to Brough and Carlisle, there is a lonely steading called the Hand of Glory. This glittering name for a moorland house of call refers back to a macabre crime. It is a title that stays in the mind and to me it has long seemed the apt, the final phrase for the fingers that can be seen in effigy stiffly clutching a quill below the unworthy bust in Stratford Church. There never was such a hand for the use of words, and such a hand, maybe, there never again will be. Nothing in our literature, nothing, perhaps, in any literature, has such a quality of supremacy, nothing is so unchallengeable, as Shakespeare's power, through that Hand of Glory, to put observation and feeling into words.

It is this very sovereignty of Shakespeare's that has made some deny him the crown. If he had been only a little ahead of the others, would there have been so much effort to prove that 'Shagsper' of petty Stratford could not have been the man? But he was so easily the best that people have found it difficult to believe that he was real. Chesterton said of Dickens that he was not a man but a mob; Shakespeare, in his use of words, was not a man but a miracle. And where you get miracles, you are bound to get doubt and denial. Nobody can say that the lines were never written; but they can and do deny that they were written by the Warwickshire lad turned strolling player. The sceptics stress the ignorance of Stratford, on which they have been sufficiently refuted. There were plenty of books and readers in the town; moreover, Shakespeare does not make the country folk in his plays illiterate. The shepherds provide a market for printed ballads as well as for baubles. Young Richard Quiney of Stratford wrote to his father Adrian in flowing and correct Latin at the age of eleven. To say that Shakespeare could not have picked up a good Ovidian Latinity at Stratford is nonsense.

It is claimed that he left no books, when all that is true is that he mentioned no books in his will. It is claimed that he showed knowledge in his plays beyond the scope of a mere actor; it can be counter-claimed that he also made mistakes unlikely to be made by great scholars of the Baconian level. A zealot for accurate learning could hardly have mentioned Aristotle amid the Trojan wars or given the Romans clocks. If it be urged that things appear in his texts which are outside the experience and information of 'a harlotry player,' the answer is that the Shakespeare whom I have endeavoured to picture, according to known facts and contemporary allusions, was certainly under patronage of the Earl of Southampton and seemingly a close friend of that nobleman too. In Southampton's house and circle he would meet John Florio, translator of Montaigne, and the wits who hovered round the brilliant Essex or the learned Bacon. With his quickness of ear and perception and strength of memory he would absorb and retain without difficulty what was said round about him. The idea of the outcast and ignoramus actor can only be supported by ignoring the dedications to Southampton and by thinking of Tudor London as a huge modern capital among whose millions genius can easily wilt unrecognised. But Tudor London was in size no more than a country town of to-day; it was a rich market for wit and melody, and to arrive at the centre of things is obviously far easier when the suburbs are few.

I have read much of the anti-Stratfordian literature, and have never questioned the integrity of its writers. All sides in this controversy share one admirable thing : they are liegemen to the Master and it is because they care for him so much that they are prepared to argue until their print and paper (and possibly the reader's patience) are all exhausted in discovering the identity of that great one.   The Baconians have had the longest say and can still fairly inquire what became of the plays Bacon was alleged to have written.   The Oxfordians, who arrived under the starting hand of Mr. J. T. Looney nearly thirty years ago and have since been industriously, even passionately, assisted by Mr. Percy Allen, Mr. William Kent, and others, have asked the same question about Edward de Vere, 17th Earl of Oxford.   William Stanley, a less widely favoured candidate, was put forward in 1890 in England and had powerful support in France from Professor Abel Lefranc.   The Stanleyans could point out two statements in letters of 1599.   'Th'erle of Darby is busyed only in planning comedies for the common players.'   Then, later, came a learned volume called *The Dyer's Hand*, by Alden Brooks, which hands the palm to Sir Edward Dyer (1545-1607).   It is possible, of course, to maintain that all these and others too put in their little bits and pieces, just as J. M. Robertson used to carve up the supposed Shakespeare texts and find pieces inserted or passages redrafted by all sorts of hands.   Those contentions are based on a curious impercipience about men and their writing.   There is one Shakespearean hand, immediately recognisable, and that is the master-hand.   Four or five men do not all perform the same kind of miracle.

The general start of the anti-Stratfordians is the strong conviction and assertion that a Stratford lad, turned playactor, could never have known so much.   There are two faults here; one is the snobbery, common in capitals, of underrating provincial towns and their culture: the other is that lack of imagination in those who cannot conceive a mind far quicker, far more mobile, than their own.   The allotment of dark ignorance to Stratford is as foolish as the allotment of a deep academic knowledge and a bred-in-the-bone courtliness to Shakespeare.   Able men are versatile men and imaginative men.   The more I see of life the more I am impressed by the extreme rapidity of apprehension which the unusually gifted man possesses. That Shakespeare, after some years on the fringe of Southampton's society (and possibly after some foreign travel in the Earl's company), would have remained slow and ignorant is unthinkable. The very reason why Southampton took him up must have been the uncanny promise and swift performance of this unique young man.

Shakespeare may very well have taken hints and ideas from the nobility and gentry of his acquaintance; he may also have worked over their manuscripts for them, for they were busy writers and undoubtedly liked to compose for their revels and perhaps, anonymously, for the supposedly shameful public theatres as well. A case in point is *Love's Labour's Lost*: the plot is original, which was unusual in the case of Shakespeare. Bored by this business of story-invention, he usually drew on chronicles and story books, agreeing with the query of a subsequent playwright, ' What the devil is a plot for except to bring in fine things ?' Professor Ifor Evans in his *Short History of English Drama* has said of this piece:

It is imaginary, but there are some references to almost contemporary French history, and much of the humour depends on topical allusions worked out in part through figures similar to those of the Italian commedia dell' arte. The play is one of the most astounding things that Shakespeare did. It is a sixteenth-century manners comedy, where the ' finer shades ' of contemporary sentiment are subjected to the light of the comic spirit by one who is new to the stage, and almost a stranger to courtly life. Nor is the world of this play previously discoverable in the drama. Shakespeare, apparently by invention, has discovered a society sophisticated and elegant, like that in Molière or Congreve.

The French history is detailed stuff. It would have been familiar to Bacon, who travelled, after leaving Cambridge in 1576, for three years with Sir Amyas Paulet, the English Ambassador in France. He visited Navarre, the scene of this play. Mr. Roderick Eagle, one of the most sensible and acute of the Baconians (some of whom Mr. Eagle would himself admit to have talked fantastic nonsense in their time), argues that *Love's Labour's Lost* was either written or inspired by Bacon. I would certainly accept the second half of the statement. Or if it was not inspired by Bacon, whose diplomatic sojourn in France could have provided some of the facts which are mentioned for no particular reason of dramatic value (e.g. the financial deals between France and Navarre), then one of the Southampton group may have been the original begetter.

This play was specially mentioned as being due for performance at Southampton's house. My theory is that it was first drafted for a private revel or masquerade with an audience of wits and grandees, to whose taste most of it is specially directed: then the author found it harder than he expected to work the conceits of his intellectual fancy into ' good theatre ' and called in Johannes Factotum, young Shakespeare the play-smith, to mend it. Shakespeare ultimately set his stamp on nearly all of it and brought in the rustic charades whose humours he renewed in *A Midsummer Night's Dream*. Once the Hand of Glory was set to work, its signature was unmistakable. It is there in everything that Berowne, flouting, love-smitten, or abashed, has to say. It is there in the dying fall of the comedy when the players troop away to the lovely cadences of

> When daisies pied and violets blue,
> And lady-smocks all silver-white,
> And cuckoo-buds of yellow hue
> Do paint the meadows with delight.

It is there, unmistakably, in Berowne's speech on Love:

> But love, first learned in a lady's eyes,
> Lives not alone immured in the brain;
> But, with the motion of all elements,
> Courses as swift as thought in every power,
> And gives to every power a double power,
> Above their functions and their offices.
> It adds a precious seeing to the eye;
> A lover's eyes will gaze an eagle blind;

A lover's ear will hear the lowest sound,
When the suspicious head of theft is stopp'd:
Love's feeling is more soft and sensible
Than are the tender horns of cockled snails;
Love's tongue proves dainty Bacchus gross in taste:
For valour, is not Love a Hercules,
Still climbing trees in the Hesperides?
Subtle as Sphinx; as sweet and musical
As bright Apollo's lute, strong with his hair:
And when Love speaks, the voice of all the gods
Makes heaven drowsy with the harmony.
Never durst poet touch a pen to write
Until his ink were temper'd with Love's sighs;
O, then his lines would ravish savage ears
And plant in tyrants mild humility.
From women's eyes this doctrine I derive:
They sparkle still the right Promethean fire;
They are the books, the arts, the academes,
That show, contain and nourish all the world:
Else none at all in aught proves excellent.

That is by the man who was to write the rest of the magnificence.
It is signed as much by the cockled snails as by Apollo's
lute.

Of course, say the Baconians: but they insist that the whole
magnificence of the rest of the plays was Bacon's. For Bacon,
read Oxford or Raleigh or Rutland or Derby or Dyer, say the
devotees of other ' possibles.' To that there is an obvious reply.
Some of these men wrote much, some little, in verse as well as
in prose. Can anything substantial be produced from their
work, however good, which can be matched with the product of
the Hand of Glory? There was nothing to stop the noblemen
writing prose and poetry of all kinds outside the suspect arena
of the theatre and Bacon was perhaps the greatest of English
essayists. But the mind behind the Essays is not, in my
opinion, the mind behind the plays: there is much in Bacon
and in Raleigh to admire, but it is admirable because it is
essentially their own.

The Hand of Glory may well have worked over the notions
of Bacon or of other men, but its glory was its own and what

it wrote it signed for itself with the lettering of its own supremacy. The idea put forward by Dr. Gilbert Slater that there were Seven Shakespeares, i.e. seven contributors to the Shakespeare canon, shows a complete lack of sensitivity to style. How on earth could there be Seven Hands, all with the same glory? It is possible to be a great venerator of Bacon and yet to feel a total conviction that he could never have approached the heights of Shakespeare's poetical achievement.

On the other hand, since we know that Bacon and his set did write plays covertly, it is fair enough to suppose that the brilliant young arrival in the theatres, Southampton's pet of genius, could have been employed to go over the efforts of the gentry, to give them a new surface of poetry, and to insert a hard core of playhouse quality. I can well imagine Bacon sitting at a public performance of the revised *Love's Labour's Lost* and saying to his friends, ' Of course it's all mine really ' —as authors do in all innocence after their work has been efficiently sub-edited and rewritten—though, of course, it was the Hand of Glory that put the sheen upon the Navarre story.

Shakespeare, it seems, was always ready to collaborate. At the height of his success he would turn to pour his angry heart into another man's tragedy of *Timon* or to inject his new taste for romance into another's tale of *Pericles*. In each case the Hand of Glory proclaims its own section of the play. That he worked with Fletcher seems likely too. If he was ready to do that when he was in full mastery of his craft, why should he not have assisted the young ' littery gents ' of the Inns of Court when he was in great need of their financial backing and social support? He knew all the time—surely the self-confidence of the Sonnets proclaims it—that he would emerge to full recognition and even immortality.

If that was the situation, it explains some of the sneers at a sneak-thief poet which the anti-Stratfordians discover in Ben Jonson and elsewhere and then attach to Shakespeare. It was a permissible jest to hint that Shakespeare was a poet-ape and play-broker, if it was known that *Love's Labour's Lost*, for example, was based on someone else's origins. We know that Shakespeare did, in several cases (e.g. *The Taming of the Shrew* and *King*

John), work on foundations already set. In *Richard II* there certainly seem to be the remnants of another (and a feeble) hand's first draft. The last scene of all, Act V, Scene 6, following close on the superb soliloquy which starts

> I have been studying how I may compare
> This prison where I live unto the world

contains stuff like this:

Northumberland First, to thy sacred state wish I all happiness.
             The next news is, I have to London sent
             The heads of Oxford, Salisbury, Blunt, and Kent;
             The manner of their taking may appear
             At large discoursed in this paper here.
Bolingbroke   We thank thee, gentle Percy, for thy pains;
             And to thy worth will add right worthy gains.
             [*Enter Fitzwater*]
Fitzwater   My lord, I have from Oxford sent to London
             The heads of Brocas and Sir Bennet Seely,
             Two of the dangerous consorted traitors
             That sought at Oxford thy dire overthrow.
Bolingbroke   Thy pains, Fitzwater, shall not be forgot;
             Right noble is thy merit, well I wot.

This is Pantomime poetry.

The only conclusion I can draw is that Shakespeare had been using an older play on this theme lying in the possession of the Chamberlain's Men and that when he had seen his King ' Spur-galled and tired by jauncing Bolingbroke ' (Hand of Glory phrasing indeed!) and left him murdered in Pomfret Castle by Sir Pierce of Exton, he could not be bothered to rewrite the clearing-up lines and left them as they stood.

So Ben Jonson and the others, perhaps in pique after some failure or when engaged in a literary wrangle, jested at the Factotum's benefit of lordly suggestions or at his usage of old playhouse scripts. Yet they knew well enough that the Hand of Glory was unique. The anti-Stratfordians have to argue that Jonson's famous tribute to Shakespeare in the First Folio is an elaborate deceit practised for motives which they cannot easily explain or define. They try very hard, but this job really does defeat them.

The portrait of Sogliardo, the essential clown, greedy for status and title (' I will be a gentleman whatsoever it costs me '), in Jonson's *Every Man out of His Humour* may or may not refer, contemptuously, to the eager invader from Stratford who so rapidly asserted himself as a man of property, family, and position. But the Folio verses by Ben Jonson are indubitably assigned to Shakespeare's glory, and only desperate invention can find reason for assuring us that they are an elaborate and false façade behind which Jonson is really honouring Bacon or Oxford or one of the others. Shakespeare, Swan of Avon, is here acclaimed as the star of poets; we are assured that he still lives with us in his Book, merits the homage of all Europe, and is ' for all time.' Well, he has had the homage, still lives, and never looked closer to immortality than at present.

The owner of the Hand came to a city already ' word-happy ' as we might say now. To the good ale of Chaucerian English had been added the wine of the Renaissance. Of these liquors the young English grandees drank deep; they came back from their Grand Tours with new clothes, new dances, new music, new words. Little wonder that the town was full of ' lisping, affecting fantasticoes ' and ' tuners of new accents.' Shakespeare disliked these ' buzzers '; he thought of them in terms of insects. Mercutio called them strange flies. Berowne described the phrases themselves as summer-flies, and the chattering fop Osric is called by Hamlet a water-fly.

Yet the flies could fascinate as well as infuriate. I think of the young Shakespeare as being no less ' word-happy ' than Mr. Wells's young Mr. Polly, of whom ' H. G.' wrote:

Words attracted him curiously, words rich in splendour, words rich in suggestions, and he loved a novel and a striking phrase. New words had terror and fascination for him. He could not avoid them, and so he plunged into them. ' Sesquippledan,' he would say, ' Sesquippledan Verboojuice. ' Eh ? ' said Platt. ' Eloquent Rapsodooce,' answered Mr. Polly.

Shakespeare soon abandoned the silken terms and taffeta-phrases of Euphuism, as I explained in my chapter on 'The Morning's War.' The absurd Armado who called the afternoon 'the posteriors of this day' and the pedant Holofernes who added 'The posterior of the day, most generous Sir, is liable, congruent, and measurable for the afternoon' had served their turn. There remained the lure of the mighty line, the playhouse surge of sound, the Rapsodooce. And Shakespeare soon proved that he could better the Marlovian instruction. No sooner was Marlowe dead than the new hand, the hand of greater glory, could turn out this for Romeo:

> Death, that hath suck'd the honey of thy breath,
> Hath had no power yet upon thy beauty:
> Thou art not conquer'd; beauty's ensign yet
> Is crimson in thy lips and in thy cheeks,
> And death's pale flag is not advanced there.
> Tybalt, liest thou there in thy bloody sheet ?
> O, what more favour can I do to thee,
> Than with that hand that cut thy youth in twain
> To sunder his that was thine enemy ?
> Forgive me, cousin ! Ah, dear Juliet,
> Why art thou yet so fair ? shall I believe
> That unsubstantial Death is amorous,
> And that the lean abhorred monster keeps
> Thee here in dark to be his paramour ?
> For fear of that, I still will stay with thee;
> And never from this palace of dim night
> Depart again ; here, here will I remain
> With worms that are thy chamber-maids;   O, here
> Will I set up my everlasting rest;
> And shake the yoke of inauspicious stars
> From this world-wearied flesh.—Eyes, look your last !
> Arms, take your last embrace !

Eloquent Rapsodooce indeed! How Marlowe would have loved to roll it out. I quote that passage for two reasons. It illustrates so vividly Shakespeare's instinctive feeling for the letter ' r ' ; time and time again he was to play on its emotional vibration, especially when linked with the letter ' o.' (I chose the phrase ' Hand of Glory ' for that reason; it is twice as effective as Hand of Brilliance or Hand of Fame.) Within three lines Shakespeare partnered amorous, abhorred—the ominous ' abhor ' was a favourite word of his for dark occasions —monster and paramour. In a moment he was back among his darling r's, with works, chambermaids, here, everlasting rest, stars and world-wearied. I do not say that, when in full flow, he deliberately said to himself, ' Wait a minute ' and pulled out a bagful of r's; but, subconsciously at least, he was seized of the letter's potency. The very name of Romeo was a gift to him. Suppose it had been ' Valentine and Juliet.' Comedy is suggested at once, whereas Romeo drives straight into the heart. The word romance has itself been a benefit to its own theme, just as the words Rome and Roman sound their clarion with consummate effect.

He would build a whole line—and what a line!—on o's and r's. A poet can easily manage emotional effects on the theme of ' dead yesterday.' ' Y ' sets a note of yearning, but ' or ' gives grief full cadence. First

To-morrow and to-morrow and to-morrow.

What simplicity and what poignance! Why had Marlowe never thought of it ?

And then

To the last syllable of recorded time.

Recorded time! Make it related time and the emotional vibration has vanished. *Macbeth* is full of such glory. ' Pluck from the memory a rooted sorrow.' Substitute mind for memory and a settled pain or a deep-set ache for a rooted sorrow and all the grief has gone out of it: and Shakespeare knew the value of the ' r ' in the word grief itself. Grief filled the room up of his absent child—not pain or woe.

The second point to notice is that Romeo, after his final

fling of Rapsodooce, dies with a string of monosyllables. Marlowe had coined the haunting line:

> Infinite riches in a little room

(The r and o do the trick again. ' Infinite riches in a little space ' would have only half the value.) Shakespeare realised, with his flawless verbal sense, and practised, with his hand of glory, the use of the single syllable. It was a point of technique that Marlowe had only partly grasped. Shakespeare was to discover and perfect the value of varying the Eloquent Rapsodooce with the Poignant Brevity. So Romeo, abandoning his organ-music, bids farewell to life with two lines in which are sixteen words of one syllable. Note Hamlet's valediction:

> If thou didst ever hold me in thy heart,
> Absent thee from felicity awhile
> And in this harsh world draw thy breath in pain
> To tell my story.

What an exquisite piece of verbal patterning is this! Here is the interlaced alliteration of h's and r's and the cunning return to the ' or ' sound in world and story; apart from felicity, so felicitously used, there is no word that is not short and simple.

Shakespeare also played on monosyllables for more than pathos; he could use them, like blows, to frighten. What more shiversome than Macbeth's ' Blood hath been shed ere now ' going on to

> the time has been
> That when the brains were out, the man would die
> And there an end ; but now they rise again.

That is the very genius of brevity: it smites even harder than does the best of Rapsodooce.

In the poetry, comedy, and tragedy of love he moved from the rhetorical to the tender simplicities, from the orotund to the exquisitely curt and plain. Could anything be less affected, less ' written up ' than this ?

Duke of Illyria	What dost thou know ?
Viola	Too well what love women to men may owe:
	In faith, they are as true of heart as we.
	My father had a daughter loved a man,
	As it might be, perhaps, were I a woman,
	I should your lordship.
Duke of Illyria	And what's her history ?
Viola	A blank, my lord. She never told her love,
	But let concealment, like a worm i' th' bud,
	Feed on her damask cheek : she pined in thought;
	And, with a green and yellow melancholy,
	She sat like Patience on a monument,
	Smiling at grief. Was not this love indeed ?
	We men may say more, swear more : but, indeed,
	Our shows are more than will ; for still we prove
	Much in our vows, but little in our love.
Duke of Illyria	But died thy sister of her love, my boy ?
Viola	I am all the daughters of my father's house,
	And all the brothers too;—and yet I know not.—
	Sir, shall I to this lady ?

There are a few long words, concealment, melancholy, monument, but line after line is packed with the shortest and most ordinary words. The Hand of Glory that created Romeo and Juliet once set that child Juliet to cry:

O serpent heart, hid with a flow'ring face!
Did ever dragon keep so fair a cave ?
Beautiful tyrant ! fiend angelical!
Dove-feather'd raven ! wolvish-ravening lamb!
Despised substance of divinest show!
Just opposite to what thou justly seem'st,
A damned saint, an honourable villain!

Now the mind behind it has discovered something new, namely that the economy of syllables can be the enrichment of emotions.

Early in his career he had had inklings.   If anything in the three plays of *Henry VI* has the certain marks of the Hand, a 'prentice Hand, but definitely the Hand, it is in the speech of King Henry upon Towton Field beginning:

> This battle fares like to the morning's war
> When dying clouds contend with growing light.

After that the King recites, very simply, the praises of escape from crowns and wars and weariness.

> O God ! methinks it were a happy life,
> To be no better than a homely swain;
> To sit upon a hill, as I do now,
> To carve out dials quaintly, point by point,
> Thereby to see the minutes how they run,—
> How many makes the hour full complete;
> How many days will finish up the year;
> How many years a mortal man may live.

> Ah, what a life were this ! how sweet ! how lovely!
> Gives not the hawthorn-bush a sweeter shade
> To shepherds looking on their silly sheep,
> Than doth a rich-embroider'd canopy
> To kings that fear their subjects' treachery?
> O, yes, it doth ; a thousand-fold it doth.
> And to conclude,—the shepherd's homely curds,
> His cold thin drink out of his leather bottle,
> His wonted sleep under a fresh tree's shade,
> All which secure and sweetly he enjoys,
> Is far beyond a prince's delicates,
> His viands sparkling in a golden cup,
> His body couched in a curious bed,
> When care, mistrust, and treason waits on him.

And then the dramatist is off again to Marlovian battle-music, with sepulchres and winding-sheets. The passage with its monotonous rhythms and its unsophisticated ' To conclude,' as though the end of a sermon were arriving, is not nearly as expert, naturally, as a similar passage in *Richard II*:

> I'll give my jewels for a set of beads,
> My gorgeous palace for a hermitage,
> My gay apparel for an almsman's gown,
> My figured goblets for a dish of wood,
> My sceptre for a palmer's walking-staff,
> My subjects for a pair of carved saints,
> And my large kingdom for a little grave,
> A little little grave, an obscure grave:—
> Or I'll be buried in the king's highway,
> Some way of common trade, where subjects' feet
> May hourly trample on their sovereign's head.

. . . .

> Or shall we play the wantons with our woes,
> And make some pretty match with shedding tears?
> As thus;—to drop them still upon one place,
> Till they have fretted us a pair of graves
> Within the earth; and, therein laid,—' There lies
> Two kinsmen digg'd their graves with weeping eyes.'

The latter speech is obviously more mature and better varied in rhythm. But the *Henry VI* speech is an indication of Shakespeare's early comprehension that there are more things in poetry and drama than Rapsodooce and the Sesquippledan attack.

Meanwhile he never abandoned his mastery of and his gusto for the good old multi-syllabled uproar of the stages. He could always fetch out that vein of his. In the great tragedies he has a wonderful capacity for blending the two styles. The Ghost in *Hamlet* both speaks in eloquent Rapsodooce himself and evokes it from others. We are back in the theatre of Marlowe with speeches like this. (But, of course, it is Marlowe glorified by the Hand.)

> Angels and ministers of grace defend us!—
> Be thou a spirit of health or goblin damn'd,
> Bring with thee airs from heaven or blasts from hell,

> Be thy intents wicked or charitable,
> Thou comest in such a questionable shape,
> That I will speak to thee : I'll call thee Hamlet,
> King, father, royal Dane : O, answer me!
> Let me not burst in ignorance ; but tell
> Why thy canonized bones, hearsed in death,
> Have burst their cerements; why the sepulchre,
> Wherein we saw thee quietly inurn'd,
> Hath oped his ponderous and marble jaws
> To cast thee up again ! What may this mean,
> That thou, dead corse, again, in complete steel,
> Revisit'st thus the glimpses of the moon,
> Making night hideous; and we fools of nature
> So horridly to shake our disposition
> With thoughts beyond the reaches of our souls ?
> Say, why is this ? wherefore ? what should we do ?

That may, or may not, thrill you to the marrow. Yet, when Shakespeare really intended to strike us to the heart in the same play, he did it quite otherwise with the lines I have just quoted, ending:

> And in this harsh world draw thy breath in pain,
> To tell my story.

It is the same with *King Lear*, the same with *Macbeth*, the same with *Antony and Cleopatra*. In each there is the consummate mastery of variation in use of words, the instinctive knowledge of when to thunder like a colossal waterfall and when to drop a pebble in the pool. At one moment we have the eloquence of Nature, even of Chaos itself:

> Blow, winds, and crack your cheeks! rage! blow!
> You cataracts and hurricanoes, spout
> Till you have drench'd our steeples, drown'd the cocks!
> You sulphurous and thought-executing fires,
> Vaunt-couriers to oak-cleaving thunderbolts,
> Singe my white head! And thou, all-shaking thunder,
> Strike flat the thick rotundity o' the world!
> Crack nature's moulds, all germens spill at once,
> That make ingrateful man!

In 8½ lines there are fourteen words of more than one syllable and ten of these have three or more syllables. Contrast that glorious tornado with this last whisper to the heart:

> No, No, No, No! Come let's away to prison:
> We two alone will sing like birds i' the cage:
> When thou dost ask me blessing, I'll kneel down
> And ask of thee forgiveness; so we'll live,
> And pray, and sing, and tell old tales, and laugh
> At gilded butterflies, and hear poor rogues
> Talk of court news; and we'll talk with them too,—
> Who loses and who wins; who's in, who's out;—
> And take upon's the mystery of things,
> As if we were God's spies; and we'll wear out,
> In a wall'd prison, packs and sects of great ones
> That ebb and flow by th' moon.

In these twelve lines there are only nine words of more than one syllable.

Then there is the Hand's dexterity with the magic inherent in the letter ' w '. All poets must have felt its persuasion to some extent. Browning's

> O lyric love, half angel and half bird
> And all a wonder and a wild desire

is Shakespearean in its alliterative pattern and most especially so in its use of ' w '. Make it

> And all a surmise and a fierce desire

and the spell has gone. Even if you write

> And all a rapture and a fierce desire

the magic is far less, even with the alliterative assistance of the r's.

Nobody has felt more keenly than Shakespeare the value of ' w.' He, too, could make strange music of this word 'wonder.' There is a thrilling beauty in Macbeth's sudden cry,

> Can such things be
> And overcome us like a summer's cloud,
> Without our special wonder?

Those lines are not among the familiar quotations from *Macbeth*. But repeat them to yourself. They have the stamp, the ring. Nobody else wrote like that. The alliterative o's and u's are part of the glorious trick: then the two w's come in to give the finishing touch of verbal magic. Constantly he returns to this letter when there is no particular need for it. Remember Feste singing of the wind and the rain, with its plangent melody of 'w' and 'r'. Suppose he had sung of the gale and the snow. The verbal sorcery has vanished.

And again take the Willow Song:

> The poor soul sat sighing by a sycamore tree,
> Sing all a green willow;
> Her hand on her bosom, her head on her knee,
> Sing willow, willow, willow.

Why sycamore? It has the combination of o and r so dear to the Hand of Glory. Why all these willows? Not only because they may be said to have a weeping look, but because there are essential tears in the letter 'w.' Other trees would have served the material purpose. But they would not have served the heart.

Return to the highest emotional levels of *Antony and Cleopatra* and you find the interplay of r and w as cogent as recurrent. As Antony's life wanes away, Cleopatra cries,

> O see, my women,
> The crown o' the earth doth melt. My lord!
> O, wither'd is the garland of the war.

Cleopatra frequently calls on her 'Women, Women.' Her

creator knew that 'girls' would not do at the moment of supreme stress.

It is lucky, no doubt, for poets that so many of their most evocative themes, war and woe, wind and water, women and wine, and farewells to the world offer them the magical letter. The trick could easily be overplayed. But Shakespeare never overplayed his strength. Hands of Glory are hands of moderation too. Watch him using all his arts at once in the farewell to Cleopatra.

> Why should I stay,

murmurs Cleopatra, and Charmian replies,

> In this vile world ?—So, fare thee well.—
> Now boast thee, death, in thy possession lies
> A lass unparallel'd.—Downy windows, close,
> And golden Phoebus never be beheld
> Of eyes again so royal!—Your crown's awry;
> I'll mend it, and then play.

The r's and o's are at their work. The line that accompanies the shutting down of those eyes that had bewitched the world, 'A lass unparallel'd.—Downy windows, close,' is a roll of drums followed by a last trump. Then comes the old device of ending on monosyllables.

Shakespeare had many fancies and preferences. I know no other writer so fond of the prefix ' dis ' or so well able to use it with beautiful effect. Disbench and disseat for unseat, discandy for melt, discomfortable, disedge, disjoin, dislimn, disorb, dispunge, dis-stain, distasted for put out of flavour, disvalue, disvouch, are some examples. They mostly occur in the later plays. The separated lovers' single famished kiss ' distasted with the salt of broken tears ' is, I think, the most striking example of this taste in prefixes: it is a line that summarises to perfection the agony when journeys end in lovers' parting.

On the enormous size and range of Shakespeare's vocabulary

much has been written. We are now so well accustomed to his magic that we hardly notice it. Yet if we try to treat familiar passages as though we are meeting them for the first time, we can always rediscover fresh sources of ' especial wonder.' I noticed that recently during a performance of *Hamlet*. The phrase ' dead vast and middle of the night ' suddenly tumbled out of the cliché status to which we had condemned it. I no longer took it for granted. ' Dead vast.' Its two dull, thudding monosyllables, the use of vast as a noun (parallelled in *Pericles*, ' Thou god of this great vast, rebuke these surges ' and in *The Tempest*, ' this vast of night '), the expressiveness of the heavy, broad ' a ' to signify the darkness of a temporal chasm, these things the Hand of Glory seized in its fluency. Shakespeare cannot have stopped to think them all out. They came to him, but not to others. So it is possible to re-read him, as no author can be re-read, infinitely; there is always some new bounty for those eyes and ears that can freshly attend upon his alms-basket of words.

Anti-Stratfordians may continue to scrape for cryptic sneers in other men's works, to puzzle over cyphers and to claim that the Real Author stood over the printers of the First Folio making them paginate the text and fix the lines so as to render alphabetical hints for posterity with their initial letters. What they must do, if they are to persuade me, is to produce evidence that their Aristocratic Substitute for Shagsper the Warwickshire lad had the Hand of Glory and wrote not finely—for of course Bacon wrote finely—but wrote also with this supreme verbal genius that raised words not only to a higher power but to the highest power ever achieved by any writer in our tongue.

CHAPTER XVI

Matters of Opinion

MAN'S age-long habit of making his gods in his own image has been transferred to his heroes. Shakespeare-worship has been moulded by the nature of the worshipper. Since Shakespeare has been accepted, beyond question and beyond criticism, as the lord of language and the sovereign poet of English tongue, his devotees have naturally seen their paragon as they want him; that is, in the likeness of themselves. So scholars have paid their veneration to William the profound, actors to William the mummer, poets to William the lyricist and sonneteer, men of the world to William the worldly. Shakespeare has thus been endowed by ' the fancy ' with every kind of virtue and vice, with learning and with ignorance, with a noble academic wisdom and with a deplorable taste for indecency, with the lofty mind of Prospero, the scholar-recluse, and with the carefree Bohemianism of a drinker and wencher about town. So when we come to examine Shakespeare's mind, his creed and his policy, in short the ' gross and scope ' of his opinion to use Horatio's phrase, we find a multitude of contradictory answers.

The Droeshout portrait of Shakespeare presents us with a lofty brow; of that, at least, there can be no dispute. What was the brain within that formidable dome? At one time Bernard Shaw denied Shakespeare any such thing as brain. Writing of the Lyceum production of *Cymbeline* (Sept. 22, 1896) Shaw had this to say of the play—Tennyson's favourite—and of its creator:

> It is for the most part stagey trash of the lowest melodramatic order, in parts abominably written, throughout intellectually vulgar, and, judged in point of thought by modern intellectual

standards, vulgar, foolish, offensive, indecent, and exasperating beyond all tolerance. There are moments when one asks despairingly why our stage should ever have been cursed with this ' immortal ' pilferer of other men's stories and ideas, with his monstrous rhetorical fustian, his unbearable platitudes, his pretentious reduction of the subtlest problems of life to commonplaces against which a Polytechnic debating club would revolt, his incredible unsuggestiveness, his sententious combination of ready reflection with complete intellectual sterility, and his consequent incapacity for getting out of the depth of even the most ignorant audience, except when he solemnly says something so transcendently platitudinous that his more humble minded hearers cannot bring themselves to believe that so great a man really meant to talk like their grandmothers. With the single exception of Homer, there is no eminent writer, not even Sir Walter Scott, whom I can despise so entirely as I despise Shakespeare when I measure my mind against his.

It has to be remembered that when Shaw wrote this outburst he was fighting a particularly fulsome and foolish kind of Bardolatry. Yet this same Shakespeare ' out-topped knowledge' for Matthew Arnold, while for a modern Cambridge scholar like Dr. Tillyard he is a noble example of the educated man, ' a poet more rather than less like Dante and Milton in massiveness of intellect and powers of reflection.' Here is contradiction indeed! Mr. Wilson Knight discovers profound symbolism, based on deep reflection, where Shaw found only ' complete intellectual sterility.' Mr. Knight agrees with Mr. Colin Still on the subject of The Tempest that this play should be exactly located as a work of mystical insight with reference to the cross-axes of Universal and Shakespearean vision. I am not sure what that means, but it certainly does not leave Shakespeare among the crass bumpkins. The Tempest has evoked endless commentary by those in search of deep wisdom and profound symbolic intimations. Certainly, it has a note of personal farewell, and Prospero, when played as the gentleman-scholar and not as a semi-episcopal bore, may acquire a superb pathos in the theatre as the voice of the poet's own tired, and now retiring, greatness. For the rest I agree with Sir Arthur Quiller-Couch that here is basically a simple story written for a wedding ceremony and based on recent sailors' stories from the far west. Shipwreck, pilots, exile, magic, young love at first sight, villainy confounded, all happy ever after. What is this but the eternal stuff of fairy tale, touched by the master-hand with tints of glory?

So, as one follows the cross-talk between the tribute-payers and the 'knockers' of the Bard, the contradiction becomes the more astounding. Coleridge called Shakespeare 'myriad-minded' and observed that no man was ever a great poet without being at the same time a profound philosopher, thereby implying that the finest of our poets must certainly rank with the loftiest of our sages. Yet many another poet has viewed Shakespeare as the child of nature, untutored in his warbling of the wood-notes, by no means philosophical in his pursuit of fancy free. Dryden spoke for Shakespeare's immediate successors when he found him 'naturally learned,' needing no 'spectacles of books' wherewith to read the world aright. Naturally learned was not the same for Dryden as properly learned.

To his contemporaries Shakespeare was, as we have seen, industriously gentle, sedulously honey'd, of 'right happy and copious industry,' as his rival Webster put it. Jonson, a little sniffy about the Stratford man's academic ignorance, had, of course, to salute him as a chief son of Nature's Family. One could go on quoting this variety of judgment with never a pause for lack of matter.

The outstanding fact is that each man follows his bent. It seems to be a form of incurable human vanity that the worshipper should always see the hero, in this case the supreme writer, as a reflection of himself. Coleridge wanted a Coleridgian Shakespeare just as the young student, perplexed with the yearnings of his years and indulging the melancholy often so dear to the salad days, will have nothing of Shakespeare the sage and is rapt, like Digges, by 'Passions of Juliet and her Romeo.' The poet hangs upon the poetry, the actor on the roles which, being immortal, can immortalise, the sensual man upon the sensuous beauty, the patriot on the trumpet-call, the High Tory on the contempt of the slippery crowd and of the common curs and stinkards who are as treacherous as odorous, the Radical on the bitter abuse of servile courtiers, of hypocritical rulers, and of unjust judges, the sportsman on the robust delight in horse and hawk and hound, and the fretful youth upon the sweet sadness to which Shakespeare so often gave most exquisite utterance. The pessimist can quote the Dark Period tragedies to the top of his bent, while the optimist is happy with the lark that tirra-lirra chants and will echo Bernard Shaw's query, ' Is it not clear that there was to the last in Shakespeare an incorrigible divine levity, an inexhaustible joy that derided sorrow ? ' The problem for the ordinary reader and playgoer to-day is somehow to fight through this tangle of contradiction and to discover for himself a reading of Shakespeare's mind and character that will agree with the known facts of his life and the general tenor of his work.

We may begin with personal characteristics. He was ' gentle Shakespeare.' The adjective recurs and it is stressed by Ben Jonson in his second line ' To the Reader ' opposite the portrait in the First Folio. By gentle was meant affable, good-tempered, sociable; Shakespeare was obviously not of the blustering, Draw-can-sir kind so common in the taverns of the time. That he was involved with others in certain troubles and hot disputes with Master Waite on the South Bank is true, but that Shakespeare was himself threatening violence is certainly not proven. Aubrey assures us that he would not be debauched, but that word, as we saw, was not so strong in Aubrey's time as in ours. The remark only implies that long sessions with tumultuous parties wearied the poet and that he pleaded health to keep away from them. But we never hear of him as proud or aloof.

He wrote fast, of course; otherwise his work would never have been done. ' His mind and hand went together and, what he thought, he uttered with that easiness, that we have scarce received from him a blot in his papers.' That was the verdict of those who knew best, his friends, colleagues and editors, Heminge and Condell. In the quick forge of his brain the hammer fell without a fumble. (Jonson might snarl that his rival would have been wise to do more blotting, but we can let that pass. Rivals will scrap and Ben had earlier given full grandeur of tribute.) *The Merry Wives of Windsor* was said to be written in a couple of weeks and well may have been; all this proves is that Shakespeare, when pressed for time, found prose the easier, for this play is scant of verse. Jonson has a passage about an unnamed acquaintance who worked in long furious bouts and then was spent for a while.

> Ease and relaxation are profitable to all studies. The mind is like a bow, the stronger by being unbent. But the temper in spirits is all, when to command a man's wit, when to favour it. I have known a man vehement on both sides; that knew no mean either to intermit his studies or call upon them again. When he hath set himself to writing, he would join night to day; press upon himself without release, not minding it till he fainted: and when he left off, resolve himself into all sports and looseness again; that it was almost a despair to draw him to his book: but once got to it, he grew stronger and more earnest by the ease.

Some have believed this to refer to Shakespeare, but we have no proof of it. It fits in, certainly, with the account of a swift flow and no revision: also with the unevenness of Shakespeare's work and the perfunctory endings after passages of highest power. But it does not quite tune in with Aubrey's report of a sedulous worker, disdaining ' sports and looseness.'

We can see that he was personally fastidious and disliked the stench and squalor of which Tudor London was prolific. Those who closely examine his metaphors and verbal images discover that he was annoyed by smoky lamps, disliked untidiness in the house, and was revolted by the ' orts ' (pieces of stale food) on unwashed dishes. Greasy and sugary foods nauseated him. He was particularly sensitive to sweat and the smell of people. The stench of the crowd was a constant grievance to his nostrils. His political leaders of the Right are always harping on the itch and the scab, the body-odour and the vile breath of the filthy multitude.

> Yon common cry of curs, whose breath I hate
> As reek o' the rotten fens, whose loves I prize
> As the dead carcases of unburied men
> That do corrupt my air!

Yet he loathed no less the sickly fawning of the courtier whose crooking of the knee he likened to the cringing of the dogs waiting round a dining-table to pick up the scraps. The most obvious and most significant of what is called the Shakespearean image-clusters is that which several times links candy with fawning and both with dogs. Many commentators have stressed the curious interaction of these words and metaphors in passages expressing disgust.

> Why, what a deal of candy courtesy
> This fawning greyhound then did proffer me!
>
> *I Henry IV*, I, iii

is an example. Hamlet talks of the candied tongue licking absurd pomp, an obvious dog-image. The defeated Antony in *Antony and Cleopatra* complains that those who spaniel'd him at heels ' do now discandy,' i.e. melt away. Shakespeare had a particular distaste for the obsequiousness of the spaniel, whom, as we saw, he not only connotes with base fawning but turns also into a verb contemptuously used. To say that he disliked dogs is nonsense: he admired the hounds of the chase. But there must have been some bitter experience of his own, some memory of dogs grovelling for sweet-meats while he himself was feeling humiliation, which drove deep into his subconsciousness and so caused the ideas of candy, spaniels, and servility to recur in company when he was writing about flattery and abject obeisances.

This fastidiousness, this hatred of excess, did much to shape his common-sense and middle-of-the-road politics. The qualities he most disliked were pretentiousness and hypocrisy. His central belief was in the natural discipline of an ordered society, that order being proclaimed by the nature of the universe. The monarchy stood to the nation as the heavens to the earth, while the stars in their courses proclaimed the sacred necessity of a stable regimen. The speech of Ulysses on this theme in *Troilus and Cressida* has been cited so often that one need not quote fully from it again. It expounds at length the necessity of ' degree,' since the heavens themselves observe ' degree, priority, and place . . . office and custom in all line of order.' Without degree and ' all line of order ' come rampant and ruinous power-politics and so ' chaos, when degree is suffocate, follows the choking.'

In short, Shakespeare proclaimed the Tudor ideal of a strong, unifying monarchy with a graded system of ' place ' below it, each place to have its rights as well as its duties, including, especially, the right to own property. We should presumably deem Shakespeare a politician of the centre for the reason that, while he is most precise in praise of discipline, his respect for degree and authority was very far from being an abject submission to rank exploited or to authority abused. His detestation of instability in the slippery mob was only equalled by his violent chastisement of the bullying official, the lecherous, sadistic beadle, the unjust judge, and all abusers of power. As Shaw has put it in his preface to *The Dark Lady of the Sonnets*:

Now whoever will read *Lear* and *Measure for Measure* will find stamped on his mind such an appalled sense of the danger of dressing man in a little brief authority, such a merciless stripping of the purple from the ' poor, bare, forked animal ' that calls itself a king and fancies itself a god, that one wonders what was the real nature of the mysterious restraint that kept ' Eliza and our James ' from teaching Shakespear to be civil to crowned heads, just as one wonders why Tolstoy was allowed to go free when so many less terrible levellers went to the galleys or Siberia.

Shaw adds later:

Then consider Shakespear's kings and lords and gentlemen! Would even John Ball or Jeremiah complain that they are flattered ? Surely a more mercilessly exposed string of scoundrels never crossed the stage. The very monarch who paralyzes a rebel by appealing to the divinity that hedges a king, is a drunken and sensual assassin, and is presently killed contemptuously before our eyes in spite of his hedge of divinity.

The acceptance of this Tudor universe is no proof of profound political speculation on Shakespeare's part. He took what was going in the way of ideas and, as was his wont, gave to it the perfect shaping that came naturally to that Hand of Glory. He saw history as a dramatist, in terms of people and character —rightly, since that was his profession—and not as an analyst of social forces, or as a student of economic and political motive. He drew on the chronicles of Hall and Holinshed for English history and on North's Plutarch for his classical plays. The anonymous author of an *Essay Against Too Much Reading* (1728) had heard some rumour of his methods.

I will give you a short Account of Mr. Shakespear's Proceeding; and that I had from one of his intimate Acquaintance. His being imperfect in some Things, was owing to his not being a Scholar, which obliged him to have one of those chuckle-pated Historians for his particular Associate, that could scarce speak a Word but upon that Subject, and he maintain'd him, or he might have starv'd upon his History. And when he wanted anything in his Way, as his plays were all Historical, he sent to him, and took down the Heads of what was for his Purpose in Characters, which were thirty times as quick as running to the Books to read for it: Then with his natural flowing Wit, he work'd it into all Shapes and Forms, as his beautiful Thoughts directed.

Now an anonymous author of 1728 is not a first-rate authority for what happened in 1598, but it is surely probable enough that Shakespeare may have used an impecunious and even ' chuckle-pated ' scholar to devil for him. Mr. Alan Keen has a copy of Hall's Chronicles (1550) with annotations which were specially centred upon and were most relevant to just those episodes on which the dramatist chiefly drew. It is not claimed by Mr. Keen that the annotations are Shakespeare's own. (Such a claim has been put forward for an annotated Holinshed (1587) by the Comtesse de Chambrun, the authoress of

Shakespeare Rediscovered and other interesting Shakespeareana.)
But it is quite possible that Shakespeare's tame historian left
traces of his hand on the copy of Hall now in Mr. Keen's
possession, since the markings run so closely, in event and
phrase, to the pattern of Shakespeare's usage of the chronicle.

It was hardly to be expected that Shakespeare would see the
Middle Ages as we see them now. The chronicles gave him
an ugly record of baronial brawling and of civil war continually menacing a weak throne: this was an obvious text
on which to base his advocacy of a country united in peace
under a strong throne. But the Wars of the Roses were the
eczema of a body not wholly unhealthy: Chaucer's England
was going on: the cathedrals were going up; the crafts in
the cities were being developed with native ingenuity and the
supplementary aid of foreign refugees; wherever there was
wool there was wealth and, where there was wealth, it went
into a modest magnificence of civic and manorial building and
into encouragement of memorable workmanship. Hardly any
of this emerges in Shakespeare's plays; it might have done
had he set his comedies at home instead of (nearly always) in
Italy, Greece, and even Asia Minor. Shaw makes this point
strongly in his preface to *Saint Joan.*

> Now there is not a breath of medieval atmosphere in
> Shakespear's histories. His John of Gaunt is like a study of
> the old age of Drake. Although he was a Catholic by family
> tradition, his figures are all intensely Protestant, individualist,
> sceptical, self-centred in everything but their love affairs, and
> completely personal and selfish even in them. His kings are
> not statesmen: his cardinals have no religion: a novice can
> read his plays from one end to the other without learning that
> the world is finally governed by forces expressing themselves
> in religions and laws which make epochs rather than by
> vulgarly ambitious individuals who make rows.

The intricate social pattern of the Middle Ages had been
broken up by the Renaissance, which let in a new classical
culture, and the Reformation, which let in the new religion.
The Elizabethans were living in a fresh light with a great

M

darkness separating them from the old light. The famous and forward-looking speech of prophecy and blessing delivered by Cranmer over ' this royal infant,' Elizabeth, in *Henry VIII*:

> In her days every man shall eat in safety
> Under his own vine what he plants: and sing
> The merry songs of peace to all his neighbours

suggest a considerable ignorance or disbelief in that Merry England before the Reformation, full of art, craft, folk-song, beef, liquor and bliss, which our modern medievalists commend to our admiration. For Shakespeare the Middle Ages meant the pillage of the countryside by the roving armies of the robber barons who would be kings, relieved—for playgoers—by the blessed intervention of a Falstaff with his knavish hangers-on and by the comedians' pretence that every peasant bullied into these senseless and interminable wars was not only pathetic but a natural contributor to comedy such as a Bullcalf, a Mouldy, or a Feeble.

Shakespeare was typical of his time in his vigorous individualism. Let there be order, he demanded, but only a limited, peace-preserving order, so that men should otherwise be free from interference with their lives and commerce. Every man is to eat in safety what *he* plants, sitting under *his* vine. No county agricultural committees, no nationalisation of the land for him! The ' kulak,' as the Communists call and denounce the free peasant, was his ideal, and his own life and investments in Stratford are sufficient evidence that he believed in thrift, provision, and self-help.

Millions of readers and playhouse auditors must have listened down the centuries to the advice given by Polonius without realising that it contained a powerful denial of the social virtues. If to our own selves we are true, announces the Chamberlain with Shakespeare's apparent approval, we cannot then be false to any man. It is possible to argue over Shakespeare's intention in the use of the word true in this passage, but plainly the general instruction is exactly that of mid-Victorian Liberalism. Follow your conscience and follow your interest: for, if each is true to his own inner light and his own material gain, both the general good and the general advantage will best be served. This is simply the traditional doctrine of the Free Churches as to spirit and of Free Trade as to matter. Shakespeare—such is the wide scope of his opinion—might be the Perpetual President of the Cobden Club as well as of the Society of St. George, and his Immortal Memory should be drunk on the Birthday by the few faithful of *Laissez-faire* as well as by the devotees of the dramatist all over the world: not that he could have happily delivered addresses on Free Enterprise; his opinions were too instinctive for the dais and the water-bottle of the lecturer.

So those who rejoice most in his glorious rhetoric about this England, a true-to-itself and world-defying demi-Eden, must face the fact that he was no profound historian, no student of social and ethical forces, no lover of a closely integrated society where each gives according to his capacity while each receives according to his need. He was a true child of his bustling time, with its new religion defying old boundaries, with its new commerce breaking through the old Guild controls, and its new learning which poured into England the verbal and narrative treasures of the old, classical Europe. He had few regrets for the England that had passed, except that servants were not as ready to work for nothing as they used to be.

Why should he sigh? He had genius and the motive and the scope to employ it freely for the advancement of himself and of his family. History had its lessons: there must be security for enterprise. History had also its treasure of raw material for a theatre-man. Always in discussing Shakespeare's mind and opinions we must remember the life-long pressure of theatrical demand. He was one of a team in which he soon held responsible leadership; he was writing for them, and Burbage surely did not want plays which buried the acting part in the historian's wisdom. It suited him, and it suited the audience, that Shakespeare's outlook on history should not be a leisurely economic survey but a swift glance at the portrait gallery. The man in the anecdote who could not say that Richard III died on the stage, but spoke of Burbage dying instead, may have been an unsatisfactory student of the chronicles, but he was just the type of customer whom any actor must love to serve. The play was the thing and the player came first.

Shakespeare's work in the theatre was not designed to be didactic. Its business was to attract by the excitement and the laughter it could provide. It is significant that the play in which Ulysses delivered his long essay in political science was a failure. Somerset Maugham has shrewdly said in *The Summing Up* that it is very unlikely that a dramatist lucky enough to have been born with the faculty of putting things in a way that makes them transferable across the footlights will also be an original thinker. The playwright works in the concrete and with the instance. ' There is no reason to expect that he will have a faculty for conceptual thinking.' Maugham has also put the point in this way:

> How can you write a play of which the ideas are so significant that they will make the critic of *The Times* sit up in his stall and at the same time induce the shop-girl in the gallery to forget the young man who is holding her hand ? The only ideas that can affect them when they are welded together in that unity which is an audience, are those commonplace, fundamental ideas that are almost feelings. These, the root ideas of poetry, are love, death and the destiny of man. It is not any sort of dramatist who can find anything to say about them that has not been said a thousand times already; the great truths are too important to be new.

This is a long way from the Higher Criticism of the donnish type. Bradley wrote profoundly indeed and is never to be left out of a student's reading, but all volumes analysing Shakespearean Tragedy in terms of the Superb Mind should be taken along with such reminders as that of Maugham, who is doubly qualified as Shakespearean critic and expositor, although he has never set up in that position. For Maugham is not only the possessor of a probing and philosophical brain: he is himself a true follower of Shakespeare in the workshop, a successful and practical dramatist. Shakespeare would have understood and applauded the judgment I have quoted. Substitute Sir Francis Bacon for *The Times* critic and a Bankside groundling for the shop-girl in the gallery; Shakespeare could only ' get ' them simultaneously by stressing ' the fundamental ideas that are almost feelings.' The emotional vibration caused by his uncanny use of words, while he dramatised the common humours, failings, and calamities of mankind, were what filled the theatre. He was writing for the players and the box-office first and for the sages second; the lover and his lass had to be considered before the wits and wiseacres.

Sometimes, as I have suggested, he may have taken over the wisdom of the wiseacres (in the form of an ill-digested script) and ' Burbaged ' it to the general pleasure. In our time we have had ' the drama of ideas,' and it was a welcome change from the fustian which it supplanted at a period when romanticism had run dry. But the conceptual and doctrinal drama will never have the general appeal possessed by the ' ideas that are almost feelings.' When Shakespeare wrote in a sonnet ' Love is too young to know what conscience is ' he stated something which is more emotion than reflection: but it is emotion that must in some form have smitten everyone who has reached the age of puberty. His plays are conceived on this plane where opinion melts into sensation. The old universal notions were enough. Great truths are not only too important to be new: they are, with genius playing on them, too serviceable to grow old.

The sects, of course, have been busy with Shakespeare's soul. With equal confidence he has been claimed by Catholic and Protestant. The Ardens were Catholics and John Shakespeare may have been; one at least of the boy's schoolmasters was known as a noted adherent of the old religion. On the other hand he had a thorough knowledge of the Genevan Bible and one feels a pressure of conviction and even of real glee behind the defiant lines, written for *King John*, but obviously acceptable to Queen Elizabeth.

> What earthly name to interrogatories
> Can task the free breath of a sacred king ?
> Thou canst not, cardinal, devise a name
> So slight, unworthy, and ridiculous,
> To charge me to an answer, as the Pope.

> Tell him this tale; and from the mouth of England
> Add thus much more,—that no Italian priest
> Shall tithe or toll in our dominions;
> But as we, under heaven, are supreme head,
> So, under him, that great supremacy,
> Where we do reign, we still alone uphold,
> Without th' assistance of a mortal hand:
> So tell the Pope; all reverence set apart
> To him and his usurp'd authority.

One feels, too, that no good Catholic could possibly have penned the words in *Henry VIII*, ' God shall be truly known, ' as a description of England under Elizabeth. This strong and simple tribute to the Reformation has the ring of authenticity.

The statement by Parson Richard Davies, made nearly a century later, that Shakespeare ' dyed a Papist ' has been accepted or dismissed according to taste. It seems to imply that he did not live as a Catholic, whatever he may have professed upon his death-bed. The phrasing of his will, the known entertainment of ' a preacher ' at New Place, the circumstances of his burial and the tributes all suggest conformity with the prevailing and reformed religion.

Whether or not this was the way of conviction it was certainly the way of safety. A man with a career to make would be as shy of professed Catholicism, especially if he was working near the Court, as of the atheism alleged against Marlowe. Shakespeare was temperamentally a man of the Centre; laughing at excesses was a very profitable part of his occupation; the satirist and comedian must find his material in the extreme and the absurd. While unlikely to stand at either of the religious poles, he was kinder to Friars than to parsons in his plays and, like all the playhouse men, he hated the fanatical Puritans, who so fanatically hated the theatre and would have ruined its servants. His humanity, his compassion, and his intense belief, expressed most strongly in his latest plays, that penitence merits mercy and that right reason takes part against the fury of revenge all suggest a generous but undogmatic faith.

In so far as his view of death can be discovered from the plays, it shows curiously little belief in any Christian heaven or hell.

The Duke in *Measure for Measure* is presumably a good Viennese Catholic; yet he definitely bids Claudio ' be absolute for death ' with the recommendation that death is no more than sleep, a sleep which evens all the odds. It is the same language as Antony's description of suicide:

> To do the deed which ends all other deeds,
> Which shackles accident and bolts up change.

Claudio's fear of death takes this form and evokes this superb passage:

> Ay, but to die, and go we know not where;
> To lie in cold obstruction, and to rot;
> This sensible warm motion to become
> A kneaded clod; and the delighted spirit
> To bathe in fiery floods, or to reside
> In thrilling region of thick-ribbed ice;
> To be imprison'd in the viewless winds,
> And blown with restless violence round about
> The pendent world; or to be worse than worst
> Of those that lawless and incertain thought
> Imagine howling!—'tis too horrible!
> The weariest and most loathed worldly life
> That age, ache, penury, and imprisonment
> Can lay on nature, is a paradise
> To what we fear of death.

It is un-Christian doctrine that spirits are imprisoned at the North Pole or are blown round about the pendent world. It was natural for the lusty young Claudio to want life and not to lie and rot. But why should he be afraid of dire punishment ? His offence in the play, that of anticipating the marriage ceremony, had been Shakespeare's own and, like Shakespeare, he was ready to put all in order by a hasty marriage.

The conception of death and of the after-life in *Hamlet* provide us with some glorious poetry, but not with any clear intimation that Shakespeare himself held clear opinions. ' To die, to sleep ' is not the Christian attitude; but the hope of escape from the world's heartache by immersion in complete unconsciousness is constantly in Shakespeare's mind. It may surely be derived from the rapture of his constantly recurring tributes to sleep that he was himself an insomniac and suffered, when he did drop off, from troublesome dreams. The benison of deep, calm sleep was ever in his mind. In his will he commended his soul to God his Creator ' hoping and assuredly believing, through the only merits of Jesus Christ my Saviour, to be made partaker of life everlasting.' But this was common form and, when his imagination was working upon death with full intensity, he showed, in his plays, a view of ' the invisible event ' which is more pagan than Christian. Yet Fripp, after saying with justice that ' No sect could claim him: he was too broad and deep for any one,' ended thus: ' He stands supreme among English laymen for his Reverend Liberalism. From his writings and from his will, we conclude that he lived, and died, a member of our National Communion, a lover of his Church in days when, before the Act of Uniformity, it included in pulpit and pew a rich variety of thought, ancient and modern, and enjoyed, if sometimes painfully, a salutary clashing of brains.'

We do not demand of our poets that they be logicians. Shakespeare satisfied himself in politics with some simple ideas about a community, unified in order under the Crown, but living freely in all personal matters. He did not work out a Philosophy of History. Being a dramatist and having to please by the provision of plays for the people and parts for the actors, he preferred to raid the chronicles for their Tussaud treasures, their wax-work villains and murderers, and then to make these dummies spring to abundant and enduring life. He was not in business either as statesman or theologian: his mind was busy but wayward, as his fancy was infinite; the hand which served his thoughts and fancies followed their deviations with one abiding characteristic—namely, that it touched nothing which it did not glorify.

T. S. Eliot has said, I think justly, that while Dante made superb poetry out of a clear philosophy, Shakespeare did the same out of a muddled one. I see no offence in calling him muddled, which is only a brief way of saying ' not a conceptual thinker.' Quite early in life he had himself—bestowing, as so often, his grandest lines on a minor character—explained that the poet's eye in a fine frenzy rolls, and as it glances from heaven to earth and earth to heaven 'the poet's fancy bodies forth the shapes of things unknown.' He then added, ' such tricks hath strong imagination.' On condition that the frenzy be indeed a fine one, shall we complain because, defying consistency, a ghostly traveller in *Hamlet* has just returned from ' the bourn from which no traveller returns ' ? It was no part of Shakespeare's purpose or profession to lay down a system of thought, like any ' bookish theoric.' He did not conceive it to be drama's function to codify politics, ethics, and creeds. He had not come, like Bernard Shaw, to tidy things up, to discourse on ethics, and to tell us the how and why and whither of society. He could have exclaimed with Walt Whitman,

> Do I contradict myself?
> Very well, then, I contradict myself.
> (I am large. I contain multitudes.)

What brain and fancy better justified that bold, Whitmanic claim? We must remember, too, that he was a man in a hurry. He bolted from one task, one masterpiece, to another. There was not much time for full, profound, consistent ' conceptual thinking.'

People have often asked me whether I could discover a clear vision of Shakespeare ? Clear, crystal-clear, perhaps not. In the case of an author who left no personal papers and whose writings are mainly in dramatic form, so that the opinions voiced can always be attributed to fictional characters, it is not easy to be precise about his views and personal traits. Yet many have believed that Shakespeare's image is fully mirrored in his work. Shaw has claimed that we know more of him than of Dickens and of Thackeray. No writer can wholly disguise himself. Apart from definite expression of opinion, his language and his metaphors betray his predilections and aversions. It is not

M*

impertinent, it is not vain, to try to find the figure behind the glorious hand.

It is a figure of seeming contradictions: yet to me at least it comes out sufficiently coherent. Many an eminent professor has written of Shakespeare as though he had never been inside a theatre, never cursed and adored the players, never despaired at a rehearsal or rejoiced at ' an opening ' where all flowed well, never worn the motley himself and relished the feel of getting his audience, never cursed his clever little critics in the galleries, and never sworn to throw the whole game up—and then been at it again the next morning. The first and simple fact about Shakespeare is that he was stage-struck, as all of his calling have to be: otherwise they would be driven frantic by the madhouse in which they work. Theatre life, with its quarrels and muddles and vanities, is a form of lunacy: but the moon-beams of that lunacy can be of a radiance that does indeed reward. Out of the tantrums and tornado or—even worse—out of the dreary flatness of a really bad rehearsal, out of the egotism and jealousy of the green-room, out of the delay and frustration and confusion inevitable in the staging of plays, grandeur may suddenly spring when the great day arrives. Then the play, which seemed to be possessed by Caliban, becomes an Ariel and ' flames amazement ' on the audience. This occasional miracle of the theatre its inhabitants know: indeed, by it they live. Shakespeare was of that company and knew the pains, the ecstasy, the magic.

I am not saying that the Elizabethan theatre, so young a growth, provided exact parallels to our own distracted theatre, bedevilled as this is with film contracts, vast salaries, and the din and blaze of publicity. No doubt they took things more easily then, fussed less over ' flops ' and were less jumpy, prickly and vain. But, even so, there must have been emotional crises, rows and recriminations. Amid all that Shakespeare was writing his texts: madhouse and miracle went together.

But he was the common-sense man always. He knew that miracles are only half miraculous; they come by taking thought and plodding on as well as by hit-or-miss methods and by the sheer luck of a moment's inspiration. He had a will of his own.

' Would not be debauched.' He had grown up among the dissolute bully-boys of the old brigade, of whom Greene was richly typical, down at heels and up in arms, cursing and quarrelling, drinking and drabbing, churning out a sufficiency of theatre-stuff to buy a stoup of liquor, and then rotting away in debt and disease. Shakespeare was fastidious; he had a nose and the filth of poverty offended it. He was going to rise clear above the squalor of Greene's death. There was always behind him, too, the sweeter smell of the countryside, for which he craved not merely as a posy-loving poet but as a man of farming stock, a devotee of ownership and possession. With the actor's and the playwright's thirst for glory he mingled the land-hunger of a peasant. He had a wife and three children to keep, a family to restore, and hard work would do it. He had a home and acres in his mind's eye and very soon they were in his hand as well.

Loving beauty, from the eye of wren to the starry floor of heaven, he loved women and paid for it. His masculine affections were warmed, too, by his eye for elegance. He opened his heart freely. He suffered deeply in body and mind in the middle reach of his life and almost laid laughter aside. He had lost his son and found a dark mistress who turned out to be a daughter of ' the sugar'd game.' He was more libertarian than libertine, for libertines fall behind with their work, and he was ever punctual with a new play, even while studying a new part to act for no good reason save his delight in the mumming of it and in roaring out the ' eloquent rapsodooce.' Libertines get into debt and he would rather a lender than a borrower be. His genius, as we see it now, far outranged contemporary awareness of it and it seems to have outdistanced his own notion of it too: there is no sign that he felt underrated as an author.

He enjoyed the freedom of an age in which an able and an active man could use his wits and make his way, prosper and buy a parcel of land, without being railed at as a verminous oppressor of the poor. He had, like Michael Cassio, ' a daily beauty in his life ' and bore himself modestly, affably, gently. Our modern taxation of honest work would have rendered speechless even that lord of all language, sacred and profane.

Hurling ridicule at politicians was a normal playhouse practice; his fellows were always ready with an epithet from the stews or the lazar-house for statesmen and officials. Shakespeare had all their loathing for beadles and bullies, for dogs-obeyed-in-office, for bureaucrats and misusers of the powers granted. Even if he could have endured to pay income-tax he could hardly have lived sane in a community of form-filling, inquisitions, and controls. For the ' looped and windowed raggedness ' of the poor he had compassion; social reform on our scale was nobody's business then and so a modern Socialist could rate him as impolitic. But he would always mix laughter with his loathing and, if the Socialist complained that the great poet was also, in his seizure of play-plots and his hoarding of malt, a considerable pirate, it can be answered that the flag over New Place was a very Jolly Roger indeed.

He could not sustain his moods. He sang love and scolded lust as none before or since. When he had looked into the pit and drawn from it the howls of hell that are in the speeches of Lear and Timon, he could with speed refresh himself with a little of that innocent botany and elementary bird-watching which he transmuted into wood-notes wild and music everlasting. Many great men have entirely lacked the quality in which Shakespeare excelled, the power to laugh at himself. In one of his early and most informative plays, he both practised word-spinning of the Euphuistic kind to perfection and then abjured it with contempt. He felt for melancholics and smiled at them; he insulted the greasy mob and then ridiculed the courtier who kept the stinkards at good distance. He preached the virtues of an ordered monarchy but presented a cavalcade of English royalty that is not much better than a rogues' gallery: ' In the midst thou shalt go safest.' It was always the comedians' precept. For them both Ally Sloper and Lord Tomnoddy, Pistol and Osric, are equally rich material. But the mockery of the extremes must be neither sour nor shrill. He said that ' ripeness is all ' and obeyed his own instruction. Shakespeare was always ready to turn about. He put a fop or a thief in the pillory of his art one day: he would take sack or small beer with him on the next.

Let the scholars call him myriad-minded, a visionary symbolist, co-equal of Dante and Milton in his scope of soaring thought, if they will. But they must not forget the player who would not give up, the writer of parts for actors coveting a laugh or ' a round,' the enchanted observer of the maltworms and of the tapsters who served them; this was a man not so much omniscient as omnivorous of the human scene. It is customary to end books on Shakespeare by remarking of him, as Agrippa said of Antony (rather oddly), that ' a rarer spirit never did steer humanity '! But Shakespeare was not at the rudder of the world and never sought to be. A more pertinent line is Romeo's, ' I'll be a candle-holder and look on.' None ever held the candle to throw a subtler ray or better recorded the shadow-play which that illumination gave. He was not for the throne of pomp or the dais of the intellectual; he preferred to be the Gentleman in the Parlour, the vagrant lodger, the man in the wings, the reporter in the royal gallery. In these positions of spectatorship he mingled three elements: a common-sense philosophy of moderation, deep feeling for all folk suffering and all things gay or beautiful, and unfailing power to find the word perfect to each place and subject. Out of this trinity came his unified perfection in the writer's art. He had his solitary moods and would evade the clatter of cups and quips when the writing fit was on him, which was often. But he was ' Sweet Mr. Shakespeare ' none the less and ' known to his own.'

Of his death we know nothing save the date. The record in Stratford Parish Church attributes to April 25, 1616, the burial of ' Will. Shakespere, gent.' The inscription on his tomb says that he died two days earlier.

As to Parson Ward's story, set down nearly fifty years after the poet's death, that he contracted a fever following some hard drinking with Drayton and Jonson, it is a case of ' believe it or not.' Dr. John Hall, who in his case-book noted illnesses of his wife, his daughter, and himself, lamentably omitted to say anything about the decline and demise of his father-in-law. We can but hope that a tired man came to his rest without pain.

It is strongly apparent in Shakespeare's work that he knew all about the terrors of insomnia. The frequent invocations of sleep seem personal and poignant and he constantly wrote of death as an easeful slumber after the fretting and the fever of life; true, that was a commonplace of the fifth acts of his time, but in Shakespeare's case there seems to be a particular urgency of feeling when he touches the topic of sleep.

His fellow-dramatist Webster put into his play-finales some lines about death so touching as to be tremendous:

> I have caught
> An everlasting cold. I have lost my voice
> Most irrecoverably.

and

> I am i' th' way to study a long silence:
> To prate were idle. I remember nothing.
> There's nothing of so infinite vexation
> As man's own thoughts.

To study a long silence! It is an actor's phrase with silence substituted for part, a brilliant irony. Sick men, those who in an English spring have caught the cold that may be everlasting, understand the infinite vexation of a whirling brain, with its recurring fancies, fears, and obsessions. Man fights for breath instinctively, but it is hard to think of Shakespeare, when the mist was about him and the sleep was upon him, resisting very stubbornly its gradual and growing occupation.

Whenever he left London the temperature must have fallen at the Globe and the Blackfriars: and now, when the news came up from Stratford that he was dead, surely one of the King's Men must have whispered the haunting line from Nashe's lyric, *In Time of Pestilence*, ' Brightness falls from the air.'

APPENDICES

APPENDIX I

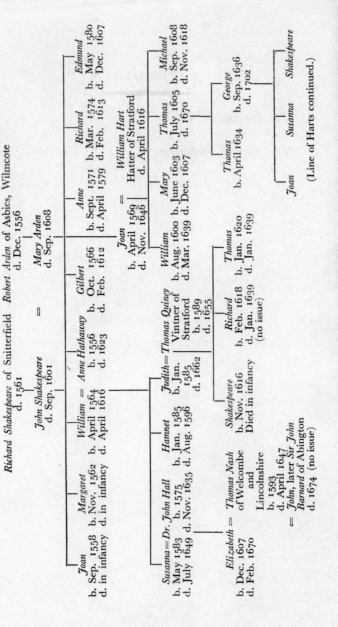

Richard Shakespeare of Snitterfield ... Robert Arden of Asbies, Wilmcote
d. 1561 ... d. Dec. 1556
... = ...
Mary Arden
d. Sep. 1608

John Shakespeare
d. Sep. 1601

Joan
b. Sep. 1558
d. in infancy

Margaret
b. Nov. 1562
d. in infancy

William = Anne Hathaway
b. April 1564   b. 1556
d. April 1616   d. 1623

Gilbert
b. Oct. 1566
d. Feb. 1612

Anne
b. Sept. 1571
d. April 1579

Richard
b. Mar. 1574
d. Feb. 1613

Edmund
b. May 1580
d. Dec. 1607

Joan = William Hart
b. April 1569   Hatter of Stratford
d. Nov. 1646   d. April 1616

William
b. Aug. 1600
d. Mar. 1639

Mary
b. June 1603
d. Dec. 1607

Thomas
b. July 1605
d. 1670

Michael
b. Sep. 1608
d. Nov. 1618

Susanna = Dr. John Hall
b. May 1583   b. 1575
d. July 1649   d. Nov. 1635

Hamnet
b. Jan. 1585
d. Aug. 1596

Judith = Thomas Quiney
b. Jan.   Vintner of
1585   Stratford
d. 1662   b. 1589
... d. 1655

Shakespeare
b. Nov. 1616
Died in infancy

Richard
b. Feb. 1618
d. Jan. 1639
(no issue)

Thomas
b. Jan. 1620
d. Jan. 1639

Thomas
b. April 1634

George
b. Sep. 1636
d. 1702

Joan   Susanna   Shakespeare

(Line of Harts continued.)

Elizabeth = Thomas Nash
b. Dec. 1607   of Welcombe
d. Feb. 1670   and
... Lincolnshire
... b. 1593
... d. April 1647
... = John, later Sir John
... Barnard of Abington
... d. 1674 (no issue)

APPENDIX II

AGES OF SHAKESPEARE	PLAYS	THEATRE EVENTS	CONTEMPORARY EVENTS
1 Johannes Factotum 1587-1592	*Henry VI*, 1, 2, 3 *Titus Andronicus* *The Comedy of Errors* *The Taming of the Shrew* *Richard III* *The Two Gentlemen of Verona*	1587 Marlowe's *Tamburlaine* 1588 Marlowe's *Faustus*	1588 Defeat of the Spanish Armada 1590 Publication of Lodge's *Rosalynde* Sidney's *Arcadia* Spenser's *Faerie Queen* (1-3)
2 Lyrical 1592-96	*Venus and Adonis* *Lucrece* *Love's Labour's Lost* *Romeo and Juliet* *A Midsummer Night's Dream* *The Merchant of Venice* Early Sonnets	1592 Plague closes theatres 1593 Theatres still closed. Much alteration of Companies. The Earl of Derby's Men become Lord Chamberlain's Men 1594 Shakespeare at the head of Lord Chamberlain's Men with Burbage and Kempe. They play at the Theatre north of the river, while the Admiral's Men, with Alleyn, act at the Rose on the South shore	1593 Death of Marlowe
3 Histories 1596-1599	*King John* *Richard II* *Henry IV*, 1, 2 *Henry V*		1596 John Shakespeare applies for a coat of arms, successfully. Hamnet Shakespeare dies 1597 Shakespeare buys New Place, Stratford Bacon's *Essays*. First volume appears

AGES OF SHAKESPEARE	PLAYS	THEATRE EVENTS	CONTEMPORARY EVENTS
4 High-fantastical 1599-1601	The Merry Wives of Windsor Much Ado About Nothing Twelfth Night As You Like It	1599 Building of the Globe Theatre by Burbage and the Chamberlain's Men. Shakespeare appears as one of the comedians in Ben Jonson's *Every Man in His Humour* 1600 Alleyn counters the move to the Globe by opening the Fortune Theatre 1601 So-called 'War of the Theatres,' professional disputes, attacks and counter-attacks between the Lord Chamberlain's Men and the Boy Players and their authors	1599 Essex fails to conquer Ireland
5 Bitter Comedy 1601-03	All's |Well that Ends Well Troilus and Cressida Measure for Measure		1601 Rebellion and Execution of Essex Southampton condemned to death, but sent to the Tower John Shakespeare dies

AGES OF SHAKESPEARE	PLAYS	THEATRE EVENTS	CONTEMPORARY EVENTS
6 The Dark Vision 1600-08 (Overlap with *Bitter Comedy*)	*Julius Caesar* *Later Sonnets* *Hamlet* *Othello* *Macbeth* *King Lear* *Timon of Athens* *Coriolanus* *Antony and Cleopatra*	1603 May. King James I 'licences and authorizes' the King's Players 1608 Aug. King's Men take over Blackfriars Theatre	1603 March. Death of Queen Elizabeth 1607 Susanna Shakespeare marries Dr. John Hall
7 Fancy Free 1608-13	*Pericles* *Cymbeline* *The Winter's Tale* *The Tempest* *Henry VIII*	1613 Globe Theatre burned	1608 Mary Shakespeare (poet's mother) dies 1613 Shakespeare buys a house in Blackfriars 1616 Feb. Judith Shakespeare marries Thomas Quiney, Vintner of Stratford 1616 April. Death of Shake- speare

NOTE ON BOOKS

THE Shakespeare literature is so enormous that it is difficult to give a selection. I can only say that the following books have helped me most:

CHRONICLES

William Shakespeare. Sir Edmund Chambers.

Shakespeare, Man and Artist. Edgar Fripp (Fripp is particularly learned on the Stratford scene and characters).

Elizabethan Plays and Players. G. B. Harrison.

Shakespeare at Work. G. B. Harrison.

The Life and Art of William Shakespeare. Hazelton Spencer.

Shakespeare's Marriage and Departure from Stratford. J. W. Gray.

Shakespeare's Life and Art. Peter Alexander.

Shakespeare—Truth and Tradition. J. Semple Smart.

Materials for the Life of Shakespeare. Butler.

William Shakespeare, A Handbook. Parrott.

Shakespeare Versus Shallow. Leslie Hotson.

I, William Shakespeare. Leslie Hotson.

Shakespeare Survey, appearing annually from the Cambridge University Press, should be watched.

IMAGINATIVE

The Man Shakespeare and His Tragic Life Story. Frank Harris.

The Essential Shakespeare. J. Dover Wilson.

The Return of William Shakespeare. Hugh Kingsmill.

Preface to *The Dark Lady of the Sonnets.* G. Bernard Shaw.

The Voyage to Illyria. Muir and O'Loughlin.

Shakespeare. Hesketh Pearson (Penguin Series).

The Real Shakespeare. William Bliss.

Shakespeare Rediscovered. Comtesse de Chambrun.

Gentleman of Stratford. John Brophy.

The Sonnets have produced a literature of their own. I have been much helped by Lord Alfred Douglas and W. Thomson on this subject.

STAGE-MATTERS

Prefaces to Shakespeare (five volumes). Harley Granville-Barker.

Shakespeare's Stage Conditions. Bradbrook.

Shakespeare's Audience. Harbage.

Shakespeare's Workshop. W. J. Lawrence.

Shakespeare and the Audience. Sprague.

Shakespeare's Boy Actors. Robertson Davies.

The Organisation and Personnel of the Shakespearean Company. T. W. Baldwin.

CRITICISM

The Approach to Shakespeare. J. W. Mackail.

On Reading Shakespeare. Logan Pearsall Smith.

Shakespeare's Plays. M. R. Ridley.

Shakespeare's Imagery. Caroline Spurgeon.

Shakespeare. Sir Walter Raleigh.

Shakespeare. J. Middleton Murry.

The ' Classics ' of Shakespearean criticism from Dr. Johnson to Bradley are too numerous to mention.

ANTI-STRATFORDIAN

Roderick Eagle I find the best of the many Baconians.

Percy Allen has stated the case with passionate devotion for the growing cohort of Oxfordians, whose early champion was J. T. Looney.

Gilbert Slater's ' Seven Shakespeares ' represents the Distributist School.

Alden Brooks in ' Shakespeare and The Dyer's Hand ' speaks for Sir Edward Dyer.

Professor Abel Lefranc is the leading claimant for the Earl of Derby and has expounded ' Le Secret de William Stanley.'